DATE DUE

MY 8 07			

DEMCO 38-296

BLACK CAMELOT

BLACK
CAMELOT

AFRICAN-AMERICAN

CULTURE HEROES IN THEIR TIMES,

1960–1980

William L. Van Deburg

THE UNIVERSITY OF CHICAGO PRESS

CHICAGO AND LONDON

William L. Van Deburg is professor of Afro-American studies at the University of Wisconsin, Madison. He is the author of *New Day in Babylon: The Black Power Movement and American Culture, 1965–1975,* also published by the University of Chicago Press, and of *Modern Black Nationalism: From Marcus Garvey to Louis Farrakhan, The Slave Drivers: Black Agricultural Labor Supervisors in the Antebellum South,* and *Slavery and Race in American Popular Culture.*

The University of Chicago Press, Chicago 60637
The University of Chicago Press, Ltd., London
© 1997 by The University of Chicago
All rights reserved. Published 1997
Printed in the United States of America
06 05 04 03 02 01 00 99 98 97   5 4 3 2 1

ISBN (cloth): 0-226-84716-0

Library of Congress Cataloging-in-Publication Data

Van Deburg, William L.
    Black Camelot : African-American culture heroes in their times,
  1960–1980 / William L. Van Deburg.
      p.   cm.
    ISBN 0-226-84716-0 (cloth : alk. paper)
    1. Afro-Americans—Social life and customs.   2. Heroes—United
  States—History—20th century.   3. Popular culture—United States—
  History—20th century.   4. Afro-Americans—Race identity.
  I. Title.
  E185.86.V34   1997
  973′.0496073—dc21   97-10837
                                                              CIP

☉ The paper used in this publication meets the minimum requirements of the American National Standard for Information Sciences—Permanence of Paper for Printed Library Materials, ANSI Z39.48-1984.

To Pops

CONTENTS

Research for this study of popular-cultural heroism began during the 1950s as neighborhood pals and I swapped Topps baseball card images of Hank Aaron and Al Kaline; reenacted aliens versus army guys battle scenes from *War of the Worlds;* and played Screamin' Jay Hawkins's classic shriekfest "I Put a Spell on You" *real loud* so as to make grown-ups think that a domestic dispute was in progress somewhere on the block. The earliest stages of the project were funded by my father, who managed a pair of movie houses in our hometown. He supplied me with free butterpop in exchange for swatting flies in the lobby and refilling the ice cream bar machine. Indeed, many a Milk Dud was consumed to the awe-inspiring sight of Johnny Weissmuller or Buster Crabbe conquering the wilderness (and the hearts of distressed damsels) in glorious Sepia-Tone. Thus, when I was a child, I didn't think as one—or so it seemed. I imagined myself a hero—just like the ones I saw every Saturday on TV or at the Michigan and Uptown Theatres. In truth, my friends and I were many different heroes. Roy Rogers, Sky King, and Rory Calhoun as Big Bill Longley the Texan were among those most frequently emulated in our playground portrayals.

In later years, my personal conceptualization of the heroic continued to evolve through devout adherence to the Chicago Bears fans' code of conduct—that is, pledging undying loyalty to Gale Sayers and Walter Payton; weekend screenings of low-budget movies at the college film society; and frequent pilgrimages to the gloriously seedy Shank Brothers music store for James Brown, Beatles, and Four Tops 45s. By this time, I had grown taller, but my heroes seemed to be more than keeping pace. How *did* they do it?

Much older and presumably more observant, I concluded my research efforts with a trip to the 1995 Grammy Awards in Los Angeles. There, while wedged into the Shrine Auditorium's nosebleed section next to an excited radio station contest winner from Cleveland, I was confirmed in the belief that the star-making machinery was a grand and glorious invention. It was clear that fandom's legendary support network remained solidly grounded and fully operational. Springsteen was there, receiving his song-of-the-year award from a covey of presenters and spokesmodels who acted as if the trophy was filled with frankincense and myrrh. Salt-N-Pepa was there, too. After getting a bit mixed up and going to the wrong podium, they hugged like cheerleaders at the end of a big game and gave ecstatic thanks to Mom. Then came Tony Bennett and Al Green; Babyface and Bonnie Raitt; Seal and Sheryl Crow—the whole multiplatinum, multiethnic *mishpocheh*. Perhaps more than anything else, it was the experience of viewing this spectacular celebration of celebrity first-hand that has sustained my faith in the power and the possibilities of the pop-culture heroic.

After the show and late-night reception, my elegantly attired wife and I stood waiting for the hotel shuttle when a slight, dreadlocked figure pushing a shopping cart filled with dumpster gleanings approached. Looking up at my tallish, tuxedoed visage, the young man smiled widely and exclaimed, "Hey, you're a movie star, aren't you!" I denied this wildly improbable notion, but he persisted. "No, you are, I've seen you somewhere," he said with serviceable sin-cerity. After I issued several more spirited rebuttals, he seemed satisfied and then proceeded to the heart of the matter: "Hey, could you help me out with a little spare change?" Of course, the "star" immediately cleaned out his pockets, receiving grateful thanks as this lone (but loyal) "fan" continued on his nightly rounds. Having spent the evening fixating on the heroic, I interpreted this mi-nor transfer of funds as follows: What I had just done for the clever panhandler, a truly famous celebrity does for us all. Each day, one or more of them "helps us out" a little and sends us on our way, happy. Thanks to my streetwise friend, I now more fully appreciate this timeless wisdom.

Back at home, I have been fortunate to receive valuable research assistance from a number of individuals and institutions. None have mistaken me for a Hollywood actor. Nevertheless, grateful thanks are extended to my university for a sabbatical leave which allowed me to delve deeply into black-music his-tory; to the Ford Foundation for a materials acquisition grant that was used to assemble a blaxploitation film library; to my department's chair, Nellie McKay, and to the Hilldale Fund for helping defray photoduplication costs; to the magazine *New Woman* for sponsoring the Grammys trip; to Steven Gietschier of *Sporting News* and Jim Danky of the State Historical Society of Wisconsin for time spent in locating hard-to-find source material; to my wife, Diane, and my colleagues in Afro-American Studies and History who put up with nu-merous, annoying inquiries about hopelessly obscure sixties minutia; to Pamela Bruton, whose skillful manuscript editing prevented a number of grammatical gaffes and infelicities from reaching the printed page; and to Doug Mitchell and the entire University of Chicago Press staff for their con-tinued support of black cultural studies.

Of Kings, Kennedys, and Culture Heroes

> We live in star-struck times, and the Kennedys were stars, and everyone
> had a swell time at the party.
>
> WILFRID SHEED

Contemplative conceptualizations of the heroic have changed a great deal since the days of Thomas Carlyle. By and large, the history of the planet no longer is considered the history of its Great Men—those "modellers, patterns, and . . . creators, of whatsoever the general mass of men contrived to do or to attain."[1] If the writings of historians provide any measure of a society's sensibilities, it seems that ours has become fully cognizant of the many limitations placed upon its greats by competing institutions and interest groups. Certainly, we are more willing than Carlyle's like-minded, mid-nineteenth-century contemporaries to permit the display of our major public figures' flaws and blemishes. Often, we seem to glory in the sight of the once mighty plummeting ingloriously to earth from their pricey abode on high.

Nevertheless, our attraction to the heroic remains strong. If not quite hero-worshipers, most of us are at least hero-conscious. Encouraged by press agents and manipulators of the electronic media, the so-called common people (*dēmos*) maintain a keen interest in learning about, celebrating, and sometimes even attempting to replicate the exploits of uncommon people (*hērōs*). Although the actual process by which certain individuals become recognized in this manner remains one of the great mysteries of contemporary mass culture, there is no question that our heroes continue to possess the ability to educate us about ourselves. Admittedly, some of these teachings may seem trivial and others downright embarrassing. But, if carefully considered, all may be utilized in our attempts to fathom the collective unconscious.

Recognizing both the challenge and the danger of traversing myth and folklore, history, and popular culture in search of cogent observations on contemporary heroes and their impact on the world, I submit that the quest is a virtuous one. With all due respect to PBS and Joseph Campbell, we seem to know a bit too much about the heroic myths of the ancients relative to what we have learned about the heroes of modern-day America. In particular, if any of us are to survive and prosper in twenty-first-century society, we must strive to learn a great deal more about our nation's racial and ethnic minority group heroes—how they mirror the folk soul, promise power to the weak, and inspire revolt against the mighty. We also will need to consider the possibility that just as the heroes of the ancient world served as a link between God and humankind, these stalwarts may be capable of serving as mediators between today's diverse, antagonistic, seemingly irreconcilable racially based interest groups.

This study considers four variants of the African-American heroic: competitive athletes; blues, jazz, and soul musicians; urban badmen; and "superhero" detectives. All rose to prominence during the 1960s and 1970s and are treated in the context of their times. I call them culture heroes—typically, but not exclusively, real-life individuals whose deeds acquire heroic dimension through popular-culture portrayals.

Since the book makes no pretense of exhausting this topic, readers should feel free to add other hero types to their personal list of those meriting examination. Neither does this work contend that any single type succeeded in becoming the perfect embodiment of composite American ideals—or even of the hopes, fears, and self-concepts of all segments of the black community. It does, however, suggest that the black culture hero had considerable impact on a national, multiracial constituency. The black heroes fueled civil rights and Black Power activism, sustained an oppressed population during desperate times, and offered a series of compelling counterproposals to majoritarian teachings. At the same time, their contributions to the nation's common cultural storehouse helped all Americans compensate for the tragic loss of their generation's most revered culture hero, President John Fitzgerald Kennedy. By doing so, these heroes accomplished a feat of Arthurian—even Homeric—dimension. Like those ancient champions, the contemporary black hero served both as a projection of dreams and as a model for emulation. Insofar as they won the fealty of an increasingly receptive white public, they established a cultural bridge between the races which could be utilized by each and every citizen.

Lest it be rumored about that I am promoting a revival of hero worship as a sort of New Age cure-all for the ills of contemporary American society, let it be noted that the possession of heroic models is no guarantor of social progress—or of individual or group activism. Creating or adopting a culture hero does not automatically turn a worm into a world-beater. Numerous additional factors are involved. But, for any person or group *not* to have heroes suggests cultural stagnation and a deficit of imagination and, perhaps, signals the onset of what Martin Luther King Jr. once referred to as a death of the spirit.

How, then, should one conceptualize the modern culture hero? What social and communal purposes do heroes serve? Do they possess special attributes which distinguish them from ordinary beings? Fortunately, students of the heroic mode have suggested numerous answers to such questions. Although some of these responses likely would have been derided even by the ancients, many are as applicable to the Age of Aquarius as to the Golden Age of Greece.

Whether fathered by the folk, created through the unfolding of historical events, or purposely shaped to meet the demands of our contemporary consumer culture, heroes tend to be larger than life. Since their fame rests upon deeds and personality traits which typically are either exemplary or exaggerated, heroes radiate a mythic aura. But, although they may be admired for their courage, charisma, or commitment to personal or group values, heroes are not gods. Their modus operandi must be comprehensible if they are to bond with their followers. Identification with such figures can be encouraged by the heroes' personal magnetism and solidified by the spark that they provide to the imagination. Seldom, however, is fealty gained through authoritarian means. Heroes serve at the pleasure of the people and can be deposed from their position of honor with remarkable ease. They are cultural genies who await our bidding.

Heroes both reflect and influence societal mores. As many commentators have noted, they are the personification of predominating ideals, the embodiment of a people's ineffable desires. While not quite "a mirror held up to a culture," a hero provides at least a partial image of a group's most cherished values.[2] A second hero may serve to reveal a different component of that value system; a third, yet another facet; and so on. But, because heroes are held in such high esteem, they also are capable of providing direction—of leading the group into new and uncharted areas of experience. Heroes aspire. Playing a role far more elevated than that of a cultural barometer, the hero stimulates us to do better, to reach our potential—and beyond.

Even if their deeds are impossible to duplicate fully, these metaphorical representations of culturally sanctioned achievement may serve as behavioral models. They have a propensity toward innovation and can help us to imagine the unimagined, to release the untapped creative energy within ourselves. Like those champions of ancient days who ventured forth from the everyday world to win decisive victories against supernatural forces, our modern heroes encourage us to step out and take risks. Then, after jolting us from our humdrum, status quo existence, they gird us as we stumble into the mysterious and frightening unknown. If we should fail in our quest, heroes offer compensatory services—consoling us and disguising our shortcomings, calming our fears, and providing temporary relief from unpleasant realities. Moreover, the culture hero's survival and continued well-being reassure us that all is not lost, that the ideals and values which the hero represents have not been discredited or diminished. Thus, the contemporary hero serves nobly as a force and a rallying point as well as an agent of change—a symbolic helpmeet in the struggle to keep the human spirit alive and full of vigor.

Since a hero is adopted by the people and in some fashion represents their hopes for the future, it is possible to conceptualize the act of hero building as an act of self-discovery and self-creation. Heroes are what people need them to be at any particular time in their group history. Therefore, the character, style, and specific attributes of heroes vary greatly over time and between groups. Heroism is constantly evolving.

To make this point, some writers have expended considerable effort in attempting to identify a "representative" heroic type in each historical period. For example, we learn that in the classical world heroes were god-men. By the Middle Ages they had become holy men. In Renaissance times they were universal men. And by the middle of the present century in our own country, we had adopted gentlemen, self-made men, and common men as heroic archetypes.[3] This makes for a very orderly, understandable presentation. Nevertheless, it also must be remembered that every era produces hundreds, even thousands, of aspiring hero candidates who compete for public favor with one another as well as with past champions. Constituencies based on region, race, class, ethnicity, gender, and age select their own favorites and present them to the larger culture. Each hero represents his or her particular interest group in the constant cultural jockeying that has become such an integral part of our modern pluralistic society.

During the 1960s and 1970s, it became obvious to all that culture heroes no longer could be conceptualized as exclusively male and macho, white and wise. In film and literature, on the nightly news, and—eventually—in the pages of history texts, these time-honored patriarchal types were joined by black and by female heroes. To complicate matters further, there were many distinctive varieties of each. Smart operators, selfless crusaders, great lovers, free spirits, technological wizards, and noble martyrs made an incredible clutter on the cultural landscape. Representing the long-suppressed longings of their creators, they engaged in an epic search for selfhood and sought to promote values deemed essential to the survival and well-being of the core group. Thus, even as these young upstarts purposely violated convention and conspired to retire the elder statesmen of the hero world, they affirmed the resources of the common human spirit.

Some said that many of these newcomers were celebrities, not heroes. Allegedly, most celebrities neither were born great nor achieved greatness through noble, daring, or even noteworthy deeds. Their fame was fabricated— the calculated, synthesized product of press agents, marketing surveys, stage lighting, and voice-overs. It more correctly could be termed notoriety. Indeed, in some cases, their chief claim to fame was their fame. If truth be told, said the critics, these ephemeral, store-bought heroes were not much better than the rest of us. Although far better known and presented, they were about as likely as one's next-door neighbor to offer a meaningful challenge to the status quo.[4]

Other commentators spared the celebrity from criticism but nevertheless proclaimed the passing of the hero. All of us, they said, were born too late. The sun had set on the age of heroes. Opinion as to exactly when this unfortunate event occurred varied, but the general impression given was that the roots of the traditional heroic ideal had been allowed to wither and die as Americans grappled with (1) the constant threat of mass destruction; (2) the rapid advance of a mythless, impersonal technology which dwarfed the individual and dulled human imagination; and (3) the spread of an enervating cultural anomie which could be traced to a noticeable decline in our sense of community and national purpose. Increasingly, it seemed, the body politic was fragmenting and the common people were finding whatever personal identity they were able to salvage in isms, institutions, and classes rather than in heroes. In such a world, the hero was thought to be either irrelevant or dangerous—a romantic delusion best consigned to cultural history's dustbin.[5]

How should one treat these two interrelated suppositions regarding the decline of heroism and the triumph of celebrity? Most assuredly, with all the respect they are due. The America of the 1960s and 1970s definitely was not the world of Frederick the Great—or of FDR, Charles Lindbergh, or Babe Ruth. Certain of the values and ideals that these traditional heroes had personified had lost their relevance and power of attraction. If this generation of Americans seemed suspicious of individuals riding white horses, hindsight reveals that even *more* care should have been exercised in keeping them at arm's length. Moreover, in a world where lives and events changed so rapidly, it was perfectly logical to believe that today's hero could become yesterday's news. To many, the presence or absence of any single hero at any particular time seemed to make little difference in the overall scheme of things. Certainly, the practice of old-fashioned forms of hero worship was not a major concern of those who were so absorbed in themselves that they perceived no benefit in forging a link between the finite and the supernatural. Neither was it likely to flower as of old in the bosoms of those who believed even a small portion of the titillating but determinedly iconoclastic screed written about high-profile public figures in gossip columns and supermarket tabloids.

But, if heroes were experiencing hard times, was their prognosis really as dire as the doom-and-gloomers claimed? Were the heroes of the mid–twentieth century less able than their predecessors to tough it out against the competition? Could they so easily be swept from the field by the tawdry glitter and spandex snap of the sixties celebrities? Not by a long shot. Although the factionalism of the era inhibited the proliferation of national heroes, it encouraged the growth of the aforementioned "segmented" group heroes. During the 1960s and 1970s, such heroes were both plentiful and powerful. Like successful corporate executives, each hoped to win and to hold a share of the national market in heroism for themselves. Romantic, but not delusional, they adapted themselves to the requisites of the modern world. Utilizing the "faceless" technology of the day to heroic purpose, this pack of pluralist James Bonds became the new champions of film and fiction. If these were celebrities, they certainly *behaved* like heroes.

In truth, the hero and the celebrity never were as estranged as some reports indicated. They long had resided in close proximity on the continuum of popular acclaim. Both owed a great deal to contrived, publicity-generating mechanisms. Over time, it is likely that a similar proportion of each group betrayed whatever standards they were celebrated for upholding. Neither faithfully represented the mundane realities of everyday life.[6]

Always problematic and highly theoretical, the dividing line between celebrity and heroism was blurred as never before by the sociological, technological, and cultural changes of the 1960s and 1970s. Big screens got bigger while politicians found their stature diminishing more markedly than that of the Incredible Shrinking Man. Nightly news coverage from Southeast Asia overwhelmed viewers with images of potential war heroes, but the warriors themselves became cynical—even angry—over the absurdity of their sacrifice and were given no parades. At a White House ceremony, presciently preserved on film for the edification of future generations, President Nixon clasped Elvis Presley's hand and made him an honorary federal narcotics agent. Confusing? Yes, indeed! Nevertheless, the heroes managed to muddle through, a bit battered but feeling no less worthy of the public's devotion. The people still needed, still wanted their culture heroes and would continue to celebrate them come hell or high camp. Those lucky enough to be tapped for this honor may not have slain many dragons, but most were capable of providing their common-folk kin with the same unique services offered by earlier generations of heroes.

No single individual manifested the essence of the modern culture hero in more compelling fashion than John F. Kennedy. And no better example of the hero's continuing importance to the American people can be found than in their overwhelming response to his life—and to his death. Kennedy serves as the logical point of departure for any study of contemporary heroes because he so completely satisfied the requisites of both traditional heroism and mass-marketed celebrity. His appeal was all but universal.

If the greatest culture hero is the one most capable of bridging the gaps between the largest number of competing interest groups, Jack Kennedy was that hero, par excellence. In a relatively short period of time, he made remarkable progress in pulling together the fragmented fiefdoms of his pluralistic domain by inextricably linking homage to himself with allegiance to the nation-state. Aided immeasurably by all of the mythmaking machinery available to one of his status and position, JFK became the embodiment of a generation's composite ideals.

Specifically, Kennedy's public persona was constructed from four key building blocks of the modern-day heroic: (1) movie star looks and appeal, (2) a sportsmanlike competitiveness, (3) the ability to maintain an aura of the humane, virtuous Everyman even while remaining a most uncommon man, and (4) physical courage and a penchant for risk taking. As a cultural force, the combination of these qualities was irresistably attractive to a nation bored by the complacency, conformity, and overall sluggish pace of the Eisenhower years.

Even without the studio-quality airbrushing which the Kennedy family portrait received from hired retainers and an adoring fourth estate, Jack, Jackie, and the rest of the clan radiated charm, glamour, and élan from every pore. From the earliest days of his candidacy it was clear that, if elected president, Kennedy would bring the dash and style of a Tinseltown star to an office long occupied by stodgy, gray-flanneled, grandfather types. Kennedy was younger and more handsome than most other major political figures of his day, the unmistakably commonplace Dick Nixon included, and his dazzling good looks had females swooning and breaking through police lines to run after his limo. They wrote to the White House for autographed photos (1,000 per week) and to his barber for hair clippings. In April 1961, a record 13,575 tourists crowded the mansion in a single day, hoping to catch a brief glimpse of his tieless, tousled-haired visage. One year later, a national campus poll showed that the nation's coeds believed their chief executive to have more sex appeal than any other male celebrity, including Rock Hudson.[7]

JFK's leading lady contributed significantly to the storybook quality of this scenario. Possessed of regal grace and queenly bearing, Jacqueline Bouvier Kennedy was well suited to her role. As one awed reporter noted, "She could be in a barn, leaning on a pitchfork, blowing the hair out of her eyes, and she'd look like Miss America."[8] At public receptions, admirers stood on chairs to get a better look at her trend-setting couturier fashions. Those unable to rub Chanel-suited shoulders with Jackie at such affairs shared her glamorous life vicariously in the pages of *Women's Wear Daily, Modern Screen,* and *Redbook.* Many adapted her stylish wardrobe to a commoner's budget. Unadorned cloth coats, A-line dresses, plain pillbox hats, and pastel pumps were seen everywhere. Others purchased Jackie (and Caroline) dolls for their children. Still others flooded her office with requests for advice on everything from wardrobe planning and makeup techniques to toilet training and ways to get their slouching teenage daughters to stand up straight and walk like ladies.

President Dwight D. Eisenhower and the president-elect, John F. Kennedy, at the executive mansion, 6 December 1960 (U.S. News and World Report Collection, Library of Congress)

Together Jack and Jackie set tongues a-wagging. But even more important, like the greatest of our culture heroes, the Kennedys allowed the public to share the moment—and the fantasy. They permitted the common folk to believe that their glamorous, video-ready image was transferable. Even as they helped invent themselves, the Kennedys helped their fellow citizens to conceptualize an American as a youthful, dynamic individual with limitless "star" potential.

Those hoping to mold themselves in the Kennedy image had to shape up and become physically fit. If they were to be like their hero, they would have to live a life of "vigah." Although plagued by a remarkable variety of physical ailments and disabilities (jaundice, appendicitis, diptheria, scarlet fever, malaria, chronic back problems, a sensitive stomach, a weak right knee, a left leg shorter than the right, numerous allergies, and an adrenal insufficiency known as Addison's disease), JFK became his era's most effective spokesperson for participatory sports activity.[9]

From his earliest days, Jack Kennedy had refused to accept the fact that he was not as strong or as talented as many of his peers. He turned out for half a dozen sports during his prep school days at Choate. At 6 feet and 149 pounds, he played freshman and junior varsity football at Harvard, was a member of the swimming team, and served on the crew that won the Eastern Intercollegiate Sailing Championship in 1938. As president, he had far less time to devote to sports but occasionally tried his hand at golf, usually shooting in the high 70s or low 80s. The Kennedy clan's touch football contests always were spirited affairs. Highly publicized, they became an essential participatory weekend sporting activity for "viga"ous families nationwide.

Intensely competitive, Kennedy not only encouraged others to engage in sports activities—on one occasion he sent top aides on a fifty-mile hike along the towpath of the Chesapeake and Ohio canal—but also adapted the spirit of athletic competition to the conduct of the nation's business. Numerous observers remarked on both the rapid pace and the length of his workday. He rushed about the office, they said, "as though he has been told he has a week to live."[10] Pacing the corridors, reading on his feet, and dictating correspondence at a rapid-fire pace, Kennedy's workday was conducted at full throttle. Said to be capable of going as long as twenty hours without rest, the president seemed at times to be in perpetual motion. Little wonder, then, that he found great pleasure in meeting star athletes and hosting receptions for astronauts. Such individuals were, like himself, symbols of discipline, toughness, and strength who could serve as positive role models for a nation of all too "soft" armchair athletes.

Because of his constant back problems, Kennedy's own preferred chair was the rocker. A potential political liability if perceived as a sign of infirmity, the president's rocking chair instead became a nationally recognized symbol of traditional values—evidence of the homespun informality prevailing in the White House.[11] In part, the public's interpretation of this symbol was influenced by JFK's promotion of physical fitness as well as by his own youthful appearance. But it also was shaped by Kennedy's remarkable ability to be seen as a modern-day Everyman—a regular guy who just happened to be president.

This particular heroic virtue was manifested in a variety of ways. First, his Boston Irish heritage provided JFK with entrée to the hearts, minds, and imaginations of millions of Americans descended from nineteenth-century immigrant stock. Even if they hadn't done quite as well for themselves as the Kennedys since their great-grandparents knocked the mud of the Old World from their boots at Ellis Island, these common folk relished the opportunity to recognize one of their own and to celebrate his successes. Media coverage of Kennedy's spring 1963 pilgrimage to the ancestral homestead near New Ross, Ireland, solidified this ethnic connection. Shortly after the president snacked on sandwiches and tea in the dirt-floored kitchen of his cousins' newly whitewashed cottage (with chickens and a pig wandering around them), one observer was so bold as to remark, "That was like Tobacco Road."[12] Perhaps so, but the moment was steeped in emotion both for Kennedy and for his many fictive kin back in the United States.

Second, the sparkling Kennedy wit encouraged belief in the notion that JFK was the first real presidential humorist of modern times. Although his political humor often was wry and ironic, White House witticisms also could be quite folksy—not unlike those told down at the local lodge hall fundraiser. One example: "I appreciate your welcome. As the cow said to the Maine farmer, 'Thank you for a warm hand on a cold morning.'"[13] Even more endearing was his ability to "take" a joke and to laugh at himself in public. Unlike the first lady, JFK seemed more amused than angered over the many Kennedy stories, songs, and skits then in circulation. Some were quite cruel, poking fun at his Catholicism ("There's a rumor going around that Kennedy has caused the State of Massachusetts to be divided into two sections: 'Low Mass' and 'High Mass.'") or Jackie's wardrobe ("Jackie not only is the nation's best dressed woman, she also is the most dressed woman"; "Jack: 'What would you like for Christmas?' Jackie: 'I don't know. What's left?'"), but the president was no snob and refused to take them—or himself—too seriously. Asked at a press conference whether he was annoyed by impersonator Vaughn Meader's satirical skits about the First Family, Kennedy replied: "I listened to Mr. Meader's record, but I thought it sounded more like Teddy than it did me—so *he's* annoyed."[14]

Comedian Vaughn Meader and his faux First Family, 1962 (record jacket, author's collection)

Third, Kennedy-the-Everyman also shared the common people's taste in entertainment. Although featured performers at White House dinner parties ran the gamut from Pablo Casals playing Schumann and Basil Rathbone reading Shakespeare to the Paul Winter Jazz Sextet and the Air Force Strolling Strings, JFK preferred the popular artists of Broadway and Hollywood. His conception of culture was more middlebrow than effete. If ever willing to escort Queen Jackie to the ball, America's popularly elected regent had little real interest in opera and was bored at the ballet. He liked "Bill Bailey" and "Danny Boy"; *Maverick* and *The Jack Benny Show;* historical biographies and Ian Fleming novels; westerns and other types of action movies. His all-time favorite film was *Casablanca.* By adopting many of the pop cultural preferences of middle America, Kennedy humanized the office of president even as he increased his popularity quotient.[15]

But, could one who lived amid such magnificence and who wielded such awesome power be convincing as an Everyman? Certainly, not all chief executives who have attempted this sleight of hand have succeeded in assuming the cloak of commonness. In Kennedy's case, the task was especially difficult. At the time of his inauguration, the president was worth roughly $10 million. The yearly after-tax income from the trust fund established by his father, Joe Kennedy, was in the neighborhood of $100,000 per year. His presidential salary brought in another $100,000 (plus $50,000 expense money and $40,000 for travel).[16] When book royalties and other miscellaneous income are added to the tally, one begins to suspect that this was one family that could afford to go someplace other than Coney Island for a summertime vacation.

Indeed, they could. But as fate and the press would have it, the glamorous Jackie was destined to take the heat for being a spendthrift. While the first lady's "household budget"—which topped out at more than $100,000 per year— seemed somewhat excessive even for one so style conscious, JFK gained a reputation for being both charitable and remarkably frugal. Good advice, it seemed, had been passed along with the Kennedy fortune. As brother Bobby once noted, all of Joe and Rose's children had been instructed in "the value of nickels, dimes, and quarters." But they also had learned to be good stewards who were "never conscious of wealth" and regarded their own good fortune as an obligation to help others. As he had done ever since entering Congress in 1947, the president donated his salary to charity. "I'm of the Establishment in the sense of where I've lived, and my schools," he would say. "But in the sense of the Anglo-Saxon Establishment—no. . . . In my case, my politics and my religion are against it."[17]

How accurate was this self-characterization? Was the extremely well-heeled JFK really such a regular guy? Did he have a sense of compassion rivaling that of Father Flanagan and an ego the size of a gnat? Could he honor and uphold

the hallowed traditions of his office and yet stoically resist the many temptations to affectation, pretense, and elitism that came with the territory? To millions of heroically inclined Americans, all of this seemed possible. Each
element rang true. Donning rose-tinted glasses, the people refused to allow
their president to appear less than the person they imagined and needed him to
be. Perhaps they hoped that by erasing the class-based divisions between themselves and Kennedy they somehow would inhibit the growth of societal alienation and creeping institutionalized depersonalization. Possibly, they felt that if
their greatest hero was an Everyman, then every man (and woman) would be
considered to have heroic potential. Whatever the underlying rationale, it was
obvious that Americans of the 1960s desperately wanted to believe in this
vision. They would have no stuffy, preening, out-of-touch snob as their culture
champion.

A far more acceptable choice was the type of individual who had gained a
solid reputation for high-spirited boldness and valor. One who willingly had
risked all for the promotion of a greater good. An undaunted devotee of
derring-do. A person made of stern stuff. Someone who, like JFK, could produce a press packet bulging with testimonials to his physical courage.

Central to the image of the president-as-risktaker were his widely publicized exploits as commander of PT 109 during World War II. Mass-marketed
via Robert J. Donovan's best-selling book, a country-flavored ballad that
reached number 8 on the hit parade in spring 1962, and a $5 million feature
film starring Cliff Robertson (Warren Beatty turned down the part), the PT
109 story was an adventure tailor-made for the creation of heroic imagery:
The valiant young commander in the water helping save his crew amid the
wreckage of their fatally rammed and splintered torpedo boat; clamping the
strap of Pat McMahon's life jacket between his teeth and towing the seriously
injured sailor to a safe haven; spending an entire night treading water in the
hope of attracting the attention of a rescue vessel; harvesting coconuts and
drinking rainwater fouled by bird droppings in order to stay alive; and, in the
end, receiving the Purple Heart, the Navy and Marine Corps Medal, and the
thanks of a grateful nation for his courage, endurance, and extraordinary leadership ability. Here, certainly, was evidence of uncommon valor. As a bonus, it
was very good theater.[18]

To the very end, when Bobby Kennedy lovingly placed a gold PT boat tie
clasp in his brother's coffin, the PT 109 episode helped shape both JFK's personal and his public identities. During the Massachusetts congressional campaign of 1946, staffers mailed reprints of a *Reader's Digest* article on his wartime
heroism to all registered veterans in the district. PT 109 pins and tie clips were
distributed during the 1960 presidential race and given out as mementos for
years thereafter. In January 1961, surviving members of the crew rode in the

inaugural parade on a float containing a mock-up of the famous torpedo boat. Once in the White House, the new president furnished his office in a nautical motif. World War II mementos included his Navy ID card encased in a glass ashtray, the Solomon Islands coconut shell upon which Kennedy had carved the SOS message that led to his rescue, a scale-model miniature of PT 109, and an oil painting depicting the Japanese destroyer *Amagiri* ramming the ill-fated ship. These tangible reminders of the epic events of 2 August 1943 helped JFK and his many admirers keep the heroic alive and in fresh focus, always available and primed for contemporary application.[19]

The popular image of JFK the Bold that was shaped by the PT 109 adventure received additional texture through later acts of daring. Like the most enduring of our culture heroes, Kennedy opted for something more than a one-night stand with the heroic. Although his administration's determined response to Soviet provocations in Cuba and Berlin caused at least one observer to equate such actions with the Greek stand against the Persians at Salamis in 480 B.C., it was in the area of civil rights that the aspects of Kennedyesque risk taking and courage most relevant to this study may be seen.[20] Here, JFK's adversary was not a foreign foe seeking to expand its sphere of influence but the domestic beneficiaries of a deeply ingrained national bigotry who were hoping to maintain their tenuous grasp on the status quo in race relations.

By the fall of 1963, those who saw their president as the white knight of the modern civil rights movement could cite the following examples of his boldness:

1. As a legislator, he supported antilynching legislation, southern school desegregation, a strong Fair Employment Practices Commission, and abolition of the poll tax. Kennedy was the first New England member of either house of Congress to appoint a black to his staff.[21]

2. When, in 1957, his best-selling *Profiles in Courage* was awarded the Pulitzer Prize for biography, he donated the $500 prize money to the United Negro College Fund.[22]

3. During his run for the presidency, Kennedy banned participation in segregated campaign meetings.[23]

4. After noticing that there were no blacks marching with the Coast Guard unit in the 1961 inaugural parade, JFK started an official inquiry which resulted in the funding of a major recruiting drive to enroll African-Americans in the Coast Guard Academy. By 1963, black recruiting officers were visiting some two hundred schools per year and making additional contacts through the National Association for the Advancement of Colored People (NAACP) and the National Urban League.[24]

5. Once established in office, the new president expanded this initiative by employing a variety of executive actions, orders, and appointments to end ex-

clusionary practices and to promote equal employment opportunity within the federal bureaucracy. U.S. Employment Offices were told to refuse "whites only" job orders. Frank Reeves became a special assistant to the president; Andrew Hatcher, the associate White House press secretary; Carl Rowan, a deputy assistant secretary of state for public affairs; and Clifton Wharton, the ambassador to Norway. In addition, Kennedy appointed five blacks, including NAACP counsel and future Supreme Court justice Thurgood Marshall, to the federal bench. At the Justice Department, the number of African-American attorneys jumped from ten to more than seventy. Overall, between June 1961 and June 1963, black employment in the upper civil service ranks increased by 88 percent. As the NAACP's Roy Wilkins later recalled, "Kennedy was so hot on the Department heads, the Cabinet officers, and agency heads that everyone was scrambling around trying to find himself a Negro in order to keep the President off his neck."[25]

6. In mid-1963, JFK launched a drive for the passage of what eventually came to be the nation's most comprehensive piece of civil rights legislation, the Civil Rights Act of 1964. The controversial bill received House Judiciary Committee approval less than a month before the president was assassinated.[26]

7. Either directly or through his representatives, Kennedy stood up to segregationist southern governors seeking to maintain color-coded educational institutions. He congratulated the citizens and officials of cities that had successfully implemented school desegregation. Kennedy was among the first public officials to promote student and faculty exchanges between predominantly white and historically black colleges.[27]

8. The president made sure that blacks were invited to White House social functions. In January 1963, the Kennedys hosted a dinner and reception commemorating the centennial of the Emancipation Proclamation. Among the 1,400 guests was the largest contingent of blacks ever welcomed at the executive mansion. Later that same year, the president treated civil rights leaders to sandwiches and coffee when they met with him at the conclusion of the March on Washington.[28]

9. In the fall of 1960, after Martin Luther King Jr. was sentenced to four months at hard labor in Georgia's Reidsville state prison, JFK's supportive telephone call of concern to a worried and pregnant Coretta Scott King was appreciated greatly by African-Americans. This politically hazardous gesture caused Dr. King's father to switch his vote to Kennedy and moved the Southern Christian Leadership Conference's Ralph Abernathy to declare that it was "time for all of us to take off our Nixon buttons." As they went to the polls in November, many blacks did just that.[29]

Although skeptics would say that certain of these highly publicized deeds were either too tentative, too halting, or too politically motivated to be accorded heroic status, most would agree that they were in some sense symbolic—and symbolism has always been a staple in the culture hero's diet. At the time, what seemed most important was that Kennedy's expansive view of the presidency included the willingness to utilize his powers of office—both symbolic and substantive—on behalf of black folk and in support of their historical political agenda. But there were only so many contributions JFK could make as the nation's chief administrator and the civil rights movement's executive branch gatekeeper. The rest, including the spark to widespread activism and long-term commitment, had to come from Jack Kennedy as culture hero. Indeed, it is here that the full value and importance of his bold, risk-taking image becomes apparent.

If he was not quite the all-powerful white knight of civil rights, he was, without question, a most impressive motivator of those who might choose to cast their lot with such a movement. For many of this generation, black and white alike, he unlocked the door to new possibilities, urging them to sample freely and then to go out, test limits, and demolish precedent. Although one might expect that a person of Kennedy's stamp would seek to maintain exclusive bragging rights to the heroic, he refused to consider risk taking an executive privilege. Like the most egalitarian of our culture heroes, JFK promoted the belief that a life of courage was within the reach of every American. "To be courageous," he wrote, "requires no exceptional qualifications, no magic formula, no special combination of time, place and circumstance. It is an opportunity that sooner or later is presented to us all." Whether it meant journeying into space or joining the Peace Corps, Kennedy urged his followers to accept life's great challenges; to respect themselves enough to recognize that each person possessed the ability to do something that would benefit some other person in a material way. As Jackie noted, his vision of human empowerment was based on the premise that "one man can make a difference and that every man should try."[30]

Perhaps this was John Kennedy's most significant contribution to the civil rights quest. Descending from Olympus, this modern-day culture hero attempted to bridge the color chasm separating his all-too-mortal subjects. Aided by the attractive power of his own multidimensional heroic image, he promoted belief in the notion that the average person was capable of great and noble deeds. According to this teaching, heroism was both universal and color-blind.

So, too, was Kennedy's popularity as reflected in the national opinion polls. Although such surveys are, at best, an imperfect yardstick by which to measure a president's abilities, they can provide a rough approximation of the people's response to the overall image (heroic or otherwise) that he conveys. A decidedly positive public image can compensate for an officeholder's less-than-sterling job performance, but a poor one may detract from even his most laudatory accomplishments. While historians will argue forever about how well JFK fulfilled the duties of his office, there likely will be far less debate over the attractiveness of his heroic persona. And the president's reputation as a courageous, movie-star-handsome sportsman who could relate to the common people even while maintaining an extraordinarily glamorous lifestyle didn't hurt him a bit in the polls. After giving him an estimated 70 percent of their votes in 1960, African-Americans ranked Kennedy just behind Dr. King as the individual who had done the most for black rights. Among all Americans, the president's approval rating reached a high of 83 percent just after the Bay of Pigs invasion in April 1961 and stayed within the 60th and 70th percentiles until the fall of 1963. As a composite, these were the best scores garnered by any chief executive in modern times.[31] Thus, even if many Americans were slow to accept Kennedy's entreaty to activism, most seemed to appreciate receiving an invitation to join him in recasting the image of the presidency.

But the nation found JFK only to lose him. Initially, the work of a cowardly assassin's (or assassins') bullets did no harm to his hero's reputation. For a time, the slain president's persona became even more resplendent than before, his exploits more frequently recalled and lovingly appreciated in death than in life. Television coverage of his funeral rites allowed almost everyone to participate in the communal ritual of remembering and grieving. The vivid, electronically transmitted images that many Americans vowed would remain with them for the rest of their lives were deeply moving and classically heroic: the continuous stream of tearful visitors filing past the catafalque; the flag-draped caisson and riderless horse; the magnificent procession of foreign and domestic dignitaries following Kennedy's body to Saint Matthew's Cathedral; three-year-old John Jr. giving his father a final salute as the band played "Hail to the Chief"; Jackie lighting the eternal flame at graveside and then passing the torch to his brothers.[32] To many mourners, the martyred Kennedy long would remain a storybook figure—a symbolic hero frozen in time and unburdened by a mortal's flaws.

Their heartfelt tributes came in many forms. Over 800,000 sent sympathy cards to Jackie. Joining Hallmarkian sentiment with personalized condolences bordering on the filiopietistic, they recalled the most noteworthy traits of their fallen leader. To some, he simply was "the best president we ever had." But for others, Kennedy already had become a saint. In life, they said, JFK had been "brave and very kind." He helped feed the poor, fought courageously for civil rights, and "saved us from many wars." Loved and honored as a "special brother," he "died like a soldier for his country." Never again, wrote one mourner, would there be "a man as great as him." Kennedy was "a hero and every good thing you could think of."[33]

Military guard of honor at John F. Kennedy's casket in the East Room of the executive mansion, 23 November 1963 (U.S. News and World Report Collection, Library of Congress)

The emotional catharsis promoted by these individual expressions of loss—and of gratitude—soon gave way to a national buying spree as Americans clamored for lasting mementos of their now sainted president. Musical tributes and recordings of Kennedy's speeches vied with Beatles and Beach Boys LPs for access to record-buyers' pocketbooks. Coffee-table picture books and praise-laden insider biographies filled booksellers' shelves. Ceramic busts, tribute charms, "eternal flame" night-lights, and memorial medals engraved with New Frontier credos became a part of an ever-growing catalogue of collectible Kennediana. In the United States alone, JFK's regal likeness appeared on a new fifty-cent piece, a $75 savings bond, and a commemorative stamp.[34] And why should it be otherwise? If the ancients could strike coins and medallions in order to perpetuate the memory of their emperors, could bereaved Americans do any less for their beloved JFK?

Certain individuals, however, discovered that it was not enough to own a Bavarian "Ich Bin ein Berliner" token or an uncirculated Kennedy half-dollar encased in plastic. Nor were they satisfied by the renaming of a public building, bridge, or highway after the former president. With little to restrain their emotional involvement in the process of mythmaking, these fans became fanatics. When memorialists turned to myth, the Kennedy story became legend.

Some likened JFK to the martyred Lincoln (but seldom to McKinley). Similarities went far beyond the fact that both died on a Friday—or that the full name of each of their assassins had fifteen letters—or that Lincoln was killed in Ford's Theatre and Kennedy shot while riding in a Lincoln made by Ford. In life, said the mythmakers, both presidents had displayed exemplary moral courage. In death, their legacy could assist lesser beings in the struggle to live up to national ideals. Perhaps, it was suggested, the two saintly leaders had perished in order to redeem and regenerate America. To make this hypothesis seem more immediate, certain of the more imaginative minds recounted instances of Kennedy effecting cures of arthritis and cancer from beyond the grave.[35]

Others concocted equally surreal stories claiming that JFK really wasn't dead at all. According to these modern-day folk legends, the president had been seriously but not critically wounded in Dallas. For the time being, he either was recuperating from his wounds in an intensive-care ward; warehoused, in a comatose state, at a secret medical facility; or resting on a Mediterranean island until such time as he could return to the United States—presumably to assist his fellow citizens in their hour of greatest need.[36]

Far more widespread was the postassassination belief that the Kennedy presidency was best—even most accurately—characterized as a modern-day Camelot that could never be reestablished. As a historical analogue, this linking of JFK's New Frontier bureaucracy with the court of King Arthur was nonsensical. But as a metaphor combining in one symbol the various heroic traits and images which had become associated with his administration, Camelot made all the sense in the world.[37]

The storybook coupling of Kennedy the Hero with Arthurian legend—or at least Lerner and Loewe's Broadway version of it—began in the presidential bedroom. Shortly after the assassination, Jackie told journalist Theodore H. White that before going to sleep, the president often had relaxed by listening to selections of his favorite music on an old Victrola. "The song he loved most," she recalled, "came at the very end of this record, the last side of *Camelot,* sad *Camelot:* 'Don't let it be forgot, that once there was a spot, for one brief shining moment that was known as Camelot.'" Perhaps there would be great presidents again, she continued, making her point, "but there'll never be another Camelot again."[38] Popularized by White and other writers, Camelot soon became far more than what Rose Kennedy referred to as Jackie's "personal, private symbol" of the couple's "romantic and glorious life together."[39] Evoking an undeniable sense of magic, it shaped, solidified, and enhanced JFK's reputation as a noble and virtuous leader of great accomplishment. The attractive power of Camelot ensured that Kennedy's heroic persona would have remarkable staying power.

Eventually, however, problems surfaced. By the mid-1970s, rumormongers and revisionist writers had begun to disassemble what they now referred to as the Kennedy myth. A murkier and far less inspiring image of the martyred president emerged. It became commonplace to hear that both JFK and the true believers in Camelot too often had confused style and substance, activity and action, toughness and strength, self-confidence and character, popular and political leadership. Although few questioned Kennedy's impact on the public imagination, a growing number of commentators held that neither lofty rhetoric nor an excess of "vigah" could substitute for concrete achievement. The heady rush to the New Frontier, they implied, had been more bust than boom.[40]

Critics scored Kennedy for being overly cautious with Congress and for neglecting to utilize fully the powers of his office in support of progressive legislation. He was, some said, "pragmatic to the point of amorality"—at best, a centrist politico whose preference for gradual, incremental change provided students of American government with a classic example of the inadequacies of liberal Democratic leadership. Moreover, Kennedy's personalization of the presidency and his "obsessive-compulsive need for power and social recognition" were said to have led the nation ever deeper into the morass of Vietnam and served to legitimize some of the worst excesses of the Johnson and Nixon administrations.[41]

The nature and extent of Kennedy's commitment to civil rights came under especially close scrutiny. Portrayed as a moderate both by conviction and by design, the former president now garnered little praise for his efforts at ending discrimination. Revisionist writers claimed that a person of his social class could not have known blacks intimately enough to fathom the depth of twentieth-century racial oppression. Certainly, his own experiences with religious bigotry had been slight in comparison. As a result, while Kennedy eventually came to oppose discrimination of all kinds intellectually, there seemed to be little in his personal experience to cause him to be truly passionate about the subject of black rights.[42]

Once in office, JFK's tendency was to favor volunteerism over coercion—a practice which gave the impression that he was promising change and stability at the same time. Some understood that the chief executive's "zig zag behavior" on civil rights was dictated by the practical need to maintain the allegiance of key southern Democrats. Others were more blunt. It was political expediency, a coward's attempt at crisis management through the appeasement of white bigots. Still others considered his cautious approach to be a violation of past campaign promises and an immediate threat to the safety of those far bolder individuals who were putting their lives on the line daily to register black voters in the South.[43]

If Kennedy truly was a man of the people, asked critics, why had black folk been forced to mount an "Ink for Jack" campaign in order to pressure him into signing an executive order prohibiting discrimination in federally assisted housing? Why had Kennedy been so hesitant to lend his support to the March on Washington? And what in heaven's name had caused him to appoint Mississippi judge William Harold Cox to a federal court post after Cox repeatedly had ignored the desegregation decisions of higher courts and had referred to blacks as "niggers" from the bench? Was Martin Luther King Jr. on target when he accused the president of "aggressively driving only toward the limited goal of token integration"? Had African-Americans, as another early skeptic suggested, been the unwitting victims of "the best snow job in history"? Indeed, were we all so dazzled by the so-called Kennedy myth that his actual failings had been glossed over, ignored, or dismissed as irrelevant?[44]

Although it may have done little to ease the doubts of those who were beginning to question Kennedy's heroism, assurances were given that heroic feats—albeit of a somewhat unconventional nature—most definitely had been performed during the time of Camelot. On numerous occasions, said these reports, JFK had exhibited a near-Herculean desire and capacity for sex outside marriage. What the predominantly male Washington, D.C., press corps once quite conveniently had relegated to the rumor mills now became a frequent subject of investigative journalism. During the postassassination years, the sensationalist press was awash in these kiss-and-tell revelations of marital infidelity: orgies in D.C. hotels, sexual conquests in the presidential bedroom, nude swimming parties in the White House pool. According to one story, Kennedy nearly was late for his 13 October 1960 television debate with Richard Nixon because he had dallied so long with a woman at New York City's Plaza Hotel. Another tale described a turned-on JFK experimenting with marijuana cigarettes before sex—joking to his blonde socialite bedmate, "We're having a White House conference on narcotics here in two weeks." A third told of the time that he had to clamber out a window and down a fire escape to avoid a pack of photographers and reporters who had discovered his hideaway on the top floor of a swank Los Angeles apartment building.[45]

From Hollywood starlets to hatcheck girls, hotel maids, and at least one practicing historian, no reasonably attractive woman seemed safe from Kennedy's advances. The sheer pace of his sex life was said to have been awe inspiring. "There's no question," recalled one intimate. "Jack had the most active libido of any man I've ever known. He was really unbelievable—absolutely incredible. . . . No one was off-limits to Jack—not your wife, your mother, your sister." JFK, said another, "was a very busy boy."[46]

For some, accounts of these numerous sexual conquests provided titillation and voyeuristic amusement, further strengthening the belief that Kennedy had possessed the physical stamina of a true hero. Others, especially those brought up short by the revisionists' assessment of his contributions to the civil rights movement, started to doubt his moral character. The desanctification of Camelot began to pick up speed. And the White House bashing, public cynicism, and national self-scrutiny brought about by Watergate did nothing to slow the trend. Even the jokes got a bit disrespectful, to say nothing of morbid:

> What did Johnson say to Mrs. Kennedy?
> "I guess Jack needed that trip to Dallas like a hole in the head."

> Did you hear what John-John got for Christmas?
> A jack-in-the-box.[47]

In some circles, it seemed that JFK, like sad-sack comedian Rodney Dangerfield, was getting no respect.

This is not to imply that all of the hero-worshipers abandoned the good ship Camelot at the first sign of troubled waters. Certainly, a viable case could be made for the continuing attractiveness of the Kennedy legend. Well into the 1980s, national polls showed the ex-president garnering considerable support from the faithful.[48] In one way or another, every subsequent president has been bedeviled by the ever-present, ever-expectant ghosts of the New Frontier.[49] But the times were changing, and Camelot, with or without party girls and hanky-panky, was fading rapidly into the mists. Rumor peddlers and revisionist historians were not wholly to blame. As a dead hero, JFK was unable to defend himself against his accusers or respond to the new social concerns of the postassassination years.

The hero of memory often adapts slowly to change—and by the late 1960s America was totally engulfed in an exceptionally divisive, violent season of change. Urban riots, foreign warfare, campus unrest, and still more political assassinations put an abrupt end to the unabashedly optimistic notion that a national sense of purpose and of community existed. To all appearances, the limits of American idealism had been reached. No single culture hero— certainly no dead martyr—appeared capable of putting our Humpty Dumpty world back together again.

Enter the black culture heroes. So uniquely representative of the group spirit that they were celebrated by all manner of black people, yet possessed of sufficient "universal" appeal to be attractive to a far larger and more diverse constituency, African-American heroes helped fill the void created by the decay of Kennedy's Camelot. Certainly, they were not alone. Culture-hero-worshipers who had struggled to maintain a mental image of JFK as a combination Paul Bunyan, Rudolph Valentino, Errol Flynn, and Jimmy Stewart as George Bailey had the option of asking *either* Jim Brown *or* Paul Newman, the Beatles, and Sean Connery as James Bond to fulfill their post-Camelot needs.

Nevertheless, if the black heroes were neither politically powerful nor popular with everyone, they made an undeniable impression on the popular culture of the era. The present study makes no attempt to manufacture black heroes out of whole cloth but simply to give overdue recognition to those whose distinctive cachet became most visible within the cultural matrix of the 1960s and 1970s. To date, their contributions to the Black Revolution and to the continuing vitality of the American spirit have been less than adequately recognized or thoroughly studied.

Black culture heroes possessed a full complement of the qualities for which John Kennedy was cherished. As standard-bearers for the modern-day heroic, they offered their followers both entertainment and ego enhancement. They were a source of in-group identity and provided an avenue to intergroup understanding. As the mainstream culture absorbed, adopted, modified, and mimicked the deeds and style of black heroes, the cultural void within society and between groups grew a little smaller. By the end of the era, many Americans of strikingly different backgrounds had elected to apply for citizenship in the black heroes' version of Camelot.

As employed in this study, "Black Camelot" serves as a metaphorical device meant to symbolize and illuminate the new world order sought by African-Americans of both the civil rights and the Black Power eras. Here, standing in stark contrast to the past experiences of most black people, was a resplendent kingdom founded on great expectations. Although many of its manifestations were as tangible as those of any political entity, this Camelot, like Kennedy's, was less a place than a state of mind. It also was more than a sepia-toned version of the Middle American Dream and would be populated by all manner (and classes) of black humanity. Not dependent on a single, precisely delineated ideological structure but rather on a diverse, interconnected set of culture-based principles, Black Camelot extended and applied the culture champions' empowering, futuristic vision to the larger society. According to this schematic model, the outer boundaries of Camelot would be reached when average black Americans were accorded the same basic rights and responsibilities as their heroes. The settlement would be considered secure when self-directed black Everymen were respected by all for being true to themselves. Designed to last much longer than "one brief shining moment," this idealized Promised Land would improve upon JFK's version. The best of all possible worlds, it would be a place of chivalry, honor, justice, and courage—a spectacular showcase for both fully realized African-American achievement and meaningful interracial cooperation.

ONE

The Black Hero's History and Humanity

"Zora," he said thoughtfully, "you must learn to read."

"What for?"

"So that you can read books and know lots of things."

"Don't white folks make books?"

"Yes—most of the books."

"Pooh! I knows more than they do now—a heap more."

"In some ways you do; but they know things that give them power and wealth and make them rule."

"No, no. They don't really rule; they just thinks they rule. They just got things,—heavy, dead things. We black folks is got the *spirit*. We'se lighter and cunninger; we fly right through them; we go and come again just as we wants to. Black folks is wonderful."

BLES AND ZORA IN W. E. B. DU BOIS, *The Quest of the Silver Fleece*

Upon his elevation to the nation's highest office in 1960, Jack Kennedy—like all previous chief executives—was escorted to the very end of a presidential queue containing numerous American political heroes. According to the dictates of history, it was here that he would start his quest for lasting greatness. Admittedly, the heroism of a fair number of those situated closer to the head of the line was apparent only to the most diligent searchers of now yellowed campaign biographies and funerary eulogies. Others continued to be recognized for contributions of substance and/or style but found their mantle of celebrity wearing a bit thin as once brilliant reputations were dimmed by the triumphs of subsequent leaders. Indeed, many ex-presidents seemed not to have aged well at all. Each year their heroism quotient diminished as they were accorded fewer and fewer paragraphs (with no accompanying photos) in encyclopedias and schoolroom texts. Certainly, it was anticipated that a splendid specimen like Kennedy would have little trouble besting and bypassing the most unfortunate of these near-forgotten oldsters in the ongoing, ever-spirited competition for public adoration and historical acclaim.

But, as we all know, each and every one of Kennedy's Oval Office competitors was a European-American male—and not very "ethnic" at that. Was this a fair test? A true challenge of Olympian magnitude? Let us say, for argument's and curiosity's sakes, that we could rewrite history and add a racial variable—a *black* president—to the equation. Would this have made JFK's task of advancing in rank any more or any less arduous? Moreover, where on our list of presidential heroes might we expect this imaginary black official to place? Above or below Polk? Nipping at Cleveland's heels? Trailing Tyler but slightly ahead of Grant? Would he (or she) be a flash in the pan or possess long-term heroic staying power?

Obviously, to entertain such questions is to engage in the most ahistorical speculation imaginable. Nevertheless, it should be noted that even guilty pleasures often have great utility in the writing of history. Stimulated by the notion of Jack Kennedy duking it out with a worthy black challenger, one conceivably might begin to formulate a series of larger, more essential questions about American culture heroes, their creators, and their constituents. For example, given the social dynamics of the situation, is it reasonable to believe that a descendant of slaves was capable of attaining the degree and type of recognition granted Kennedy even *before* he became president? To probe further, one might ask whether a fair-minded observer would be likely to find a larger percentage of hero types within one population than in another. Indeed, what are the chances of locating a completely fair-minded observer? Can we, then, posit the existence of racially defined "cheering sections" for different varieties of culture heroes? And, if this is the case, is it possible to determine how heroism is defined and measured within each advocacy group? More specifically, is black heroism essentially the same as white—or significantly different? And has this been the case from the beginning? To a remarkable degree, the (typically unreflecting) responses that most Americans have made to perplexing questions such as these have been determined by racial identification and ethnic loyalty. Ultimately, to tell the story of heroism in America, one is obliged to go beyond a recapitulation of the jockeying of white elites for public favor in the political, corporate, or entertainment sector. The *real* story lies in a far less frequently told tale of interracial confrontation and conflict—of epic struggles between heroic representations of group interests and ideals.

Throughout American history whites have guarded access to the national pantheon of heroes with an unwearied vigilance. Often, these cultural gatekeepers have opted to define the heroic in a manner which effectively excluded all but white males from consideration. African-Americans responded by developing certain aspects of what some have termed an oppositional culture. While blacks by no means rejected all—or even most—mainstream notions about heroism, they did stand firm on one issue. A black skin, they declared, was no barrier to heroic stature. Indeed, in some cases, it was deemed a prerequisite.

To begin to understand both the nature and the importance of this long-term, culture-based battle royal, it is useful to return to what one certified American celebrity, Clayton Moore's Lone Ranger, in all likelihood would have referred to as "those golden days of yesteryear." At the opening of the twentieth century, the nation's chief culture heroes were far less likely than those of today to feel the sting of constant, invasive public scrutiny. A man was still a man and a hero a (white male) hero. Nobody thought about going through the garbage to look for evidence of scandal. No army of paparazzi stalked the hero in search of salacious snapshots. Typically, all but the most sensationalist scribes of the day accorded national political heroes a mannered but heartfelt respect. On occasion, this ultradignified treatment bordered on the filiopietistic. Most seemed to feel, however, that this was the least that could be done for governmental greats who, under a somewhat different administrative model, would be presented to the public in full-dress, scepter-toting splendor. Certainly, this was a halcyon age for the culture hero and none received a more splendid remembrance than the Republic's very first patriarch, George Washington.

For example, in *Hero Tales from American History,* a marvelous encapsulation of turn-of-the-century hagiology, Henry Cabot Lodge and Rough Rider Theodore Roosevelt waxed poetic over the many virtues of Lincoln and Grant, Daniel Boone, Stonewall Jackson, and Colonel Robert Gould Shaw (but far less so over those of Shaw's black 54th Massachusetts Regiment troops). Nevertheless, their most enthusiastic—and some of their most over-ripe—prose was reserved for the revered master of Mount Vernon. Here, one can ascertain the outlines of the majoritarian culture's preferred portrayal of the politician-cum-statesman become legend. Here, in a nutshell, were the fundamental components of American heroism circa 1900.

In Lodge's account, the prepresidential Washington was vigorous, self-directed, and bold. Born into a poor family, he was forced by circumstances to leave his widowed mother and "go out into the world to fight for himself." Ably rising to the challenge, Washington "plunged into the wilderness," where he quickly became an expert hunter, woodsman, and Indian fighter. At a time when his pampered peers were just leaving college, young George was displaying his considerable leadership ability on the battlefield. With "reckless daring" and "cool courage" he exposed himself to great danger. Indeed, so often did enemy bullets pass through his clothing without doing harm that both the French and their Native American allies concluded that he "bore a charmed life." According to Lodge, these military feats proved that the "adventurous spirit of his race" coursed strong within the future president.[1]

By 1776, this bold representative of European-American virtue had won the respect and confidence of all. The veritable embodiment of the American Revolution, Washington was said to have been central to its success. During the war he became the "idol of the country and of his soldiers." After peace and in-dependence were established, he at first resisted the overwhelmingly popular notion that he should head the new nation-state. General Washington, it was said, had "no vulgar longing" for personal power. Nevertheless, after witness-ing the financial and administrative chaos of the Confederation, he agreed to accept the call to national leadership. With a vision at once far more refined and considerably more expansive than that of of the vast majority of his contem-poraries, Washington began to chart America's destiny. After eight years at the task, the hard-driving president had compiled a most impressive catalogue of achievements on behalf of the Republic and its citizens.[2]

Duly noted were the personal attributes that enabled this particular Found-ing Father to succeed on such a grand scale. Physically striking, the first presi-dent was tall, handsome, and "powerfully made." An educated but not especially learned man, he led a life of action. As portrayed in Lodge's battle-field narrative, Washington was habituated to "swimming icy streams" and "feared no exposure or fatigue." Although by nature possessed of "strong de-sires and stormy passions," he nevertheless succeeded in keeping these "fiery impulses" from overriding his keen sense of justice and compassion. It was said that those who knew him well found Washington to be "all that was kind and gentle." His heart continually went out to the poor and oppressed. Moderated and governed by an "iron will," the president's more volatile tendencies were compensated for by a sensibility that permitted neither self-aggrandizement nor self-deception. Thought to be the very "soul of truth and honor," Wash-ington possessed a moral character that was deemed pure and "free from spot." Certainly, in the collective historical memory which Lodge and Roosevelt were attempting to invigorate, Washington rightfully stood "among the great-est of his race."[3]

But, was Lodge talking about the human race or the Caucasian race? Did prevailing assumptions about racial evolution and Anglo-Saxon superiority exclude blacks from the field of heroism? In an era of expansionist fervor, po-litical disfranchisement, and racial segregation, could a people who Lodge's coauthor believed were "200,000 years behind [the whites]" produce culture champions of Washingtonian stature?[4] Then as now, responses to these ques-tions would vary depending upon whom one asked and how heroism was defined. To black intellectual and activist W. E. B. Du Bois, Lodge's contempo-rary, the answers were as obvious as the white ethnocentrism and cultural chauvinism that permeated early-twentieth-century historical writing.[5]

Believing that the Universal could be found in the Particular, Du Bois was an outspoken proponent and popularizer of African-American heroism. As a member of an oppressed, politically powerless people, he recognized the social utility of dynamic role models who could provide inspiration and, hopefully, racial uplift in troubled times. But, as a firm believer in the precept that genius was the exclusive preserve of no single variety of the human species, he could not discount the possibility of white heroism. Certainly, throughout history white folk had worked hard to document its existence, even its omnipresence. What he would do—as essayist, historian, novelist, poet, and playwright—was to compare and contrast the black and white heroic.[6] Perhaps, he hoped, each race could learn from the other. If such "instruction" helped each separate group to reach its own internal potential, the progress of all humankind would be advanced. Eventually, both a cultural synthesis and a reciprocal world order might be realized. Here, Du Bois revealed his well-known sense of double consciousness. The "double self" of the African exiled in America was composed of "two souls, two thoughts, two unreconciled strivings; two warring ideals in one dark body."[7] More important, however, was the manner in which his critical analysis of heroism revealed deeply felt racial loyalties. To Du Bois, it was unmistakable that black heroism was superior to white.

Although the notion that the various races possessed special attributes was widely accepted by early-twentieth-century intellectuals, Du Bois's reading and interpretation of this patently racialist concept were distinctive and exceptionally fine textured. Because he expressed himself in a diverse array of literary formats and genres, his opinion on such matters sometimes appears contradictory, his message mixed. Indeed, one puzzles at the origin of certain conceptualizations. Had he been a ready recipient of Social Darwinist precepts while in training at Harvard? Was he at all influenced by the rise of German nationalism? Did Du Bois inherit the Ethiopianist/black nationalist tradition of Edward Wilmot Blyden, Alexander Crummell, and Martin Delany? Or was he a messianic visionary, charting his own course through the world of ideas? The precise intellectual mix could be argued endlessly.[8] But one thing is certain: he believed fervently that black people were destined to make a significant and lasting contribution to world history.

According to Du Bois, the African-American "seventh son" truly was gifted—and with more than a "veil" and "second-sight." Blacks were a race of artists, endowed with a unique sense of beauty—of sound, color, and "spiritual joyousness." A "tropical" love of life not only enabled members of the race to benefit from the therapeutic properties inherent in laughter, song, and dance but also led them to place a premium on the development of personal qualities such as honesty, humility, faith, and compassion. Like his own mother, whom Du Bois described as a "kind face[d]" woman of infinite patience, blacks had triumphed over life-destroying forces with a "curious determination" that was masked by racial "softness." Their laughter in the face of adversity was deemed a sign of courage, not of buffoonery. African-Americans were not hardened by centuries of struggle against man and nature, and their contribution to Western civilization was more aesthetic and spiritual than technological or military. But it was an element essential to its survival. The black community was said to provide an "oasis of simple faith and reverence" in an artificial and hypocritical land.[9]

On at least one occasion, Du Bois gave public thanks that to the best of his knowledge no "Anglo-Saxon" blood flowed through his veins. Contrasting dramatically with his idealized ancestral race, the U.S. branch of the Anglo-Saxon family tree was said to be horribly diseased. Its contamination of American culture was in an advanced, critical stage. Indeed, to Du Bois, the term "Anglo-Saxon" (or "Teuton") stood for all that was wrong with contemporary society. Self-centered and boastful and with a taste for "the tawdry and flamboyant," these white people were masters of deception but were incapable of camouflaging their essential meanness of spirit. They always seemed to be preoccupied with war or the preparation for war. When not directly engaged in conquest for commerce's sake, their energies were expended in creating a drab, dehumanizing, domestic workplace that was capable of sapping even the most vibrant life force. Deprived of God's greatest gift to humankind—the spirit of laughter—this pale-skinned, joyless race caused numerous problems for others. According to Du Bois, theirs was a history of "murder, theft, rape, deception, and degradation." Burdened by an "overweening sense of the I and the consequent forgetting of the Thou," whites had yet to overcome this terrible legacy of "Liquor and Lust and Lies."[10]

As one might expect, the Anglo-Saxon's heroes shared these unfortunate attributes. They, too, had deified Self and adopted "kill or be killed" and "might makes right" as behavioral watchwords. With "moral obtuseness and refined brutality," these soldiers and strong men had advanced Western civilization by imperialism and slavery. Theirs, said Du Bois, was the "cool logic of the Club"—individualism gone berserk, might transformed into the most sacred right at the expense of human brotherhood. Although portrayed by generations of Anglo-Saxon chroniclers as indomitable "guardian[s] of a people's All," champions of white-authored history texts such as Bismarck, Gladstone, Chinese Gordon, or Jefferson Davis could be considered bold *and* admirable only by "lopping off their sins." And this Du Bois refused to do.[11]

Instead of acceding to a further deification of the white culture heroes' "impetuous manhood," the black historian offered a counterproposal. He urged whites to consider the unique qualities that African-Americans brought to heroism. Perhaps, after careful consideration, they would deign to allow blacks to become coworkers in the kingdom of culture, to share their racial gifts with the mainstream, and to thereby provide a much-needed complement and corrective to Anglo-Saxon "hardness." Without the leavening, humanizing component of blackness, white Americans—led by their brash and bloodied culture heroes—likely would continue to act more as destroyers than as agents of civilization. In Du Bois's vision, *true* heroes were those whose "strong passions" were tempered by the African-Americans' "softness."[12]

For blacks, Du Bois's message contained a prophecy, a warning, and an encouragement to action. He suggested that it was highly unlikely that the fortunes of the black race would improve materially if the Lodge-Roosevelt model of heroism continued to hold sway. Throughout history, African peoples had been among the chief victims of white heroism. Indeed, from a black perspective, the "fiery impulses" and "reckless daring" of even a Washington were far too unpredictable, too volatile, too dangerous to countenance. Rarely had white-race champions endowed with these traits proven to be "kind and gentle" in their dealings with other groups. All too often, the "iron" in their wills had served as a bludgeon, not a self-governing mechanism. Certainly, the rise of white elites to positions of high status within American institutions may not, in every case, have been the result of "vulgar longing," but the resulting allocation of political, economic, and social power most definitely had worked against blacks' best interests. In this context, the whites' highly touted "honor" was that of thieves.

Attracted to the subversive notion of "carving God in night/painting hell in white," Du Bois urged his people to break the Anglo-Saxon heroic mold. In place of "might makes right," he suggested that they substitute a more race specific and far more ennobling axiom: "the blacker the mantle the mightier the man." He challenged black folk to maintain their racial and cultural identity, to cherish their unique gifts. Against considerable mainstream opinion to the contrary, they were to conceptualize themselves as the "spiritual hope of this land"—a strong yet "deliciously human" people who could serve as the "harbinger of that black to-morrow which is yet destined to soften the whiteness of the Teutonic to-day."[13]

To many whites, however, this seemed a fanciful notion, a wasted effort. Here, they believed, was a classic example of wishful thinking. If the essential components of a black heroic tradition actually existed, why, at this late date in human history, weren't they more widely recognized? Why weren't there any black heroes in the (white-authored) history books, atop finely patined statues, or on the nation's money? Perhaps, as Du Bois suggested, it was because "lions have no historians." On the other hand, it may have been due to the fact that mainstream textbooks all too often portrayed black-, red-, and yellow-skinned peoples as "uncivilized and bizarre" while individuals of the Caucasian persuasion were presented as "kindly and distinguished-looking philanthropist[s]."[14]

Thus, even as they were being encouraged to raise up leonine but decidedly humanistic race heroes for the edification of their contemporaries, African-American writers were forced to do battle with a long-standing and exceedingly influential countertradition. Actually more a mental block than a mind-set, this white perspective on the black world defined African peoples as non-heroic in (and by) nature.

The fundamentals of this tradition have been detailed by a host of modern-day researchers. What they have uncovered in the maw of our popular culture repulses late-century liberal sensibilities. It has disgusted and angered blacks for generations. Insinuating themselves into our lives through all manner of pre-sentation and influence—stage, screen (large and small), music, literature, art, and advertising—an irrepressible gaggle of black nonheroes has swarmed about us. With rustic charm and comic bufoonery they attempt to captivate and control the unwary—to win us over to their view of the black personal-ity.[15] The most memorable of these white inventions include the following:

Noble Savages/Tragic Mulattoes. Heroic only in a sacrificial or existential sense, the Noble Savage was among the earliest variants of black portraiture to appear in Anglo-American literature. Aphra Behn's *Oroonoko* (1688) un-leashed a flood of sentimental writing depicting Africans as unspoiled children of nature whose descent into New World bondage could only serve to awaken human sympathies.[16] Fully capable of heroism in their Edenic homeland, these gentle beings nevertheless were unable to cope with the harsh demands of plantation life. Instead of rebelling or running away, they tended to weep, swoon, fall into a melancholy stupor, or go mad. Cowed and defeated by pow-erful whites, some, like Behn's African prince, Caesar, acted the tragic victim and committed suicide. Those who survived slavery's cruelties longest made their final soliloquies especially poignant by speaking of shattered dreams and lost opportunities:

> Oh! had we died upon our native plain,
> Stretch'd like brave heroes, by our tyrants slain!
> Oh! had our blood smoak'd on each ruffian spear,
> And thus sav'd us from sin, insult and fear;
> But now we meet a shameful shocking fate,
> Unworthy of the brave, the bold, the great.[17]

Noble and contented while in Africa, weak and wretched in America, these literary children of sorrow encouraged reform-minded whites to view the African-Americans' plight as pitiable, but they also affirmed the notion that blacks were weak-willed, hothouse transplants to the white hero's domain.

Later, light-skinned, mixed-race characters met a similar fate. Typically por-trayed as a beautiful young woman who had been raised and educated as "white," the tragic mulatto lost her privileged position when spiteful enemies discovered that she was marked—however faintly—with the "ineffaceable curse of Cain." Even if she had managed to acquire some form of racial double consciousness, it proved to be of little use once her "secret" was revealed.

As described by Zoe, the heroine of Dion Boucicault's Louisiana plantation drama *The Octoroon* (1859), the prognosis for this condition was bleak:

> Of the blood that feeds my heart, one drop in eight is black—bright red as the rest may be, that one drop poisons all the flood; those seven bright drops give me love like yours—hope like yours—ambition like yours— life hung with passions like dew-drops on the morning flowers; but the one black drop gives me despair, for I'm an unclean thing—forbidden by the laws—I'm an Octoroon![18]

Such virtuous but unfortunate women often died in shame or committed suicide after failing to regain their original status. Seemingly, it was "white blood" which provided the tragic mulatto with physical beauty, above-average intelligence, and whatever heroic virtue and staying power she possessed. It was "black blood"—and the larger society's aversion to it—which caused all the problems. Eventually, this deeply troubled, racially star-crossed figure became as much a theatrical convention as the stage whisper.

Loyal Servants. Not so long ago, Mammy, Old Black Joe, Aunt Jemima, Uncle Wabash, and other unctuous octogenarians graced the labels of our syrup bottles, coffee cans, peanut butter jars, and soap powder boxes; legions of nattily attired lawn jockey statues added style, if not good taste, to even the most modest estates; the Cream of Wheat chef was touted as "De Bes' Known Nigger in De Worl'"; and seemingly decent people whistled catchy ditties such as "Snowball," "The Dusky Stevedore," and "That's Why Darkies Were Born" on their way to eat at one of the West Coast's Coon Chicken Inn Restaurants. And this was just the tip of the iceberg.[19]

Loyal, ever-ready-to-please blacks have been one of America's most enduring popular-culture icons. Both as artifact and as image, their benignly comforting countenances have provided generations of whites with a simple but increasingly hard-to-come-by commodity—selfless, often enthusiastic, subservience. From the antebellum stage to postwar local-color novels to early film sets, these kindly, imitative beings embraced servility as the proper organizing principle of their lives. For example, in the two-part Hollywood drama *His Trust* and *His Trust Fulfilled* (1911), an elderly servant saved his master's family from their burning home and then sheltered them in his own tiny cabin throughout the Civil War. Willingly, he sacrificed his own meager savings so that young Missy could be properly educated. In the end, Old George, played by a white actor in blackface, saw that his master's daughter was safely wed to a prosperous English cousin and then, finally, turned to his own affairs. As a reward for his long and faithful service, the elderly bondsman received the bridegroom's grateful handshake and his master's saber. Back at his cabin, the loyal servant could be seen fondling the treasured sword, happy in the realization that he had not betrayed his owner's trust.[20]

Unctuous "Uncle" archetype on postcard
from the South (author's collection)

Uncle Remus revisited? *Gone with the Wind* in embryo? It really didn't matter.
Both the basic intent and anticipated response were the same. Whenever and
however presented, compelling displays of black obsequiousness allowed audiences to experience a vicarious interracial kinship. Here, as numerous story
lines revealed, black and white could become as close as "two fibe-cent pieces in
one dime."[21] Content with their lot, servants rarely questioned the dynamics of
the relationship. To tell their story, it seemed that novelists, screenwriters, and
historians forever would be obliged to "follow the tracks they have made in the
history of another people."[22] Only when the meek came into possession of the
planet could such individuals be considered either self-directed or heroic.

    Comic Minstrels. Sambo, Tambo, and Jazzbo Jim. Rastus, Topsy, Zip Coon,
and Jim Crow. Stepin Fetchit, Willie Best, and Rochester Van Jones. All were
variants of the black American comic minstrel type. Each of these revered cultural figures sported individualized costumery and possessed certain unique
peculiarities. On occasion, some were accorded a modicum of dignity and
allowed to display their wit and shrewdness. But the trait that both defined
and connected them was a seemingly innate ability to provoke gales of side-
splitting laughter. Whenever they appeared, audiences *expected* to be entertained. As a late-nineteenth-century ad for Whallen and Martel's minstrel
extravaganza *The South before the War* (1892) breathlessly promised, ticket buy-

ers would be treated to "whoops of terpsichorean ecstacs [*sic*]." They would be privileged to "see the colored folk shuffle their enormous feet on sanded floors, do live jigs, sing, and do comical antics of niggerdom."[23] It was an irresistible package that lost little of its attractive power—and reached even larger audiences—when the minstrels abandoned the vaudeville stage and took their shtick to the big screen and network television.

Obviously, the minstrel's pop-eyed obtuseness, garish clothing, love of big words, and habitual mumbling mispronunciations were designed to tickle the

THE SLAVES IN THE CORNFIELD.

Comical cornfield malingerers (W. L. G. Smith, *Life at the South; or, "Uncle Tom's Cabin" as It Is* [Buffalo: George H. Derby, 1852])

funny bone. Make no mistake, even black audiences chuckled at radio comics Amos 'n' Andy, Sam 'n' Henry, and Molasses 'n' January. But there was a sinister side to these "dusky delineators of devastating dumbfoolery."[24] Their humorous antics camouflaged a hidden agenda that had little to do with mirth and merriment. In addition to their unparalleled ability to galvanize a laugh meter, these comical figures served as mechanisms of social control and agents of white psychological security.

Minstrel comedians not only put other blacks down, glibly referring to friends and associates as "fools" and "niggas," but also adopted demeaning personal names such as Asbestos, Eight Ball, Prince Orang Outan, Smoke, Mushmouth, Uncle Anthracite, and Bon Bon Buddy the Chocolate Drop. Many were physical grotesques, described by one radio comedy character as "short, dark, and repulsive." With "beef stake lips" and a mouth that stretched "from ear to ear," the minstrel was tailor-made for sight gags that belittled an entire race.[25] And if this gaping red trench wasn't filled with watermelon, whiskey, or chicken, it very likely was engaged in loose talk, braggadocio, or uninhibited childlike expressions of glee. Rarely were informed opinions on issues of concern to *real* people forthcoming. Indeed, this was the minstrel's great burden. They were fit only to be jesters and buffoons.

To quote that untutored sage Andrew H. "Andy" Brown, these comical blacks possessed no "zecketive-billys" and could not hope for success in the business world. Prone to confusing footballs with watermelons, they were unlikely to be enshrined in any sports hall of fame. Unable to fathom the intricacies of modern politics, they were unelectable.[26] A bit of dialogue from *Amos 'n' Andy* sums up the minstrel's prospects for rapid socioeconomic advancement:

> SAPPHIRE: George, I know why you're a no-good bum. It's on account of your association with Andy Brown. Why don't you try to meet a nicer class of men?
>
> KINGFISH: Well, I ain't got da opportunity to meet em, they's all workin'.
>
> SAPPHIRE: Well, that Andy Brown is the cause of it all. What has he ever accomplished?
>
> KINGFISH: Well, yesterday, he had a run of thirteen balls in da side pocket without leanin' on da table.
>
> SAPPHIRE: Now, that's exactly what I mean: Andy hangin' around a pool table all day. Why don't he go to a cultured place like a public library?
>
> KINGFISH: They ain't got no pool table dere.[27]

In the minstrel's world, the glass ceiling of racial stereotyping—not segregation, job discrimination, or disfranchisement—limited the African-American's possibilities. Here, both the reality of black impoverishment and the omnipresence of black unrest were denied. Stripped of self-respect by the role they were forced to play endlessly, comic minstrels seldom became "regusted" enough to strike out against myth and convention. For the most part denied even the compensations of conscience and community, they could not hope to compete with nonminstrels—economically, politically, socially, or sexually. The working out of this cleverly scripted story line allowed whites to maintain their self-penned reputation as a uniquely wise, hardworking, and beautiful people.

Cowards. Black cowards have always been well represented in popular-culture portrayals—if only because their ilk also could be found skulking among the noble savages, comic minstrels, and loyal servants. But even after this double counting is taken into consideration, the sheer number of characters exhibiting pusillanimous traits continues to amaze. Their tremulous antics have led generations of Americans to believe that African-Americans have no capacity for heroism.

Cowardly black literary and theatrical characters were terrified of grave-yards, haunted houses, funeral parlors, and any other locale where one was likely to experience a brush with mortality occasioned by an encounter with an unfriendly spirit. When frozen in the icy grasp of superstition-driven horror, their hair stood on end, eyes bulged, and teeth "chattered with affright." Some temporarily turned chalky white with fear. On such occasions, this seemingly uncontrollable response to the unknown forces of the universe made even Ichabod Crane appear intrepid.[28]

At other times, it was the challenge of life, not the spirits of the departed, that caused their knees to quake. Cowardly blacks made loyal slaves in part because they were too weak-willed to test the waters of the mysterious world beyond the plantations. Early accounts of Underground Railroad operations, for example, lauded the brave, self-sacrificing white conductors and their families but described slave escapees as having a "timid and fearful look, like that of hunted animals." Ignorant, half-clothed, and hungry, they were said to have "skulked and stumbled along half the way to Lake Erie" before (quite accidentally) finding sanctuary among northern friends. If left to their own devices, few would have made good their escape. Indeed, after reading such portrayals of the fugitives, one cannot help wondering what motivated these pitifully ill-prepared, perpetually bewildered beings to attempt a northward journey in the first place. Perhaps it was because they were among the most spirited and resourceful of a race adjudged by many to be "unenlightened and submissive by nature."[29]

Of those who reached the free states, a fair proportion lived to regret their precipitous action. Both ante- and postbellum expatriates soon sought to effect a return to "massa, friends, and home." Often, sorrowful fugitives could be found on the minstrel stage, reminiscing about the days when they would "sit under de shade ob de tree and listen to de little birds sing," read their Bibles, and tip their hats to "de white folks as dey passed by." Northern society—and its new challenges—seemed to have no attractions that could compete with the "land where cotton grows," the "land where milk and honey flows." Dixie, they firmly believed, was "heaven here below."[30] And why shouldn't they? For several generations, proslavery ideologues had taught that African-Americans were constitutionally unsuited for risk taking. They were, asserted the influential southern historian U. B. Phillips in 1929, "more or less contentedly slaves, with grievances from time to time but not ambition."[31] As radio's most famous cabbie, Amos Jones, noted after pulling up roots in the rural South and moving to the big city, a competitive existence in the industrial North wasn't for everyone. "Sometimes Andy," he lamented, "I wish I was back down in Georgia workin' for Mr. Williams, yo' know it. We didn't have a worry in de world den."[32] There, it seems, little was expected of timorous blacks because southerners recognized and had adapted to their supposed racial limitations.

As might be expected, these stereotypically timid, psychologically hamstrung beings made poor soldiers. Inept in freedom, they became cowardly in wartime. Black minstrel characters were shown to be reluctant to enter the Civil War fray even if it meant bringing about an end to racial slavery. In A. C. D. Sandie's "Ole Uncle Abrum's Comin'," newly liberated bondsmen appeared more interested in creature comforts than in the Union army. As their masters fled from the Yankee invaders, leaders of the slave community urged their brothers and sisters to "git into de parlor / As fast as yer can, / And set upon de sofy / Wid yer feet on de divan." Allowing white northerners to take most of the risks, the blacks in such songs were perfectly willing to "fight de South / . . . / All by de 'word ob mouth.'" Few wartime heroes would emerge from their ranks because, in the popular-culture view, "de Niggas would rather *run* dan fight, / . . . a Nigga will be Nigga, you kin neber make him white."[33]

Brutes. Although they usually were more than willing to pick a fight, brutish blacks often had enough in common with black cowards to be considered blood brothers. Both character types were disadvantaged by the fact that their innermost directional compasses were controlled by external forces. Kept vivid through postbellum literary depictions of black "savages," ethnological displays of "primitive" African villages constructed for museums and international expositions, numerous sepia-tinted Tarzan movies, and 1950s windup toys such as Tom Tom the Jungle Boy and the spear-carrying Pango Pango African Dancer, popular visions of blacks as a dangerous and uncivilized people have withstood even the most determined frontal attacks by revisionist scholarship and educational television.[34]

Some, like Civil War era novelist John Townsend Trowbridge's apelike

Cudjo, were natural barbarians who practiced the "fire-worshipping fanaticism" of their ancestors and looked far more like "demon[s] of the cave" than human beings.[35] If somewhat uncouth, their personalities did contain a bit of the noble savage. Their worst crimes might be the mangling of standard English and the unauthorized appropriation of a stray chicken or two. As was demonstrated by Margaret Sullavan in the 1935 film *So Red the Rose,* such characters' hereditary disability could be controlled with relative ease. One well-placed slap to an angry slave's face could quash a plantation revolt, sending the insurgent back to his accustomed work, tail between legs.[36]

On the other hand, certain brutish characters seem to have been made so by nurture, not nature. They existed at the pleasure of powerful whites and were forced to do the dirty work of their overlords. Typically, no slave "community" sheltered them or provided alternative values and role models. In the words of one late-nineteenth-century history text, the human sensibilities of such individuals were "dwarfed and distorted by oppression and ignorance."[37] Hardened by the cruelties of black life, they had become unfeeling, incorrigible villains.

In Harriet Beecher Stowe's *Uncle Tom's Cabin* (1852), two unforgettably evil black slave drivers named Sambo and Quimbo personified the axiom which held that "the slave is always a tyrant, if he can get a chance to be one." Trained in savagery and brutality by cotton planter Simon Legree, Sambo and Quimbo hated each other and in turn were feared and despised by the rest of the slaves. Ably illustrating Stowe's contention that "brutal men are lower even than animals," the demonic duo participated in orgies of drunken debauchery with their master, treated the slave women as sexual playthings, and gloated with "fiendish exultation" at the whippings that they meted out to errant field hands and house servants. In this manner, a northern reformist writer popularized the notion that black personality could be perverted or destroyed by white oppression. According to Stowe, African-Americans could be "unman'd" and turned into "things" through the normal operation of the slave regime.[38] Audience response to later black villains such as filmmaker D. W. Griffith's rampaging, feral bucks or certain of historian Stanley Elkins's repressed, co-opted Sambos suggests that whether made brutes by nature or by nurture these debased creatures were unlikely to be treated as heroes by an adoring public.[39]

★ ★ ★

The Noble Savages, Loyal Servants, Comic Minstrels, Black Cowards, and Brutes of American popular culture were noisome impediments to the growth and development of an African-American heroic tradition. Serving as disincentives to both heroic conceptualization and action, most of these literary and theatrical archetypes approached heroic stature only in their service to

CASSY MINISTERING TO UNCLE TOM AFTER HIS WHIPPING   Page 198.

Uncle Tom after his "breakin'" by Sambo and Quimbo (Harriet Beecher Stowe, *Uncle Tom's Cabin; or, Life among the Lowly* [Boston: John P. Jewett, 1852])

whites or in the mocking, pseudoclassical names with which they were burdened. As a result, they were far better suited for the denigration than the elevation of black Americans' self-image.

If it was unlikely that creations such as Epaminondas, Pompey, and Professor Julius Caesar Hannibal could convince whites that blacks were capable of gallantry and valor, perhaps African-American novelists, playwrights, poets, and historians would be able to influence national public opinion in that direction. In 1903, with a keen understanding of the stakes involved, W. E. B. Du Bois asserted that a central problem of the twentieth century was that of the color line—"the relation of the darker to the lighter races."[40] As the century progressed, it became clear that one way in which black intellectuals and creative artists intended to grapple with this vexing problem was to continue firing popular-culture salvos at the color barriers to heroism.

In order to define, sustain, and promote the concept of a viable African-American heroic, Du Bois joined with like-minded "race men" (and women) to conduct research in black history. Extending the tradition established by nineteenth-century literary and library societies and early black writers such as Robert Benjamin Lewis, James W. C. Pennington, William Cooper Nell, and William Wells Brown, they formed study groups, sponsored lectures, and lobbied educational institutions to include black history in the school curriculum. Organizations such as Philadelphia's American Negro Historical Society, the Bethel Literary and Historical Association of Washington, D.C., the Negro Society for Historical Research, and the American Negro Academy encouraged lay interest in the black past and paved the way for the formation of the Association for the Study of Negro Life and History (ASNLH) in 1915.[41] As noted by ASNLH founder Carter G. Woodson, the overarching purpose of these varied activities was to ensure that blacks escaped "the awful fate of becoming a negligible factor in the thought of the world."[42]

Like their antebellum predecessors, these African-American researchers recognized that efforts in this regard would be aided materially if they first succeeded in authoritatively documenting the nature and extent of black heroism through the ages. "Every race that has counted for much in history has had its heroes," they said. "Every nation that has helped to build civilization got its inspiration from within. . . . Negro achievements must be taught to the young men and women, if they are to learn to labor and to achieve, to do and to dare."[43] African-Americans of the early twentieth century recognized that they had to create a usable past in order to provide for a bright, productive future.[44]

Responding to what they perceived as mainstream historians' tendency to manipulate the truth to the disadvantage of others, black scholars complained loudly. Whites, they said, not only controlled access to elite educational institutions, advancement within the professions, and access to scholarly publishing but also had succeeded in spawning a historiographical monster. By melding historical exposition with prevailing stereotypes, white academics had created a sterile hybrid which alternately ignored and mocked black contributions to American history. As Kentucky State College historian Lawrence D. Reddick noted in a 1934 study of texts used in the public schools of sixteen southern and border states, few of the books covered the African-American experience in any detail. Even fewer treated black people as individuals or personalities. Most illustrations of blacks were pictures of groups or "types," typically docile slaves standing in the cotton patch. Reddick concluded that the overall presentation was biased and simplistic. Verbal and visual stereotypes filled valuable space which could have been used to document the African-Americans' role in national development. As a result, the white historians' portrayal of black people was "altogether unfavorable."[45] Similar conclusions were reached by later generations of black scholars who continued to marvel at the white researchers' facility for crediting their own ancestors with another group's historical accomplishments.[46]

But these outspoken scholars did more than complain. They acted. Joining the fruits of their research with theatrical forms of presentation, they spread the black-history gospel beyond the academy and its formally educated constituency. Twentieth-century black-history pageants complemented revisionist studies of the African-American past, providing a visual and emotional dynamic that even the most skilled textbook author seldom succeeded in generating. The goal of their creators was to utilize the forms of conventional historical pageantry to create a meaningful African-American folk drama. In doing so they hoped to counteract the effects of white-run community pageants, which often borrowed stock routines and stereotypes from the minstrel stage.[47] Like the pageants of other ethnic groups, these black community entertainments presented inspirational tableaux of individual and group achievement. They also introduced many to an important interpretive notion. As W. E. B. Du Bois claimed in an address delivered in Louisville in 1900, "the unquenchable fire of civilization" may have been "gathered, conserved, and augmented" in Europe, but it first had been kindled in the black kingdoms of northeast Africa.[48] In this view, white folks were latecomers to racial heroics.

Presented to New York City audiences during the National Emancipation Exposition in 1913, Du Bois's own "The People of Peoples and Their Gifts to Men" was typical of the black-history pageants that were to follow. Each of its six acts celebrated a significant contribution that "the eldest and strongest of the races of mankind" had made to world civilization. The pageant transported theatergoers from Iron Age Africa to the splendid palaces of the Nile and then on to the court of Mansa Musa, king of medieval Mali. As the modern era dawned, the "gifts" of Humiliation, Struggle, and Freedom were presented. In these tributes to blacks of more recent times, the African-American fight against slavery and racism took on epic proportions. By the end of the show, the forces of Greed, Vice, Luxury, and Cruelty had been defeated. In their place stood symbolic figures of "the Laborer, the Artisan, the Servant of Men, the Merchant, the Inventor, the Musician, the Actor, the Teacher." The chattels had risen from the "valley of the shadow of death," proving that this courageous dark-skinned people could "bear even the Hell of Christian slavery and live."[49]

Challenged by Du Bois to consider the "dramatic possibilities of the Negro's story," later pageant directors added a veritable cavalcade of black heroes to the list of notables.[50] At Emancipation Day celebrations, Negro History Week observances, and national church conventions, Sojourner Truth, Gabriel Prosser, Nat Turner, Harriet Tubman, Crispus Attucks, and Benjamin Banneker were received with the same mixture of awe and unequivocal gratitude that white ethnics typically displayed toward European-American culture heroes such as William Tell, Leif Eriksson, or Christopher Columbus. These inspirational character studies celebrated both the past and the future by defining the struggle for black equality as a lifelong commitment which could not fail. Progress was ensured as long as each individual remained, like the esteemed Frederick Douglass, "an ardent fighter for the freedom of his people . . . courageous in the midst of dire adversity."[51]

Motivated by these compelling displays of heroism in support of group advancement, black Americans expanded their field of vision even further, seeking out contemporary figures for honorific treatment. Utilizing their considerable powers of discretion, they anointed current favorites as living legends. Those fortunate enough to be selected varied greatly in terms of regional, occupational, and ideological affiliation. They fit no unitary mold. Each placed an individual cachet on black heroism. But all had the heroic "it"—the capacity to be envisioned by others as a person who was capable of great things, remained undaunted by adversity, and appeared ever willing to be tested by life's challenges.

Among the most celebrated and colorful of this stalwart band were two men who, at first glance, seemed to have little in common with the "average" black citizen of the early twentieth century. Certainly, casual admirers, doubting skeptics, and even confirmed critics had ample reason to believe that Father Divine and Marcus Garvey were "special" people. The most committed followers, however, tended to narrow the gap between themselves and their champions, conceptualizing the hero as a culturally sanctioned representative of the "folk."

No black public figure of the day worked more diligently at the task of advancing his celebrity to ever more rarified heights than Father Divine. Born George Baker Jr., self-christened Reverend Major Jealous Divine, and known to his disciples as God come to Earth, this charismatic New Thought preacher-reformer led the international Peace Mission movement from the early 1930s until his death in 1965. Seeking to promote racial justice and equality, he taught that blacks could assert control over their own destinies and overcome oppression through mind power. At the movement's Depression era peak, Divine estimated that some 22 million disciples were "believing in ME and calling on ME."[52]

From the lips of the faithful came numerous confirmations of their religious hero's divinity. True believers told of Divine's miraculous healing powers. "Thank you, Father," one would proclaim, leaping up to testify at a Peace Mission banquet. "Father, you gave me your own blood transfusion. I bled till there was no more blood. My intestines were rotten . . . I was nothin' but the skin and the bones. . . . God . . . you gave me that blood transfusion!" Others held signs aloft during parades up Lenox Avenue, New York, claiming that "Father Divine raised me from the dead" or, somewhat less grandly, "Father cured me of sniffing snuff." Although he modestly asserted that perfect faith would ensure perfect health regardless of his own efforts, it seemed that no ailment or affliction could exist for long in this holy doctor's presence.[53]

For evildoers there was neither cure nor reward, only punishment. Unexpected things happened to those who dealt unfairly with Divine or members of his flock. For example, on one summer's trip to the Long Island shore, Father and Mother Divine attempted to rent a cabana but were turned away. Blacks were barred from the beach. "Well, if I can't swim, no one else will either," he told the attendant and headed home. According to his own recollection of the incident, within a week a tarlike substance of unknown origin washed ashore, closing that stretch of beach for the remainder of the season.[54] On another occasion, a "Red Tide" of dead fish shut down Miami Beach bathing facilities shortly after resort owners had refused Peace Mission followers access to them. As Divine was fond of noting, such remarkable coincidences "do not just happen. They happen just." Swift, certain retribution was the movement's "administrator of equity."[55]

Although less awe inspiring, the more "worldly" aspects of Father Divine's persona also served to increase his popular appeal. Not unlike other celebrity-heroes of the day, he was a splendid self-promoter. Playing to the press and utilizing a variety of publicity stunts—even airplanes trailing inspirational messages—the black preacher manipulated the media like a Hollywood publicist. His every bold claim seemed custom-made for use as a banner headline. Whether unilaterally declaring his hometown of Philadelphia the world's capital, taking credit for the invention of the hydrogen bomb, or relating how he had defied and outwitted thirty-two lynch mobs over the years, Father Divine continually forwarded a compelling and heroic self-image.[56]

The Peace Mission leader's grand displays of wealth commanded respect even as they served to discredit received notions about African-Americans' "place" in the social order. In 1938, for example, he struck a blow against both racial stereotyping and residential segregation by acquiring Spencer's Point, an elegant 500-acre country estate directly across the Hudson River from the Hyde Park mansion of President Franklin Roosevelt. Asked for a comment on his new residence, he quipped, "I couldn't have a finer neighbor, could I?"[57] If surrounding property owners were somewhat nonplussed, black folk reveled in the irony of the situation.

Women were especially impressed. Despite the fact that he was barely five feet tall, bald, and quite squat, Father Divine radiated a "star quality" that females found attractive. These Depression era protogroupies chased after his limo, grabbing at the door handles and chanting "He's God, he's God." They sang tribute songs ("Father Divine is walking in the land / . . . / Got the world in a jug / And the stopper in his hand"), threw kisses, and proclaimed their undying love and devotion. Many, it was said, appeared to experience sexual orgasms while caught up in a Peace Mission rite known as "vibrating."[58]

Some boyfriends and spouses groused about the hypnotic effect Divine had on women. "All my wife does now is stand around droolin' at that man," one disgruntled mate was heard to complain. But, in general, believers of both genders credited their leader with significant accomplishment. When they sang "Father is on the mountain, Father is in the sea, / Father is down in the valley, saving humanity," they were describing how the diminutive preacher had restored their human dignity.[59] As one "outsider" observed in 1932, Divine's "confidence in himself has been the keynote of his entire teaching and it is this belief that he has succeeded in imparting to his many followers."[60] Unlike other predominantly African-American religious sects of the twentieth century which simply made God black, followers of the Peace Mission movement made a black man God—and then proceeded to appropriate a portion of their greatest hero's divinity for themselves.

While the Peace Mission attracted a significant white following, Marcus Garvey's Universal Negro Improvement Association (UNIA) was a vehicle for the promotion of black nationalism. If Father Divine envisioned a color-blind democracy, championed complete societal integration, and considered race an artificial mental construct fostered by negative thinking, Garvey was the high priest of pan-Africanism and racial separatism for his 1920s generation. When the two ideological swords crossed, sparks flew as in a Homeric era battle of the Titans. Garveyites termed Divine's movement a "colossal racket" and labeled the good Father a "wicked contriver of deception"—a blasphemer who dared to declare himself omniscient.[61] Responding very much like an angered and vengeful deity, Father Divine invoked his doctrine of righteous retribution on the slanderers. Those who denied his divinity, he said, have "signed their own death warrants and have directed destruction to those they love."[62] It was all so, shall we say, epic.

Nevertheless, this spirited disagreement between the two camps should not be allowed to obscure important similarities. Both men (1) headed up large-scale, multifaceted organizations which embraced capitalism and economic nationalism while aggressively forwarding programs of social action and racial uplift; (2) were compelling platform speakers who employed biblical imagery to make themselves the unifying center of their respective movements; and (3) used their positions of influence to promote feelings of self-worth and unity among their predominantly lower-class followers. Father Divine came to personify God among his constituency, but Garvey's ceremonial military attire and assumed title (provisional president of the African Republic) conveyed the impression of earthly royalty only one step removed from immortality. Indeed, the colorful pan-Africanist's supporters often apotheosized Garvey, hailing him as a prophet and comparing him to Jesus, Gautama, and Muhammad.[63] Little wonder, then, that the Peace Mission movement attracted thousands of former UNIA members following Garvey's deportation from the United States in 1927. Undoubtedly, New Thought doctrine reminded them a great deal of the times when their now exiled leader would thunder: "Up, you mighty race! You can accomplish what you will!"[64]

Although he could not work miracles, as a culture hero Marcus Garvey had at least one significant advantage over Father Divine. He had a well-documented earthly history to which his followers could relate on an intimate level. As God incarnate, Divine did not live "in time or seasons." He claimed to have been "intangible, invisible, and without form" until he was "combusted one day in 1900 on the corner of Seventh Avenue and 134th Street in Harlem."[65] While most impressive in theological terms, such assertions limited Divine's ability to share inspiring stories of youthful struggles against adversity with potential converts. The UNIA leader had many to share—and these more easily placed him in the company of traditional secular heroes.

Born into the bottom third of Jamaica's tripartite system of racial classification, Garvey learned from an early age that struggle against the status quo and servility, not the vaunted mulatto escape hatch, were the only options available to members of his dark-skinned caste. His father—a strong, stern type prone to stubbornness and argumentation—was among his earliest teachers. Said to be descended from Maroon stock, Marcus Garvey Sr. seemed determined that the youngster bring credit to the legacy of those ex-slave ancestors whose guerrilla warfare against British foes was such an integral part of early Jamaican history. The Garvey's eleventh child was destined for great things, he boasted. Any boy "born under the planet Leo . . . when the Sun is in the ascendancy" was certain to be "a leader in his line."[66]

To ensure this outcome, the elder Garvey—a stonemason by trade—provided harsh but character-building lessons in coping with adversity. For example, on one occasion young Marcus was helping construct a vault for a planter's son who had died of pneumonia. At lunchtime, the father climbed the ladder and immediately pulled it up, leaving the boy alone in the dark. Cries of "Pa! Pa! I am down here" went unanswered. Although he imagined that the menacing spirits of the dead were all about him, the hungry, exhausted youngster eventually fell into a fitful sleep. When Pa Garvey returned to awaken him, Marcus understood the purpose of his ordeal. "Boy," said the father, "this is a lesson to teach you never to be afraid."[67] It was one that he would not soon forget. Years later, Garvey claimed that while many had tried, none of his elementary school peers ever bested him in physical confrontations. "I was never whipped by any," he wrote. "I simply refused to be whipped. I was not made to be whipped."[68]

In 1901—the same year in which the fourteen-year-old was called "nigger" for the first time—Garvey left school for the world of work. Here he would broaden his base of observation and begin to grapple with the thorny problems of caste and class. His adversaries were numerous and powerful: wealthy land barons; white-owned shipping interests and fruit companies; a pliant, business-oriented press; and a privileged class of African-American elites whom he adjudged to be "moral cowards . . . afraid to speak to their people on the pride of race."[69] All seemed part of an unholy conspiracy to keep darker-skinned, less-educated blacks down, unable to think for themselves or produce leaders of their own.

Travels throughout Central and South America brought the young activist into close contact with these powerless, leaderless workers of the mines, tobacco fields, and banana plantations. Greatly moved by what he had witnessed, Garvey sensed their collective need for an advocate and volunteered his services. Before long, he was attempting to organize the exploited laborers, writing for reform newspapers, and haranguing government authorities for expanded educational opportunities for workers and their children. Guided by the glorious vision of "a new world of black men, not peons, serfs, dogs and slaves, but a nation of sturdy men making their impress upon civilization and causing a new light to dawn upon the human race," he founded the UNIA in the summer of 1914.[70]

It was an institution built to heroic scale. From its conception in Garvey's unanswered questions, "Where is the black man's Government? Where is his King and his kingdom?" to its incorporation under the laws of New York in 1918, the UNIA promoted racial uplift through a program designed to unite "all the Negro peoples of the world into one great body." Slogans such as "One God! One Aim! One Destiny!" and "Africa for the Africans!" rallied supporters' idealism. Recalling their proud racial past, Garvey stoked the fires of anticipation for that historic day when black folk would establish "a country and Government absolutely their own."[71]

Throughout the 1920s, tens of thousands of African-Americans cast their lot with Garvey, helping organize over seven hundred domestic UNIA branches, investing over $750,000 of their savings in Black Star Line Steamship Corporation stock, and contributing to their communities through service with the Universal African Black Cross Nurses, Universal African Legions, and other uniformed Garveyite auxiliaries. By the middle of the decade, the UNIA's founder could boast of being able to marshal twenty times the support given to all other black membership organizations combined. "Every second Negro you meet," he declared, "if not an actual member, is one in spirit."[72]

From all appearances, the membership was appreciative and enthusiastic— at least until serious financial, administrative, and legal woes began to drain support. Loyal followers praised Garvey for his grit, determination, and willpower.[73] They penned tribute poems ("Marcus Garvey Our Moses," "Garvey's Fame," "Homage to Garvey," etc.) and marveled at his trance-inducing oratorical skills.[74] To many, he "personified the possibility of the fulfillment of a dream latent in the heart of every Negro." As one admirer recalled, just the sight of the proud black leader and his splendid entourage was inspiring. "When Garvey rode by in his plumed hat," he wrote of a 1921 Sunday afternoon parade down Cleveland's Central Avenue, "I got an emotional lift which swept me up above the poverty and the prejudice by which my life was limited."[75]

Indeed, Garvey's chief appeal and contribution, like those of many heroes, were inspirational and must be viewed apart from programmatic accomplishments or failures. He captured the imagination and harnessed the enthusiasm of his core audience, directing their energies toward the restoration of racial pride and group solidarity. Even staunch critic E. Franklin Frazier admitted as much when he observed that the UNIA addressed certain deep-seated human needs. The black sociologist wrote that it gave members "what they want—the identification with something that makes them feel like somebody among white people who have said they were nobody."[76] Spokesperson for the cumulative grievances of his colonized people, Garvey provided a living example of the aggressive self-assertion they desired but had not dared express.

Although special consideration has been given to Father Divine and Marcus Garvey, it does not follow that these two men were the only race champions of their day. But they were exceptionally compelling figures and suitably representative of the type. Many other larger-than-life figures could be found outside religion and politics. Typically, such individuals claimed no prophetic gifts and did not aspire to any sort of messianic role in human history. Although not treated as divinities, the twentieth-century heroes of stage, screen, and sports commanded considerable respect and garnered widespread adulation. Most, if encouraged, would step down from the culture hero's pedestal long enough to mingle with the folk, to share common concerns, and, whenever possible, to act on behalf of group goals.

The most beloved of these figures made a point of touching base with the common folk on a regular basis. As noted by the multitalented Paul Robeson, there, at home among their people, culture heroes could "feel the press of all that is around." They could work to preserve their cultural birthright from the creeping affectations of celebrity. The most fortunate might even be able to experience the warm glow of old-time fellowship and reconnect with their earliest feelings of community. As they strengthened the bond that joined them to "the long, hard march" of black history, the culture hero would be rejuvenated and the homefolk reassured that their idols actually were their friends.[77]

Nevertheless, the "folk" often exhibited a vexing and quite random tendency to bemoan their heroes' humanity even as they celebrated it. Some pointed out that many otherwise resplendent representatives of the black heroic were encumbered by certain of the same weaknesses and imperfections which plagued other mortals. When the need arose, they said, these flesh-and-blood heroes might have to enlist allies whose powers could compensate for their most critical inadequacies. On such occasions, it was suggested that they turn to the black folk heroes of legend. These seasoned veterans of the crusade to overturn demeaning racial stereotypes were ever ready to assist in mapping new strategies for the culture wars.

Black folk heroes came in all shapes and sizes. Most were adult males, but they could be slave or free. All owed a great deal to the animal tricksters of the rural southern heritage and to an even earlier West African vernacular tradition that was re-created from memory and preserved via oral narration throughout the slave era.[78] Like Br'er Rabbit and his anthropomorphized compatriots, they instructed as they entertained. Each character had important didactic and wish-fulfillment value. Collectively, these heroes formed the cast of a folk-culture shadow drama in which group representatives transcended or reversed real-world social roles. Typically, they employed guile, wit, cunning, and deception—as well as physical strength—to best better-equipped, higher-status foes. Their modus operandi suggests that black Americans believed these particular adaptive behavioral traits had considerable contemporary relevance. To twentieth-century African-Americans concerned about formulating effective coping strategies, such subversive behaviors still seemed options worthy of consideration. Although an individual folk hero's approach to surviving against the odds was not always intended to serve as a literal guide for action, his typically proactive response to life's challenges encouraged behaviors that were antithetical to white-determined norms and expectations. The black folk hero made it clear to all that he would accept no hierarchical order or value system that was not a reflection of his own cultural identity.

Who were these stalwarts and exactly how did they evidence heroism? Among the most remarkable physical specimens was Henry Peterson, familiarly known as Old Pete. A frequent subject of conversation among Florida blacks of the early twentieth century, Pete's claim to fame was his (literal) hard-headedness. According to local oral lore, the powerful black man's skull was an inch thick and as strong as iron. Often, he would use it to split thick pieces of lumber and to crack coconuts open for sport. Only a stranger or a fool risked betting against him in a butting contest with one of his neighbor's billy goats. On one occasion, Old Pete, the railroad yard janitor, was said to have fallen asleep in a repair shed, using the track as a pillow. Unexpectedly, a switch engine pushed several cars into the building. The wheels of one rolled right over Pete's powerful pate. A second car derailed after bumping up against this ultra-hard obstacle. Hearing the racket and fearing the worst, panicked coworkers ran to the shed only to find Pete still napping peacefully. When awakened and told what had happened, he sat up, rubbed his eyes, and remarked, "Dawgone, mah head does feel kinda funny." Other tales had him using a ship's anchor for a pickax, singlehandedly stopping a runaway train, and pushing a grounded ship off a sandbar. In his spare time, Pete wrestled alligators and uprooted bee trees to get at the honey more easily. According to legend, he fathered fifty-six children.[79]

Just as physically prepossessing and even more widely celebrated was a steel-drivin' man named John Henry. Songs recounting his exploits were well known by the 1880s, having their probable origin in the advance of the Chesapeake and Ohio Railroad through the mountains of West Virginia a decade earlier. In subsequent years, he was memorialized by both black and white creative artists. Poets, painters, and playwrights found inspiration in John Henry, touting him as a "nachal man" worthy of emulation. Folk, country, and blues singers produced hundreds of recordings which described his fiercely competitive nature and chronicled his relationship with sweetheart Polly Ann. Importantly, the authors of illustrated children's books made sure that each new generation was introduced to the heroic deeds of the Black River country's favorite son, a resolute and fearless black man born with a hammer in his hand.[80]

While the defining event of John Henry's life remains his epic contest with a steam drill at Big Bend Tunnel sometime between 1870 and 1872, it is the tantalizing ambiguity of this legend that has made it so broadly appealing. Depending on the interpreter, here was a tale pitting man against machine, black against white, labor against management, and/or southerner against Yankee. Little wonder, then, that there came to be almost as many variations in the recounting of the drilling contest episode as there were descriptions of the victorious, but tragically martyred, John Henry.

Interpreters have claimed that he was either "short and brown-skinned," a "yaller-complected, stout, healthy fellow," or "six feet two . . . straight as an arrow and . . . 'black as a kittle in hell.'"[81] One account asserted that he weighed forty-four pounds at birth. As an adult, he was said to tip the scales somewhere between 150 and 312 pounds, give or take a few hundred pounds.[82] When allowed to speak for himself, the voluble John Henry seemed genuinely pleased to expound upon the magnitude of his natural gifts. "I'm big and bad and had ought to be chained, and I comes f'm I don't know whar," he boasted. "I weighs a ton, and my name is writ in my hat! . . . My bones is made outn solid steel and my muscles is made outn rubber. . . . My feet don't tetch de ground."[83] Clearly, here was a figure who commanded attention.

John Henry maintained his remarkable physique by cultivating a heroically healthy appetite. Even as a youngster, he could more than hold his own at the dinner table. According to one account of his early life, the rapidly growing boy wore his parents to a frazzle at mealtime. "Bring me four ham bones and a

John Henry strikes a pose for young readers, 1965 (author's collection)

pot full of cabbages," he demanded. "Bring me a bail of turnip greens tree-top tall, and . . . a pone er cold cawn bread and some hot potlicker to wash hit down." Typically, this hearty fare would be followed by additional helpings of peas, hog jowls, and biscuits dripping with molasses.[84] Fortunately, the struggling family's burden eased as young John began to fend for himself. Eventually, he learned to live off the land, hunting bear, rabbit, and wild pig, thirstily emptying honey-filled lakes of their nectar, and completely denuding trees whose branches were filled with biscuits and flitterjacks. As one admirer noted, understating the case considerably, "Gee-hee, hee, dat nigger could eat!"[85]

This massive intake of food enabled John Henry to perform numerous feats of strength. He regularly bested all comers in weight-lifting and spike-driving contests, easily hefted 600-pound bags of sugar onto riverboats, and, on one occasion, managed to pick 4,500 pounds of cotton in a single day. Capable of driving steel with a 20-pound hammer in each hand (and sometimes with one clenched between his teeth), the Bunyanesque laborer kept a half dozen men busy running back and forth to the tool house for sharpened drills. Although he wielded his hammer with such speed and force that he wore out two handles per shift, John Henry never seemed to tire. "Jes gittin' soople," he would say at the midpoint of a ten-hour day. "And jest gittin' started to sweatin'."[86]

A third, equally memorable African-American folk hero evidenced none of John Henry's attraction to the Protestant work ethic. Neither did he partake of Old Pete's predilection to perform remarkable physical feats. Instead, the slave hero known as John (or Jack) met most personal challenges through a finely tuned talent for transcendent trickery, verbal quickness, and sleight of hand. John's forte was one-upmanship. His goal was to turn every situation to his own advantage. As often as possible, he hoped to see the bottom rail come to rest on top.

By the time of the Civil War, John's reputation for superior cleverness already was well established. In slave quarters' cabins, woodland labor camps, and urban dram shops, black people buoyed their self-confidence by telling, retelling, embellishing, and adapting stories in which the slave trickster got the best of Old Master. Through the John tales, African-Americans shaped in-group behavioral standards, shared survival techniques, and expressed forbidden feelings—all the while getting a good laugh at whites' expense. Since John was only slightly larger than life, practical application of his teachings was a real possibility.

In his pioneering 1853 novel, *Clotel,* William Wells Brown utilized this form of indirect, mocking humor as a vehicle to comment upon contemporary southern economic relationships. In one scene, an infamously cruel slaveholder named John Peck sought to convince a group of northern visitors that his field hands were "happy, satisfied, and contented." To win the slaves' goodwill for the day, Peck treated each to a dram of whiskey. In return, the hands were to drink to their white overlord's health or offer a complimentary toast in the presence of the assembled guests. Although initially delighted at their professions of contentment, Peck met his mental match when he offered the cup to Jack—the "cleverest and most witty" slave on the farm. "Now, Jack, give us something rich," urged the slaveholder. "We have raised the finest crop of cotton that's been seen in these parts for many a day. Now give us a toast on cotton; come, Jack, give us something to laugh at." Taking the whiskey in his right hand and putting his left to his head, the bondsman began to "scratch his wool" like the bumbling blackface stooges of minstrelsy. Then, he toasted his master's agricultural achievements with a slyly worded critique of southern labor exploitation:

> The big bee flies high,
> The little bee makes the honey;
> The black folks makes the cotton,
> And the white folks gets the money.[87]

Here, the slave trickster helped Brown demonstrate that the Old South's preferred system of capital accumulation rested upon an inglorious foundation of selfishness and greed.

Postbellum generations continued to take great delight in recounting these stories of the weak outsmarting and humiliating the strong. And why not? Although built around the commonplace occurrences of nineteenth-century plantation life, many are timeless examples of folk wit and wisdom. For example, in one classic tale John and Old Master were taking a wagon load of cotton to auction when the slaveholder was bitten on the back of the neck. Crying out in pain, he asked what sort of creature had attacked him. "Nothin' but a common horsefly," John replied calmly. Refusing to believe his black servant, the white man became contentious. "That weren't no horsefly," he crabbed. "Horseflies go after mules and jackasses." But John stood his ground, a strategy which only added to his master's consternation. "John," he barked, "You aren't calling me some kind of a mule or jackass, are you?" Seeming to sense that the situation was deteriorating, the slave backpedaled: "No, sir. . . . You don't 'pear to be neither a mule or a jackass. Ain't nobody round here ever say anything like that. All I knows . . . All I knows . . ." Old Master took the bait. "All you knows is *what?*" he shouted. Pausing, John scratched his head and then delivered a patent trickster punch line. "All I knows," he said, "is I never hear tell that a horsefly can be fooled 'bout such things."[88] Zing! For the moment, John had his master exactly where he wanted him.

Even when the trickster conned a fellow slave, important educational purposes were served. Such tales encouraged constant mental vigilance and taught that oppressed peoples were well advised never to let their guard down, even among friends. In one story of this type, a bondsman bragged to his companion that he had "peeped up under Ole Miss's drawers." Predictably, the disbelief which this revelation elicited prompted him to elaborate. "Well, Ah sho done it," he responded defensively. "Ah stopped and looked jus' as long as Ah wanted tuh an' went on 'bout mah business." After learning that this blatant, indecorous act had gone completely unpunished, the slave's friend vowed that he was "goin' tuh look too." Of course, when he attempted to do so, all hell broke loose. Some days later, after recovering from the thrashing he received, the gullible victim sought an explanation. "How come she never done nothin' tuh *you?*" he asked. "She got me nearly kilt." Shaking his head, the trickster responded in mock disbelief: "Man, when Ah looked under Ole Miss's drawers they wuz hangin' out on de clothes line. You didn't go look up in 'em while she had 'em on, didja? You sho is uh fool! Ah thought you had mo' sense than dat, Ah claire Ah did." Beyond its entertainment value, this tale revealed that deceptive behavior could be employed successfully in a variety of contexts. Indeed, as every black storyteller's audience knew, the African-American experience was composed of an ongoing series of conflicts with a variety of foes. Most of the confrontations resulted in no more than tempo-rary, often inconclusive victories. But in order to survive with one's faculties intact—to live to fight another day—black folk had to heed the trickster hero's advice. Since most weren't blessed with superhuman powers, they had to cultivate the gift of wit and become well versed in the tactics of indirec-tion. Only then could they hope to expose and defeat the pervasive myth of inherent white superiority.[89]

In retrospect, the study of African-American folklore reveals that the con-ceptual boundaries between art and life often blurred, becoming indistinct and, ultimately, meaningless. For many blacks, it made perfect sense that tradi-tional folk heroes and real-world acquaintances often appeared on opposite sides of the same cultural coin. Both possessed an empathetic understanding of the burdens borne by the underclass and had nothing but contempt for those who wielded societal power unjustly. Indeed, after correcting for superhuman traits, the task of distinguishing between these two categories of African-American heroes seems an exercise in semantics. The story of Caroline "Caddy" Gordon illustrates this point.

Progenitor of a Philadelphia family whose roots extended to antebellum Lynchburg, Virginia, Caddy was said to have possessed two characteristics that made her life as a slave unusually precarious: she was an incorrigible runaway and beautiful enough to make white women mad with jealousy. These traits combined to earn the young, light-skinned girl numerous whippings with a cat-o'-nine-tails. According to granddaughter Marjorie Lawson, these brutal punishments never stopped her from attempting to escape—and she refused to cry when whipped.[90]

After Emancipation, Caddy continued to persevere. Her inability to read or write was compensated for by hard work and an avid entrepreneurial spirit. In addition to serving as a midwife to both black and poor white families, she made a regular circuit of local restaurants and the "good houses on the other side of the tracks." Rummaging through the garbage, she would pick out slightly overripe fruit, take it home, remove the spotted portions, and make pies and preserves. Then, she would return and sell her wares to the same people who had thrown the fruit out as waste. Honesty, diligence, and thrift earned the ex-slave the respect of the entire community.[91]

According to great-granddaughter Kathryn Morgan, Caddy was an even greater inspiration to her relatives. Transmitted orally across four generations, accounts of her tenacious struggle for survival served as "buffers to overcome fear, anxiety, and anger." Often, her spirit was invoked when everyday obstacles seemed insurmountable. Through her example, Caddy provided family members with a much needed antidote to the "poison of self-hate." But couldn't the same be said for Father Divine or trickster John? Weren't these celebrated culture heroes the obvious choices to call upon when psyche-strengthening (or soothing) services were required? Not in the opinion of Caddy's great-granddaughter. Blacks were fortunate that their group folklife contained so many inspirational narratives. But, as she noted, "they did not belong to us, as did the legends of Caddy." Every other folk hero "belonged to the world but Caddy was ours."[92]

While genuine concern for and frequent contact with the black community could cause celebrities like Paul Robeson to be treated like fictive kin, Caddy *was* kin. Moreover, by no means was she unique. Many African-American families had a Caddy—or a Clovis or an Aunt Charlotte—occupying a stout branch on the family tree. Perhaps they couldn't dispose of an evildoer with the flick of a superstrong wrist like Old Pete, be memorialized in a black-history pageant like Marcus Garvey, or hope to win international acclaim as a "race man" like W. E. B. Du Bois. But they weren't without resources—or cultural influence. When other hero candidates seemed too distant, otherworldly, or otherwise unapproachable, these authentic, family-based champions could be relied upon to help dispute the contention that blacks were a race of cowed, timorous beings who blindly and thankfully accepted any scraps that fell from white folks' cultural banquet table. Caddy and other heroic "Everymen" were the folk culture's ultimate answer to confirmed skeptics who, against all other evidence to the contrary, maintained that the oppressed lacked the courage to reject white America's skewed, pessimistic view of their human potential.

As can be seen from the examples drawn from black history, folklore, and contemporary life, twentieth-century African-Americans were not without resources when it came to the marshaling of culture heroes. In their quest for personal dignity and group advancement, they created a resplendent array of symbolic champions whose actions and goals were at once similar to and strikingly different from those of white American heroes. Their most salient characteristics were readily apparent to those socialized within the black folk culture. But most whites understood little about African-Americans' choice of hero figures, the rationale used in their selection, or the specific purposes they served. To learn more, nonblacks would have had to break down the mental barriers created by a segregated social order. To begin this daunting task, all involved would have been wise to consult Du Bois. At the beginning of the 1960s, the black scholar's pioneering conceptualizations still provided a valuable interpretive guide to the black heroic.

As was the case in Du Bois's own day, however, most blacks continued to respond in a positive fashion to selected white heroes. Indeed, what person of any era born and bred in the United States could resist the historical allure of that "immortal . . . saint and martyr of Harper's Ferry" (John Brown) or fail to honor the "mighty Homer of the lyre of war" (Abraham Lincoln)?[93] What American—of any ethnicity—was so estranged from the Judeo-Christian tradition that he or she would refuse respectful tribute to biblical giants such as Joshua and Samson, Moses and King David, or "Brudder Daniel" and "Sister Mary"?[94] And what possibly could be gained by turning a deaf ear to musical tributes celebrating white working-class heroes such as Casey Jones?[95] Certainly, as poet Paul Laurence Dunbar wrote of antislavery reformer Harriet Beecher Stowe, these were "prophet[s] and priestess[es]" whose exemplary lives dared not pass unnoticed.[96]

Nevertheless, a deeply felt need to promote the virtues of their race against the mainstream culture's constant barrage of negative stereotypes gave blacks both suitable inspiration and ample justification for promoting group attributes through their own heroes. Notwithstanding a diversity of appearance and appeal, those chosen shared several traits. Typically, the African-American hero was a bold, self-starting individual who, with only slight encouragement, could be persuaded to take charge in any troublesome situation and thereby serve as a rallying point for the group. As conceptualized by twentieth-century black poets, novelists, and playwrights, antebellum slave rebels set lofty standards in this regard. Although caught and eventually hanged for his role in a Virginia slave conspiracy, Gabriel Prosser's example of resistance to oppression was seen as inspirational. To the end, he refused to countenance surrender. "I'm after getting up a crowd of don't-care niggers and punishing them white folks till they hollers calf-rope me," said Arna Bontemps's Prosser in *Black Thunder* (1936). "I'm out to plague them like a hornet. God's against them what oppresses the po'. I ain't fixing to quit now."[97] Even in death, wrote poet Robert Hayden, Prosser remained a "Flame-head of / Rebellion" capable of igniting the idealism of future generations.[98]

Similarly, Nat Turner's "angry stab for freedom" was deemed the work of a prophet, not a madman.[99] According to playwright Randolph Edmonds, Turner put both antebellum and modern-day whites on notice that black people "ain't willing tuh be wurked lak a mule in de fields, whupped lak a dog, and tied tuh one farm and one Moster." Neither would they allow their children to grow to adulthood knowing "dat dey is slaves 'cause we ain't gut guts nuff tuh fight."[100] As shown in a John Henrik Clarke poem entitled "Sing Me a New Song" (1948), the Virginia bondsman's spirited challenge to white hegemony "inspired / Ten thousand black hands to reach for freedom."[101]

Encouragements to perseverance, struggle, and racial solidarity also appeared in dramatic reconstructions of abolitionist Frederick Douglass's life. Here, the black hero took on an additional role as a determined champion of educational uplift. For example, in Georgia Douglas Johnson's 1935 play, *Frederick Douglass,* the young slave was shown to have an unquenchable thirst for knowledge. He scavenged scraps of newspaper from the streets of Baltimore, dried and pressed the damp, wrinkled sheets, and then cajoled white playmates into helping him learn to read. When asked whether he had feared for his safety, he replied coolly: "[Whites] caught me an' nearly killed me many a time. They took all my papers away, but pshaw! I whirled right around an' found some more an' learned harder than I ever had." Far from selfish in his motivation, Douglass's overriding goal was to learn all that he could in order to help his "poor down-trodden people" escape the yoke of ignorance and bondage.[102] Correctly conceptualized as "gleams of light shining out of the dark," strivers such as Douglass hoped that others would learn from their example.[103] Then, utilizing hard-won skills in support of black progress, others, too, could become effective freedom fighters.

Black women shared this burden of racial leadership. Chief among those memorialized by twentieth-century writers was the tireless Underground Railroad conductor Harriet Tubman. "She's jes lak a angel," noted a slave admirer named Catherine in one 1935 play. "Ah don' know no other slave what's got free an' come back all the way from Canada nine or ten times to git others free—an' wid 'em watchin' foh huh, too." If angelic, she was one of the most stolid and iron-willed of the heavenly host. Black authors called her "fiery, dark and wild" and noted that plowing, digging ditches, and driving oxen had made Tubman "stronger than anyone else in the county." Rejecting suggestions that she occupy her time in traditional women's pursuits, Harriet risked all to lead her black brothers and sisters out of bondage. When, on one occasion, the grateful slaves began to kneel and kiss her dress, Tubman gave a stern warning. There was no time for such emotional displays. The task ahead would require courage and fortitude. "Git up off o' yo' knees," she ordered. "We's got to be startin', an' the way is long, Ah tell you. Once started, you gotta go on or die—thar ain't gonna be no turnin' back." For this antebellum black Moses, there would be no rest until the Slave Power surrendered the deed to the Promised Land.[104]

Other female characters shared Tubman's heroic tenacity and were shown to be similarly infused with an unshakable racial loyalty. Some, like the six-foot-tall, pipe-smoking Sojourner Truth, were as physically powerful and no less outspoken than than the courageous Underground Railroad operative.[105] Nevertheless, many black writers recognized that muscle mass was no measure of a person's spirit. The inability of a female field hand to outpick or outplow her male counterparts did not necessarily disqualify her from becoming a group leader and role model. Certainly, even in prefeminist days, it was possible to conclude that those who carried "the seed of the coming Free" need not possess the same qualities as male hero figures.[106]

In support of this viewpoint, dialect poet John Wesley Holloway's ode to the "Black Mammies" of the Old South claimed that these hardworking domestics and heads of black families were assured of a rich, heavenly reward. Their privation and sacrifice had not gone unnoticed by a just God. According to Holloway's vision, on Judgment Day "dar'll be a bunch o' women standin' hard up by de th'one" rubbing elbows with George Washington, "Fathah Lincoln," and the other notables.[107] The traits that enabled Mammy to aspire to this lofty rung on Jacob's ladder were said to include neither extraordinary uppityness nor exceptional upper-body strength. Instead, the poet cited her unwavering faith in God and an untiring devotion to family:

> She'd de hardes' road to trabel evah mortal had to pull;
> But she knelt down in huh cabin till huh cup o' joy was full;
>
> . . . .
>
> An' she prayed huh chil'en freedom, but she won huhse'f de bes',
> Peace on eart' amids' huh sorrows, an' up yonder heabenly res'![108]

Never doubting the promises of "de Lawd" or straying from earthly commitments, such women made indifferent insurrectionists. Neverthless, they provided black youth with examples of dignity, pluck, and endurance. In many cases, their Bible-based view of the future radically transformed existing temporal relationships. As Holloway sagely concluded, "blessed, good ol' Mammies must 'a' been of noble birt'."[109]

Intelligent, innovative, courageous, and committed, both black male and black female culture heroes were born leaders. As they worked to rally and inspire their people, time-honored stereotypes were put to the test and discredited. But what distinguished the African-American hero from competing European-American models? Each color-coded group contained a superabundance of seers and strivers. Were there any differences that truly mattered? Again, Du Bois provided an answer.

The black historian's conceptualization of racial heroism transcended the notion that an A. Philip Randolph or Mary McLeod Bethune could perform difficult leadership and motivational tasks as brilliantly as a John L. Lewis or Eleanor Roosevelt. In many respects, neither the nature of their deeds nor their ability to boost group self-esteem differed markedly, but the black and white culture champions were—like the rest of society—separated by race. Even by itself, this sociocultural fact of life was a matter of considerable significance. Supplementing and adding definition to their other characteristics, African-American heroes were said to possess a unique, fully developed humanity that differentiated them from the heroic representatives of other ethnic groups. To a remarkable degree, all black heroes shared this quality. If Du Bois described the distinctive but hard-to-define attribute as a racial "softness" or "spiritual joyousness," others posited the existence of a "black aesthetic." In the 1960s and 1970s, the word on the street was that blacks, but not whites, had "soul."

No one knows the precise origin of the notion that African-American traits could be viewed in a positive manner, but the concept was widely disseminated long before Du Bois challenged Henry Cabot Lodge's celebration of the white heroic. Undoubtedly, the notion was prompted by black disagreement with one or more of the following misguided and contradictory cultural assumptions:

Among blacks, racially defined virtues tended to be minor—or negative—ones.[110]

African-Americans were a highly imitative people, many of whom longed to be white.[111]

Because they did not fit the white heroic model and often strayed from an allegiance to mainstream values, black America's heroes more correctly could be termed antiheroes.[112]

Even when representatives of both races exhibited the same traits (e.g., bravado, intelligence, charisma), whites invariably employed the trait in a productive manner, whereas blacks tended to utilize it for base or selfish purposes.[113]

Certainly, there were a variety of Catch 22s within the popular culture. In the stark, either/or world of the American cultural imagination, blacks alternately were portrayed as (1) passive beings (cowards, victims, servants, and minstrels) to be mocked, pitied, and despised or (2) spirited but brutish savages whose disgusting behavior virtually mandated racial slavery and segregation. On the other hand, as evidenced in Lodge's romanticized view of the bold but compassionate George Washington, whites could—and did—have it both ways. It was in response to these widespread misperceptions and abuses that African-Americans turned the tables and began to develop a tradition of oppositional interpretive portraiture.

Black writers scrutinized the careers of "representative" whites and, in many cases, found their jewel-encrusted hero's chalice to be less than half full and thoroughly polluted with racism. By no means was it overflowing with virtue. As Du Bois suggested, this was one of the hazards of dealing with Anglo-Saxons. According to black critics, the superstition-ridden ancestors of these rude and untrustworthy people had lived in caves "either naked or covered with the skins of wild beasts." The most degraded creatures imaginable, they were said to have made the nighttime "hideous" with savage shouts. European skies were darkened by the smoke from their altars of human sacrifice. Centuries later, the heirs to this ignoble tradition would cross the Atlantic, steal land from the Indians, and force innocent Africans into perpetual servitude. Condemned by their own bloody history, the New World Anglo-Saxons retained in principle, if not in manner, "all the characteristics of their barbarous and avaricious ancestors." As William Wells Brown concluded in 1865, "Ancestry is something which the white American should not speak of, unless with his lips to the dust."[114]

But blacks were different. While Anglo-Saxon "CONVICTS . . . DRUNKS AND SODOMITES" occupied themselves in rape and pillage, the ancestors of modern-day African-Americans were "filling the world with amazement" by building great civilizations and shaping lasting humanistic value systems. Black-run societies such as ancient Egypt were seen as showcases of racial achievement. Here, it was said, the arts and sciences flourished amid a noble and generous people. Possessed of "true greatness," these black forebears were credited with having done more to "cultivate such improvements as comports to the happiness of mankind, than all the descendants of Japhet[h] put together." According to black researchers, it was the conquering white colonialists' determination to erase this proud historical record that prevented the Africans' signal contributions to world culture from being more widely recognized.[115]

Black intellectuals held that the Afroworld's decline as a locus of civilization and power could be attributed to Anglo-Saxon technological advancements and to the greed of capitalist slaveholders. African-Americans had become hewers of wood and drawers of water by force, not by choice or through any hereditary disabilities or "gifts." To validate this point, defenders of blackness worked to identify noteworthy racial qualities that had survived both the collapse of African empires and a subsequent involuntary diaspora. Like Du Bois, they highlighted traits which elevated blacks to a supernal moral plane, separated from and situated high above oppressor peoples. Withstanding the tests of time most fully were the virtues of patience, kindness, artistic creativity, and "spiritual fervor." The genius of the race, it seemed, was an often cited ability to soar "the great world of the spirit" even while struggling to be released from earthly bonds.[116]

While a white observer might be tempted to conclude that this racially defined "instinct for beauty" reflected an unfortunate overrepresentation of "domestic" or "feminine" virtues, blacks felt otherwise.[117] Perhaps, they suggested, misconceptions about black racial characteristics were the result of the burdensome economic and social pressures that had been placed upon several generations of African-American creative artists. In order to authenticate the preconceptions and enhance the egos of mainstream audiences, black writers and entertainers often had been forced to play fools and servants, to expound at length—and in dialect—about their supposedly carefree song-and-dance–filled lives.[118] Then again, perhaps it was all the result of white lies. According to the ethnic artists themselves, black people had managed to effect a unique and functional symbiosis between aestheticism and activism.

As shown in *Dark Explorers,* a 1948 radio play by Richard Durham, the people of the diaspora were neither savage nor sissified. A metaphoric tale of the strong black men who accompanied Spanish conquistadors to the New World, Durham's script pointed out that heroic kin of modern-day African-Americans were integral to the exploration and settlement of the hemisphere; that these heroes could be "rebellious, biting, scornful, angry, cocky, as the occasion calls for"; but that, in addition, they possessed a sympathetic, nurturing humanity which contrasted greatly with the hard-hearted ruthlessness and greed of European adventurers.[119]

Durham's black characters advised the white explorers "not to bite off too much of the earth," to leave indigenous peoples "something more of [themselves] than a hateful memory." They refused to listen. Instead, blinded by visions of wealth, fame, and empire, they "thundered in," warring against and despoiling ancient Indian civilizations. Everything they touched "turned to loot, blood and gold."[120]

Although blacks helped blaze the way for European settlement, they were said to have evidenced an even greater heroism by rebelling against the whites' cruel methods. Among the noblest were Raylon, an expatriate African gunsmith who marched with Cortez in Mexico, and a slave named Stevan, hired by a Spanish merchant explorer to locate the fabled seven cities of gold. Sickened by the adventurers' treatment of the Aztecs, Raylon deserted and went to live with the Indians. Instead of appropriating their wealth, he taught the villagers how to plant and harvest wheat. Similarly, Stevan wanted nothing to do with "the plunder that would follow me." After receiving a warm welcome from the natives, he abandoned his mission, took his freedom, and sent word to the Spanish that henceforth he could be found "on the side of the Indians here, not on the side of the plunderers." Recalling that he "never looked back at the old world" with its misaligned values and perverted notions of progress, Stevan spoke for all of Durham's black characters when he added, thankfully, that "it never caught up with me." Despite their encounters with evil, the heroic trail-blazers emerged intact, their humanity uncompromised. Given the coercions and temptations involved, this, in itself, was a significant accomplishment—an act of heroism worthy of remembrance.[121]

While not every African-American culture hero could be as reflective and unswervingly principled as Durham's black explorers—especially when involved in life-and-death struggles with oppressors—the vast majority seemed to possess many of the same humane virtues. Even if readily apparent only in their relationships with family, friends, and followers or in their symbolic defense of societal underdogs, the black champions' high regard for the things of the spirit came shining through. Dissembling slave heroes, for example, may have been portrayed as desperate men who neither gave nor expected quarter, but seldom were they given to the loathsome, unprincipled behavior which their creators attributed to white exploiters.[122] Even the physically awesome John Henry evidenced a characteristic racial "softness" that went to the very core of his being. His heart, it was said, "were as tendah as a woman's." Although "big and bad," John Henry didn't "mean no harm." Indeed, he gladly would give his last crust of bread to a hungry child or sit up all night at the bedside of a sick friend.[123]

As such characterizations reveal, racial nobility would not be selfishly squandered, sacrificed to carnal urges, or bartered for short-term gains. Far too much was at stake. The black culture hero's eyes remained fixed on a greater prize. Committed to achieving a freedom that would come only through reliance on traditional group values, the heroes typically took the high road. Each time they did, time-honored group mores were reinforced and white-authored stereotypes refuted.

Whether attributed to nature or nurture, the complexity of the black hero's persona allowed African-Americans to lay claim to an emotional and intellectual completeness denied them by most whites. As poet Melvin B. Tolson noted, it also freed them from blame and encouraged them to assume moral superiority over a race adjudged guilty of creating "Okies for *The Grapes of Wrath*" and the "slum that breeds a *Native Son*."[124] In the revisionist revelation that the people of the African diaspora were neither a childlike nor a savage race but in many respects a superior one, black nationalists found support for an activist program that emphasized distinctive racial and cultural characteristics. They urged that African-Americans separate themselves from the corruptions of the white world. On the other hand, black pluralists and integrationists could hope that the new understandings would help break down ancient barriers to interracial communication, drawing all Americans closer together.

But how readily would nonblacks accept these iconoclastic assumptions of black nobility? Could they come to terms with the notion that their own heroes were flawed and incompletely human? Certainly, a positive and accepting response to these questions was more eagerly anticipated by pluralists and integrationists than by those of the nationalist persuasion. Nevertheless, to be realistic, blacks should not have pinned their hopes on a speedy and bloodless capitulation. However deeply felt, blacks' righteous cultural chauvinism would not easily—or by itself—convince whites to abandon their own culture heroes or to attribute negative behavioral traits to them. The tendency to focus the spotlight of acclaim exclusively upon the champions of one's own group (and to camouflage or overlook their imperfections) was as prevalent in white as in black America. Many nonblacks had considerable difficulty relating to an outspoken activist like Marcus Garvey. Most had insufficient contact with Caddy's world to extend more than a brief, paternalistic gaze in her direction. Others found it hard to cheer on folkloric tricksters who were busily engaged in victimizing and making fools of white surrogates.

Miraculously, this mainstream mentality did not cause the creators of black culture to recant. They would withstand the storm, maintaining that black America's unique synthesis of activism and aestheticism could provide the spiritual boost so desperately needed by a nation in peril. Until whites came to a similar conclusion, African-American culture heroes would continue to champion these vital racial traits, promoting an ethic of leadership, loyalty, courage, and psychological well-being within the group. Keeping both their options and the cultural door open in anticipation of the eventual rise of a less-intolerant society, black heroes offered splendid visions of "new frontiers" long before JFK arrived on the scene. When key political, social, and mental roadblocks began to crumble during the 1960s, they, like Kennedy, would be well positioned to open new avenues of interracial understanding. The guiding lights of Black Camelot possessed great personal magnetism, were competitive and courageous, and, as often as practicable, sought both wisdom and guidance in the folkworld of the African-American Everyman. Moreover, just as Du Bois had claimed, they were "deliciously human." It was essential that each of these traits be carefully nurtured and maintained if the black heroes were to succeed as modern-day cultural mediators and agents of change.

CHAPTER

TWO

Championing the 1960s Cultural Revolution

Who will uninvent the Negro? For nearly four hundred years the black man's personality has been under attack, his selfhood devastated. Ever since he was brought to this country in chains he has constantly been given the ultimatum: "Deny your humanity or perish!" Where are the artists and prophets who will undo this white destruction? Who will write the songs for us to sing of our black heroes?

JOHN OLIVER KILLENS

Even without John Kennedy, Americans of the late 1960s were in no immediate danger of perishing from acute hero deprivation. Pretenders to the Camelot throne were everywhere, all promoting themselves as the next big thing and guaranteeing bountiful rewards to those who wished upon their rising star. All enriched their followers' fantasy lives, vicariously satisfying a variety of emotional needs and helping compensate for the unanticipated loss of JFK.

Although most never would acquire the late president's cobralike powers over the national press, real-world risktakers did their best to attract and maintain the fourth estate's undivided attention. Some, like Moon walker Neil Armstrong, saw their heroic efforts rewarded with glowing media tributes and an avalanche of memorabilia. Others, such as United Farm Workers' leader César Chávez, consumer advocate Ralph Nader, and the National Organization for Women's Betty Friedan, received far less universal acclaim but could be viewed as legitimate New Frontier legatees. Their combative approach to social change stood out in bold relief after the nation's pantheon of activist political heroes was all but denuded of Kennedys through Bobby's June 1968 assassination and the dousing of Teddy's presidential hopes at a Chappaquiddick bridge the following summer.

Hollywood film stars did their best to compensate for any heroic shortfall. In darkened auditoriums and living rooms from coast to coast, Americans were assured that all was well. Neither Russkie spies, THRUSH terrorists, nor evildoers such as the Riddler and Catwoman would benefit from this leadership lacuna as long as Napoleon Solo, James Bond, Derek Flint, and Batman were on the scene. Equipped with the latest in supermodified sports cars, eighty-three function cigarette lighters, and attaché cases bristling with concealed weapons, they were bad news for video villains but a boon to storekeepers. Bond-O-Matic water pistols, 007 cologne ("makes any man dangerous"), and the more than five hundred Batman products introduced to eager consumers in 1966 *alone* made cash registers ring. Although the popularity of most commercial spin-offs was faddish and short-lived, *Hawaii Five-O* action gear, *Secret Agent* comics, and *Man* (and *Girl*) *from U.N.C.L.E.* lunchboxes strengthened the bonds of loyalty between consumers and their favorite culture heroes.

Nowhere was this merchandising fact of life more apparent than in the field of popular music. Here, during the mid- to late 1960s, the Beatles reigned supreme. Following their February 1964 appearance on *The Ed Sullivan Show,* the Lads from Liverpool led a British invasion of the American airwaves. Before the end of the year, thirty of their songs had hit the charts and *Meet the Beatles* was on its way to becoming the best-selling LP in U.S. history. A series of silly but fresh and often engaging films followed.

The acclaim garnered by these merry moptops encouraged countless other youthful vocalizers to grow their hair, outfit themselves in groovy Carnaby Street garb, and form rock groups named after insects or small woodland animals. Soon, their streaming, gleaming, flaxen-waxen images filled the pages of *Datebook* and *Rolling Stone,* were seen weekly on NBC's *Hullabaloo,* and— along with those of John, Paul, George, and Ringo—almost completely obviated the need for wallpaper in teenagers' bedrooms nationwide. Collectively, the young popsters rejuvenated a stagnating U.S. recording industry, established new standards for dress and attitude, and became an important cultural reference point and source of inspiration for an entire generation.

In like manner, the sports stars of the late 1960s loomed larger than life. Throughout the popular culture, the swift, the skilled, and the just plain anatomically awesome were celebrated for both their physical prowess and their ability to provide fans with a Sunday afternoon psychic vacation from real-world concerns. Underdogs everywhere experienced euphoria when a cocky "Broadway" Joe Namath and his upstart New York Jets defeated the Baltimore Colts in Super Bowl III. Ninety-six-pound weaklings had their day in the sun when, during the summer of 1966, a spindly nineteen-year-old Kansas college student named Jim Ryun returned the world record in the mile run to the United States for the first time in thirty-two years. Similarly, all could bask in the glow of figure skater Peggy Fleming's stunning performance at the 1968 Winter Olympics. She was awarded the country's only gold medal. In each case, those who identified with a victorious athlete shared his or her exhilaration and success, forming a fantasy world connection with fame.[1]

Given the remarkable ability of these nonblack newsmakers to rise to the occasion of their own historical moment, one legitimately might ask if there was room in the limelight for black culture heroes. Considering the plethora of possibilities, was there a need for them? Initially, far more blacks than whites would offer enthusiastically affirmative responses to such queries. However, as the 1960s turned into the 1970s, the African-American heroes' ability to honor the promise of their own talents began to be recognized and respected outside the group culture as never before. The mainstream media scrutinized their every offstage, screen, or field move, continually troubling them for intimate lifestyle details and copiously documenting every verbalized wisp of personal opinion. Soon, Americans of all ethnicities were engaging in the most delicious gossip imaginable about the heroes' confidants and contretemps.

On occasion, this heightened level of attention seemed to create friction with the more territorial-minded white culture champions. As a *Batman* script would have it: AARGH! BIFF! KAPOW! ZWAPP! Nevertheless, white and black gradually became accustomed to sharing the spotlight. Time and events would reveal that even an uneasy coexistence could be mutually beneficial. Certainly, black heroes continued to instruct and inspire their own, both shaping and reflecting African-American group norms. But, in addition, having gained improved access to the mainstream, they were in a position to communicate their views and values to a far more diverse audience. Although whites retained the option of rejecting all but the most familiar faces, it was not outside the realm of possibility that the black heroes' new, higher, more positive profile would be utilized to promote a cross-cultural reevaluation of *all* the good townspeople of Black Camelot.

The single most important force propelling these dramatic sociocultural trends forward was a black cultural revolution of unprecedented scope and vitality. During the summer of 1966, Black Power arrived on the national news scene, its angry birth cries reverberating throughout the popular media. Although initially the concept seemed unfamiliar, somewhat foreboding, even fearful to many, Black Power's ideological roots ran deep. Inextricably intertwined with Afro-America's historical struggles for freedom, the essential spirit of the movement was the product of generations of black people confronting powerlessness—and surviving.

Early spokespersons had expressed the sentiment in a variety of ways. Before the Civil War, for example, free blacks met the reality of oppression by forwarding the notion that it would be wise to "combine, and closely attend to their own particular interest."[2] In militant fashion, reform conventions made it clear that African-Americans would speak for themselves and fight their own battles, if need be, no matter what the odds. "If we act with our white friends," said one New York group, "the words we utter will be considered theirs, or their echo."[3] Conscious of their shared experiences and cultural traits, blacks aimed to foster an empowering sense of group identity by forming fraternal, mutual-aid, and cooperative organizations. It was hoped that the creation of viable, autonomous institutions would unify black communities, improving their chances for survival and growth.

Some expanded upon these ideas and pumped for the establishment of a separate homeland. The concept of providing the people of the diaspora with a nation-state alternative to white American exclusivism, discrimination, and racism was formulated prior to the Civil War, most notably by Martin Delany and Henry Highland Garnet. It was reinvigorated late in the century by African Methodist Episcopal bishop Henry McNeal Turner and flowered during the 1920s in the pages of Marcus Garvey's *Negro World*.[4]

While much of this talk concerned a black-sponsored African return, more domestic Edens also were discussed. Benjamin Singleton's efforts to form black enclaves in Kansas during the 1870s earned him the sobriquet "Pap: Moses of the colored exodus," and the dream of turning Oklahoma into an all-black state was promoted through the planting of dozens of black towns—certain of which drafted restrictive (no whites) covenants. Plans to create a black nation within a nation were carried into the twentieth century by Cyril Briggs, founder of the African Blood Brotherhood, by the Forty-ninth State movement of Chicago lawyer Oscar Brown, and by Elijah Muhammad's separatist vanguard, the Nation of Islam.[5]

As grassroots examples of black solidarity and wish fulfillment, the re-settlement projects encouraged the growth of an African-American self-determination ethic. For supporters of these movements, centuries of unjust white rule proved that there could be no peace—or true freedom—in the world until black folk relocated to a "state or territory of their own—either on this continent or elsewhere."[6]

Other precursors of modern Black Power promoted unity and autonomy with a message of cultural self-definition. As opportunities for engaging in open displays of creative expression expanded, nineteenth-century African-Americans' sense of racial loyalty was evidenced in black-authored literary productions that were guaranteed to foster racial pride. Securely grounded in a rich folk heritage, African-American poets, novelists, essayists, and dramatists fought back against those who presumed to *"think* for, dictate to, and *know* better what suited colored people, than they knew for themselves."[7] In addition to bringing new dignity to the portrayal of black life, they employed language as a weapon of liberation, adding their voices to those demanding the use of "African" or "colored" rather than some slurred variant of the Portuguese *os negros*.[8] Convinced that blacks were a beautiful people, some even dared compare their physical characteristics with those of whites. As their works reveal, the boldest among them concluded that the lank-haired, sharp-featured European-American was but a pale imitation of nature's ebony-skinned crown of creation.[9]

Providing a worthy activist legacy for both the Harlem Renaissance authors of the 1920s and the Black Arts movement of the 1960s, these early voices spoke of an end to accommodation and prophesied the coming of a new day in which black people would wield considerable societal power. As they strived to capture the essence of "what it means to be colored in America," the creative artists looked into the racial soul, liked what they saw, and thereby became vehicles for the promotion of heightened self-esteem and psychological well-being.[10] By rejecting white formulas, highlighting and praising group characteristics, and wholeheartedly committing themselves to liberation, culture makers proved themselves the equals of black activists who preached a more institutionally focused political revolution. Born of a positive racial identity and a keen aesthetic sensibility, their heady, infectious confidence in fellow blacks influenced lives and events far beyond the literary community.

Thus, although the mainstream media often made them seem like revelations from a recently uncovered Book of the Dead, remarkably few of the principles guiding Black Power spokespersons of the 1960s were wholly new constructions. Indeed, that the modern movement burst upon America's consciousness when it did should have been foreseen. Most of the preconditions for the revitalization, dissemination, and acceptance of an insurgent group consciousness had been met by the midpoint of the decade.

During the civil rights era, black Americans had succeeded in liberating an unprecedented amount of "social space" within which the most fortunate among them could develop a sense of self-worth. As they worked to enlarge this space, they came to understand that the nation was at a crossroads. Increasingly, black and white lives dovetailed. In many places, the two communities had begun to prove that they could coexist and work together for the common good. Racial "firsts" were becoming commonplace. Nevertheless, there still were too many barriers of too many different kinds, and they were toppling too slowly. African-Americans no longer were awestruck every time they learned that a token black had been promoted to the post of assistant vice president for minority affairs at General Motors or that Lyndon Johnson had appointed a "brother" to a minor diplomatic post. They wanted to know the time and place of their own triumph over both institutional racism and the burden of everyday insults. Thus, when black Americans broke with established patterns, tested new ideologies and approaches for proper fit, and began to chant "Black Power," they actually were saying "me power," "us power." They were seeking total release from the psychological and cultural baggage they bore as a minority people. This was a broad and swelling sentiment, difficult to encapsulate and easily misinterpreted.

It is tempting to explain the rise of the modern Black Power movement by focusing on disillusionment and despair. Often, Afro-America's shift from civil rights to Black Power has been portrayed as a bleak descent into "pessimism and even cynicism." According to this view, by the mid-1960s, a core of black activists had begun to question whether the federal government ever could become an effective promoter and protector of civil equality. Others were becoming skeptical of the white liberals' value to the movement in the South. Still others had lost faith in the ability of black moderates to spur renewal in northern ghettos. In black communities, both large and small, frustration was building as the high hopes of earlier years proved illusionary. Their aspirations thwarted by unemployment, poverty, and white intransigence, urban slum dwellers expressed their alienation and anger by lashing out in the precipitous manner characteristic of frustrated but functionally powerless masses. Driven to the breaking point by the slow pace of progress, they "express[ed] their own sense of futility" by rejecting the integrationist ethic. The Black Power revolution, it was said, emerged out of a "gloomy atmosphere" in which the African-American people increasingly regarded themselves as doomed victims of modern-day neocolonialism.[11]

However downbeat, much of this tale is true. Certainly, it is justifiable—even mandatory—to include disappointment, discouragement, and disgust in any account of Black Power's 1960s origins. Many activists had reached an intellectual and emotional impasse by mid-decade. They were tired, perplexed, and mad as hell at white America. Governmental foot-dragging, increasingly sophisticated legal evasions, widespread poverty, de facto segregation, and the inability of Martin Luther King's crusade of love and nonviolence to put an end to white-sponsored terrorism virtually guaranteed frustration. But the rallying cry "Black Power" was far more than a sorrow song or a synonym for black Jacobinism. To understand the movement as such is to permit despair to reign supreme as a causative force. Critically distorting the movement's character and meaning, this narrow perspective fails to plumb the depths of activist sentiment or to establish a connection with the sphere of culture. The energizing, soul-satisfying aspects of psychological and cultural liberation are forced into the background, giving the impression that they were tributary, not foundational, to Black Power's overall thrust. The movement thereby is trivialized and made one-dimensional. Indeed, by discounting the more positive aspects of the empowerment process, one risks divesting African-American group culture of much of its characteristic vigor and resilience.

Similarly, there has been a great deal of confusion over the definition of terms. Some adherents boldly proclaimed that the meaning of "Black Power" was self-evident. Whites, they said, understood its essence because they had deprived blacks of it for centuries. Any African-American who claimed not to understand its basic implications was either a fool or a liar. Lexicographic confusion over Black Power was considered part of a conspiracy to discredit the movement.[12] Nevertheless, despite these confident assertions, there was considerable backpedaling when it actually came time to define the concept. Some seemed to view it as an almost totally existential doctrine. Others considered it a freshly minted variant of the traditional African-American freedom agenda. As attentive students of modern-day realpolitik, most sought to adapt Black Power to their own purposes.[13]

The black activists of the 1960s were a contentious lot, part of an idealistic but combative generation, fated to come of age in an increasingly litigious so-

Black Power pamphlet, 1967 (author's collection)

ciety. In many respects, they resembled those quarrelsome early-twentieth-century black ideologues who had been likened to "crabs in a barrel." None would allow another to climb out, but on every attempt, all would combine to pull the hopeful escapee back inside.[14] Certainly, the activists knew a good thing (Black Power) when they saw it and would sacrifice the ideal of establishing a comprehensive, universally agreed-upon definition in order to place their individual cachet on the term.

Even though name-calling was common and each of the movement's major factions seemed to take considerable pleasure in questioning the motives and methods of their ideological competitors, there nevertheless came to be an unexpectedly broad agreement on at least one major component of "Black Power." By both definition and necessity, the term had a great deal to do with psychological liberation. Power, said the Black Panthers' Huey P. Newton, was "the ability to first of all define phenomena, and secondly the ability to make these phenomena act in a desired manner." Seeking freedom from the psychological burdens imposed by societal opinion makers, he would claim the right to define white and black and to assign blame and praise as his personal muse saw fit. In doing so, he hoped to provide a mental antidote to despair that would be capable of infusing black Americans with an empowering sense of individual and group pride.[15] Shared by many other Black Power spokespersons, this passion for definitional and interpretive power better represented the views of the average African-American than did frustrated—and widely reported—cries of "get Whitey."

Central to the Black Power experience, the concept of self-definition was a fundamental component of the "revolution of the mind" that activists believed was a prerequisite for the successful implementation of their (numerous and varied) plans for revolutionizing society. Before black people could hope to become influential in world affairs, they had to define themselves. They had to win and then exercise the right to reject organizational structures, values, and methodologies that emanated from sources outside the black experience. Even commonplace concepts such as "truth" and "beauty" had to be newly cast before they could be employed in the cause of African-American empowerment.[16]

During the late sixties and early seventies, Black Power's chief psychological component most often was referred to as "black consciousness" or "the new blackness." This life-renewing mind-set was available to each and every African-American irrespective of ideological preference or economic status. Acquired through a multistage process dubbed the "Negro-to-Black conversion experience" by black psychologists, its core assumptions were as follows: After first questioning and then rejecting received interpretations of the world order, formerly self-hating "Negroes" would begin an in-depth involvement with blackness by striving to affirm their racial personhood and shape their environment. No longer would they meekly respond to white stimuli. In addition to critiquing regressive mainstream values, their mandate was to reorient black life, to create new symbols and directives capable of guiding future generations. These were to be drawn largely from the black experience. For example, traditional color associations would be reversed and black lifestyles elevated in status. A far more functional value system emanating from and fully adapted to the unique folk world of the African-American would be put into place.[17] As the entire range of human emotions was called into play, those who had succeeded in acquiring a "significant sense of self" now could begin to feel "alive for the first time." Before long, they would be "speaking up, standing tall, and thinking big."[18] Certainly, to become fully conscious of one's blackness was considered a most healthy psychosocial development.

Activists believed that a thoroughgoing response to this self-definitional call to "collective manhood" was essential to the acquisition of Black Power. Self-direction, assertiveness, and pride in heritage would remove the negative connotations of race which long had served as a constraining psychological and social force. Whites, of course, might still factor supposed racial limitations into their own plans for continued societal domination, but black people endowed with black consciousness no longer would play by the old rules. Energized by their new, pragmatic philosophy, they would dare to be pro-black—to look, feel, be, and *do* black. Thus, by progressing successfully through the consciousness-raising process—by formulating a positive racial identity through self-definition and self-assertion—individual blacks would play an important role in acquiring material manifestations of power for the group. The belief that this could be accomplished—that widespread identity transformation was capable of unifying black America in common cause—buoyed the spirits of Black Power advocates. It was their hope and expectation that the revolutionary psychological process of *becoming* black would initiate a social revolution of great magnitude. In doing so, they would be fulfilling the dreams of those earlier generations of strivers whose determined efforts had fallen short of total liberation.[19]

Black activists understood that the power to define extended into the sphere of culture. Considerably less threatening to whites than the average well-armed guerrilla warrior, black culture nevertheless had promoted resistance and survival during slavery, offered spiritual sustenance throughout the segregation era, and provided a foundation and reference point for the early civil rights movement. During the Black Power years, the socially and economically disfranchised learned that they could define themselves through various forms of cultural expression without paying obeisance to "Whitey." By utilizing cultural forms as weapons in the struggle for liberation, black creative artists worked to fabricate a much needed structural underpinning for the movement's political and economic tendencies. Whether represented by subversive slave folktales or sixties soul serenades, African-American culture was the central, irreducible, irreplaceable element in the ongoing struggle for psychological freedom and empowerment.

A surprising number and variety of Black Power voices contributed to the formulation of these broad understandings. Despite obvious temptations to do otherwise, many expressed a desire to link politics and culture in support of national liberation. For some, especially pan-Africanists, culture defined a unique community, widely dispersed by the diaspora but joined by virtue of its ancestry, its value system, and its struggles against white colonial domination. Centuries of European meddling had obscured this primal unity, but the universals of black culture transcended local differences and geographic boundaries. It was held that recognition of these precepts not only would enable those of African heritage to better appreciate black cultural qualities but also would encourage them to cultivate the liberating egalitarian and communalistic principles of political and economic organization embodied in the pan-African culture.[20]

Others, including many attracted to revolutionary nationalism, felt that whatever their theoretical or ideological relationship, culture and politics were anything but antithetical in practice. The white power elite, they said, always had understood how to manipulate language and art in order to forward political views. Undoubtedly, every cultural act was political in some sense. The essential question was whose political interests would be served. In this context, Black Power could be seen as a challenge to whites' modus operandi—a movement of reaction against white cultural domination concomitant with political domination. Properly cultivated, black culture was capable both of posing an alternative to white values and of revealing to African-Americans the way in which their oppression must be brought to an end. Lacking sufficient cultural consciousness, even a successful political revolution stood in danger of erosion, or even total reversal, through an infiltration of white culture-borne values.[21]

Still others, especially those evidencing cultural nationalist tendencies, believed that if isolated from each other, neither black politics nor the black aesthetic was likely to free the black nation. Culture, like politics, could serve as an instrument of change. Nevertheless, uninformed by righteous revolutionary political thought, the black artists' creations stood in danger of being considered "white art"—reactionary and supportive only of the political status quo. In truth, said proponents of this viewpoint, Black Power had to be both a cultural and a political revolt. To free the nation was to free the culture—and vice versa. Since culture could be seen as a "whole way of life" encompassing the economic, political, social, and aesthetic aspects of a people's existence, the work of black creative artists was deemed capable of accomplishing liberation in the temporal, as well as in the "spiritual," realm. Certainly, on an individual level, it would be difficult to become involved in the revolutionary process without simultaneously beginning to look at both oneself and others in a new light—with a revised vision of self and society provided by an empowering group culture.[22]

Recognizing that culture sometimes takes the role of politics among the disfranchised, Black Power era artists and intellectuals strived to reconcile ethics and aesthetics. Serving as a vital communications link between advocates of various "political" persuasions, they articulated and popularized a new group consciousness through what the influential black psychiatrist Frantz Fanon called a "literature of combat."[23] Seeking to speed black empowerment via "a radical reordering of the western cultural aesthetic," promoters of the late-1960s Black Arts movement worked to develop a dynamic, functional black aesthetic that would put an end to the "alien sensibility" which long had tainted African-American cultural expression.[24]

Beyond its recognized utility as a conceptual and critical tool, this race-specific aesthetic was valued as a means of "helping black people out of the polluted mainstream of Americanism."[25] In this context, the chief concern of Black Arts participants was not the relative beauty of a particular melody, play, or poem but rather the degree to which the work facilitated Negro-to-Black conversion. Convinced that "there is no better subject for Black artists than Black people," they utilized their own street experiences and on-site interpretations of communal mores as subject matter. Black art was to be created out of the experience of African-American life and conveyed to audiences in a language they could understand. By creating meaningful rituals of ethnic identity and self-worth, these imaginative anthropologists of the Afroworld hoped to teach black people important truths about themselves. The expectation was that eventually all would come to view blackness as a blessing, not a curse. Indeed, it was this appreciation for the beauty of African-American life that most clearly defined the black aesthetic—a unique cultural sensibility that was thought to be most evident where the artist-community bonding was most complete.[26]

Recasting Afro-America's often distorted image in a consciously black mold, Black Arts writers created a celebratory literature of inspiration and uplift. They highlighted the distinctiveness of African-American group culture—along with its unique symbols, myths, metaphors, and heroes; extolled the virtues of black lifestyles and values; and promoted race consciousness, unity, and pride. Relying upon the "spirit of blackness" ever present in their folk heritage for guidance, these activist authors refused to stand aside from the contemporary fray in order to pursue their muse. Instead, they provided their audiences with a series of easy-to-follow thematic road maps to both personal and group empowerment. As they developed new characterizations and themes, the black artists' works became agencies of spiritual renewal—metaphors for actual lifestyle transformations.

By way of contrast, the European-American aesthetic was widely perceived as arid, stagnant, and debilitated. "They stop and say the greatest happens to be Shakespeare or Bach or Michelangelo," noted one commentator. "They stop around the 15th, 16th, 17th or 18th century, and only once in awhile will somebody [more recent] sneak in."[27] Having run its course, the white aesthetic was considered an anachronism—a "dry assembly of dead ideas based on a dead people." Any remaining relevance and spark could be traced to theft or plagiarism from other traditions. Far more concerned with the preservation and veneration of artifacts than with the creative act itself, this dominant sensibility was held to negate expression in favor of reflection. Separating art from life and artists from their audience, it aptly mirrored the perceived hollowness of white life. Obviously, the taint of this outmoded ethos was to be avoided at all costs.[28] From this perspective, it was easy to agree with Black Arts poet-dramatist Amiri Baraka: "The white man is not cultured. He knows neither James Brown nor John Coltrane."[29]

But one didn't have to be a celebrated playwright, an editor at Broadside Press, or a founding member of the Organization of Black American Culture to proclaim the existence of a distinctive African-American point of view through cultural expression. Throughout the era, Black Arts priest-necromancers proved to be remarkably adept at convincing everyday people that they could help bring about "the destruction of the white thing" by simply being themselves.[30] Perhaps this was due to the fact that Black Arts activists hammered away so diligently on the themes of self-acceptance, the beauty of blackness, and the necessity of effecting a "psychic withdrawal" from mainstream values and assumptions.[31] Perhaps their success was related to the confidence that they placed in the common folks' ability to "sustain, assist, and inspire" art.[32] On the other hand, perhaps it had something to do with the popular, widely debated notion that all blacks had soul.

Essential to an understanding of the culture of Black Power, soul was the folk equivalent of the black aesthetic. If there were beauty and emotion in blackness, soul made it so. If there was a black American mystique, soul provided much of its aura of sly confidence and assumed superiority. Soul was sass—a type of primal spiritual energy and passionate joy available only to members of the exclusive racial confraternity. It was a "tribal thing," the emotional medium of a subculture. To possess a full complement of soul was to have attained effective black consciousness. Since every Negro was considered a potential black person, this experience was available to all African-Americans. But, try as they might, most whites were incapable of reaching the same state of awareness. Because few outside the culture sphere knew what it was like to grow up black in an experiential sense, their strivings toward soulfulness invariably fell short of the mark. For outsiders, soul defied both imitation and codification. Often, even an adequate definition of the concept was hard to come by. It was neither as literary as "Negritude" nor as threatening as "Black Power." It was more like red beans and rice, nappy hair, and Saturday night at the Apollo.[33] Du Bois would have considered it a uniquely life-affirming "spiritual joyousness."

During the Black Power era, the self-defining capabilities of soul were nowhere more evident than in the soul style that originated in and was authenticated by the urban black folk culture. Here, in-group forms of personal expression were developed which not only conveyed necessary social information but also could be utilized to promote a revitalized sense of self. Uninhibited in their expression of blackness, the truly soulful were exhibitionists par excellence. They didn't simply *walk* down the street. They strutted and *flowed* from place to place, radiating an aura of aloofness, detachment, and emotional invulnerability. Resplendently outfitted in supercool threads and a "righteous" natural hairstyle, soul people found great pleasure in "giving and getting skin." Indeed, their complex handshakes existed in a multitude of variants, each strikingly expressive of close comradeship and mutual bonding. Executed with great flair and rhythmic perfection, these rituals of nonverbal communication served as kinesic counterpoints to the rigid, purportedly robotlike mannerisms of "uptight" whites. Whatever their specific attire or method of greeting, sixties soulsters assumed a compelling, no-holds-barred swaggering pose as they bop-bop-bop-de-bopped down the road to empowerment.[34]

Eager to promote what they considered to be a positive group image, most of Black Power's grassroots supporters remained relatively unconcerned as to whether the traits they celebrated were "real" or heavily colored by the idealism and romanticism of the era. They were even less interested in white opinion on the matter. All were joined in the belief that their common culture gave meaning to life and could be a valuable asset in the liberation struggle. Informed by these uplifting notions, black folk placed the imprimatur of soul on more than a few of their favorite things. As Black Power percolated through the hinterland, eventually bumping up against and selectively infiltrating the mainstream, all manner of African-Americans claimed that they possessed a full quotient of the dynamic soul style.

By the early 1970s, many newly Black Negroes had cast aside their Teflon and Silverstone for cast iron and earthenware, bought up all the collard greens, black-eyed peas, catfish, and chitterlings in sight, and rushed into their kitchens to cook by "vibration." Double-blind taste tests might have proved otherwise, but to the culturally sensitive taste buds of black Americans, white folks' attempts to duplicate this spicy ethnic cuisine always seemed to lack that indefinable "something" that authentic soul food possessed in abundance.[35] Others put down their Johnny Mathis albums and took a heart-stoppin', soul-sockin' journey down the African-American musicological continuum, stopping at those points on the radio dial where "boss" jocks played the Temptations, Sam and Dave, and Aretha long into the night. Stations offering superficially soulful white imitations of this "poetry of the black revolution" were bypassed quickly.[36] Still other soul people took African names, helped paint powerful, symbolic images on community center "walls of respect," and listened with increasing interest as race-conscious preachers assured them that God smiled on all their efforts because he too was black and comely.[37] Taken together, these grassroots manifestations of soulfulness revealed the degree to which the cultural expression of "average" African-Americans could be utilized to project, symbolize, celebrate, and interpret a revolution in black consciousness.

Far more than an "index of repudiation" or the grudging recognition of a forced "separate development" within segregated institutions, this widely expressed desire to preserve and honor black distinctiveness, to define the world in black terms, spoke of a perceived need to shield the group spirit from the insistent siren call of a white-inspired and white-dominated consumer culture. To promote psychological wellness, activists urged that black folk embrace their own forms of cultural expression, molding them into a varied but recognizable "style" that was "uniquely, beautifully, and personally ours." It was hoped that after realizing they were no more able to express their "Peopleness" in a white cultural context than a barnyard fowl could "find his chickenness in an oven," the newly culture-conscious blacks would conclude that the opposite also was true. No other group could duplicate their culture, lifestyle, or worldview. In this fashion, they would proceed to redefine both themselves and society with bold, empowering, revisionist strokes.[38]

Widespread acceptance of these principles suggests that the Black Power movement can be conceptualized most accurately as a revolt of culture that was powered by a reawakened racial consciousness. Thus, "Black Power" is best understood as a broad, adaptive cultural term serving to connect and illuminate the differing ideological orientations of the movement's supporters. Like the American Revolution or the Civil War, Black Power was as cultural as it was political. It involved both a contest for the control of institutions and a clash of divergent "national" identities. From a historical perspective, it was a contemporary militant manifestation of the long-standing divergence between black and white American cultures, between each group's distinctive "shared way of life." Both the European- and African-American cultures provided a symbolic basis for group cohesion as well as a stimulus to political mobilization. But, for too long, blacks had been told that they had no cultural heritage worthy of respect. In response, the black activists of the late sixties sought to protect the essence of blackness from what Student Nonviolent Coordinating Committee (SNCC) leader Stokely Carmichael termed "the dictatorship of definition, interpretation and consciousness."[39] They demanded important changes in extant patterns of cultural hegemony and sought to effect them by building outward and upward from a core of group values. Purporting to represent both themselves and the less-vocal members of their constituency, the supporters of Black Power pitted their shared worldview and standards of conduct against those of the colonizers. With renewed determination and vigor, they sought to complete the irrepressible quest for independence of thought and deed that had been thwarted so many times in the past. Fully aware of the transforming potential of cultural self-definition, sixties activists utilized all available forms of cultural expression to forward their message of self-actualization. Often, it was the black culture hero who was delegated to deliver these vital missives of the cultural revolution.

It was appropriate that an incipient revolution promoted via black cultural forms and grounded in a soulful black aesthetic be led by a vanguard of African-American culture heroes. Fortunately, there was an abundant supply from which to choose. The number of martyred, exiled, or persecuted fifties and sixties activists was capable of keeping organizers of memorial celebrations and writers of tribute verse occupied for years. Among the recently departed, none received a more splendid hero's send-off than Malcolm X, also known as El-Hajj Malik El-Shabazz.

As the most visible and vocal spokesperson for the Nation of Islam during the early 1960s, the fiery Muslim leader had provoked considerable anger, apprehension, and fear both among whites and within mainstream civil rights organizations. Even after leaving the Nation to form the more orthodox Muslim Mosque, Inc., and the Organization of Afro-American Unity, his outspoken pronouncements on "the Black Revolution" continued to generate fear and loathing in high places. Apparently, a spirited critique of bourgeois, integration-minded "professional beggars" and their white liberal friends, combined with support for community control initiatives and talk of self-defense "by any means necessary" grated on many tender ears and egos.[40] Upon his assassination by ideological enemies in February 1965, Malcolm was described by *Newsweek* as "a spiritual desperado . . . a demagogue who titillated slum Negroes and frightened whites."[41]

On the other hand, his street-smart rhetoric had an almost visceral appeal to a young, black, economically distressed constituency. Here, following his death, Malcolm's influence expanded in dramatic, almost logarithmic fashion. For many, the fallen Muslim minister became a Black Power archetype, reference point, and spiritual advisor in absentia. Loyal supporters incorporated his image into community murals and invoked his name whenever they wanted to add legitimacy to their own blueprints for revolution. At Chicago's Malcolm X College, they even exhibited his shiny black Oldsmobile like a treasured work of art within one glass-walled hallway. To the most devoted, Malcolm was a totemic being, possessed of supernatural strength and wisdom. He was the martyred but soon-to-be-triumphant redeemer, a Fire Prophet, the ghetto-man in heroic proportion.[42]

As tends to be the case with culture heroes of all types, Malcolm X soon acquired additional heroic dimension through the instrumentality of the popular-culture marketplace. Posters, sweatshirts, greeting cards, and even bumper stickers bore his likeness and the inscription "Our Shining Black Prince" or "St. Malcolm." Black college students held festivals on his birthday. Some observed Dhabihu—a cultural nationalist holiday meaning "a sacrifice" in Swahili—and participated in annual commemorative services. Others eagerly awaited theatrical treatments of what screenplay author James Baldwin called "the great jungle" of Malcolm's life story.[43]

Carried to succeeding generations via his widely read, mass-marketed *Au-*

Ad for Malcolm X T-shirts (*Sepia* magazine, 1979)

tobiography (1965), several volumes of collected speeches, and spoken-word recordings such as *Message to the Grass Roots* (1965), the black leader's self-interpreted personal history was a godsend to creative artists in search of edifying examples and motivational messages.[44] Although physically unable to add dimension to his own popular legacy, there was no shortage of literary commentators willing to do so on his behalf.

African-American writers conceptualized "Brother Malcolm" as a self-help messiah whose all-too-brief time on earth was spent teaching his people to be "their own salvation."[45] Some, like poet Etheridge Knight, said that they barely were able to "control the burst of angry words" welling up within as they reflected on the day "Judas guns" ended his life. Although shocked and deeply saddened by the loss, most were not devastated. His spirit lived on, they believed, swirling "around us / In the vital air, inspiring all." Born into "a long line of super-cools, doo-rag lovers & revolutionary pimps" who "tol' it lak it DAMN SHO' IS!!" this culturally beatified Malcolm transcended mortality through the empowering wisdom he shared with his followers. "Brother of all black mankind," he virtually "became his people's anger."[46] As interpreted by Nate, a raging, militant character in William Wellington Mackey's play *Requiem for Brother X* (1966), his words were pure revelation: "POWER! THAT'S THE KEY," he shouted; "POWER IN THE HANDS OF MILLIONS OF BLACK PEOPLE ALL OVER THE WORLD. . . . That's the key, you know: BLACK PEOPLE PROUD OF BEING BLACK!"[47] In this manner, as both subject matter and inspirational guide, Malcolm helped carry the Black Power message to the people.

Ably assisting in this endeavor were the men and women of the Black Panther Party. Founded in Oakland in 1966 with a core membership of fewer than a hundred, the Panthers' penchant for the dramatic soon carried their image and influence far beyond the Bay Area. Chapters formed in England, France, and Israel and in such unlikely places as Des Moines and Halifax. By the fall of 1970, the party was operational in at least thirty-five cities in nineteen states and the District of Columbia.[48] Both the Panthers' notoriety and their attractive power among young blacks stemmed from the group's militant panache and the response they garnered from the (black and white) establishment. Whether making a dramatic appearance on the floor of the California state assembly to lobby against gun control legislation or rallying to guard Malcolm X's widow on a West Coast visit, the typical Panther cut a dashing, heroic figure.

They were youthful. In 1968, for example, the top-ranking leadership ranged in age from twenty-six to thirty-four, and second-level leaders were between twenty-one and twenty-six. Sixteen- to twenty-one-year-olds predominated among the rank and file.[49]

They were well dressed. The original Panther uniform—black leather jacket, slacks, shoes, and beret; powder-blue shirts with scarves or turtleneck shirts; dark glasses optional—had great symbolic value. It spoke of organization, discipline, unity, and commitment to the cause of black liberation. As a bonus, the full complement of Panther garb looked simply marvelous—especially when worn by male-model-quality hunks like Huey Newton and Bobby Seale.

They were outspoken and, to say the least, vivid in their expression of grievances. Whether instituting inner-city "survival programs" to help alleviate the intolerable conditions created by black America's "capitalistic, imperialistic exploiters," organizing armed citizens' patrols to monitor the behavior of "racist pig cops," or boasting of how their revolutionary, socialistic program would provide the wherewithal for formerly huddled masses to "seize the time and deliver themselves from the boot of their oppressors," Panther spokespersons were confirmed advocates of in-your-face politics. Utilizing the harsh but descriptive "language of the ghetto," they railed continually against the twin tyrannies of race and class, hoping thereby to nurture the seed of what they hoped would become a Black Power juggernaut.[50]

Above all else, they were armed to the teeth, employing their arsenal of weapons both as a self-defense mechanism and as an aid in recruiting "the brothers on the block" to the organization. Terming guns an "extension of our fanged teeth that we lost through evolution," party leaders conducted classes in the use of firearms, held close-order drill, and studied literature on guerrilla warfare techniques. Recognizing that they wore the group's reputation for armed militance whenever they donned their uniforms, recruits made certain that they knew how to defend themselves against all comers. Upon leaving the training session, a typical Panther delegation might have in its possession several shotguns, a couple of M-1 rifles, and all manner of handguns. If challenged by the police, they would coolly recite the applicable legal codes to the officer as an interested crowd of prospective members assembled, eyes bulging at the sight of bold, dignified, heroic young blacks facing down armed white authority figures.[51]

Although the Panthers declared that they did not intend to use their guns to "go into the white community to shoot up white people" but only to defend themselves against unjust attack, their ultramilitant image caused problems.[52] Failing to explain the group's rationale and raison d'être, the mainstream media focused on the party's seeming preoccupation with weaponry and confrontation. They were "black racists" and, according to the FBI's J. Edgar Hoover, the number one threat to the internal security of the nation. Harris surveys conducted in 1970 and 1971 showed that about 60 percent of whites and 20 percent of blacks considered the Panthers to be a "serious menace" to the country.[53]

"ONE OF THE GREAT CON-
TRIBUTIONS OF HUEY P.
NEWTON IS THAT HE
GAVE THE BLACK PAN-
THER PARTY A FIRM IDEO-
LOGICAL FOUNDATION
THAT FREES US FROM
IDEOLOGICAL FLUNKEY-
ISM AND OPENS UP THE
PATH TO THE FUTURE."
Eldridge Cleaver
Minister of Information
Black Panther Party
U.S.A.

Minister of Defense Huey P. Newton in Black Panther Party pamphlet (State Historical Society of Wisconsin)

Although the militants' popularity quotient improved whenever youthful African-American respondents were polled, both the Black Panther brass and Malcolm X—also a frequent victim of skewed, panicked news coverage—remained unlikely candidates for mass adulation.[54] The same could be said for the heads of the Revolutionary Action Movement, Congress of Racial Equality, Republic of New Africa, Us, and SNCC. With the exception of a relatively small number of Students for a Democratic Society (SDS) ideologues, rogue Muslims, and Brown Berets, most nonwhites found them far too threatening.

In addition, African-Americans who continued to find solace and hope in the nonviolent philosophy of the martyred Dr. King tended to consider their brand of activism unacceptably divisive and incendiary. As a crowning blow, women on the verge of initiating their own liberation movement took issue with the male militants' presumption that females should be willing to tolerate continued gender-based discrimination. Increasingly, they refused to be limited to their assigned role as babymakers for the revolution.[55] Because of these factors, leading Black Power figures had to be content with serving as role models for a limited constituency. They were not fated to become the type of universally acclaimed heroes who could succeed in bridging the culture gap between black and white America.

Nevertheless, although many opinion makers derided the Black Power leaders, considering them far longer on style than substance, hindsight reveals that one should not deprecate the contributions that "style" can make to a movement of racial self-definition. In the context of a budding cultural revolt, style carried considerable weight—especially when it could be related closely to aesthetics or soulfulness. It was manifested in a variety of group cultural expressions—from hair and clothing styles to cooking techniques, speech patterns, and rituals of nonverbal communication. As promoters of an uplifting, celebratory ethos, trend-setting "political" militants were the uncrowned heads of a revolution in black consciousness whose broad, societal impact was cumulative. If not immediately successful as facilitators of full-fledged empowerment, the Black Power leadership corps was in the vanguard of a movement which produced tangible psychological effects on black minds and left a distinctive cachet on all of American culture. Rather than dramatically breaching the barriers separating communities and worldviews, many of the concepts and understandings which they promoted filtered into the larger culture incrementally, in spurts and stops. Certainly, this process was not completed by the time "whatever happened to . . ." profiles of key Black Power personalities began to appear in the popular press during the mid-1970s.[56]

As sociologist Herbert H. Haines's study of the relationship between black radicals and the civil rights mainstream has demonstrated, militants like Malcolm X and the Black Panthers created a "positive radical flank effect" in 1960s political affairs. They helped generate a crisis in American institutions which made the legislative agenda of "polite, 'realistic,' and businesslike" mainstream organizations more attractive to societal decision makers.[57] By applying these understandings to cultural affairs, one can see how the mere presence of these outspoken activists could encourage skeptical black moderates and fearful whites to treat the Muse of Black Power with respect.

Part of a diverse group of specialists in consciousness-raising, the political militants "softened up" black audiences so that less-abrasive, more user-friendly practitioners of the black necromancer's art might taste success. In addition, they bluntly informed those socialized outside the African-American culture sphere that clown time was over. If Uncle Tom or Topsy ever deigned to make another stage appearance, it now seemed likely that they would be wearing "boss" dashikis, talking "bad," and looking for an argument. Unaccustomed to having their favorite, most comforting icons toppled in such a precipitous fashion, whites were given considerable incentive to learn all they could about these strange, uncommonly spunky black folk. More often than not, they sought instruction through familiar forms and from those who would present the movement's lesson plan in a somewhat less confrontational manner.

Who, then, was responsible for taking the empowerment message to black holdouts, doubters, and naysayers, hoping ultimately to convince them of its compatibility with the traditional civil rights agenda? Once the noisy political activists had whites' attention, which African-American culture hero would be assigned the task of completing their "education"? Was there a black hero waiting in the wings whose appeal was so broad that he or she could challenge Batmen, Bonds, and Beatles for national media attention and the affection of the general public? And what race champion, if any, possessed the precise combination of commitment, cajolery, and plain old roll-with-the-punches high spirits needed to keep the revolution of culture and consciousness alive and well during tough times?

During the latter half of the 1970s, the answers to such questions seldom were forthcoming, largely because they rarely were asked. By this time, the Black Power movement stood in danger of vanishing from the public consciousness. Guided by the familiar adage "out of sight, out of mind," most Americans—both black and white—now expended far fewer brain cells contemplating the "radicals" than they had in previous years. As the nation experienced a welcome hiatus from urban rioting and as the most vocal of the political activists were either "rehabilitated," exiled, or permanently silenced, both the press and the public lost interest in Black Power.[58] Like hippies, yippies, and other segments of the interracial community of "the great unwashed," black militants no longer were news. As a result, once deprived of a regular regimen of angry blacks waving lists of nonnegotiable demands at reporters, the average American couch potato slipped easily into a post-Vietnam stupor.

At the time, this seemed a reasonable response to a seemingly outdated sixties "phenomenon" that had run its course. After all, how many 'fro-headed, bandolier-bedecked Black Panthers had won seats in Congress or joined the boards of major corporations? How many independent nation-states had followers of Malcolm X carved out of the Deep South? Nevertheless, it would be incorrect to conclude that the Black Power ethic was in total eclipse. Given the fact that the movement never was as successful in effecting institutional, as opposed to psychological, change, and that it rarely influenced politics as dramatically as it did cultural affairs, one reasonably can conclude that its "political" leaders simply finished a poor second to other types of black heroes both in terms of longevity and in the competition to expand the movement's influence beyond its initial constituency.[59]

Informed by this perspective, it becomes plausible to believe that the aforementioned TV-watching, snack-consuming couch potatoes actually had been witnessing the working out of the empowerment process nightly without ever realizing it. Whenever they watched a soul singer perform, took in a black-cast film, or urged their favorite professional sports team on to victory, they were being presented with compelling audiovisual portraits of fully actualized African-Americans. During these years, African-American musicians stopped crooning syrupy white folks' ballads, film stars refused to engage in burnt cork tomfoolery, and athletes cast off their apolitical jock mind-set. In doing so, they helped energize and educate people of color while irrevocably altering white perceptions of black personalities and possibilities.

Possessed of individually apportioned mixtures of essentialist and universalist appeal, these and other pop-culture practitioners of the black heroic were no less promoters of self-definition than the political separatists and revolutionary nationalists whose raging images had flickered across the same middle-American television screens. Although acting out the psychodrama of black empowerment according to their own scripts, these entertainment world culture heroes were influenced greatly by the political activists' style and message. Indeed, sometimes it was difficult to distinguish one from the other. On occasion, they were one and the same. As major players in the cultural revolution of the 1960s and 1970s, they, too, radiated the "me power," "us power" ethic which coursed throughout the land. In the indirect, subversive fashion favored by folk-culture tricksters, they joined in promoting black unity and psychological wellness. It was their hope to consign both black "invisibility" and all-too-recognizable stereotypes like Mammy and Little Black Sambo to oblivion. At the same time, many of their number sought to break through racial barriers, to decolonize (white and black) minds. Due to their representational and symbolic nature, the culture heroes' success or failure would affect a great deal more than prime-time ratings points. In Black Camelot, primacy in cultural affairs was a matter of the utmost importance.

CHAPTER

THREE

Sports Superstars

God made us all, but some of us are made special. . . . Some people have
special resources inside, and when God blesses you to have more than others, you have a responsibility to use it right.

MUHAMMAD ALI

The life of a post-JFK-era black culture hero was rough-and-tumble, super-
competitive, and so filled with burdensome obligations and ceaseless frustration that it is a wonder more didn't come to look back upon the bad old days of
the 1930s, 1940s, and 1950s with nostalgic longing. To succeed against both
the odds and the competition was a major challenge. This had always been true.
Now, however, it seemed that aspiring heroes had to be everything to everyone
all at once, endlessly, and without complaint. In addition to advancing the
black revolution, they were asked to entertain the mainstream without bowing
to traditional racial etiquette or perpetuating negative stereotypes; to remain
true to themselves, their craft, and their historical role even as they voluntarily
put principle and honor in harm's way by courting the national media. Fortunately, the dawning of the Age of Aquarius had filled personal horizons
with the intoxicating glow of we-can-teach-the-world-to-sing-in-perfect-
harmony idealism. And if the common people felt this way much of the time,
their culture champions made a career of ignoring impossibilities.

Because of their long-standing involvement with the heroic, sports heroes
are among the most experienced instigators of idealist initiatives. Foes of failure, they resent retrogression and chafe at changelessness. Never resting until
victory is assured, the athlete-hero has long been recognized as possessing in
abundance the type of never-say-die attitude that is so highly valued by institutions and groups seeking to make their mark on world affairs. During the
1960s and 1970s, an ever increasing number of black superstars won recognition as formidable competitors in the athletic arena. Both the history and the
sociology of competitive sports virtually guaranteed that this new visibility
and acceptance would have considerable impact on prevailing notions of race
and status.

Demigods of the Sports World

In a sense, the ancient Greeks were to blame for all of this. Even the most spirited critic of the chauvinistic belief that every marvel of modern-day Western culture can be traced to some faded image on a Grecian potsherd must admit that the golden agers developed their fair share of seminal understandings about the relationship between sports and society. In addition to providing us with just about all of the essential terminology (e.g., *aethleo* and *gymnos*—but not "slam dunk," "seventh inning stretch," or "Go Hawgs!"), the Greeks were pioneers in conceptualizing athletes as culture heroes.

A normal diversion for the warrior class of Homer's day, sports contests were well integrated into a rugged Mediterranean lifestyle that also included clearing the seas of monsters and making roadways safe from highwaymen. It was believed that the gods not only followed these contests but also intervened on behalf of certain competitors. Returning the favor, the Greeks held numerous athletic festivals in honor of Zeus (Olympic Games), Apollo (Pythian Games), and Poseidon (Isthmian Games). In historic times, the greatest sculptors and painters of Athens immortalized the victors, public feasts were held to celebrate their accomplishments, and boy choirs offered triumphal hymns of praise *(epinikia)* during the magnificent processions which welcomed champions to their native cities.

Although they competed as individuals, athletes were seen as representatives of these communities—and were suitably rewarded by a grateful citizenry. In addition to olive, laurel, or pine wreaths, festival event winners could hope to bring home bronze shields, cloaks, tripods (three-legged cauldrons), and vessels of olive oil. Beginning in 594 B.C., Solon offered 500 drachmas—a sum equal to the cost of 500 bushels of grain—to any Athenian who brought credit to the homefolk by winning an Olympic event. As one might have predicted, before long the most-accomplished athletes were being offered inducements to compete for states other than their own, and festival organizers were busily wooing the "big names" with cash advances. Purists, such as the sixth-century B.C. philosopher Xenophanes, complained bitterly about the prizes, free meals, and other benefits which accrued to the most successful, but to little avail. Even at this early date, the connection between sports, celebrity, and commerce was well established.[1]

Surviving descriptions of Greek sports heroes also sound remarkably "modern"—if one allows for the somewhat freer interplay between the gods and humankind that was taken for granted by the ancients. After adjusting for changing times and beliefs, certain of these personality profiles seem the work of imaginative press agents devoted to the cause of making their clients into legends through media manipulation and puffery. There was, for example,

Euthymos, a fifth-century B.C. boxer (and river god's son) who once defeated a ghost to win the hand of a fair maiden; Olympic wrestling champion Amesinas, whose sparring partner was a bull; the towering pancratium specialist Polydamas, who was said to be capable of stopping a speeding chariot dead in its tracks by seizing it with one powerful arm; a youthful pugilist named Glaukos, who, on one occasion, astonished his father by using his fist to hammer a bent plowshare back into shape; and Milo, a huge, sixth-century B.C. wrestler who could burst a band placed around his temples by inhaling and causing his veins to swell. A devoted disciple of Pythagoras, Milo is credited with saving the philosopher's life by singlehandedly bracing a crumbling building's superstructure until all of its occupants had escaped.[2]

Other sports demigods may have been star performers in the arena but were said to possess certain of the same unpleasant personality traits which continue to be seen in their modern-day counterparts. Certainly, large egos were not uncommon among the ancients. A case in point is that of the legendary Theogenes, an early-fifth-century B.C. boxer and pancratiast who reportedly won between 1200 and 1400 festival events during his lengthy career. According to Plutarch, he was ambitious to the point of arrogance, displayed an excessive love of praise, and was extremely quarrelsome. Needless to say, the fans loved him. Theogenes was worshiped as a deity after his death and was said to possess magical healing powers. Another prime example is a Cyrenian sprinter named Eubatus. After having been promised success by an oracle, he was so confident in his abilities that he commissioned his victor statue to be made *before* the games and took it with him to Olympia when he went to compete in 408 B.C. And then there was Dioxippus, who, after winning the Olympic pancratium in 336 B.C., caused a stir by ostentatiously ogling women in the crowd lining the streets of Athens for his victory procession. Finally, one must consider the gigantic boxer Epeius, who, on one memorable occasion, declared in all immodesty: "I am the champion. . . . For I tell you this straight out, and it will be a thing accomplished. I will smash his skin apart and break his bones on each other. Let those who care for him wait nearby in a huddle about him to carry him out." After this splendid buildup, the match undoubtedly was standing-room-only.[3]

The Sociodrama of Athletic Competition

While all the hype and hoopla, egomania and excitement of today's sports world was here in embryo, primed and ready to be passed down through the ages as part of the European-Americans' colorful folk-cultural baggage, ancient Greek conceptualizations of the heroic necessarily were modified as they were adapted to the New World order. By modern times, Americans had developed their own unique understandings about the interface between athletics and everyday affairs. Thus, sociologists can tell us many things about the nature of sports that the ancients probably knew (and were too busy to write down), but their focus and database are brutally contemporary. The researchers' findings are wholly applicable only to the type of technologically advanced, media-driven consumer culture that took firm root in the United States during the 1960s and 1970s. Here, competitive sports—and sports heroes—fulfill several key sociocultural functions essential to the fans' mental health and general welfare.[4]

First, and most obvious, sporting events are meant to entertain. Whether participant or observer, the devotee obtains pleasure, refreshment—even inspiration—from sport. Upon entering the athletes' symbolic universe, fans exchange the humdrum and ho hum for a chance to participate in splendidly staged, culturally sanctioned rituals. Even if the thrills are largely vicarious, they can be deeply felt and memorable. Perhaps this is escapism—a brief, but whole-souled denial of unwelcome demands placed upon former children by the adult world. But, if so, it is an escape into a parallel universe whose governing principles add perspective to our own. In this fantasy world of play and performance, we are encouraged to imagine what it would be like to live in a golden age in which the societal directives are unambiguous and equitable, the social roles are both fulfilling and glamorous, and the sociodrama of daily existence is intense but unthreatening and ultimately rewarding.

For some, to linger in such a lush locale is either an admission of defeat, a mechanism for avoiding the more complicated, far riskier problems of real life, or, at best, a diverting amusement. From the same events, however, other fans receive an emotional charge capable of energizing tired, run-down psyches and of replenishing depleted stores of self-esteem. With the assistance of the "winners" with whom they identify and become ego-involved, such individuals may no longer rest comfortably with the less-than-ideal status quo. Upon their return to reality, they might even decide to reach out for a new "personal best"—to aspire to be winners themselves. In doing so, each of these newly rejuvenated spiritual athletes becomes a distinct threat to any orthodoxy or institution standing in the path of individual accomplishment.

Sociologists also tell us that sports reflect many of the controlling assumptions which govern the prevailing economic and political order. In this respect, they are more a societal mirror than an alternative universe. During the late 1960s, competition between social groups was becoming intense. Often, the athletic arena itself was turned into a hotly contested terrain of social meanings as representatives of regional, ethnic, and gender-based constituencies sought to advance in the great pennant race of life. Competitive sports offered Americans a much-needed guidebook and survival manual to both interpersonal and intergroup relations. As the most astute players understood, the trick was to be *informed* about and yet not *controlled* by the reigning value hierarchy, to learn its composition and function well enough to avoid an unwilling imposition of any unpalatable tenets, and ultimately to wrench a modicum of personal free-dom from the invasive presence of this mainstream mentality. By mastering the ground rules, one became credentialized for competition. Like the greatest sports heroes of the day, successful secular competitors were disciplined and hardworking. They were able to handle bad luck, intense pressure, and defeat without whimpering or making excuses. Mentally fit, they were fully prepared to enter the fray and prove themselves worthy of acclaim.

Like the larger society of which it was a part, the sports world of the 1960s and 1970s provided a showcase for individual, as well as group, effort. But, for both participants and observers, one's identification with a particular team in-evitably involved shared loyalties and collective activity. Athletes often stood alone in the spotlight but were widely perceived to represent—even embody—entire cities or regions. Separated by race, class, and geography, fans nevertheless managed to join in common cause whenever they rooted for their favorite clubs. Sports, then, involve people jointly and constitute a social force with the potential for linking and unifying disparate elements within the general popu-lation. They can, if properly cultivated, give the alienated a new identity and sense of belonging. The shared language, lore, and ritual of competitive sports constantly reinforce these tendencies—as do corollary activities such as joining touchdown clubs, trading baseball cards, and wearing team caps and T-shirts. Moreover, each time victorious teammates embrace, slap palms, pat each other on the behind, or run victory laps arm in arm, equally jubilant fans are provided with compelling visual images of strong, independent entities with healthy egos rapturously bonding via collectively affirmed feelings of triumph and re-lief. Clearly, sports divide winners and losers, but their emphasis on cooperation and teamwork provides symbolic resolution of the ever present conflict be-tween individual initiative and the cooperative ethic.

In any era, the contribution made by sports to the formulation and dissemi-nation of national values would be worthy of mention, but this was especially true of the decade following John Kennedy's assassination. As the first baby boomers entered their college years, athletic enterprise became a megaforce on the American scene. Before long, the specter of lost youth loomed before these onetime children of the New Frontier. Hoping to postpone the in-evitable, they jogged, played racquetball, and aerobicized with cultlike fervor. Always alert and responsive to new trends, Madison Avenue marketing execu-tives fueled this fitness fever by using youth, thinness, sex, and guilt to sell a wide variety of consumer goods.

Spectator sports also began to take on a decidedly entrepreneurial cast as record crowds jammed stadiums and arenas. By 1974, both college football and major-league baseball were attracting over thirty million fans per season, nearly twenty-five million watched college basketball, and interest in professional football, basketball, and hockey was at an all-time high.[5] In addition to broadcasting an ever lengthening schedule of league games, the major TV networks developed an entirely new entertainment genre which critics quickly dubbed "junk sports." During the early 1970s, programs such as *The Superstars, Dynamic Duos,* and *Celebrity Challenge of the Sexes* showed accomplished athletes competing in events outside their specialties and pitted Hollywood celebrities against one another in a variety of outdoor, schoolyard-quality games. Viewers who tired of these often amusing, if not particularly skillful, matchups could switch channels and watch spirited competition in wrist wrestling, logrolling, and snake hunting on ABC's long-running *Wide World of Sports.* At the end of the decade, the networks were broadcasting 1,356 hours of sporting events per year—a 90 percent increase from 1970.[6] With the rapid growth of the ESPN and USA cable channels, the overexposure of "jock culture" became a real possibility.

But for faithful devotees, it seemed that there never could be enough sports. For many, "the big game" provided a primary reference point for conceptualizing the heroic. Such individuals would eat and sleep sports, lacing conversations with locker room proverbs (when the going gets tough, the tough get going; a quitter never wins, a winner never quits; "lose" is a four-letter word) and utilizing the play-by-play announcer's argot ("bomb," "blitz," "blast," "manhandle," "outhustle"). The most avid might even bird-dog their favorite teams, waiting expectantly outside stadiums for a nod or an autograph and descending in predatory packs upon unsuspecting athletes at airports.

Devoted followers came from all walks of life. Even the nation's chief executives sought somehow to appropriate JFK's reputation for athletic "vigah" by paying close attention to the sports section of the morning papers. Lyndon Johnson was no rabid fan, but he did voice the opinion that Gerald Ford had played too long without a helmet during his years as an offensive lineman at the University of Michigan. As president, Ford engaged opponents in a sort of blindman's bluff version of public links golf, whereas his successor Jimmy Carter liked to jog and watch good ol' boys race stock cars. But it was a former benchwarmer for the Whittier College Poets football team named Richard Milhous Nixon who made the greatest display of sports addiction. At a time when it was deemed politically astute for national leaders to honor the memory of sainted figures such as Knute Rockne or Babe Ruth and to make annual pilgrimages to stadiums and halls of fame, Dick Nixon served as high priest of the sports world shrine. Not only were well-known athletes recruited to work on his campaign, but once in the Oval Office, the conservative Republican sought to bolster a shaky "Everyman" image by continuing to cultivate their friendship at every (photo) opportunity. Throughout his White House years, Nixon basked in the looming, radiant presence of visiting superstars, jumped at the chance to phone effusive congratulations to winning coaches, and, on three occasions, personally presented the annual award for the nation's top-ranked college football team. Stories of the president being diverted from official tasks to greet a favorite athlete or simply to "talk sports" and reminisce with equally avid fans are legion.[7]

What was it that both the influential and the unpretentious found so irresistibly compelling about athletic competition? In addition to the psychological, sociological, recreational, and promotional factors already mentioned, one certainly must give credit to the sheer attractive power of sports heroes. During these years, the hero arguably was the single most significant contributor to the growth of national sportsmania. This was understandable because there was such a varied selection from which one could choose a personal favorite. Among the most popular were charismatic individuals whose acumen for garnering off-field publicity was as well developed as their athletic skills; reliable practitioners whose consistent performance over the years made them the "gentlemen" of the game; normally faceless journeymen types whose outstanding play on some rare but fondly remembered occasion sparked their team to victory; and against-the-odds underdogs whose competitiveness and unexpectedly prolific output belied disadvantages of size or experience.[8]

Some of these heroes received additional media attention as members of one of several sports "dynasties" which flourished during the 1960s and 1970s (e.g., the UCLA Bruins and Boston Celtics, the Green Bay Packers and Pittsburgh Steelers, and the New York Yankees and Oakland A's). But, whatever their uniform, sports world royalty tended to possess one or more of the following traits which set them apart and made them memorable in their own right: speed, power, grace, strength, coordination, agility, flexibility, endurance, accuracy, balance, rhythm, vitality, efficiency, fortitude, preparation, dedication, hope, and courage.[9] Gifted with a superabundance of such attributes, the most charismatic athletes of the day exuded an anticipatory emotional force capable of energizing audiences simply by entering the game.

A Cavalcade of Black Champions

Each year, more and more African-Americans were found among this skilled, celebrated elite.[10] The social importance of such a development far outweighed the fact that a few especially gifted individuals were able to garner fat signing bonuses and wear Super Bowl rings. Noteworthy heroes had three times the athletic ability of JFK; the aggressiveness, self-confidence, and ego of the most flamboyant Black Power podium-pounders; and the unharnessed potential to be every bit as much a "race man" as black political figures like Du Bois or Garvey. Updated versions of ancient Greek champions, they were larger-than-life representatives of their communities whose increasingly prominent role in the American sports fantasy world encouraged homefolk to envision and then to strive for the realization of individually defined "personal bests." Many of these staunch competitors came to understand the ground rules of social interplay and advancement so well that they became inspiring teachers and activist role models. Indeed, their style and level of performance held considerable pan-racial attraction. Employing the shared values, rituals, and language of sport, African-American heroes stood their ground and even advanced into hostile territory. Although the opposition was equally determined, the black athletes' charisma, courage, and "extra effort" moved all Americans a step or two closer to the resolution of long-standing intergroup conflicts and the planning of new cooperative initiatives.

In truth, African-Americans had participated in competitive sports for several generations. Despite being subjected to separate leagues, surly spectators, second-class travel accommodations, and spotty press coverage, black stars garnered considerable acclaim even before the 1960s. In the last decades of the nineteenth century, sprint bicycling champion Marshall W. "Major" Taylor was earning $20,000 per year from racing, Joe Gans reigned as world lightweight boxing champion, and jockey Isaac Murphy rode three Kentucky Derby winners home to victory. During World War I, Brown University's Fritz Pollard and Paul Robeson of the Rutgers Scarlet Knights were named to Walter Camp's All-American football team.[11] Indeed, by the end of the Great Depression, black sports fans could boast of an abundance of talented athletes whose national reputations would have been even greater had they not been forced to toil for "Negro League" teams like the Pittsburgh Crawfords (baseball) or the Harlem Renaissance (basketball).

If the white media often cast top performers such as home run king Josh Gibson or women's tennis and basketball star Ora Washington in the long shadows of their celebrated white counterparts, African-American fans placed them square in the spotlight. The faithful did their best to fill the fleabag parks in which barnstorming baseball clubs practiced their art, turned out 10–15,000 strong for a weekend Rens game, and crowded college fields for Thanksgiving Day matchups between Fisk and Tuskegee or Lincoln and Howard. In the late 1940s, more than 50,000 fans attended the black baseball leagues' East-West (all-star) games—so many that additional cars had to be added to trains bound for Chicago.[12]

Eventually, the big leagues got the message that blacks were box office. Exclusion was exchanged for cautious, token integration as football (1946), baseball (1947), bowling (1949), tennis (1950), and basketball (1950) dismantled long-standing color barriers. But none of this came without struggle, the careful weighing of alternative approaches, and considerable reflection upon the nature and outcome of previous meetings between the sports establishment and black heroes. Especially instructive in this regard were the experiences of Jack Johnson, Joe Louis, and Jackie Robinson. Each, in his own way, helped de-

termine the character and agenda of a "second wave" of sports world desegregation that took place from the 1950s through the 1970s. Moreover, the manner in which these role model pioneers conducted themselves as they were
projected into the public consciousness provided the black stars of this later period with invaluable instruction (both positive and negative) in athletic etiquette.

Some consider bad-boy boxer Jack Johnson to be the hero who never was.
Others call him a credit to the race, but one who was before his time—a world-
class black champion fated to perform for a stridently racist mainstream public
that had great difficulty conceptualizing, to say nothing of tolerating or admiring, an outspoken Negro athlete. Most find Johnson both controversial and
difficult to pigeonhole. All agree that this colorful fighter who held the world
heavyweight title between 1908 and 1915 was a hard act to follow.

Flamboyant and outspoken both inside and outside the ring, the preening
pugilist shamelessly directed attention to himself at every opportunity. A true
hedonist, he dressed ostentatiously and expensively, employed a corps of servants to care for his every need, and was especially fond of big cars, vintage
wines, late-night parties, and pulchritudinous women. During his fights,
Johnson kept up a steady stream of taunts and insults designed to unnerve and
humiliate opponents. "Who told you you were a fighter?" he would ask deri-
sively, laughing between gold-capped teeth. "Who taught you to hit? Your
mother? You a woman?" He could be merciless even in victory. Instead of offering sportsmanlike praise of a defeated foe, the black champion often would
continue his critique for the benefit of reporters. "He is the easiest man I ever
met," he said of fallen titleholder Tommy Burns in 1908. "I could have put him
away quicker, but I wanted to punish him."[13]

On numerous occasions, Johnson's flouting of "acceptable" behavior got
him into trouble with the authorities. He appeared in traffic court at least
twenty times and was involved in a half dozen serious car accidents prior to the
crash that killed him in June 1946. Lawsuits ranging from breach of contract to
extortion, assault, and smuggling plagued him throughout his career. In 1912,
he was charged with violating the Mann Act, eventually serving a year in Leav-
enworth prison for paying prostitute/paramour Belle Schreiber's way from
Pittsburgh to Chicago and setting her up in an apartment so that she could
practice her trade.[14] To the irrepressible Johnson, all of this was like water off a
duck's back. Indeed, he was far more likely to joke about an alleged transgres-
sion than to accept blame or express regret for having broken the law. "Stand
back, Mr. White Offisah," he would tell a traffic cop as he was being written up
for speeding, "and let dem colored peoples hab a look at me."[15]

Many African-Americans liked what they saw when they fixed their in-
credulous gaze upon this swaggering, boisterous figure who carried himself as

if an invisible heavyweight crown had been placed permanently atop his clean-shaven head. Fans celebrated Johnson's victories with almost as much gusto as did the champ himself, parading, blaring automobile horns, shooting off fireworks, and carpeting their hero's path with flowers. According to all reports, the crush and excitement in the streets were incredible. As common people caught victory fever, their ego involvement in the heroic enterprise became apparent. To awe-inspired celebrants, this "brawny son of African lineage" seemed "the greatest cullard man dat ever lived."[16] By first convincingly defeating symbols of European-American superiority in the ring and then defying white standards of behavior for African-Americans outside it, the powerful boxer became a highly visible exemplar of racial prowess.

Jack Johnson (Library of Congress)

To others, however, Jack Johnson was something of a racial embarrassment. African-American critics scored the champ for his lack of humility and his troublesome public conduct. Some considered his preference for white lovers an insult to black womanhood and his disregard for bourgeois values a threat to Booker Washington's accommodationist entente with mainstream elites. Certainly, the specter of white backlash and reprisals—even a bloody race war— loomed over every interracial title defense.[17]

Nonblacks had even less tolerance for the uncompromising iconoclast. The challenge that Johnson presented to both middle-class values and the prevailing racial order caused them great discomfort. In response, angry whites screamed verbal abuse, sent death threats, and engaged in random antiblack violence. No stone was left unturned in the search for a "white hope" capable of ending the champion's reign. At the same time, fearing that Johnson's example might be adopted by others, white lawmakers and the molders of public opinion elected to play "good cop–bad cop" with their African-American constituents. While some acted the paternalist—counseling blacks about the dangers of profligacy, false pride, and "disastrous ambition"—others occupied themselves with the crafting of coercive antimiscegenation legislation. In the wake of Johnson's decisive victory over former titleholder Jim Jeffries in 1910, it was even suggested (by none other than sports enthusiast Theodore Roosevelt) that prizefighting be banned throughout the United States. Then, presumably, the threat posed by uppity blacks would disappear. The decency and time-honored social decorum favored by both white Americans and "intelligent colored folk" would be preserved.[18]

Therefore, whether one considers Jack Johnson to have been too far in advance of the times for his own good or simply to have had too big a head for his hat, it is clear that he would not—perhaps could not—unite black and white in the common bonds of hero worship. To white contemporaries, Johnson's unrestrained behavior provided the perfect justification for segregation. He was the prototypical "bad nigger" and had to be excised from the sports world. Many African-Americans—even those who received considerable psychological gratification from his victories in the ring—felt that the champ was a loose cannon. Unpredictable and egocentric, he had too many white friends to be trusted with the mantle of group leadership. Indeed, he never really sought such a role and tended to distrust other successful blacks who could have served as "political" advisors and allies. Moreover, after it became apparent that Johnson took a fall in his 1915 title fight with "white hope" Jess Willard, onetime supporters began to question whether he could be considered a true sportsman. No fellow boxers, black or white, attended the ex-champion's funeral— or even sent a final floral tribute.[19]

Jack Johnson's star may have been extinguished prematurely because it burned so intensely, but he did leave a legacy for subsequent generations. Actually, it was a warning. To those with aspirations for the spotlight, his many troubles served as pointed encouragements to self-scrutiny, sobriety, and the avoidance of excessive taboo-tilting. No professional athlete took this message to heart more fully than Joe Louis.

The dominant force in heavyweight boxing during the 1930s and 1940s, Louis succeeded in combining an exceptional ring record (twenty-five title defenses) with a very attractive public persona. Although plagued by those members of the national press corps who persisted in quoting him in minstrel dialect and lampooning his appearance through grinning, large-lipped cartoon caricatures, Louis's potent left jab and carefully monitored behavior caused him to be best known as the "Brown Bomber," not, as some would have preferred, "Shufflin' Joe" or "Jungle Killer." Eventually, he would earn over $4.5 million from boxing, appear in Hollywood films, and have monuments and public buildings named in his honor.

Unlike Johnson, Joe Louis was a team player—a quiet, unassuming man who became a symbol of national unity at a time when the very existence of the United States was being threatened by economic depression and an alliance of powerful foreign enemies. In part, he came by these traits naturally. His family tree, strengthened by the genetic contributions of "blacks, some whites, and a few powerful Indians," was a veritable DNA rainbow coalition. Socialized from an early age to understand and appreciate a sense of place—as in "you have your place, and I have mine"—young Joe and his kin got along well with the whites of Alabama's Buckalew Mountain region because they never "crossed the line." As Louis noted in his autobiography, this approach to life spared his family "the angers and hurts and lynchings" that were common throughout the South during the World War I era.[20]

But the nonconfrontational, down-to-earth image so widely celebrated by a white press and public also was a conscious creation of the adult Louis and his backers. As representative-at-large for black America, he knew and abided by the rules: live and fight clean; don't gloat over fallen opponents; never go into a nightclub alone or have your picture taken with a white woman. Press releases touted the boxer's devotion to daily Bible reading, his mother, and thrift; his aversion to cigarettes and strong drink. A tutor helped enhance this "official" image by coaching him in grammar, history, geography, and math.[21] By highlighting—and sometimes exaggerating—his natural tendencies toward modesty, decency, and discretion, Louis became a model of middle-class virtue, acceptable to a broad cross section of sports fans.

The interracial appeal that caused both northerners and southerners to claim Louis as a native son was nowhere more apparent than in the days following his stunning one-round knockout victory over "Der Schlager" Max

Schmeling in June 1938. Touted as the symbol of Aryan supremacy by Hitler's propaganda mill, Schmeling had blemished the American's spotless record by putting him down for the count in the twelfth round of a 1936 matchup. During the intervening months, the Brown Bomber took the heavyweight title from Jimmy Braddock while the Germans quickened the pace of their rearmament and territorial expansionism. News of the Nazis' suppression of civil liberties and intensified persecution of Jews alarmed Americans, setting the stage for an epic confrontation which resulted in what was perceived as the triumph of good over evil.

For many, a deeply analytical appreciation of the fact that a black boxer had convincingly defeated the representative of an alleged master race was made impossible by the bout's stridently nationalist overtones. On fight day, pickets paraded outside a packed Yankee stadium proclaiming "Down with Hitler and Mussolini" and urging the government to "Oust Hitler's Agents and Spies"; the American Jewish Committee called for a boycott of the event; and rumors circulated that not only had der Führer promised to make Schmeling minister of sports if victorious but that trainer Max Machon had a Nazi uniform secreted away in his closet.[22] Angered by inflammatory statements about black inferiority said to have originated in the Schmeling camp, Louis encouraged the Nazi-baiting by draping himself in Old Glory. He informed fans that he was fighting "for America against the challenge of a foreign invader. . . . It is the good old U.S.A. versus Germany."[23] Finding it difficult to resist the temptation to embarrass the Germans, sports enthusiasts agreed, hailing the victory as a national triumph.

African-Americans were especially pleased with the outcome of the contest. But, then, they had been in Louis's corner all along. More often than whites, they tended to interpret major chapters in the black boxer's rags-to-riches life story in the context of racial, rather than global, politics. Each successful ring appearance served as a symbolic benchmark of progress for the group as a whole. "For years whites have kicked Negroes about," an eighteen-year-old high school student told Howard University sociologist E. Franklin Frazier in the mid-1930s, "and I'm happy somebody came along who could kick the stuffings out of the toughest 'hombres' the whites could put up against him."[24] It is likely that similar sentiments fueled the enthusiasm of the jubilant throng which goose-stepped through the streets of Harlem in 1938, giving mock-Nazi salutes and shouting "Heil, Louis!" In addition to being major social events in themselves, his fights stirred the emotions and, at least for a time, provided release from psychological constraints.

Ironically, the premium that this generation of African-Americans placed on such black-over-white victories was exacted in the form of an additional mental burden that was placed atop those already being shouldered by the black athlete. The press hailed Louis as a "black Moses" and ecstatic fans shouted "Joe, you're our Savior," and "Show them whites!" whenever he ventured near an adoring, autograph-seeking crowd.[25] As the Bomber trained for his 1935 bout with fascist poster boy Primo Carnera, he became the black world's bulwark against Italian interventionism in Africa. "Lots of black groups came up to camp telling me that I represented Ethiopia," he recalled in later years. "They put a heavy weight on my twenty-year-old shoulders. Now, not only did I have to beat the man, but I had to beat him for a cause."[26] Not even the church provided a sanctuary from these pressures. There, one Sunday morning, Louis was surprised to find that he was being used as an example to illustrate a sermon on the doctrine of gifts. According to the Baptist preacher, Louis was "one of the Chosen." As such, he was said to be gifted with the ability to uplift the spirit of the race; to impress upon the world that "Negro people were strong, fair, and decent."[27]

To this already substantial list one must add a final, equally burdensome responsibility—one that, sooner or later, all symbolic heroes must face: historical accountability. In Louis's case, future generations would demand to know whether athletic accomplishments led to tangible socioeconomic gains for the African-American people. Did his pummeling of Schmeling have value beyond the symbolic? Would the atmosphere of interracial goodwill generated by the events of June 1938 cause any substantive shifts in racial hegemony or consign even a single pejorative stereotype to history's dustbin? And how adept would white Americans become at equating Hitler's Aryan nationalism with that of their own Anglo-Saxon inheritance?

For the time being, such questions remained unresolved. When black and white went to war as segregated brothers-in-arms, Louis continued his work at bridge building. He appeared in armed services promotional films, contributed considerable sums to service charities, visited GIs in hospitals, hawked war bonds, and fought nearly 200 exhibition bouts overseas. Mustered out of the army as a technical sergeant in 1945, the model soldier received the Legion of Merit for "exceptionally meritorious conduct in the performance of outstanding services" abroad. He reentered civilian life better known and more universally respected than ever before.[28]

To a more limited degree, the same could be said for black America as a whole. Wartime gains could be seen and felt. The Nazis' bad example *had* made an impression on whites. At the same time, African-Americans' many contributions to the Allied military effort provided both a cogent rationale and the organizational impetus for peacetime expansion of civil rights. While ancient barriers to black advancement weren't exactly tumbling right and left, deepening cracks were everywhere apparent. Nevertheless, despite these encouraging signs, it soon became clear that even though the international sports

Pvt. Joe Louis says_

"We're going to do our part ...and we'll win because we're on God's side"

Joe Louis as symbol of national unity during World War II (Library of Congress)

confraternity might bring honor to a black symbol by enthusiastically applauding "the first American to K.O. a Nazi," it would take far longer than the two minutes and four seconds needed to dispose of Max Schmeling for racial discrimination to be defeated.[29]

What, then, was this particular culture hero's relationship to social change? Hazarding the use of additional sports metaphors, it can be said that Joe Louis scored no quick knockouts. But he did help black folk to stay on their feet, off the ropes, and even to win a few rounds in these awkward preliminary bouts of the 1930s and 1940s. Perhaps one should ask no more of a hero so encumbered by the excessive demands of overzealous supporters. Certainly, the Brown Bomber was in tune with the times and played his symbolic role well. As was noted in a 1935 *Crisis* editorial, while it would be easy to "fall into enthusiastic error" by reasoning that the success of one black person ensured progress for all, it was impossible to deny that Louis's noteworthy efforts in "interracial education" had helped to alter "the usual appraisal of Negroes by the rank and file."[30] His acceptance by the mainstream didn't exactly cause everybody to be somebody, but it did help make African-Americans seem less unfamiliar and consequently less threatening to whites. In many ways, Louis was the best role model available to those, in any field, who sought to effect change through a series of small victories.

Although he dared not berate whites for their bigotry and, in most cases, felt uncomfortable in going beyond a mild-mannered appeal for equal opportunity, the black champion did display his dissatisfaction with the race relations status quo and thereby helped to make inroads against prejudice outside the ring. He would act against stereotyping by refusing a photographer's request to pose with a huge slice of watermelon. He turned down the chance to stay in a "white" hotel if the management declined to extend a similar welcome to other blacks. During the war years, he participated in a National Urban League radio appeal for "fair play" in the job-rich defense industries and, when in uniform, insisted that military personnel treat him with all the respect due an American soldier. Later, during the early 1950s, he went out of his way to expose patterns of discrimination on the pro golfing tour.[31] In each case, Louis eschewed emotional displays of pique. To do otherwise would have been out of character. As the soft-spoken culture hero noted in responding to critics, "Some folks shout, some holler, some march, and some don't. They do it their way; I do it mine. I got nothing to be 'shamed of. I stand for right and work for it hard 'cause I know what it means not to have the rights what God give us."[32]

But the questioning voices—typically of a younger generation—did have a point. Although Louis's low-key, incremental approach to improving race relations embodied considerable social realism, it let white people off the hook, revealing the limitations of "good behavior" and "preparation" in effecting social change. Knowing that they were unlikely to feel the heat of righteous public anger against injustice, whites could toast the black culture hero one day and tell "coon" jokes the next with impunity. To celebrate Louis's accomplishments made incompletely egalitarian Americans feel moral in the face of Nazi racism and provided them with a partial, temporary resolution of their ambiguous feelings toward people of color. Certainly, it was far easier to praise a black champion of the arena than it was to sacrifice skin-color privilege in everyday life.

Fortunately, most blacks had the good sense not to blame Louis for white folks' inconsistencies and hangups. Along with their hero, they believed that "things would be a lot better for our country if all the people would pull together like one big team," but until this dream became social reality they would continue to honor those culture heroes who identified with blacks personally and with all Americans representationally.[33] In a 1963 interview, the ex-champion noted that his old adversary Max Schmeling once had been quoted as saying that a good German could beat any colored man in the world. Louis recalled that after defeating the German fighter he did, indeed, feel like "every colored man."[34] And this, of course, allowed his fans to feel a bit like Joe Louis as they savored the shared experience.

Thus, it should surprise no one to learn that a remarkable array of African-American movers and shakers—from Lena Horne and Maya Angelou to Malcolm X and Jesse Louis Jackson—have testified to the positive influence that the Brown Bomber has had on their lives. Typically, little mention is made of the degree to which Louis fell short of activist models adopted by later generations. Instead, most speak of the ways in which his triumphs strengthened and inspired, instilled new pride in blackness, and instigated personal revolutions of rising expectations.[35] Without question, these high-achievers have taken Louis's advice to heart. Like their hero, they, too, learned from the negative messages conveyed by cultural stereotypes and Jack Johnson's unfortunate example: "Don't look like a fool nigger. . . . Look like a black man with dignity."[36]

Although they appreciated the Bomber's wise counsel, minority group athletes seeking to desegregate other sports arenas during the late 1940s found that neither his prominence within black America nor his popularity among whites was transferable to any appreciable degree. No matter how dignified their walk, opposition surfaced whenever the question of signing a Negro was broached. At times, it seemed as if every league official and franchise owner in the land was determined to reinvent the wheel rather than assume that they could profit from adopting boxing's model of integrated competition.

Major-league baseball was an especially tough nut to crack. Fears of driving away fans, undermining team unity, lowering the quality of play, and destroying the Negro leagues (whose teams often rented stadium time from white clubs) discouraged experimentation. It would take an innovative executive like the Brooklyn Dodgers' Branch Rickey and a stalwart player/candidate such as Jackie Robinson to alter traditional patterns of racial exclusion.

A four-letter man at UCLA in the early 1940s, Robinson barnstormed with the Kansas City Monarchs after the war, earning a reputation as a superb competitor. Although he was not the best player in the Negro National League, Rickey's scouts believed that he was the "right type" of black athlete and could succeed in the big show. The former army lieutenant neither smoked, drank, or caroused. He was intelligent, articulate, and poised. Hopefully, he would become another Joe Louis—a level-headed sportsman whose character and competitiveness would assuage the fears of those opposed to the integration of organized baseball.[37]

But Robinson was his own person, not a clone of Louis. He had a quick temper and a history of responding in an aggressive fashion to perceived racial slights. For example, while stationed at Fort Hood, Texas, during the war, it was his principled refusal to "get to the back of the bus where the colored people belong" that led to a series of heated confrontations with white military authorities and a 1944 court-martial.[38] Even though acquitted on all charges (insubordination and refusing to obey the orders of a superior officer), Robinson's defiance of southern racial etiquette suggested that the black ballplayer could, on occasion, be as openly disrespectful of white authority as Jack Johnson.

To ensure that Robinson's proud nature would not compromise the success of the Dodger organization's experiment in integration, Rickey met with the prospective rookie in August 1945. Prior to formalizing a contract, the two men engaged in a frank discussion that quickly passed into the folklore of American sports. The gentlemen's agreement reached that day served as a litmus test for future African-American participation in big-league baseball and had important implications for the further development of the black heroic in sports.

For three hours, Rickey lectured Robinson on the key responsibilities and prospective burdens of the first black big-league rookie. Noting that there was far more to the game than revealed in any box score, he warned of abusive spectators, cold-shouldering by teammates, and beanballs. Adding emphasis to his commentary, the Dodger president engaged in role play, acting out the part of an imaginary opponent involved in an ugly spiking incident at second base. "How do you like that, nigger boy?" he sneered, describing the white player's response to the sight of blood trickling down the black infielder's leg. Then, having tested for composure under pressure, Rickey produced a copy of Italian priest Giovanni Papini's *Life of Christ* (1923) and had Robinson read about the wisdom of turning the other cheek—how it confounded adversaries, spared one from receiving additional blows, and represented a type of moral courage said to be the rarest form of bravery.[39]

In response, the black athlete asked what, by now, seemed an obvious question: "Are you looking for a Negro who is afraid to fight back?" Rickey's reply was stern and to the point. "Robinson," he said, "I'm looking for a ballplayer with guts enough not to fight back." Indeed, what he sought to impress upon his young recruit was the necessity of avoiding any and all physical confrontations until his reputation as a big-league-caliber player had been firmly established. As Rickey noted years later: "It took an intelligent man to understand the challenge—it took a man of great moral courage to accept it and see it through. He was both. . . . For three years (that was the agreement) this boy was to turn the other cheek."[40]

During the 1947 and 1948 seasons, Robinson made a determined effort

to adhere to these behavioral guidelines. He remained stolid in the face of racial taunts ("Hey, snowflake, which one of the white boys' wives you shackin'
up with tonight?" "Hey, coon, do you always smell so bad?"), employed his
lightning-fast reflexes to escape brushback pitches, and exercised the utmost
diplomacy when discussing other players with members of the press. On numerous occasions, he repressed his true fighting spirit, swallowing his pride so
that the "noble experiment" could succeed. "Until the time comes when a
Negro player can go out and argue his point as well as any other ball player," he
told a reporter in mid-1948, "I hope that all of us are able to bite our tongues
and just play ball." As teammate Duke Snyder noted, there was nothing dis-
honorable or cowardly in this approach to the psychological war being played
out on the Ebbets Field diamond. The black ballplayer simply employed an indirect, unorthodox fighting technique. He "dished it out" by ignoring the insults of his enemies.[41]

Nevertheless, by September it was apparent that Robinson was growing
restive under Rickey's restraints. Attempting to "argue his point" to umpire
Butch Henline, the black first baseman was ejected from a late-season game.
Sensing the threat to their "almost-filial relationship," the Dodger president issued what he termed "an emancipation proclamation," terminating the pact
before the start of the 1949 campaign. "Jackie," he said, "you're on your own
now. You can be yourself now." When he arrived at training camp in Florida,
the "new" Jackie Robinson was still flush with the liberating glow of this personal day of Jubilee. "They better be prepared to be rough this year," he announced, "because I'm going to be rough on them."[42]

For the rest of his career, Robinson remained true to his word, tangling repeatedly with umpires and opposing players—even managers and league officials. In 1952 he made headlines by accusing the New York Yankee front office
of discrimination, pointing out that they were the only remaining Big Apple
club with a lily-white roster. Addressed even after his retirement in January
1957, baseball's exclusionary practices would be a recurring theme in Robinson's interviews and writings.[43]

On occasion, his markedly changed, aggressive behavior was explained in
terms that any fair-minded person could understand and accept. "I had too
much stored up inside me," he said of his earliest outbursts. "I wasn't able to
squawk when I thought I had a squawk coming." However, at other times, he
seemed willing, even eager, to sacrifice understanding and goodwill for the
chance to act the bold, cross-bearing crusader. "Think of me as the kind of
Negro who's come to the conclusion that he isn't going to beg for anything,"
he told one reporter. "That he is reasonable, but he is damn well tired of being
patient." In this manner, Robinson came to represent a rising cadre of outspoken and ever more combative black leaders.[44]

Many, including a fair representation of African-Americans, lamented the loss of the "old" Jackie and continued to believe that he had a moral responsibility to "go slow." Fearing that his militancy would jeopardize blacks' tenuous position in the sports world, they counseled continued restraint and reminded him of his "obligations" to the race. But, although he readily acknowledged that his actions sometimes exceeded the bounds of athletic propriety—that when he would "get hot" there was a tendency for him to "pop off and say a lot of things I shouldn't say"—Robinson refused to be silenced. This disinclination to play the obsequious, pinstriped Uncle Tom had surprisingly little negative impact on his overall standing within the baseball community.[45]

From the first, African-American supporters had worn their "I'm for Jackie" buttons with pride. They showered their hero with gifts and awards, listened attentively to his New York radio show, and devoured every word of his "Jackie Robinson Says" column which appeared in the *Pittsburgh Courier.* Some female fans sent him embarrassingly personal professions of love, while others compared his wife, Rachel, to Eleanor Roosevelt.[46] For this loyal core, the black star maintained a timeless aura of celebrity. They would keep asking one another, "How'd Jackie do today?" long after he began to frustrate traditionalists with his oppositional approach to civil rights.[47]

While it is likely that the composure, tact, and restraint displayed during his first two seasons with the Dodgers made it possible for Robinson to become an all-American hero, it also is reasonable to believe that consistently stellar performances on the field contributed importantly to his success in winning the respect of white fans. Although many remained more comfortable with Joe Louis as a black heroic model, the ballplayer's skill, mental toughness, and flair for the dramatic could be appreciated even by those who considered him too brash for his own good.[48] From 1949 to 1954, he ranked alongside the St. Louis Cardinals' Stan Musial as the National League's most dominating player—and greatest drawing card. Rookie of the Year (1947) and Most Valuable Player (1949), the black star was elected to the National Baseball Hall of Fame in 1962 with a career batting average of .311 and nearly two hundred stolen bases. Eventually, his image would appear on the nation's postage stamps and his name on schools, street signs, and community centers throughout the country.

If not as successful as Louis in uniting Americans in common cause, Robinson's shake-'em-up attitude forced whites to grapple with their prejudices and to reexamine fixed assumptions about the nature of black leadership. Bridging the gap between historical eras, he informed all within earshot that the heroic representatives of the Afroworld no longer would be hamstrung by tradition or compromise. They had been on their best behavior, running from Jack Johnson's ghost, long enough. In the future, if there was to be marked improvement in race relations, whites would have to be the ones to constrain their natural tendencies, consider carefully their "moral responsibilities," and strive to be the "right type" of American. For the sake of the national "experiment" in desegregated living, whites needed to be able to conceptualize blacks as assertive, self-directed, truly equal partners in progress. Although he held no public office, Jackie Robinson effectively introduced sports fans to the political realities of a new day.

Sports Heroes in an Activist Era

African-American athletes who came of age during the civil rights and Black Power years cited Robinson as a major influence both on their decision to enter competitive sports and on the choice of tactics adopted to counter societal racism. He "gave us our dreams," they said, and told of how the baseball pioneer's proud, fiery example inspired them to stand up and speak out against injustice.[49] Further removed in time and attitude, earlier sports figures held far less attraction. "I saw Joe Louis in Omaha when I was a little kid," recalled St. Louis Cardinal pitcher Bob Gibson. "I was going into the movies as he was coming out. . . . He is the only celebrity I can recall seeing when I was little and, frankly, I was more excited about going to the movie than I was about seeing Joe Louis." In terms of image and style, Robinson remained the "main man" of this activist generation.[50]

Nevertheless, the case for Robinson as role model can be overstated. Athletes of the "second wave" claimed a diverse array of personal heroes—not all of whom regularly wore sweat suits to work. For example, Boston Celtic Bill Russell's boyhood favorite was Haitian king Henri Christophe. Although revolted by his cruelty, Russell admired the ex-slave's shrewdness and indomitable will, noting that the story of his successful struggle against Napoleon's army taught him that "being black was not just a limiting feeling." After reading the *Autobiography*, UCLA basketball great Lew Alcindor found "a star to follow" in Malcolm X. Eventually, this personal journey led him to the Islamic faith. Upon his conversion, he took the name Kareem Abdul-Jabbar and vowed to follow the example of his black Muslim hero in "[taking] a stand speaking the truth." Somewhat more eclectic in his selection, Oakland A's pitcher Vida Blue greatly admired Martin Luther King Jr., the Kennedy brothers, and soulster James Brown. As a youngster, he dreamed of becoming "the first big black quarterback in pro football" by succeeding Johnny Unitas as signal caller of the Baltimore Colts.[51]

Family members also figured into the heroic equation. The sports stars of the 1960s and 1970s had fond memories of strong, supportive, adventurous kin. Fortunate to have been reared among a contingent of long-lived, "high-quality" storytellers, Bill Russell recalled listening, transfixed, to accounts of the Monroe, Louisiana, clan's brave World War I era military contingent, of a great-grandmother who helped fellow slaves escape to the North, of their family logrolling champion, and of the mysterious Grandpa King, who was said to have "special connections" to haints and other members of the spirit world. The most memorable, however, was Grandpa Russell, an obstreperous old gentleman whose claim to fame rested on his seeming inability to abide by the code of behavior drawn up for early-twentieth-century southern blacks. The African-American farmer's tricksterlike deception of a racist sheriff's deputy and his shotgun-wielding rebuff to Klan interlopers were only two of many frequently recounted tales of uncommon boldness which made the future NBA superstar nearly "burst with pride." As an adult, Russell continued to feel fortunate that he was of the same lineage as one who would respond to a white bully's forceful physical challenge with an equally determined "You and who else?"[52]

If other superstar families weren't always blessed with such a splendid array of ancestral hero types, most could point to at least one or two individuals whose extraordinarily vigorous response to life's challenges made them worthy of emulation. As Abdul-Jabbar noted, such kin served as vital agents of socialization, encouraging the development of self-worth in young family members and preventing them from feeling inferior "no matter what kind of propaganda is being laid down." Certainly, not all of these champions were as tough as Dodger catcher John Roseboro's father—who was said to have been able to put out lit cigarettes in his palm without blinking—but the "heroes' heroes" typically were of a stature and disposition that would have made even a Jack Johnson or Jackie Robinson pause and offer their respects.[53]

Emboldened by this impressive, multigenerational support network, the athletes of the 1960s and 1970s set out to accomplish great things. Refusing to remain in the shadow of their predecessors, they hoped to rewrite sports history by compiling their own list of "firsts." Despite the fact that the territory to be traversed often was as unfamiliar and foreboding as that which greeted the first Moon walkers, they carried on bravely. Soon, records—and white exclusionist assumptions—were falling right and left. Certain of these accomplishments seemed monumental and therefore garnered considerable national press coverage. For example, by 1966, outfielder Frank Robinson had become the first African-American major leaguer to capture baseball's triple crown (batting average, home runs, runs batted in) and the first player to be honored as Most Valuable Player in both the National (1961) and the American (1966) Leagues. In 1974 he became the sport's first black manager. During these same years, Atlanta Braves home run king Henry Aaron became the highest paid player in baseball (1972), and seven foot two inch Lew Alcindor of the Milwaukee Bucks became the first athlete in all of American sport to sign a contract in excess of one million dollars (1969). At times, it seemed that each day's sports section altered a page or two in the history books.[54]

Not as widely reported, other breakthroughs had less to do with high salaries, Heisman trophies, and Hall of Fame inductions than with newfound recognition and acceptance at the grassroots level. Many stars of the "second wave" were the first of their race to play for high school, college, or semipro teams. Others, like Vida Blue—the favorite son of Greater Mansfield, Louisiana—were the first blacks ever to have their pictures appear on the front page of hometown newspapers. Some, such as three-time Olympic gold medal–winner Wilma Rudolph, broke the color barrier at the banquet hall as well. A gala Clarkesville, Tennessee, celebration held in her honor after the 1960 Games was the first nonsegregated social event in that city's history. As African-American sportswriter Wadie Moore Jr. noted, the black athletes of the 1960s "integrated life" as well as sport. Community-wide acknowledgment of black achievement helped create an interracial constituency for the African-American heroic even as it encouraged black youngsters to press on— to develop their talents in emulation of these sports world pioneers.[55]

Inevitably, high praise also served to swell the size of the black hero's ego. As the following examples illustrate, it wasn't long before the quote of the day was as likely to come from a loquacious, opinionated black player as from a white one:

> All baseball has done for me? What about all I've done for baseball.— Henry Aaron[56]

> I became the best catcher in the league in the 1960s. . . . I made a lot of all-star teams and deserved it.—John Roseboro[57]

> I can play this game. I can play it better than anyone. I will make a lot of money playing this game. . . . Later, I want to be an actor. I don't think there's anything beyond my reach. About now, I'm going to reach out for some sisters.—Spencer Haywood[58]

> I am the best in baseball. This may sound conceited, but I want to be honest about how I feel. . . . I can do it all and I create an excitement in a ballpark when I walk on the field. I like that just fine. . . . Everything I do makes the news.—Reggie Jackson[59]

Racial barriers in the competition for bragging rights were dismantled permanently during these years, a change lamented primarily by those with a low tolerance for loud, overbearing jocks of any kind. For the rest of America, it seemed refreshing that "color" was being added to the sports world in more ways than one.

Sensing the commercial potential of these self-affirming voices, business agents began signing black stars to personal service contracts. Soon, athlete-celebrities were making pitches for every type of consumer product imaginable—from Simmons Beautyrest, Coca Cola, and American Express (Arthur Ashe) to Black Heritage Natural Hair Sheen (Walt Frazier). Some marketed their own clothing and tennis shoe lines. Others smiled and waved to the crowds and cameras from atop holiday parade floats sponsored by major breweries. More than a dozen launched theatrical careers in eminently forgettable blaxploitation films such as *Dr. Black, Mr. Hyde* (Bernie Casey, 1976), *Soul Soldier* (Rafer Johnson, 1970), *Black Jesus* (Woody Strode, 1971), and *Boss Nigger* (Fred Williamson, 1974). A select few, notably the "300-pound Perry Como," Roosevelt Grier, were permitted to indulge their wildest rhythm and blues fantasies by cutting record albums, which typically bubbled far beneath the *Billboard* Top 100. All of this feverish activity revealed that William Morris and like-minded agencies had discovered there was a growing market for bulked-up black talent. As one astute executive from the Magnavox Corporation noted in 1974, athletic pitchmen had become attractive properties because they were heroes "at a time when America is looking for a hero."[60]

For their part, the heroes were looking to extend spheres of influence wherever and whenever possible. This convenient—and classically American— marriage of personal and business agendas pushed the most aggressively

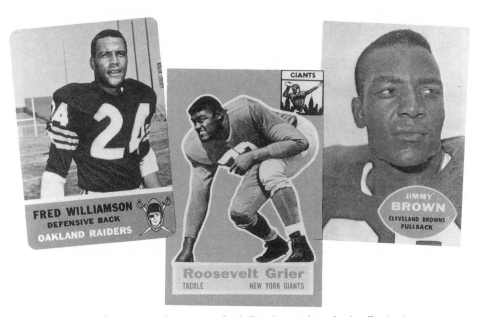

Future film and recording stars on football trading cards (author's collection)

aspiring athletes toward true pop-culture celebrity status. Before long, their everyday walk became the stuff of contemporary legend. Balladeers recounted spectacular performances:

> If you are looking for a hero
> Exciting and new
> There's a boy in Oakland
> Name of Vida Blue
>
> He throws a fastball
> Like it's shot from a gun
> Everybody's talking
> That he's number one. . . .
>
> Killebrew, Yastrzemski
> And Gates Brown too
> Can't buy a hit
> Off of Vida Blue[61]

Comedians in search of fresh material for skits elaborated upon their prowess: "Why, he's so tough that even his fingernails have muscles. . . . [His] mother told me that he was just a normal kid—except he liked to ram his head into fire hydrants."[62] Even a clinical, bare-bones description of a star athlete's physical attributes could cause amazement. Indeed, how many college sophomores were over seven feet tall, weighed more than 220 pounds, wore a size 16D sneaker, and slept in a bed seven feet six inches long? Few, other than Lew Alcindor and soulmates Paul Bunyan and John Henry.

As one might expect, biographical studies of black sports heroes also flattered and astounded. In particular, biographies written for young people during the 1960s and 1970s tended to facilitate uncritical acceptance of the glamorous, larger-than-life portraits which originated in other forms of cultural expression. Such works were fabulous, formulaic creations which nevertheless provided readers with a deliciously deceptive sense of knowing the subject intimately. Here, the composite All-African-American athlete was shown to be a "quiet, good-looking boy" gifted with "Goliath-like strength," "bubbling humor," and a "jaunty walk." With matchless speed and grace, this prototypical black champion played the game "as if he had invented it." A dominating force in any lineup, he not only served as an inspiration to his teammates but also attracted huge crowds of admirers to the stadium weekly. Certainly, such a "complete athlete" was "well on his way to smashing every record on the books."[63]

Although neither as closely tied to actual personalities and events nor as heavily laden with starry-eyed superlatives, many of the works of sports fiction published during this era also served to instruct readers in the possibilities of the black heroic. But, unlike the sports biographers, novelists writing for an adult audience seemed to have studied both the Game of the Week and the gossip columns carefully.[64] Consequently, they endowed their African-American characters with an eye-opening array of attributes and behaviors.

This body of literature introduced fans to the incredibly vain superstar-hoopster-to-be Silky Sims; enigmatic Mason Tidewater, a sensitive and highly educated mulatto pitcher who became murderously violent when called a "make-believe nigger"; Joe Louis "José" Brown, a thirty-eight-year-old rookie catcher masquerading as a Latino; the volatile power forward Isaiah "Muley" Bishop—"a massive man with a neck like a python"; Morningside Robbins, an all-NFL offensive tackle from Dallas who raged in grief over JFK's assassination; and fallen innocent Mack Davis, a basketball sharpshooter whose budding professional career was ended by a fixing scandal but who nevertheless won acclaim as "Plastic Man"—hero of the local schoolyard pickup games.[65] Like the colorful nonfictional protagonists of Jim Bouton's *Ball Four* (1970) and Leonard Shecter's *The Jocks* (1969), each in his own way served to debunk the flawless, standardized portrayal of star athletes derived from juvenile literature.[66] In doing so, these sports world figures helped close a reality gap which otherwise may have prevented readers from realizing that even though blemished and scab-kneed they, too, possessed heroic potential. To paraphrase the fanatical sports-buff narrator of Frederick Exley's *A Fan's Notes* (1968), such literary characterizations constituted an "island of directness in a world of circumspection."[67] Offering sobering instruction in the reality of human—and heroic—diversity, these fictional athletes taught an important truth. In the real world, a black superstar could be a homeboy homebody with a high I.Q., a blotting-paper memory, and a refined appreciation for the classics; a recalcitrant, street-smart "outlaw" with a decidedly bad attitude; or anything in between.

The heroes themselves may not have been fond of admitting it, but they knew all too well that a harsh reality lurked in the spotlight's shadow, largely unaffected by image-shapers' efforts to craft superhumans from mere mortals. As Henry Aaron once noted, there was a "dark side" to being a celebrity.[68] In addition to the day-to-day inconveniences of competitive athletics (e.g., living out of a suitcase; forcing oneself to be "up" for each game; playing with pain), the sports world elite were subjected to a seemingly endless series of annoyances capable of transforming even the most levelheaded individual into a psychosis-ridden basket case.

The most youthful stars—naive high schoolers forced into premature maturity—received an early baptism into these less-than-savory aspects of American sport. Recruiters from top university teams were their chief nemesis. Since the best prep players were tracked for up to three years and received a gaggle of scholarship offers, the pressure to "sign" could become intense. At a time when their peers were scrambling to line up a date for the big dance, they were mapping strategies for eluding fans after the big game and fending off the rude advances of overzealous alumni boosters and assistant coaches. Indeed, the sifting and winnowing involved in compiling a short list of prospective colleges could become a career in itself. Actually, it was more like *Truth or Consequences* on TV. Each of the contenders offered a "clean" program with national visibility, promised a top-notch education, and talked a great deal about *tradition*. Without exception, they vowed to treat the new recruit just like family. Certainly, it all seemed too good to be believe—and much of it was.[69]

After deciding on a college, harried prep stars faced the prospect of repeating this ordeal within four years. In the interim, they had their first close encounters with a truly predatory press corps. As the talent pyramid narrowed, the number of sharks in the media pool increased dramatically. No longer were the assorted prep phenoms merely hometown news. They now represented—hopefully personified— "state" or "old ivy." Apparently, this justified incessant journalistic harassment.

Although, at first, the expanded press coverage was pleasing to young egos, reporters' shallow, repetitive queries could become maddening over time. Rarely were the players asked questions designed to elicit intelligent, incisive, analytical commentary. More often, they were forced to struggle with "How do you feel after this tremendous victory?" or "Do you think Witkowski's 35 points hurt you tonight?" As former University of Kansas basketball star Wilt Chamberlain once noted, after a lengthy bombardment of inanities such as these, "it's no wonder your only response is a monosyllabic mumble. And that, unfortunately, is all the public has to judge your intelligence by."[70] According to this view, print and broadcast journalists were central to the creation of the "dumb jock" stereotype—a negative image of the competitive athlete that could affect even sports world culture heroes.

In addition to fielding questions from pesky reporters, the stars of college sport were obliged to "press the flesh" with the general public. This burden would increase upon promotion to the professional ranks. Indeed, the best-known pros often complained that they were treated more as trophies or icons than as living, breathing human beings who just happened to be successful athletes. Late-night callers seeking endorsements, contributions, free personal appearances, or other favors infringed upon the heroes' private lives and disrupted the regimen of mental preparation required for game day. Restaurant meals were interrupted by Polaroid-toting diners in search of souvenirs. Crowds of pushy, pen-waving autograph hounds formed instantly whenever the star dared emerge from locker room, hotel, or stadium.

Caught up in the moment, some fans could be downright obnoxious. For example, Meadowlark Lemon of the Harlem Globetrotters recalled the time a man chased him into an airport washroom, thrust a scrap of paper under the stall door, and declared in panic, "I'm late for my plane and my son would never forgive me if I didn't get your autograph." On another occasion, a female fan asked him to sign her program while he was on the bench during a game. When he declined, she hit him with her purse.[71] In a similarly bizarre case, the Boston Celtics' Bill Russell was awakened from a sound sleep one vacation-day morning by a motel switchboard operator who complained that he was delaying the departure of a tourist group which had been waiting in the hallway outside his room. Apparently, they had assumed he would rise early to greet them.[72] Certainly, Henry Aaron spoke for many of his peers when he noted that fame's "dark side" could force an athlete to develop "all sorts of defense mechanisms." In the hope of avoiding "complete surrender of a normal and private life," they might, at minimum, seek to deflect attention from themselves by wearing sunglasses or some other type of disguise when mixing with the public. For his part, Aaron sometimes put his right arm in a sling so as to appear unable to sign autographs.[73]

Although justifiable, such deceptions could backfire, creating additional problems. To some degree, elaborate "defenses" sheltered the stars from their fans. But they also created friction with teammates. Well-paid, frequently feted sports figures who avoided crowds like the plague (but who were more than pleased to see their regal profiles on the cover of *Sports Illustrated*) ran the risk of being considered distant and arrogant. Newspaper headlines that focused on team "sparkplugs" rather than on the team as a whole added to clubhouse public relations problems. Such superstars often were held to higher standards of accountability than less established players and wound up shouldering the blame for poor overall team performance. Oakland A's power hitter Reggie Jackson accurately described the perplexing situation by noting that "when your face is on the front of *Time* magazine and your guts are spilled out all over the inside, it's hard for people to accept you for yourself." Far too often, he complained, bigname players were placed on a pedestal. Then, after failing in some fashion to meet the unrealistically high expectations of press and public, they were taken to task—charged with being a "bighead ballplayer," spoiled rotten by success.[74]

Piggybacked atop the burdens borne by all-star-quality athletes were tribulations of a more race-specific nature. In addition to the frustrations of being misquoted in dialect and receiving solicitations from *both* the March of Dimes and the Black Muslims, African-American heroes of the second wave were subjected to a number of indignities which "old-timers" would have found disturbingly familiar. Although many 1960s and 1970s stars were born too late to experience firsthand the trauma of, say, spring training in the segregated South, many could relate bone-chilling stories about their own personal encounters with both unreconstructed bigotry and newer, more subtle forms of racism. In a very real sense, Jim Crow continued to send in key plays long after being relegated to the sidelines.

Hammerin' Hank Aaron was among those capable of providing a comparative perspective on generational changes in American race relations. When he broke into baseball in the early 1950s, African-American players were refused cab rides in Florida training-camp cities and were advised not to drive their own cars at night. They were quartered in overcrowded, all-black boarding-houses which were politely, if somewhat inaccurately, referred to in the press as "carefully selected private homes." Some newspapers would not even print their pictures. In more northerly locales, matters improved to the extent that black players were allowed rooms in the same hotels as their teammates. But, according to Aaron, these always seemed to be "in a blind spot, looking at some old building or a blank wall so nobody can see us through a window." Often, a screen was placed around them as they dined. When this was not done, white patrons tended to glare at the black athletes as if they were "some kind of strange creature[s]."[75]

In 1973, as he closed in on Babe Ruth's record of 714 lifetime home runs,

Hammerin' Hank Aaron on baseball trading cards (author's collection)

the thirty-nine-year-old Atlanta Braves' slugger must have experienced a sense of déjà vu. The specter of seeing the Babe's achievement eclipsed by a Negro brought out the worst in a relatively small but fanatical cohort of sports fans. Despite issuing a disclaimer that he had no intention of making people forget the hallowed Ruth—that he simply wanted "to be sure they remember Hank Aaron"—the black star was subjected to a withering storm of abuse. Racist catcalls from the stands and hate mail addressed to "Dirty old nigger man" and "Dear Nigger Scum" greeted Aaron daily. The anonymous correspondents urged early retirement ("Go back to the jungles," "retire or die!") and asked, "How about some sickle cell anemia, Hank?" As the season wore on, stadium security had to be increased. The FBI was called in to investigate a rash of death threats—some of which predicted that his next home run would be his last.[76]

Although the burden was lifted when he finally hit number 715 into a wildly cheering standing-room-only crowd at Atlanta Stadium in April 1974, Aaron never would forget this traumatic ordeal. In retrospect, one particular missive received during his epic quest stands out, effectively telescoping past and present. Of the accomplished professional athlete, a vindictive amateur poet wrote:

> Hank Aaron,
> With all that fortune,
> and all that fame,
> You're a stinkin nigger
> Just the same.[77]

Apparently, for some individuals, little had changed over the years. The conceptualization of the American hero had yet to transcend race.

Racist acts, however, did not have to be this obvious to be felt and resented. Less blatant manifestations of inegalitarian attitudes continued to plague black athletes throughout the period. Even more elusive and difficult to fathom than professional basketball's "unwritten law" of the 1950s (which held that no team should sign more than two or three blacks lest fan support dwindle), the neo–quota system known as "stacking" limited access to some of sports' most desirable jobs.[78]

During the 1960s and 1970s this relegation of black athletes to certain positions—and their near exclusion from others—was more easily charted than given rational explanation. In 1967, 83 percent of major-league infielders, 94 percent of pitchers, and 96 percent of catchers—but only 41 percent of outfielders—were white. By 1975, the representation of nonblacks in infield positions had dropped to 76 percent, but the outfield still was almost 50 percent black. Pitching (96 percent) and catching (95 percent) remained overwhelmingly white. At the end of the decade, an African-American player was 8.8 times as likely to be an outfielder as a pitcher.[79] Equally glaring disparities in position assignment existed in professional football. In 1975, for example, all but three of the NFL's eighty-seven quarterbacks were white—as were sixty-nine of seventy punters and placekickers.[80] Why?

As in the larger society, lingering racial stereotypes continued to foster exclusionist tendencies throughout the sports world. Here, the primary stumbling block was the black athletes' so-called Sambo image. Although certain of the slapstick routines performed by black barnstorming vaudevillians did little to discredit the stereotype, Samboism was nourished by more than the tons of confetti which several generations of Globetrotters had tossed into the laps of surprised spectators. Visions of Sambos-in-sweats were merely extrapolations from far older models. Once as ubiquitous as smiles on the faces of minstrel end men, the Sambo stereotype ever so gradually was turning into a type of guilty pleasure. But it still packed enough punch to call into question African-Americans' capacity for heroism.

Myth held that the Sambos' innate gifts were substantial but in many ways "incomplete." Brawny but not brainy, instinctive but seldom reflective, they were considered raw talents. Black boxers, for example, were said to have hard heads and weak stomachs. Runners were blessed with speed rather than endurance. Hyperextensibility (double-jointedness) and an abundance of white muscle fibers provided tremendous leverage and spring for jumping, but inadequate lung capacity caused black swimmers to be labeled "sinkers." Often, blacks' deeply ingrained laziness caused them to stray from the strict training regimen required of top performers. Moreover, no matter how physically intimidating, hardly any made good leaders. In sum, like their nonathletic pop-culture forebears, these fleet-footed, slow-witted Sambos were considered to be better at playing games than competing with whites.[81]

Scouts and coaches influenced by these traditional teachings could feel justified in targeting blacks for positions that required speed, "good instincts," and aggressiveness but that made relatively few intellectual or leadership demands. "Central" or "control" slots (i.e., pitcher, catcher; quarterback, kicker, linebacker; point guard) would be reserved for white players with more fully developed cognitive skills. These beliefs were perpetuated by the tendency of youthful aspirants to emulate existing role models, and it would take considerable effort to break the white athletes' on-field decision-making monopoly and convince sports world mythmakers that African-Americans actually developed most of their "natural" gifts in much the same manner as whites—through disciplined training.

African-American athletes met the adversities of their chosen vocation in decidedly nonstereotypical ways. Some adopted an aggressive approach to discrimination, returning their detractors' ill-will with the speed and alacrity of a grand-slam hit off a fastball. On occasion, ignorant, unthinking remarks could be dismissed with a quick retort. Such was the case when Bob Gibson was asked if he was a minister and he replied coldly, "Why? Because I'm not dirty?"[82] More often than not, however, spirited verbal and/or physical confrontation ensued.

Black athletes who responded to taunts of "nigger" and "boy" with counterinsults knew they were on shaky ground in regard to sports world etiquette. But they also understood that an injustice suffered silently was one that was certain to be repeated. Rejecting the notion that their "image" would be damaged if they responded to racist provocation in an assertive fashion, such individuals believed that being a "credit to the race" involved a good deal more than dressing well and speaking in complete sentences. As noted by Bill Russell, who once broke an opposing player's ribs for calling him a "Black Gorilla," the prevailing system of racial hegemony often made it extremely difficult to do "the gentlemanly thing." In this context, to "raise the question"—to shun accommodation and to enter into "the arguments, the tensions, the slanders, the violence" of a competitive world order—became a sign of both wisdom and racial loyalty. According to Russell, blacks could win respect only by fighting back.[83]

Others preferred to engage in more indirect, "defensive" techniques. Convinced that most "real" victories were psychological, they sought to outmuscle their enemies mentally.[84] Here, the survival skills of the rookie Robinson and the rabbit Br'er were melded into a game plan that relied less on biting rejoinders and brute strength than on gaining and maintaining tactical advantage. Like a running back who disguises his injuries so that opponents will not suspect that he is playing hurt, these heroes eschewed anger and held their tongues. When they did speak out, it was to dismiss racists as "little men," unworthy of their contempt. Utilizing righteous anger to fuel personal accomplishment, they "played their guts out" as a rebuttal to discriminatory acts. Of course, this added greatly to their mystique. As St. Louis Cardinal outfielder Curt Flood made clear in explaining this approach, "When you have answered insult and rejection with a .340 batting average, you have done something more than philosophical. . . . Your achievements have emancipated you."[85]

What caused an individual athlete to favor defense over offense—or vice versa? Although fully capable of modifying their actions as circumstances changed, most heroes evidenced a preference for one technique over the other. For some, the decision was a function of personal style. Like one's honor, the choice would be defended with considerable vigor. "I'm just as aware of the injustices done to the black man as anyone," asserted an angry but articulate Wilt Chamberlain. "I just don't believe you help things by running around, saying how evil Whitey is." In similar fashion, Henry Aaron made it known that he had no intention of "stir[ring] up trouble" or becoming a lawbreaker in order to "draw attention to myself for any cause." Nevertheless, he was determined to stand up for his beliefs—namely, that the best way to fight bigotry was to "be good . . . , play good. Play so good that they can't remember what color you were before the season started."[86]

Without completely disregarding philosophical or tactical considerations, others seemed to be more tellingly influenced by early life experiences and role models. "I think I'm pretty much the joint creation of my father, of a few friends . . . , and of smart advisors," wrote tennis star Arthur Ashe. "Daddy is a self-respecting no-nonsense type, and maybe I get some attributes from him. He's just not quarrelsome about anything or with anyone. He told me to respect everyone, even those who don't respect me." More outspoken than Ashe, the New York Jets' Johnny Sample was shaped by similar forces. As recounted in his autobiography, growing up in the segregated South of the 1940s and 1950s had a profound and lasting effect on his approach to black-white power relationships. "The agony and embarrassment that I've seen black people suffer put a hardness in me that made me what I am," he wrote in 1970. "I saw so many black people get pushed around I swore to myself that no man, white or black, would ever take advantage of me." According to Sample, discrimination molded his character "as much as a coach teaching me how to block, run, or tackle."[87]

A third possible determinant was age. Like the civil rights moderates of the late 1960s, athletes socialized during the first wave of sports world desegregation sometimes remained wedded to once successful "pioneering" approaches which now were being dismissed as passé and counterproductive. Some, of course, managed to sidestep the generation gap by permitting black liberation rhetoric to raise their consciousness. Typically, such individuals declined to take to the streets in hot pursuit of honkies. But, like Willie Mays, they also vowed "not [to get] mad at the people who do."[88] Refusing to believe that Black Power would solve all of America's racial problems, they at least understood both its attraction and its potential to force significant modifications in white behavior.

Other "first wavers" had considerable difficulty dealing with change. They were hesitant to pass the baton of group leadership to an activist generation who apparently had no use for "indirect" tactics and seemed unconcerned about bringing "credit" to their race in the traditional fashion. By adopting these views, sports world veterans risked being perceived as hidebound Uncle Toms and Aunt Minnies—pliant dupes of the European-American establishment. The divisive nature of these perceptions, misperceptions, rumors, and fears was nowhere more evident than in the heated debate which erupted in 1968 between Jesse Owens and supporters of the Olympic boycott movement.

The winner of four gold medals at the 1936 Berlin Olympics, Owens became a household name after sportswriters reported that Hitler had snubbed the black track-and-field star by refusing to shake his hand at the victory ceremony.[89] Upon his return to the States, the new American hero was showered with confetti and applause, expensive gifts and speeches of praise. He was named Associated Press Athlete of the Year and secured the services of an agent to arrange endorsement and public appearance contracts. Although eventually eclipsed by Joe Louis's rising star, Owens managed to attach his own to the coattails of an increasingly influential cadre of American cold warriors. During the Eisenhower years, the "Buckeye Bullet" campaigned for Republican politicians, made goodwill tours of India, Australia, and the Far East, and spoke often of the threat posed by international communism. By the time of the 1968 Games, the fifty-five-year-old legend was part-owner of a Chicago public relations firm and had become a fixture on the banquet circuit. His inspirational talks made it clear that he considered himself "an American first and a black man second." Unkind wags called him an "eternal glad-hander" and a "professional good example."[90]

Former boxing champ Jack Dempsey displays a Jesse Owens poster promoting physical fitness during World War II (Library of Congress)

Representing a constituency that was both puzzled and disgusted by the riots and demonstrations of the late 1960s, Owens was proud to be out of step with those whose lifestyle and political philosophy were shaped by what he derided as "blackthink." To the former Olympian, African-American "extremists" like Stokely Carmichael were either "colored con men" or "the new George Wallaces"; "skin-deep" loyalty was ugly, not beautiful; and "hair shirts" were far less effective in spurring black economic advancement than the time-honored work ethic of the "silent black majority." Critical of Johnson era welfare initiatives ("get[ting] something for nothing") and quick to dismiss the threat posed by Black Power militancy as "the biggest of black herrings," he willingly served as a lightning rod for the raucous rebuttal of the revolutionary rank and file. Certainly, Owens's penchant for dressing in the Stars and Stripes did little to endear him to those who sought to use the Mexico City Games as a forum for social protest.[91]

The organizational infrastructure of the Olympic boycott movement began to fall into place at a black youth conference held in Los Angeles on Thanksgiving Day 1967. "Liberation is coming from a black thing" was the theme of the gathering, and, most appropriately, one of the workshops focused on the question of black participation in the upcoming Games. About fifty of the two hundred delegates were college athletes. Following lengthy deliberations, the rationale behind the new Olympic Project for Human Rights was presented to reporters by Harry Edwards, a black, twenty-five-year-old assistant professor of sociology at San Jose State College. For years, he noted, African-American athletes had been major contributors to the success of the national team. Despite these selfless efforts, they continued to experience discrimination. Boycott supporters were not purposely banding together to "lose" the Olympics for the United States. They simply, but firmly, were saying that it was time for black athletes to stand up for themselves and refuse to be "utilized as performing animals for a little extra dog food." By doing so, the activists hoped to publicize the plight of poor blacks throughout society. After all, Edwards asked, "What value is it to a black man to win a medal if he returns to the hell of Harlem?" Self-definition, dignity, and power for every African-American in every sector of society were the ultimate concerns.[92]

Specific demands made by the leaders of the Olympic Project included a ban on competition between American teams and teams from apartheid states such as South Africa and Rhodesia; appointment of a black member to the U.S. Olympic Committee and an additional black coach to the U.S. team; and expulsion of the International Olympic Committee's "racist" president, Avery Brundage.[93] Initially, these proposed reforms garnered remarkably broad-based support. Following a December 1967 meeting in New York City, Martin Luther King Jr. of the Southern Christian Leadership Conference and

Floyd McKissick of the Congress of Racial Equality agreed to serve as advisors. Speaking at a rally in Oakland, Student Nonviolent Coordinating Committee and Black Panther leader Stokely Carmichael referred to the Olympics as "that white nonsense" and claimed that no black athlete "with any dignity" would go to Mexico City. Support also came from SNCC chairperson H. Rap Brown, the Us Organization's Ron Karenga, and from scores of lesser-known black activists.[94]

Despite the enthusiasm generated by these endorsements, it soon became obvious that the boycott plan would not win universal acclaim. Encouraged by newspaper headlines which screamed "Negro Hothead Threatens Games Boycott," opponents of the movement marshaled their forces in preparation for a counterstrike. Harry Edwards's apartment was trashed and sewage dumped onto the seats of his car. Soon, hate mail and death threats began pouring into the Olympic Project offices. "Dear Traitor," began one. "I'd rather have our country finish last, without you, than first with you." Others mocked the boycott effort: "Thanks for pulling out of the Olympic Games. Now I can again be interested in our U.S. team. I quit being interested in watching animals like Negroes go through their paces." Still others vilified the activists and expressed the hope that they would "get [their] bloody heads bashed in." Finally, in what must have been the ultimate insult, bribes of more than $125,000 were offered to Edwards if he would disavow the movement and call off the boycott.[95]

As it turned out, Black Power sentiment was very much in evidence at Mexico City, but it was not ordered according to the activists' original plan. Believing that their cause would be harmed by the appearance of disunity, some athletes had argued that there should be no boycott without the full participation of all blacks selected to the U.S. team. Unable to heal divisions within their ranks, alternative guidelines eventually were developed: athletes could compete but would wear black armbands and refuse to participate in victory celebrations. Later it was agreed that all participants should protest in their own ways, preferably focusing their actions around the victory stand ceremonies.[96]

Thus, when sprinters Tommie Smith and John Carlos mounted the awards platform to receive their gold and bronze medals on 16 October 1968, both were shoeless and wore black, knee-length stockings and a black glove on one hand. Smith had a black scarf around his neck. When the band began to play the American national anthem, they bowed their heads—seemingly to avoid looking at their country's flag. At the same time, their gloved fists shot skyward. Later, Smith explained the symbolism of their actions. Their raised arms stood for the power and unity of black America. The black socks with no shoes symbolized the poverty that afflicted their black compatriots. Black pride was represented in Smith's scarf, and the gesture of bowed heads was a remembrance of those who had perished in the black liberation struggle.[97]

Having been warned by Brundage that no political demonstrations would be permitted during the Games, the two medal winners were ordered to leave U.S. quarters in the Olympic Village. But this did not end the Olympic Project protest. Following the expulsion of Smith and Carlos, all three U.S. medalists in the 400-meter dash wore black berets on the victory stand, avoiding censure by removing them for the playing of the national anthem. The world-record-breaking 1,600-meter relay team wore black berets and gave a clenched-fist salute. Broad jumpers Bob Beamon and Ralph Boston stood shoeless and wore long black socks to protest both the condition of blacks in America and the treatment of their now-banished teammates.[98]

Harry Edwards had harsh words for those who refused to join in such acts of principled defiance. They were cop-outs—members of "a controlled generation" who had been brainwashed so long and so completely about sports' supposedly beneficent role in their lives that the very idea of using athletics as a forum for protest seemed mystifying to some and criminal or treasonous to others. As if to warn against association with blacks thought to possess this "highly illusionary perspective on sports," Edwards placed a "Traitor (Negro) of the Week" poster on permanent display in his San Jose State office. At its center was a picture of former Olympian Jesse Owens.[99]

As might be expected, Owens was somewhat less than enthusiastic about receiving this dubious honor. In fact, he saw little value in any of the activists' displays of discontent. A consultant for the U.S. Olympic Committee, Owens had stumped for funds to support the American team and, for months, just as vigorously had denounced the boycott movement in public lectures, in the press, and on radio and television. Sports and politics, he maintained, were incompatible. Drawing upon personal experience, he noted that Hitler "didn't accord Negroes and Jews the same courtesies he did others who came to Berlin [in 1936]," but such pointed affronts only made the minority group competitors "more determined to prove that, in the eyes of God, we were every bit as good as any man." By taking a radically different course of action in 1968, activists were doing an injustice both to themselves and to their country.[100]

Standing firm in the belief that African-Americans could "bridge the gap of misunderstanding more in athletics than anywhere else," Owens was pleased to offer the following postmortem on the Mexico City protests: The whole affair, he wrote in 1970, had been a tempest in a teapot—another "black herring" blown all out of proportion by a sensationalist press. For a time, Smith's and Carlos's "Nazi salutes" had made "sick headlines" but in the long run had proven to be of about as much consequence as "two grammar school kids trying to create a tidal wave by skipping stones in the Pacific Ocean." The boycott had fallen "flatter on its face than a one-legged hurdler." In retrospect, the damage done by the militants' "vicious, unfair, destructive" blackthink philosophy was minimal. The events of October 1968 now were but "a dim memory for most."[101]

Was this an accurate reading of recent history or merely the wishful thinking of one whose mind-set and ideology remained frozen in the social context of an earlier era? Certainly, there were those within the black youth culture of the late 1960s who would have disagreed with Owens's assessment of the situation and challenged his assertion that "the only time the black fist has significance is when there's money inside." For them, Black Power was more than a "plaything, profit-thing or ego-thing" fueled by self-hatred and a "lust for revenge."[102] From the perspective of these young idealists, the Mexico City demonstration, if not quite an unqualified success, was a success nonetheless. The boycott struck a nerve throughout America, rudely informing white and black alike that displays of black discontent could not be confined to courthouse steps or ghetto street corners. African-American activism would not be limited to matters of politics but would percolate throughout all areas of social and cultural life.

Just as important, the Olympic protest brought a new recognition of sports' importance as a shaper of personal values. Through their participation in or identification with the Olympic Project, many became transformed, empowered individuals. As noted by boycott spokesperson Lee Evans, the effects of this mental and spiritual reformation could be dramatic. "A few years ago," he told a journalist in 1968, "I didn't know what was happening. My white junior college coach used to tell colored boy jokes and I'd laugh. Now I'd kick his ass."[103] By rejecting Owens's approach and adopting an updated version of Jackie Robinson's protest ethic, youthful African-American heroes sought to speed the removal of white America's headlock on blacks in the sports world. Like the combative Dodger star, they, too, were tired of being patient and refused to beg for scraps from an entrenched sports establishment which persisted in conceptualizing them as Sambos.

Muhammad Ali: "The People's Champion"

No heroic representative of this activist generation possessed greater potential to eradicate these lingering problems than Muhammad Ali, née Cassius Clay. At a time when "old-school" champions such as Jesse Owens were taping "Do you know me?" commercials for American Express, Ali was perhaps the most immediately recognizable person on the planet. He symbolized gentleness and strength, unbending principle and unaffected wit, and his influence transcended both sports and racial politics. Obviously, the opinion of one who could "float like a butterfly, sting like a bee" (and by doing so earn more money from boxing than all previous heavyweight champions combined), had to be considered carefully. For many, this self-proclaimed "Supernigger," who likened himself to both ancient Roman and African-American folk heroes in his own playfully boastful poems, was "the people's champion"—the very personification of Black Power era heroism.[104]

Like many other sports heroes of the 1960s and 1970s, Clay/Ali appeared larger than life but, in reality, had struggled to rise from humble beginnings. He never had to battle crippling childhood illnesses, as did O. J. Simpson (rickets) and Wilma Rudolph (polio). He was better provided for than, for example, young Spencer Haywood, who regularly went to bed hungry, received his first Christmas present at age sixteen, and was functionally illiterate until high school.[105] Nevertheless, Clay's early days in the West End section of Louisville were no picnic. The meager earnings which accrued from his father's sign-painting business and his mother's job as a domestic afforded few luxuries. The Clay family never owned a car that was less than ten years old, had no money to repair a leaking roof or crumbling front porch, and wore mostly secondhand Good Will store clothing. Young Cassius let his peers think that he raced the bus to school each day because he was getting in shape for boxing. In truth, bus

Ad for Muhammad Ali T-shirts (*Sepia* magazine, 1978)

fare seldom was available—except to shuttle "Bird" Clay back and forth to cook for white folks and to clean their dirty bathrooms.[106]

Eventually, ring earnings alleviated these economic ills, but problems caused by racial prejudice were less easily remedied. As did other black champions, Clay learned early in his career that fame was but an imperfect shield against boorishness and bigotry. Proud as a peacock at having emerged victorious in the light heavyweight boxing competition during the 1960 Rome Olympics, the eighteen-year-old fighter wore his gold medal everywhere. It was, he wrote, "the most precious thing that had ever come to me. I worshipped it. It was proof of performance, status, a symbol of belonging, of being part of a team, a country, a world." One day, however, he was brought up short when a Louisville restaurant owner refused him service. "I don't give a damn *who* he is!" the white man blustered. "We don't serve no niggers!" Neither the impressive *"pugilato"* medal with its red, white, and blue ribbon nor Clay's polite introduction of himself as "the Olympic champion" could buy the youthful hero a burger and shake that afternoon.[107]

As a stunned and embarrassed Clay exited the "whites only" establishment with his friend Ronnie King, a second crisis situation developed. Adding insult to injury, a group of motorcycle toughs began to mock the black fighter. "Hey, Olympic nigger!" "You still tryin' to get a milk shake?" "I got your milk shake, Olympic!" they shouted across the parking lot. After considerable verbal sparring, the white bikers demanded the gold medal as a "li'l ole souvineer"— something to mark their brief encounter with a bona fide celebrity. A knock-down, drag-out fight ensued. Although he and his buddy emerged victorious, Cassius was devastated. Hurt more by disrespect than by the gang members' fists and chains, he found that his once treasured victory token had lost its allure. It now seemed "ordinary, just an object," a "cheap piece of metal and raggedy ribbon." Tearing the medal from his neck, Clay tossed it off the Jefferson County Bridge and into the murky waters of the Ohio River. "It wasn't real gold," he told his astonished companion. "It was phony."[108]

Hardened by these early encounters with the twin perils of privation and discrimination, Clay was well prepared for later bouts with adversity. In addition to the potentially humbling experiences which are the lot of all competitive athletes (i.e., heckling, defeat, bad press), the ex-Olympian bore an additional cross. Actually, it was a crescent. His 1964 conversion to the Nation of Islam made Clay—now Muhammad Ali—scores of new enemies. By adopting and conscientiously defending the unconventional religious doctrines and separatist political beliefs of Malcolm X and Elijah Muhammad, he risked total ostracism from the mainstream boxing public. Certainly, most sports fans were unaccustomed to having their heroes lecture them on the evils of pork and blue-eyed devils, ridicule the notion of Jesus' virgin birth and resurrection, and, with a straight face, predict the imminent destruction of the white world while demanding a separate homeland for "Asiatic" blacks.[109] His sermonizing on Christ's "burnt brass" skin color and on the extent to which "white blood" had weakened the black race made more headlines than converts.[110]

Ali's lengthy, well-publicized campaign to avoid military service on the grounds that he was both a conscientious objector and a minister of the Muslim faith generated even more animus. Claims that he "like[d] preaching better than fighting" because he devoted some 160 hours per month to his "true" vocation did little to still the clamor. In this heated atmosphere even hard-core supporters were given to wonder whether their hero was being true to his new Islamic name—which, in the language of the faithful, denotes one deemed "worthy of respect." Irrespective of his ringsmanship, the champ was said to be setting "a very poor example for American youth." Soon, calls for stripping Ali of the world heavyweight title he had earned by outboxing Sonny Liston in 1964 became deafening.[111]

Effectively exiled from the ring between 1967 and 1970, the spunky fighter greeted these setbacks with the courage of a true American hero. Serving as his own paragon of virtue, Ali took the high ground against charges that he was a draft-dodging black supremacist. "Islam means peace. Yet people brand us a hate group," he noted sadly. "That is not true. Followers of Allah are the sweetest people in the world." He credited the teachings of the Nation with changing his life and giving him the internal fortitude to "live righteous in the hell of North America." One day, Ali believed, this devotion to principle would cause him to be recognized as "a great man in history."[112]

The odds that this bold prophecy someday would come true began to improve in 1971 after the U.S. Supreme Court reversed his conviction for refusing army induction. They improved further after he assumed the role of an underdog striving to regain his title from interlopers such as Joe Frazier and George Foreman. Eventually, through hard work, personal charm, and an unerring sense of the historical moment, Ali made good his claim to being "the only man in history to become famous under two different names." Like an unjustly deposed monarch skillfully executing a master plan to recapture the throne, he vanquished Foreman in 1974 and subsequently garnered a treasure trove of major sports awards. Amid an outpouring of goodwill and talk of letting bygones be bygones, the new heavyweight champion was acclaimed "the greatest athlete of his time and maybe all time and one of the most important and brave men of all American time."[113]

The passing of two additional decades has modified this glowing appreciation only slightly. Given the major controversies which dogged him throughout the 1960s, Ali was remarkably successful both in salvaging his career and in advancing the cause of all black Americans. He shared the burdens of his people and willingly entered into disputes similar to those that would engross—and sometimes destroy—his activist contemporaries. According to Black Panther Eldridge Cleaver, Ali was a "genuine revolutionary"—a leader "in harmony with the furious psychic stance" of 1960s black America.[114] Like coreligionist Malcolm X, he introduced many to the basic tenets of Black Power. But, unlike the martyred Malcolm, Ali survived the (character) assassination attempts and was able to continue his work—inspiring the Olympic boycotters and motivating jocks and nonjocks alike to engage in acts of principled opposition to the Vietnam War. Through the terms of nine U.S. presidents, the champ spoke his mind—mercilessly skewering "brainwashed" black "white hopes" and tirelessly promoting black pride and pan-African unity. In the ring, he utilized techniques of psychological warfare against opponents which other determined black strivers could adapt to real-world canvases.[115]

Ali's black-is-beautiful rhetoric ("I so pretty they ought to make me a natural resource"; "I'm so beautiful I should be chiseled in gold") served as a race-specific corollary to the more universally applicable axiom which held that "humble people . . . don't get very far" in life.[116] As manager-trainer Angelo Dundee once noted, "he could give Norman Vincent Peale lessons on the power of positive thinking."[117] Upon his return from exile, a growing number of nonblacks clamored for the champ's wisdom on such matters of head and heart. Ali explained the attraction simply but effectively: "Everyone wants to believe in himself. Everyone wants to be fearless. And when people saw I had those qualities, it attracted them to me."[118] Humanized by his struggles against adversity, Ali emerged from the depths of popular disfavor as both a lion-hearted hero and the prototypical hail-fellow-well-met. While some die-hard types continued to hold a grudge on the basis of his long-term nonconformity, far more admired and appreciatively savored the gifts of spirit, principle, and determination that he brought to a beleaguered post-JFK, post-Vietnam society. Perhaps a bit less bombastic and narcissistic, but no less charming or approachable than in earlier years, Ali became the 1970s sports world's Superman/Everyman.

Strivers All

In truth, many black athletes of the 1960–80 period were known to possess similar attributes. Alternatively reflecting and helping shape the social and ideological currents of their day, this generation of African-American sports heroes was celebrated by the European-American mainstream with an openness and enthusiasm that would have astonished first-wave pioneers. Gifted with drive and determination, charisma and considerable entertainment value, they utilized the shared language, lore, and ritual of the sports world to widen the gap made by their forebears in white America's pop-culture defenses. Many burst through to daylight in triumphant vindication of past defeats.

At the same time, black race champions retained their unique, symbiotic relationship with the African-American community. Like Ali, most claimed to be rejuvenated and strengthened whenever they returned to their roots to play pickup games with young admirers or to give inspirational speeches to the brothers on the block. Without question, the homefolk appreciated the flow of charitable dollars generated by such visits. Typically, the heroes' largess helped fund academic scholarships, stock food pantries, and fight disease.[119] But less tangible gifts also were exchanged.

Black sports heroes brought hope to the discouraged and, as dynamic role models, helped motivate those with low self-esteem. Like the Chicago Bears' Gale Sayers, who on one occasion confidently added the notation "these must go" to a list of major rushing records which he kept pinned to his wall, all African-Americans were to accept challenge; to be strivers in the game of life.[120] Acting with the same degree of self-assurance which Ali displayed each time he declared that an opponent "must fall in the round I call," they were to campaign against skin-color privilege and work to dispel white myth.[121] Those who accepted the heroes' challenge and studied their activist playbook thoroughly increased their chances of scoring an upset victory over entrenched prejudice. In the process, they helped educate whites in the ways of the modern, competitive world.

By and large, the experiences of the black sports heroes support NFL Hall-of-Famer Jim Brown's contention that "the more successful a Negro is, the more difficult it becomes for him to accept second-class citizenship."[122] But perhaps even more important than the growth of self-esteem within any one individual is the potential that such an awakening holds for cumulative, group empowerment. During the 1960s and 1970s, the centrality of sport in American society virtually ensured that the black athletes' self-affirming, proactive approach to life would have a significant ripple effect. With remarkable speed, their dispute with the status quo spread beyond traditional sports world boundaries, promoting psychological wellness within black communities, jarring white perceptions a bit closer to reality, and forever altering the context of American racial relationships. Proving themselves able instigators of change, black champions brought credit to an increasingly interracial heroic guild whose long history of inspiring common folk to greatness was in no way diminished by their presence in the winner's circle.

CHAPTER

FOUR

Heroic Hustlers and Daring Detectives

"You're something else. Mr. Black Dude. All secrets, fast hands and feet,
heavy friends in high places. . . . Whatever happened to the shuffling,
lawsy-me darky who used to wait on everybody hand and foot?"
                    URSULA JANIS TO ROBERT SAND, THE BLACK SAMURAI,
                                IN MARC OLDEN, *The Deadly Pearl*

Into each culture hero's life some villainy must fall. Like death and taxes, this is
axiomatic—an inevitability. Sooner or later, the people's champion either will
engage in an epic struggle with an external source of great evil or face the
equally daunting prospect of battling personal demons. On occasion, beleaguered Everymen are forced to confront both of these challenges to their
moral authority and vision simultaneously. If their victories sometimes seem
incomplete, it may be because heroes and villains share many noteworthy attributes. Both camps contain lookers and strivers: the bold, the beautiful, and
the eternally restless; rugged individualists of all sorts wedded to a cause and
determined to take no prisoners. In order to defeat an unprincipled villain, a
hero may opt to employ crude, deceptive, or otherwise unsportsmanlike tactics. In the process of losing to a hero, the villain-as-foil (or scapegoat) helps to
promote the victor's values and agenda—thereby becoming a force for "good."
As evidenced by the European-Americans' noble outlaw champion Robin
Hood and by those variants of black American folk tradition which portray the
normally stalwart John Henry as a carousing womanizer with mayhem on his
mind, the heroism-villainy continuum can be a most convoluted construc-
tion.[1] Can we be blamed for confusing right and wrong, divinity and deprav-
ity—or for concluding that one person's hero most likely is another's villain?

In tune with the spirit of the times (and at the request of popular-culture
consumers everywhere), numerous such heroically inclined antiheroes and
bad good guys of color prowled the shadowy recesses of the cultural landscape
between 1960 and 1980. Chief among them were tricksterlike urban badmen—hustlers, dealers, pimps, hit men, gangsters, assorted revolutionaries—
and several squad rooms full of roguish but ever vigilant detective types.

Melding traditional and race-specific components of heroism, they helped define both a historical era and a racial aesthetic. Taken together, their impact on American cultural affairs was considerable. Not only did the most memorable of these characters engender sly satisfaction and numerous button-bursting bouts of pride within Afro-America, but the very ease—and style—with which they managed to join seemingly incompatible aspects of heroism and villainy also served to advance universalist ideals.

Ironically, nowhere were these tendencies more strikingly visible than in darkened Hollywood screening rooms and neighborhood movie palaces during what came to be known as American filmmakers' "blaxploitation" period. As a result, Tinseltown's "take" on the black heroic becomes an unavoidable point of departure for any reflective evaluation of the era's heroic hustlers and daring detectives.

Cinema and Social Banditry

Long attached to demeaning portrayals of African-Americans as Noble Savages, Loyal Servants, Comic Minstrels, Cowards, and Brutes, commercial filmmakers nevertheless were opportunistic enough to recognize the attraction of new images. They also were wedded to the always compelling notion of making a decent return on their investment. Like the splendid athletes some of them actually were off camera, black actors responded with alacrity whenever a suitable casting call beckoned. Over time, a surprising number of these enterprising, equally opportunistic thespians managed to transform ostensibly formulaic or stereotypical roles into profitable, star-making vehicles. As novelist, dramatist, and frustrated screenwriter James Baldwin once noted in a spirited critique of the Hollywood establishment's "cowardice and waste," this, in itself, was a heroic feat. Against considerable odds, these black screen pioneers created "indelible moments . . . miraculously, beyond the confines of the script: hints of reality, smuggled like contraband into a maudlin tale." When released completely from the stultifying restraints of tradition and stereotype, they were certain to "hit their stride," thereby helping usher in a new era of American cinematic excellence.[2]

Their potential to do so was apparent from the very beginning. Early black independent filmmakers such as Noble Johnson and Oscar Micheaux may have operated on shoestring budgets and settled for something less than the ideal in terms of performance and production values, but their commitment to the notion that African-Americans could be viable movie stars was exemplary. Although roundly criticized for mimicking white Hollywood's ways, for instituting a skin-color caste system in their all-black films, and for refusing to focus exclusively on the "better side of Negro life," these "underground" entrepreneurs nevertheless can be credited with nurturing the first generation of black cinematic heroes.[3]

By the end of World War II, black theatergoers had become accustomed to spending their Saturday afternoons with a panoply of suavely sensual love gods; not-too-dark-skinned divas, sirens, and vamps; and bold action heroes— a fair number of whom now received their paychecks courtesy of white- backed film corporations. Some black leads, such as Wild West rodeo bull-dogger Bill Pickett, hoped to trade on their real-life adventures by offer- ing moviegoers a big-screen approximation of the "death defying feats of courage and skill" for which they already were well known. Others, such as singing cowboy "Two Gun" Louis Jordan of Tympany Five fame, created new personas ("When he's not singin', he's shootin'. When he's not shootin', he's lovin'") even as they tapped into an existing fan base.[4]

Producers, publicists, and assorted media wags both encouraged and, un- wittingly, frustrated the budding stars' efforts to formulate distinctive, readily recognizable theatrical cachets. Their tendency was to provide African- American screen personalities with white "reference points" for promotional purposes. Thus, during the 1920s and 1930s, Lorenzo Tucker was known to many as either the "black Valentino" or the "colored William Powell"; Ralph Cooper as the "bronze Bogart"; Ethel Moses as the "Negro Harlow"; Nina Mae McKinney as the "black Garbo"; and Bee Freeman as the "sepia Mae West." Without question, this hard-to-break Hollywood habit had a certain utility. Black newcomers could hope to enhance and solidify a preselected "image" via association—however peripheral—with a well-known white celebrity. On the other hand, this method of labeling and pigeonholing black talent did little to highlight African-American cultural characteristics—or to promote their encapsulation in film. Beyond helping to spread the word that blacks could aspire to roles other than Mammy and Uncle Tom, the practice of- fered only minimal encouragement to innovations in filmmaking. And, with- out such innovation, there was no compelling reason for mainstream audiences to sample a black-cast film. For the most part, white moviegoers re- mained altogether satisfied either with musical, comedic Toms and Mammies or with the original, "authentic" Bogarts and Garbos.

The postwar era brought important changes to LaLa Land. America's trau- matic encounter with the racial supremacists of the Third Reich—and exten- sive lobbying by Walter White of the National Association for the Advancement of Colored People (NAACP)—ensured that the crudest black cinematic stereotypes were too dated to have continued relevance or box of- fice appeal. Although civil rights leaders denied that they were asking the ma- jor studios to cast blacks as "superhuman heroes," their insistence on "broadening the treatment of the Negro in the moving picture" appealed to many during this season of heightened social consciousness.[5] The resulting spate of "message movies" such as United Artists' *Home of the Brave* (1949), MGM's *Intruder in the Dust* (1949), and 20th Century Fox's *No Way Out* (1950) helped create an environment conducive to the further evolution of the African-American heroic.

The new black champions of the 1950s and early 1960s were not quite cookie cutter copies of their Anglo counterparts, but most were decidedly integration oriented. Their ascendancy within the Hollywood hero hierarchy— indeed, their very existence in mainstream movies—made the all-black film an anachronism. To patronize theaters showing such fresh, inspiring fare seemed almost a vote against bigotry. With societal incivility on the decline, it was believed that only the worst sort of race-baiting Neanderthal could oppose granting equal citizenship rights to any of the refined, amiable, paragons of propriety played by Sidney Poitier.

The first African American to win the Academy Award as Best Actor (for his portrayal of dependable, good-hearted handyman Homer Smith in the 1963 film *Lilies of the Field*), Poitier's ongoing refinement of the ebony saint persona made him one of the most reliable box office draws of the day. He seemed, noted *Newsweek*, "not merely a man, faulted and quirky like the rest of us," but rather "a candidate for the Nobel Prize in niceness, a composite Schweitzer, Salk and Christ colored black for significance."[6] Before changing times and perceptions brought claims that his clean-cut characterizations of racial respectability were passing into self-parody, Poitier managed to engage the mass imagination with solid portrayals of morally and intellectually superior black heroes. Here, aided by top billing and adequate promotional budgets, were conscience-stirring visions of talented—if sometimes bland and passionless— African-Americans whose potential was limited only by the white world's outmoded double standards.

Eventually, however, the rise of Black Power made integration-oriented studies of black manhood seem equally dated—or, in the not-to-be-misunderstood words of one black film critic, like "warmed over white shit."[7] Rejection of this civil rights era interpretation of the heroic reflected the increasingly separatist orientation of activist discourse. Although guaranteed to boost black expectations of fair treatment, the "message" in the message film cycle was directed primarily to whites. Even as they were being entertained, mainstream audiences were offered instruction in various aspects of the "Negro problem." Indeed, they were comforted to learn that black folk were "just like us"—a perspective made particularly believable in films like *Pinky* (1949), *Lost Boundaries* (1949), and *Imitation of Life* (1959), which cast European-American actors as light-skinned African-Americans agonizing over the question of "passing" as white.

Black moviegoers, on the other hand, needed no Hollywood crash course in the nature of the color line, its history, or its impermeability. By the mid-1960s, some were becoming skeptical of integration as an all-purpose panacea and of sacrificial nonviolence as the preferred approach to black empowerment. Many were beginning to hope for more frequent displays of passion, pique, and principled outrage at social injustice from stalwarts such as Poitier. If possible, it was suggested, film representations of insurgent political impulses should take place in true-to-life community settings, reveal issues and emotions central to the black experience, and all the while remain untrammeled by the imposition of white definitional tendencies. In an attempt to satisfy these increasingly insistent demands, filmmakers joined the on-site grittiness and low-budget, first-take inexactitude of the earliest films made especially for black audiences with the didacticism of postwar message movies. A melding of these two cinematic styles produced the brash, colorful—sometimes crude and clueless—blaxploitation genre.

Depending upon how one defines its parameters, the blaxploitation cycle consists of between 55 and 175 titles.[8] Especially popular with inner-city audiences during the first half of the 1970s, these action-adventure dramas tended to deify the black male, to vilify the white male, and to objectify women of all races. Although they forwarded a pop-culture version of real-world dissatisfaction with the status quo, the majority of these films are most profitably viewed as modern-day morality plays—not as documentaries on the black urban condition. Here, in a context shaped at least as much by wish fulfillment as by plot structure and dialogue, bold and beautiful representatives of the underclass repeatedly succeeded in turning the tables on grossly stereotypical white evildoers.

Some of these films were the hardscrabble product of independent African-American filmmakers committed to "the decolonization of black minds" and to the further development of community-based talent and technical skills. Refusing to privilege white fantasies or accept dominant paradigms of representation, the most idealistic of the independents sought to make films of cultural resistance which would inquire into African-American subjectivities and bring to the foreground issues central to the health and continued survival of the black community. Drawing strength from their "insider" understanding of group values, they were determined to resist the dictates of established cultural bureaucracies.[9] Most blaxploitation films, however, reached theaters only after receiving input and approval from white producers, directors, and screenwriters; white-owned studios; or representatives of white-controlled distribution networks. Thus, the notion that this mini-boom in ethnic filmmaking was "exploitative" is easily understood. Although they boasted black story lines and casts, the films were said to be compromised by external controls. In this view, the Hollywood establishment was simply up to its old tricks, sensational-izing current events, co-opting indigenous styles, and ham-handedly skewing potentially militant messages—all in the ongoing quest for "good box office."

While there is considerable merit to these charges, it should be noted that even "compromised" imagery can be made to serve activist purposes. This was especially true during the Black Power years. Blaxploitation epics often were more than what critic Pauline Kael has termed "a funky new twist" on tired story lines. Their racial content was more than "a slant, a shtick."[10] Contrary to the belief of historians such as Thomas Cripps, these films did more than "tease" youthful audiences by dramatizing revenge "as though it were a form of winning."[11] Such films addressed not only commercial but psychological, institutional, and personal agendas.

As a commercial proposition, the films were—at least for a time—a sure bet. With the industry awash in red ink, Hollywood deal makers hoped to lure free-spending young blacks to midtown theaters by recasting "guilty pleasure" for-mula flicks into blaxploitation blockbusters.[12] Typically produced on the cheap by independent filmmakers, in the United States and abroad, sleazy es-capist fare such as *Flesh Feast* (1971), *Werewolves on Wheels* (1971), *Satan's Cheer-leaders* (1977), and the 1979 trash fest *Vampire Hookers* made few claims to technical or dramatic excellence. But they often turned a handsome profit. Black-cast contributions to the motorcycle gang (*The Black Angels,* 1970; *The Black Six,* 1974), women's prison (*The Big Doll House,* 1971; *The Big Bust-Out,* 1973), and horror (*Blacula,* 1972; *Blackenstein,* 1972) genres were designed to do the same in venues which had been left empty by a season of white flight to the suburbs.[13]

Nevertheless, beyond these supply-side matters of dollars and cents lay other considerations—most notably, questions concerning audience recep-tion and response. What, one reasonably might ask, were moviegoers to "take home" from a blaxploitation film? Did the dynamic, larger-than-life images and vivid displays of black bravado provide African-American viewers with anything more than a short-lived ego boost? If some perverse marketing mir-acle managed to draw substantial numbers of white (and gentrified black) cineasts to the films, what would *they* think of such goings on? Defenders of the blaxploitation genre—typically those who acted in or directed the films—suggested possible answers.

First, they reminded critics that the subject under discussion was, after all, the *entertainment* industry. Here, the learning environment was different from that which one experienced in a college classroom or while attending a church service or political rally. Without guilt or trepidation, viewers would "take" whatever they wished from a given movie and leave the detritus beneath their seats along with crumpled Dixie cups and half-eaten boxes of popcorn. Nevertheless, "instruction" was taking place. This was said to be true for both mainstream and black-oriented productions. Whether the action centered on John Wayne or John Shaft, feature films fostered fantasies, helping to develop and to decode dreams. And, as James Earl Jones, fresh from playing the first black U.S. president in *The Man* (1972), pointed out, "there are a lot of people who need those fantasies."[14] Rejecting the idea that black filmmakers were obliged to be educators in the traditional sense, *Super Fly* (1972) director Gordon Parks Jr. summed up the matter with the following observation: "People who come down from Harlem and plunk down their three dollars don't want to see drip 'n' drab. They want to be entertained. And, if they see superheroes with fast cars and fancy clothes, well, that's the American dream—everyone's American dream."[15] Rarely did a blaxploitation film's specific "message" depend exclusively upon the political orientation, the artistic acumen, or even the original intent of the messenger. In many cases, it reached its intended audience in an almost subliminal fashion—interacting with other previously received wisdom while respondents were caught up in the action, immersed in a world of believable make-believe.

Suggestions that the films were deficient because they provided no more than a temporary and wholly superficial blush of ego enhancement also elicited a spirited response. Defenders claimed that neither audiences nor cast members were being exploited to any greater degree than would be the case in a mainstream context. Unsuspecting moviegoers were not being "set up" for real-world disappointment. On the contrary, black films brought tangible benefits to the entire African-American community. They provided an otherwise unavailable training ground for neophyte actors, producers, directors, writers, and technicians. Once a "track record" had been established, such individuals would become industry leaders—"marketable commodit[ies]" who then could "go out and demand things."[16] Moreover, according to blaxploitation mainstay Fred Williamson, even the lowest of low-budget films could be credited with confounding racial stereotypes, thereby improving the odds for permanent enhancement of group self-esteem. Indeed, just "showing people that a black man is not being knocked down and stepped on" was thought to be "a hell of a lot better than anything our submissive fathers ever did."[17] In this view, black movies were empowering. Like most forms of art, they had many nonaesthetic attributes and could help bring about social change. A truly effective film, noted veteran actor-director Ossie Davis, "not only moves us, it makes us move."[18]

Finally, concerns about negative reactions to the films were dealt with in summary fashion. Typically, they were ignored or ridiculed. Aspersions cast by whites were said to reflect either professional jealousy or "a very subtle kind of racism."[19] It was assumed that black detractors were "handkerchief-heads" who had not yet succeeded in casting off the accommodationist mind-set. Most, Fred Williamson suspected, were "bourgeois niggers who drive Cadillacs and earn $40,000 a year."[20] More than mere rhetorical bravado, such responses reflected noteworthy Black Power era trends in group dynamics and psychology. The blaxploitation supporters' aggressive rejoinders evidenced growth of the very sort of self-awareness, confidence, and esteem thought to be promoted by the films themselves.

When one focuses on these psychological aspects of the cinematic experience, a packed movie house becomes something more than the exhibitor's cash cow. Hollywood might seek to order, rearrange, or otherwise manipulate elements of popular concern in its quest to create a profitable entertainment package, but opinion is not simply imposed on an audience from above. Moviegoers are notoriously strong-willed. They also are unpredictable, fickle, self-centered, and terribly demanding. For the most part, they care far less than professional observers about subsidiary issues such as the degree to which a particular film mirrors societal conditions or whether its backers are "committed to liberation." In addition to entertainment value, what many are seeking is information and inspiration. Through films, they sample various ideas, ideologies, and styles. Eventually, they hope to find confirmation of self and of their own worldview.

As allegories for their specific moment in history, movies are encoded with the language of dreams. Even when the proffered messages are flawed or incomplete, suitably motivated film buffs somehow manage to amend the cinematic document—in effect completing it and providing personal relevance. In this fashion, Black Power era consumers/audiences joined their own visions of reality (and fantasy) with those offered by producers/artists. When the match was a good one, theatergoers could hope to gain reassuring visions of previously unacknowledged or unexpressed desires, fears, and fantasies. Under the right conditions, an evening of B-grade blaxploitation could initiate life-transforming changes in a receptive audience. It was through this working of popular-culture alchemy that the black heroic was transmitted, received, and applied to individual lives.[21]

Blaxploitation era movie heroes were constructed from elements both tried and true and decidedly unconventional. On occasion, it seemed as if they had just emerged from one of William Alexander's celebratory By-Line Newsreels. All confident smiles and spit and polish, these shameless scene-stealers commanded immediate, respectful attention. In this regard, their portrayals owed a great deal to strong, yet remarkably sensitive types played by Paul Robeson in the 1930s, by James Edwards and Juano Hernandez in the 1940s, and by William Marshall, Woody Strode, and Ivan Dixon in the 1950s and 1960s.[22]

Other black heroes clearly were part of a newer cinematic wave. First glimpsed in iconoclastic depictions of rough-hewn rakes and taciturn tough guys offered up by Brock Peters, Yaphet Kotto, and Jim Brown, this macho man stylization of the African-American heroic became de rigueur during the early 1970s.[23] Like the tight-lipped, violence-prone vigilantes and lone wolf cops made popular by Clint Eastwood and Charles Bronson in films such as *A Fistful of Dollars* (1964), *Dirty Harry* (1971), and *Death Wish* (1974), these black champions often were guided by idiosyncratic or countercultural codes of honor. Most evidenced their masculinity by playing it rough and oh-so-coolly cynical. They scowled a lot and avoided intimacy, but their true emotions were hard to gauge—even during sex or after beating up on Whitey. Ultimately, this volatile combination of stoicism, survivalism, and sensuality proved extremely attractive at the box office. Hoping to update his image, even Sidney Poitier donned a leather jacket, shades, and a surly, dyspeptic look (in *The Lost Man,* 1969). Needless to say, some appropriations of the militant, hypermasculine style were more believable than others.

Female love interests in the blaxploitation films sometimes acted as if they were attempting to join the pinup goddess aloofness of Lena Horne with the overt sexuality of Eartha Kitt and Dorothy Dandridge. Some slyly witty femmes even managed to toss in a few stinging wisecracks à la Pearl Bailey. Most, however, were firmly fixed in the "phallocentric gaze," which students of modern film culture have identified as a major hindrance to the development of fully realized cinematic portrayals of women. In terms of both filmic representation and reception, male definitions dominated. Attractive female characters in supporting roles were to be looked at, desired, and possessed. At all times, they were expected to subordinate their own needs to the prerogatives of the male culture hero. Presented as passive, erotic objects pleasing to the hyperactive and voyeuristic male gaze, such characters contributed importantly to the creation of a Hollywood fantasy world in which the woman as ornament, victim, or spectacle could hope to influence events only through her sexuality. Her main concern—and what she did best—was to satisy the patriarch's lusts and to boost male egos on both sides of the camera. While it is common to hear that the sexism of these years was an unavoidable by-product of Black Power machismo-making, the fact is that such egregious misogyny could have been avoided. In time, critics would come to view the filmmakers' tendencies as less a natural response to the daily humiliations of black men in a white-dominated society than as blaxploitation's hostile counterproposal to the women's liberation movement.[24]

No Black Power era film had a more profound impact on blaxploitation portraiture than *Sweet Sweetback's Baadasssss Song* (1971). Filmed in southern California in nineteen days by onetime kazoo-playing street busker, French-language novelist, and expert media tease Melvin Van Peebles, *Sweetback* told the story of a clever black picaroon on the lam.[25] After witnessing the savaging of a young brother on the block by two racist cops, Sweetback (played by Van Peebles) gets sweet revenge. Thereafter, he is transformed from a pleasure-seeking sexual athlete to a self-actualized Black Man on a quest for freedom south of the border. Van Peebles's protagonist doesn't actually do or say a great deal during the lengthy, often dreamlike and allegorical chase sequence. But, here, style and vision—not the complexity of the plot—drive the filmmaker's message home. Indeed, the street-smart, sartorially splendid hero conveys an *esthétique du cool* which resonates with political wisdom. Relying on native wit, on an inexhaustible reservoir of sexual energy, and on his contacts within the black community, Sweetback eventually succeeds in outdistancing his adversaries.

Filmed in a grainy, sometimes jerky and disconnected cinema verité approximation, Van Peebles's episodic "hymn from the mouth of reality" promoted a race-based ethic of survival by any means necessary. It encouraged the decolonization of minds and the growth of self-knowledge. Aglow with the

Melvin Van Peebles (*Sepia* magazine, 1972)

first rays of Jubilee's dawn, the controversial film taught that "if you can get it together and stand up to the Man, you can win."[26]

Despite receiving its share of negative reviews from critics of all racial backgrounds and ideological stripes, *Sweetback* recouped its $500,000 production cost in record time.[27] Boosted by Van Peebles's voluble campaign to rid the film of its Motion Picture Association of America "X" rating and by aggressive marketing of movie-related paraphernalia, *Sweetback*'s first-run gross of over $10 million astounded pundits.[28] This unanticipated box office bonanza provided Hollywood with a commercially viable model for the further development of the genre.

Subsequent blaxploitation heroes did not all share Sweetback's monadic lifestyle. Not all were as uncommunicative, emotionless, and unattracted to prepackaged political ideologies. Nevertheless, most had a bit of Van Peebles's stolid but quick-witted creation somewhere in their makeup. They entertained and instructed. Whether male or female, heroic hustler or daring detective, the blaxploitation champions relished the chance to join forces in support of a subversive psychological revolution. Magically turning alleged racial debits into assets, they engaged their audience's most wistful retaliatory dreams. As Van Peebles noted, films featuring such proud, black stalwarts were, by definition, "victorious." Despite their shortcomings (and excesses) they allowed African-American theatergoers to "walk out standing tall instead of avoiding each other's eyes." Here, courtesy of a newly invigorated black heroic, people of color finally were getting a chance to see "some of their own fantasies acted out"—technicolor visions of black folk "rising out of the mud and kicking ass."[29]

That "outlaws" like Sweetback could be considered heroes should come as no surprise. All who live in the complex, post–Ozzie and Harriet world have been introduced to such characters via newspapers and novels, teleplays and theatrical films. Indeed, students of the folk heroic speak often of "social bandits"—noble robbers, resistance fighters, insurrectionists, and avengers who break rank and risk all in order to rid their homeland of corrupt leaders and unresponsive governmental systems. Whether real or imagined, such figures are considered holy beings by confirmed admirers; holy terrors by avowed enemies. Partaking fully of the warrior tradition, they are tough and self-reliant. Although their boldness sometimes shades into excess, they are regarded as true criminals only by those who fear a just social order. As agents of change, they may kill or maim, but they do so in order to enhance the existence of those consigned to a state of living death. Their acts of terror inspire fear—proving that even societal underdogs are capable of exerting awesome, death-dealing power. If captured, social bandits are assured of their followers' active assistance in regaining precious freedom. Should they perish in the attempt, story and song immortalize—and often greatly enhance—their deeds. In such situations, memorials may come from roguish compatriots who also find great virtue in badness; fellow idealists who, while deeming the outlaw's methods reprehensible, share a similar vision of the "good" society; and individuals from all walks of life who find themselves attracted to the bandit's audacious approach to surmounting life's adversities.[30]

During the years 1960–80, both European- and African-American novelists and filmmakers joined pro-bandit support groups such as these in record numbers. In doing so, they helped redefine heroism and villainy, melding the divergent concepts into a composite, potentially activist ideal. But motivation and commitment often were problematic. Although well positioned to influence national affairs, most creative artists were in the business of leisure-time entertainment, not full-time revolution. Moreover, they were well attuned to the public's simultaneous fascination with and repulsion by such deliciously subversive figures. They loved to toy with their audience—to keep them guessing. Thus, it sometimes became difficult to distinguish social banditry from other, far less noble acts of avarice and aggression. In certain novels and films, vengeance seemed to differ little from wanton cruelty; violence appeared to be employed more for titillation than for group liberation or societal regeneration. In the worst-case scenario, a social bandit might seize the day only to become a hapless countercultural emperor without a stitch of new clothing to wear. Stripped of their nobility and joie de vivre, such figures risked being thrown into the pop-culture holding tank with all manner of antiheroic riffraff.

Fortunately, a most arresting assortment of black badmen soon entered the fray, guns blazing and fists flying. They appeared regularly in low-budget blaxploitation flicks and in the most prurient of pulp fiction. Eventually, they also could be found in more widely disseminated entertainment fare. Hoping to put an end to the crisis in cultural representation, they sought to set the record straight. Unembarrassed to sing their own praise, such fictional and theatrical characters worked overtime to provide a rationale for modern-day social banditry. For the better part of two decades, they were among the most visible champions of this unconventional lifestyle.

In order to gain a better understanding of how these legatees of Sweetback helped shape American expressive culture, one would be well advised to group them into two separate but overlapping categories: outlaws and revolutionaries. As will be seen, the first contingent typically adhered to an underworld variant of Horatio Alger's consumerist dream. The second sought to overthrow the very system which created and nurtured our American materialist ethic. Together, they provided a potent one-two punch—a wake-up call, if you will—directed against all who dared question the malleability and staying power of the black heroic or who sought to restrict it to "proper" forms of racial representation.

Outlaws

The black badmen of film and fiction were neither traditionally nor at all times obviously heroic. In many cases, an accurate interpretation of the outlaw hero's behavior was dependent upon time, place, and the experiential background of their audience. Cryptic messages forwarded via costumery, dialogue, and action were made even more difficult to decode by the fact that many such characters were masterful tricksters. In this respect, they reflected the African-American oral tradition which held dissembling proto-outlaws like the Signifying Monkey and Shine in high regard. Like these well-known folkloric precursors, the mischief-making urban badmen of the 1960s and 1970s utilized both mental agility and physical prowess to triumph over great odds; took considerable pleasure in besting and humiliating societal elites; and—despite their proclivity to talk about other people's mothers "in a scandalous way"—typically "live[d] to signify another day."[31]

Often, as also was the case with outlaws of oral lore such as Stagolee ("a mean son-of-a-bitch"; "a bully frum his birth") and train-robbing desperado Railroad Bill ("so desp'rate an' so bad, / He take ev'ything po' womens had"), the social bandits' most telling weaknesses and personality flaws were revealed when they made contact with a stereotypically normative hero.[32] But, are there lessons to be learned from such disclosures? Were the badmen admitting to inherent deficiencies in physical prowess, moral character, or humanity? Could they hope to inspire and instruct in heroism even in defeat?

Questions such as these would seem odd to a committed fan caught up in the action. Those most easily impressed by the physical trappings of heroism likely would consider them intrusive and altogether ridiculous. In terms of appearance and lifestyle, black outlaw heroes could match physiques and Porsches with the noblest, most law-abiding popular-culture champions. Although black male gangsters, pimps, hit men, and hustlers came in all shapes and sizes, those with the greatest heroic potential were resplendent specimens indeed. Young, strong, and full of confidence, they were toned and groomed to perfection. Rippling muscles, large but carefully trimmed naturals, and a "fancy-prancy equine stride" were sure attention-getters. Even slightly graying elder statesmen of the group maintained a powerful, godlike presence—making it seem as if they were perpetually "encased in a shaft of light."[33]

Financially empowered via a wide variety of illicit income-producing schemes, the badmen could afford more than a few of life's little luxuries. Some, like *Super Fly*'s lank-haired pusherman Youngblood Priest (Ron O'Neal), unashamedly proclaimed themselves "gorgeous" and tooled about town in dazzling, whale-sized Caddys, Rolls, and Lincolns. Others proved that they were "down cats" by overfurnishing their penthouse apartments in the latest crushed velvet, faux French provincial, or neo-Roman decor. Still others consumed conspicuously at the clothiers'. Tangible proof that they had rejected the "square" lifestyle, their wardrobes were filled to overflowing with silk shirts, wide-brimmed hats, long leather coats, platform shoes with four-inch heels, French-cut jackets, and designer bell-bottoms. Typically, such ensembles were both extremely pricey and extraordinarily vivid. In *Willie Dynamite* (1973), a cop trailing one such flamboyantly attired suspect remarked with a mixture of disbelief and awe, "Whatever happened to criminals trying to be inconspicuous?"[34]

Shared tastes in exotic cars and flashy clothes did not denote uniformity of characterization. The black outlaws of film and fiction were individualized via offbeat habits and personality quirks. For example, pulp fiction author Joseph Nazel's dapper Iceman always dressed entirely in blue. Roosevelt Mallory's lone wolf "Hitmaster," Joe Radcliff, sported rose-colored glasses and habitually quaffed beer for breakfast. In *Riot* (1969), coolly heroic con Cully Briston (Jim Brown) was said to have a "bad mouth"—from which at all times dangled a trademark toothpick. Two of Robert Beck's black pimp characters were devoted pet lovers: "Sweet" Jones's sleek ocelot sported a collar studded with precious stones; Horace Jenkins, a.k.a. King Tut, unwound after a hard day of procuring by tossing live hamsters into his tank of pet piranhas. Perhaps the quirkiest of all was Dolemite, leading-man Rudy Ray Moore's campy, theatrical hustler hero. Prone to jive talk and bathroom humor, his Muhammad Ali–like taunts ("You're a bad motherfucker, this I can see. But now it's time for you to bring your ass to me") gave due warning to anyone foolish enough to meddle in the boisterous ex-con's business affairs.[35]

The outlaws' rugged individualism and their ethic of high living had analogues in the world of legitimate capitalist enterprise. Indeed, here were risk-takers, black movers and shakers whose dreams of acquiring great wealth and social status were in no way compromised by the fact that their upwardly mobile paths crisscrossed the nation's most depressing ghettos. They were aspiring magnates of materialism who needed no Wharton School credentialization to understand that organized crime occupied an unhallowed but secure place on the continuum of American business systems. The overlords of the urban underworld provided goods and services people wanted, took considerable pride in the corporate structures and complex distribution networks they created, and fought vigorously to maintain their share of a very specialized market.

Like their alleged societal betters who resided just across the line separating ill-gotten from hard-earned wealth, black badmen valued sound business practices. For example, numbers bosses, such as Donald Goines's Eldorado Red, put in long, dangerous hours in order to establish themselves in the trade. Completely self-educated, Red had worked his way up from "dime and two-bit plays" to become CEO of a smoothly running organization that took in be-

Super Fly–influenced clothing (*Sepia* magazine 1972)

tween $5,000 and $10,000 daily. The key to his success: a reputation for straight-talking honesty, personalized customer service, and promptness in paying out winnings. In return, Red was provided the wherewithal to buy a new flame red Cadillac each year and to live in a beautiful $80,000 home complete with backyard swimming pool. Like many a good pulp fiction parent of means, Red hoped to teach his teenage son the rules of the numbers game and turn the business over to him upon retirement.[36]

Pimps, too, were portrayed as heroic strivers. Ambitious enough to amass a bankroll "so big when you walk down the street it's gonna look like your pockets got the mumps," they likened their stables of prostitutes to "a large corporation filled with qualified stockholders."[37] Hoping to garner "Mack of the Year" honors, the most calculating and ambitious developed a basic set of business practices which helped elevate their supervisory role in the world's oldest profession to a self-defined status far above that of robbers, dope peddlers, and other less "together" badmen. As administrator, it was the pimp's responsibility to set "production" quotas, to cut deals with other hustlers, to discipline poor workers, and to establish "quality control"—thereby maintaining the business's good reputation. So as not to suffer early burnout, they often delegated authority for recruitment and training to a "bottom woman." She was expected to "pull" young prospects ("the very best of hustling girls") who, ideally, would be endowed with both bountiful physical assets and the Protestant work ethic. Pimp-executives who succeeded in scaling the heights of this low-life profession tended to approach their job with great gusto. They had to. The competition was similarly motivated. Like Goines's hero Whoreson Jones, they at all times strived to "pimp with a passion," considering it their life's work and "destiny."[38]

But why not utilize these primal drives and organizational skills in more traditional pursuits? Why would such clever, talented individuals choose to ply a trade in a shadowland world where the term "cutthroat competition" was not hyperbole? For some, the choice was easy because they believed there was no choice. They engaged in social banditry because it paid well—far better than any flunky day job to which a black man, denied equal access to white-controlled institutional career ladders, could reasonably aspire. Recognizing that "everybody in both worlds kissed your ass black and blue if you had flash and front," social outlaws were quick studies when it came to sizing up the prevailing social system: there were only haves and have-nots, hustlers and squares, grifters and suckers. To be a winner—to "etch themselves a place in the jungle" (or escape it altogether)—they had to work hard at being acquisitive. As noted by the strong-arm gangland functionary played by Fred Williamson in *Mister Mean* (1977), a popular motto within this outlaw guild was "If the price is right, the job is right." Evidencing relatively little of a more traditional hero's upbeat idealism, such characters would, instead, "go for the big buck." With icy charm, square-jawed determination, and a confirmed belief in the utility of pragmatic cynicism, they would surmount white racist constraints through illegal acts.[39]

Although adhering to the commonsense, down-home principle that it was "better to be a taker than one of those who got took," most African-American badmen *did* have standards. The value system that guided them was not normative or approved by the NAACP or the Boy Scouts. But neither was it the law of the jungle or an exacting approximation of ethical norms accredited by corporate America. According to one very successful drug dealer, the key to getting ahead in the underworld was simple—and self-affirming. His advice: learn how to play "the white man's game," but "use your own rules." In certain cases, skeptics would be justified in believing that such counsel was little more than a self-serving gangland apologia—a criminal's flimsy rationale for continuing to practice a most dangerous and aberrant lifestyle. Nevertheless, to the social outlaw, aggressive, acquisitive, antisocial behavior was justified on several counts. Often, they conceptualized themselves as underdogs—disadvantaged outsiders struggling for survival against corrupt, hypocritical agents of white power. In this context, to follow their own race-specific code of conduct was to approach the heroic.[40]

Rule 1: Uphold family and community values.

To many admirers, heroic outlaws were the personification of ghetto manhood. Upwardly mobile, yet grounded in communal values assimilated during their early years in the 'hood, black badmen never really left this spiritual home. The glamour, adventure, and danger of their romanticized lives separated such ideal types from the masses, but their worldview was broad enough to encompass everyday concerns of family and friends. This combination Superman/Everyman was perceived by ghetto residents as a fellow victim and struggler against "the system"—a somewhat more dashing, more successful coconspirator whose "crimes" were not considered socially harmful.

First loyalty was to self, but fealty to family often was a major concern. If not exactly the Waltons of Watts, many of these fictional and filmic black family units managed to muster a modicum of cohesion and stability—thanks to the concerted efforts of badmen kin. Some began criminal careers specifically to provide for loved ones. Earnings from illegal activities were used to support a jobless, perpetually defeated father, to keep a bright, younger sister in school, and to supply an aged mother with a few well-deserved and long overdue luxuries. Here, the outlaw's aim was to break through social constraints and seize a piece of the American Dream. Their share could be substantial. In *The Mack* (1973), for example, one underclass mom received a yacht basin condo from her doting pimp son. *Black Caesar*'s (1973) game-legged mobster, Tommy Gibbs (Fred Williamson), bought his mother the posh Upper East Side apartment in which she had worked as a maid. On other occasions, the badman's requisites seemed inexplicably modest—even Middle American. As a temporarily down-and-out "one-man death squad" from Los Angeles (Fred Williamson) noted in *Mean Johnny Barrows* (1975), the needs of a hit man and his family were quite basic: "A home. Some land. Something I can own that nobody can ever take away from me." Whatever the prize, recipients of the outlaw's largess were eternally grateful—repaying acts of kindness with expressions of admiration. Indeed, the daughter of fictional hired gun Daddy Cool spoke for many such relatives when she asserted that outsiders' negative impressions of her outlaw father were certain to change dramatically once they experienced "the kindness underneath the cold front that he put out to strangers."[41]

Potential converts to the Church of the Badman included almost any ghetto resident. To be sure, pushers, pimps, and gangsters provided various services for extended "families," but the social outlaws' volunteerist ethic often reached far beyond these job-related fictive kinship networks. Typically, ghetto streets, alleys, and vacant lots had served as the youthful outlaws' playground, school, and even home. Having learned many important survival techniques during their earliest years in the community, adult badmen vowed to return the favor. Like Iceberg Slim, all who somehow managed to survive childhood in this "savagely familiar place of spiritual warmth . . . pathos, conflict and struggle" were thought to possess a variant of the same proud "street nigger soul." In the spirit of black brotherhood, badmen made these long-suffering central-city residents the beneficiaries of numerous do-gooder initiatives. On occasion, as in the 1974 heist flick *Thomasine and Bushrod,* a helping hand would be extended to members of other oppressed ethnic groups. In the gritty, low-budget youth gang movie *Together Brothers* (1974), it even was offered to black cops.[42]

In addition to risking life and limb in heroic struggles against outsider crime bosses intent on infiltrating the ghetto, African-American badmen sought early retirement (sometimes an early grave) for racist police officers and defended black elected officials against palace coups. In Robert Beck's *Death Wish* (1977), two such stalwarts concocted a scheme in which an anti-Mafia commando unit would hold up dope dealers and rob numbers banks to fund a community drug rehabilitation clinic. In MGM's *Cool Breeze* (1972), the proceeds of a $3 million diamond heist were earmarked to help local "soul brothers" establish a black people's bank. Elsewhere, conscientious outlaw benefactors could be seen delivering antidrug messages to urban teens and buying groceries for the poor. In *The Mack,* a splendidly caped and coifed John "Goldie" Mickens (Max Julien) distributed monthly cash awards for regular school attendance while lecturing young admirers on the evils of pimpdom. He urged them to study hard and become doctors or lawyers.[43]

Obviously, one would be wise to factor self-interest into the outlaw's carefully calculated game plan. Urban badmen were not professional altruists. Typically, they sought rewards more tangible than a brass plaque or a pat on the back from their alderman. Admiring gazes from teenage wanna-bes and local lovelies didn't pay the rent—or even the biweekly tab on their leased Porsche roadsters. The social bandits' benevolences seldom led them to abandon their quest for control of inner-city markets in illicit goods and services. Rarely tiring of profiting from the weaknesses of fellow urbanites, most confirmed criminal types couldn't even give up the habit of wasting a troublesome "street nigger" or two from time to time. Nevertheless, their many acts of compassion and their displays of concern for community uplift suggest that even the roughest-looking ghetto stud possessed a touch of nobility.

Rule 2: Respect the code of conduct for your chosen profession.

Black outlaws adhered to no universal standard of criminal ethics. Specific behavioral guidelines were attached to each underworld job description. As he advanced up the big-city crime ladder, an individual might be obliged to master the intricacies of several different codes. Those who became specialists in one area tended to denigrate the ethical standards of other vocations. For example, pimps considered dope peddlers to be cruel and uncouth—most definitely lacking in savoir faire. A proud procurer would supplement his income with drug money only to get "over the hump" in times of dire fiscal crisis. For their part, drug dealers found mackmen far too self-congratulatory and took exception to the commonplace pimp notion that "whores would die if you didn't exist to accept their money." Not surprisingly, grifters rejected the ethics of both groups, preferring to turn a dishonest buck by telling "beautiful lies." Still, each criminal guild was proud never to have (knowingly) granted membership to rapists, hypocrites, or warmongers. Abdicating responsibility for "the mess in the world," all believed their own value system superior to that of white underworld counterparts. Such individuals—indeed whites throughout competitive, materialistic America—were thought to be criminally lacking in moral fiber. They could not be relied upon to hustle and scheme by "the book." Unlike black social outlaws, many white people seemed either unaware or unconcerned that society was governed by "certain codes" and that when these behavioral norms were violated, "a man had to make a stand."[44]

According to fictionalized black badmen, the following rules were essential to the proper functioning of their respective specializations. Such customary codes of conduct served to regularize relationships both within the urban crime network and between criminals and "straights." As substitutes for statutory guidelines followed by the law-abiding mainstream, they helped the badmen distinguish between approved, forbidden, and value-neutral acts. Call it good sportsmanship for bad people.

Confidence Men. Maintain your composure. Keep your mind "honed to razor sharpness" at all times. Repay debts. Never cheat a fellow grifter—they may return the favor. Don't mumble. Speak clearly so the mark can hear every word of your con. Try not to waste sympathy on a mark. Most are thieves at heart and would play the con themselves if they only knew how. Avoid marks who stutter, are cross-eyed, or dress entirely in black.[45]

Drug Dealers. Don't whine. Don't cop out. Be tough. Play it cool. Be loyal to members of your distribution network, but maintain your independence from outside suppliers. Remember that friendship is an opportunity to take advantage of those foolish enough to offer it. Heroin is to be sold, not used. Addiction is the junkies' problem, not yours.[46]

Hit Men. Keep your identity a closely guarded secret. Always be prepared; that is, carry sufficient firepower and extra ammunition. Avoid hitting cops or civilians—it brings too much "heat." Don't try to play both sides of the street at the same time. Watch your back.[47]

Pimps. Pimping is not a charm contest. Somebody has to lose when somebody wins. A good pimp is his own best company. He rarely displays emotion. Never let a whore get the upper hand, call the shots, or disrespect you in public. Don't quit a whore. Cast adrift, they become a "ticking bomb."[48]

Policy Men (Numbers Racket). Make few promises, but keep them all. Pay off promptly. Maintain cash reserves for "administrative expenses" (i.e., bribing cops). Don't buck the syndicate—unless you can win.[49]

As one might expect, none of these job-related codes were sacrosanct. Since there was at least as much temptation—and subsequent backsliding—here as in more highly respected occupations, rules often were disobeyed. Even if they only abided by the spirit of the black bylaws, however, social outlaws gained an important psychological victory by having them in place, available for ready reference. Those who were so inclined could point to the various underworld guidelines as examples of self-definition and self-governance. Moreover, whenever such codes were contrasted with the irrationality and hypocrisy thought to be endemic in mainstream communities, allegedly immoral men (and their admirers) were provided with a self-actualizing sense of moral superiority—one customarily associated with heroes and hero worship.

Rule 3: At all times oppose the enemies of black manhood.

Whatever their own failings, black bandits saw white-on-black crime as the greatest problem facing contemporary Afro-America. Of special concern was an alleged white conspiracy to psychologically emasculate African-American males by keeping them poverty-stricken and powerless. Hammered home in numerous blaxploitation films and novels of "ghetto realism," their case against the white establishment was rooted in the nation's troubled racial history. A people whose exploitative ancestors had enriched themselves through transatlantic slave mongering could not be entrusted with control of black economic affairs. Neither could they be granted carte blanche to shape the male heroic in their own image. Cheated out of their birthright by earlier generations of "jive crackers," black outlaws of the 1960s and 1970s would refuse to be defined or constrained by the pale-skinned usurpers' conceptualization of a "real" man.

Phoenixlike, heroic social bandits (i.e., descendants of "ancient kings and emperors") would rise from the inner-city jungle floor to vindicate black manhood. In the process, they would revitalize the ghetto economy and preserve the integrity of African-American communal life.[50]

Because black outlaws lacked extensive training in revolutionary theory and maintained the most tenuous of ties with left-leaning activist ideologues, they rarely offered any sort of coordinated approach to "getting Whitey." Nevertheless, their scattershot efforts at economic and psychological liberation caused many problems for white bad guys. At times, it must have seemed as if several swarms of pesky, extremely angry, and unusually well armed black bees were buzzing about their neatly creased fedoras, threatening to disrupt the Mob's disingenuous schemes for exploiting the ghetto and thereby further emasculating black male breadwinners.

Badmen fought on several fronts simultaneously. While Harlem mobsters launched lightning attacks on crime world representatives from Little Italy, black gang leaders massed unsmiling squadrons of young toughs hell-bent on escalating the violence.[51] Determined to rout the "peckerwoods"—and by doing so prove themselves "the greatest and the baddest on the planet"—inner-city policy men and drug dealers soon joined in. Wielding racial slurs like *nunchaku,* the latter group worked especially hard at eliminating competing sources of supply. At the same time, they helped debilitate the enemy by surreptitiously substituting heroin for cocaine in sales to whites.[52] Before long, the badmen's numbers were increased further by the arrival of several splendidly uniformed contingents of pimps. As undercover operatives, they hoped to exploit the foe's weakness for comely black flesh. Both economic and psychological warfare was waged as the sly, smooth-talking warriors showed "cold-ass white broads" just how much pleasure their disloyal menfolk were having "moaning and groaning" in the embrace of black prostitutes. Some took Whitey's women as spoils of war while others repaid historical debts by being "awful tough" on the European-American members of their stables.[53] All in all, it was a colossal fracas. As one outlaw soldier of fortune asserted in *The Black Godfather* (1974), African-American men would never assent to emasculation. A line would be drawn in the dust of vacant ghetto lots whenever their manhood was threatened. "Ain't no room for the both of us," he boasted—responding to a white racketeer's economic challenge. "I want to control my own destiny. . . . His power ends where he sees the first black face."[54]

Nevertheless, even if the rout was on, Whitey held a potential trump card. In times of extreme duress, the emasculators could call upon members of a female fifth column to reinforce their ranks. Having suffered the slings and arrows of murderous matriarchs and vengeful vixens all their lives, African-American badmen were well aware that such a move would further frustrate their efforts to preserve the ideal of black manhood. To prepare for this on-slaught, they threw up defenses against both black and white women.

Pimps were in charge of building this fail-safe antifemale superstructure, but other badmen contributed to the effort. They bonded in brotherly agreement on basic principles: women were to be excluded from the ranks of heroes, serv-ing the glorious cause of preserving and elevating black manhood only in aux-iliary capacities. Often, they staffed battle stations on their backs or were relegated to song-and-dance duty on underworld USO tours. Outlaws be-lieved assignments such as these were an appropriate utilization of a woman's gender-based talents and the best, perhaps the only, way to guard against female domination.

To discourage alliances with whites, black badmen kept their women on a short leash. After formally pledging fealty to their pimp, whores were expected to become dutiful, uncomplaining servants—interested only in feathering the lordly pimp's nest. It was considered a grave offense to hold back or spend any of the night's earnings without permission. Failure could result in a minor tongue-lashing ("Stand up straight when I talk to you! . . . You got a helluva lot o' nerve! Comin' up to me, money funnier than Redd Foxx. . . . I'm gon' stick my foot in your ass in the next five seconds if you don't pull my money out from wherever you got it!") or in slaps, kicks, and coat hanger beatings.[55] There would be no coddling. Complaints were greeted with a terse, "So whatta you want, bitch, a medal for doing your whore duty?"[56] Intimations of independence were quashed and the malefactor reminded of her continued need for patriarchal oversight. As one exemplary disciplinarian from the pimp's school of hard knocks noted bluntly, "You don't think, woman. I do your thinking for you."[57] Driven by misogynist tendencies and fearful of a whole-sale defection to the enemy, such individuals brooked no challenge to male authority. They viewed all women as whores and treated every act of disobedi-ence as the most heinous affront to black manhood imaginable.

Hoping to ensure a sweeping victory in this underworld battle of the sexes, outlaws supplemented strong-arm tactics with sweet talk. Those with an "air-tight game" bragged of having "a Ph.D. in the logical evaluation of ho charac-ter."[58] Utilizing specialized skills gained through many semesters at the University of the Street, black badmen made wide-eyed claims that they were averse to brutality but sometimes had to resort to harsh corrective measures for the woman's own good—"to make her suffer so that painful guilt for her bitch dog existence can be relieved."[59] Whenever possible, they said, goals for re-cruitment and retention of female employees would be met by wooing, not whipping. As revealed in the 1975 film *The Candy Tangerine Man,* this soft-sell approach could become downright saccharine. "You been workin' for the wrong dude," cooed a slick Sunset Boulevard procurer known as the Black

Baron. "You know, I ain't askin' you to choose me, cause that's gotta be your own decision. But I tell you one thing. None of my ladies are anything but totally content. I will make you happy, wealthy, and wise. Choose me and you got the whole world by the asshole." The most manipulative mackmen followed up with promises of "insurance" policies against tough tricks and of "retirement" plans in which aging prostitutes would be given "somethin' respectable" to do during their autumnal years.[60] All was in the service of self, however. While remaining "a puzzle, a mystery" to women, the badman's ultimate goal was to "control the whole whore. . . . to be the boss of her life, even her thoughts."[61]

For the most part, the distaff side of this popular-culture pimpdom remained suitably subservient. Fascinated by the charismatic outlaw's fast-lane lifestyle and in need of protection against déclassé "chili chump[s] with no rep[s]," womenfolk seemed to cherish every moment spent in his heroic presence. They clamored for attention—especially that of the carnal variety—and were visibly turned on by violence. Some literally begged to be tied down for "correction." However, despite repeated claims that their only goal in life was to "be your little dog and make you a million dollars," such women typically were deemed untrustworthy.[62] Having written the definitive book on duplicity, social bandits could spot a fraud at twenty paces. Ever vigilant, they steeled themselves against the "love con" by keeping all potential backstabbers, sharp-tongued shrews, and subversive women's libbers either at arm's length or under their thumb. Attractive females were to serve as "stepping stones" to wealth and status.[63] The outlaw code sought to prevent them from becoming the badman's ball and chain.

Rule 4: Survive (by any means necessary).

Obviously, this straightforward, elemental directive superseded all others. Dead men were incapable of following *anyone's* code of conduct and told no tales. To avoid this fate, black badmen had to be vigilant, fleet-footed, and quick on the draw. Like action-adventure heroes everywhere, they parried their enemies' low blows by marshaling all available resources and then fighting back tooth and nail. Given the odds, they were wise to employ their wits as well. If the badmen couldn't outmuscle their opponents, they would seek to keep them "conned, confused, bamboozled and fascinated."[64]

An artfully deceptive adversary, the outlaw trickster was described variously as a "tough nut," a "cool customer," and a "slippery SOB."[65] Strategies of stealth employed in the cause of survival were equally varied. The versatile villains of film and fiction eluded formidable foes by donning clever disguises and using decoys. They avoided entrapment by lying through their teeth and playing possum. On occasion, as was evidenced in *Live and Let Die* (1973) when

Mr. Big (Yaphet Kotto) employed voodoo scare tactics to shield his opium-producing poppy fields from the prying eyes of Agent 007 (Roger Moore), subversive aspects of the rural folk culture were relied upon to confound and intimidate.[66]

Badmen also utilized pejorative cultural stereotypes to mask their real intentions. Given the average Whitey's confirmed belief in black subservience and docility, it was remarkably easy to disarm a technologically sophisticated but sociologically obtuse enemy. For example, in *Hell Up in Harlem* (1973), African-American crime lord Tommy Gibbs (Fred Williamson) infiltrated a Mafia compound in the Florida Keys by posing as a mild-mannered house servant. In *The Black Godfather,* the clever J.J. (Rod Perry) organized an information-gathering network of domestics, calling them his Maintenance Guerrilla Force. As waiter-in-disguise Gibbs remarked just before doing in the white hoods, "Just goes to show you don't know who's doing up your socks and underwear."[67]

Such individuals were, indeed, survivors. Early life experiences, as well as on-the-job training, had convinced them that the trickster's motto—"be quick or be dead"—contained all the wisdom needed to beat the odds.[68] If at all possible, they would escape harm through deception, finesse, and the long con. Postponing open confrontation with better-equipped forces until such tactical maneuvers had evened the odds, heroic trickster-outlaws evidenced their manhood via mastery of a manipulative mental game of chance.

Nevertheless, even the most quick-witted scoundrels were certain to encounter their share of adversity. Following the badman's code to the letter was no guarantee of either early retirement or eventual enshrinement in the Old Outlaws' Hall of Fame. Due to their competitive, risk-taking nature, all could expect to be subjected to numerous physical and psychological tests. Indeed, both their heroism and their humanity were, at least in part, defined by the manner in which they met challenges and accepted disappointment and failure.

In addition to life-and-death struggles with white mobsters and law enforcement personnel, black badmen had to contend with jilted lovers, jealous spouses, and greedy, duplicitous partners in crime. Pimps complained about the uncertainties of their profession, the long hours, and the high stress.[69] Hustlers hated to lose, but were even more afraid of going "con goofy," that is, lying so often and so convincingly that one lost touch with reality.[70] Hit men and others intimately involved with syndicate operations always seemed to be looking over their shoulders for ambitious small-time hoods who wanted a promotion bad enough to kill for it, or for vengeful "family" members seeking to retaliate for some never forgotten personal affront.[71]

Beset by multiple challenges, many badmen were forced to grapple with the day-to-day problems of an Everyman even as they attempted to solve more specialized conundrums guaranteed to test the mettle of a Superman. For example, pimp extraordinaire Willie Dynamite (Roscoe Orman) not only had to worry about younger, flashier competitors stealing his women (and thereby ruining his reputation) but also was obliged to evade the numerous snares set by an aggressive district attorney and two determined vice cops, keep an ex-streetwalker turned social worker named Cora (Diana Sands) from luring away and rehabilitating a sweet young thing he was grooming for big-time street action, and remain calm while being subjected to the incessant moralizing of his mother, who disapproved of her son's nontraditional lifestyle.[72] Physically taxing, mentally draining, and decidedly discouraging, these vocational vexations sometimes exceeded the badman's capacity to cope. Worn down to a less-than-heroic frazzle, they were likely to be caught and punished. In such cases, one had to wonder if the good guys in the white hats didn't, in fact, have a lock on Lady Luck. Could outlaws anticipate even a face-saving Pyrrhic victory amid these dire scenarios and against such long odds? Perhaps it was impossible to be both bad and heroic after all.

If blaxploitation filmmakers and the creators of paperback ghetto gothic confessionals were to be believed, there was nothing to worry about. Certainly, there was no reason to panic. The badmen weren't about to throw in the towel and meekly slip away into the shadows. They were made of sterner stuff. Like good pop-culture alchemists, they would transform loss into gain. Even after embarrassing weaknesses were revealed, they were determined to stand tall. In defeat, badmen claimed victory and retained essential elements of their heroic persona. How was this possible?

For some, adversity spelled opportunity—a chance not only to experience the adrenaline rush of new and greater challenges but also to offer instruction in crisis management. If handled properly, that is, with both superhero style and a grim determination to survive the ordeal, punishment could be edifying. Badmen brought to justice as a result of their own carelessness were quick to urge circumspection. "Life was never even and without difficulties," the chastened criminals told their fictional peers. "Let some shit start to slide and it would catch you in the landslide every time."[73] From prison cell and ghetto flophouse the word went out to outlaw understudies across the land: never overreach while underestimating the strength of an enemy; never trust a Whitey or be caught napping by a black competitor; never lose the "hunter's instinct"; and always proceed with caution.[74] Appendices to the badman's code, these admonitions served as a user's guide to fine-tuning the art of outlawry and a ringing declaration of commitment to the survival of the badman breed.

To be sure, this sage advice from scarred veterans was greatly appreciated. Up-and-coming criminals, disturbers of the societal peace, and all manner of miscellaneous malcontents manifested their gratitude by making the all-wise old-timers their role models. Such men, they said, were born underdogs but proved to be "as smart as they come." Typically, they "left nothing to chance."[75] Punishment incurred for a momentary lapse in judgment in no way diminished their heroism. On the contrary, the badman's brief misstep revealed his essential humanity and served to promote bonding among like-minded individuals.

These lifestyle studies in crime and punishment contained a somewhat different lesson for the average filmgoer and pulp fiction fan—most of whom professed little interest in pursuing an outlaw avocation. Certainly, the array of punishments meted out to careless criminals (loss of reputation, beatings, drug addiction, jail terms, death) served as an inducement to righteous living. But beyond the understandable desire to avoid incarceration and pain lay a near universal need for instruction in transcendence.

Perhaps recognizing that individuals from all walks of life could benefit from their vividly recounted tales of affliction, iconoclastic heroes like Iceberg Slim and *Super Fly*'s Youngblood Priest volunteered their services as pop-culture channelers. Specialists in beating the odds, they were especially effective in revealing how even a "besieged black man, an embattled nigger, in racist America" could survive life-threatening encounters with adversity—and then proceed to build a new and better future.[76] For example, following a particularly dark night of the soul during which he somehow managed to survive the spirit-sapping brutalities and indignities of prison life, Slim described how he was catapulted past the limitations of the pimp mind-set through a "dramatic personal act." Guided by "a strong sane voice inside," he was able to abandon the "counterfeit glory" of his outlaw past, quitting the "worthless, dangerous profession" before he became "a broken, diseased shell."[77] In Priest's case, dissatisfaction with the dirty business of drug dealing stemmed largely from the fact that it was controlled by a corrupt white syndicate boss. "That man owns us," he complained. "To him we're not real. He'll just use us and then kill us." Here, the arduous process of gaining release from the ghetto cocaine culture's shackles began when the badman hero realized his deep-seated need to win personal freedom—to "get into somethin' else, get my head straight." Ultimately, liberation was attained through the working out of a carefully orchestrated plan to "stick it to The Man." Applied and interpreted in a global sense, this triumph over mob domination signaled a victory for all who desired "just to be free." As Priest made clear in a spirited coming-of-age proclamation addressed to the powers-that-be: "You don't own me, pig."[78] Thus, in the end, both badmen made good by transcending aspects of the human experience which diminished their potential for greatness. They lived to tell their tales as they shaped new lives for themselves and their loved ones. Unbought, un-

bossed, and ultimately victorious, such protagonists served as inspiring, if unorthodox, avatars of African-American heroism.

Revolutionaries

Popular-culture outlaws of the 1960s and 1970s established few firm friend-
ships with black revolutionaries. From the outlaws' perspective, any talk of
melding these discreet constituencies into a unified black "movement" necessarily involved consideration of two separate but equally troublesome issues:
(1) maintenance of an acceptable comfort level when mingling with militants
and (2) determining the degree of support to be given to specific activist initiatives. Most black criminal types had somewhat more difficulty grappling
with the former than the latter, but both potential pathways to unity were
strewn with thorns. As dyed-in-the-wool spotlight seekers, their open acknowledgment of the revolutionaries' leadership abilities was limited to the
faintest of praise and laced with unwelcome advice. As devoted capitalists,
their commitment to programmatic militance was eroded by a prerevolution-
ary mentality that sometimes confused "the struggle" with expansion of a
badman-dominated service economy.[79]

To a committed African-American revolutionary, the average urban outlaw
was far too captivated by materialism and had to be forcibly discouraged from
playing "punk games." Seldom was imitation viewed as flattery. Outlaws were
suspected of mouthing militant rhetoric only to provide convenient cover for
their own criminal activities or to attract new recruits for the underworld. As
was said to be the case with Donald Goines's teen gang leader, Prince, such individuals were hoping to "ride to the top of the hill" on the newly fashionable
coattails of black awareness. If discovered, such duplicity was roundly condemned, and the offending party adjudged guilty of "frontin' our people off."
Few militants bought the line that crime, in and of itself, served as a major threat
to white supremacy. Indeed, in some circles, African- and European-American
vicelords were considered equally inimical to the success of the coming revolution. As a result of these concerns, alliances and mutual-assistance pacts were
entered into only when the proud militants could be brought to admit that
criminals had access to far more cash than they could ever hope to acquire by
"selling a two-bit newspaper on the streetcorners or by passing around a tin cup
at a rally." Even so, marriages of convenience were few and far between.[80]

Nevertheless, their mutual standoffishness did not forever condemn outlaws
and revolutionaries to work at cross-purposes. After all, heroic figures always
have been prone to independence of mind and are famous for picking quarrels.
Often, their net worth to a particular constituency is calculated on the basis of
individual, rather than collective, acts of bravery. Moreover, when in an espe-

cially ebullient mood, most—like their real-world contemporaries—somehow managed a show of noblesse oblige. A few were even overheard using the Aquarian platitude "different strokes for different folks." Through trial, struggle, and error, they eventually learned that goals could be accomplished in a variety of ways.

Further mellowed by frequent applications of Black Power idealism, the various bandit clusters revealed that they could address personal agendas in a manner that would complement, rather than contradict, the initiatives of others. If pimps targeted individual johns and if gangsters operated largely in the context of warring "families," revolutionaries tended to conceptualize the division between "us" and "them" in both race-specific and class terms. Black youth gangs occupied a constantly shifting no-man's-land between the various camps. But whenever organizational structures and petty differences could be put aside, it became clear that the enemy remained the same. There was strength in numbers, and members of each contingent were determined to get Whitey's. Together—but in separate units—they could do battle with White Power as they advanced ever closer to Black Camelot.

What were members of the revolutionary contingent *really* like? If outward appearances alone were allowed to tell the tale, one likely would conclude that these social-bandit soldiers marched to the beat of their own drummer. Unlike their criminal colleagues, the black militants' aversion to the acquisition and display of great wealth caused them to eschew sartorial splendor. Proudly understated in their manner of dress and personal display, they favored olive-green fatigues, pullover sweaters, and black berets. Formal occasions might find them slipping into a tan service uniform (epaulets optional) or, as was the case with *Uptight's* (1968) bearded B.G. (Raymond St. Jacques), donning rimless spectacles and a Nehru jacket. They drove standard Detroit-issue vehicles instead of pricey pimpmobiles. For the most financially disadvantaged, this might involve tooling around in a real beater. For example, in *The Final Comedown* (1972), the comings and goings of aspiring guerrilla warrior Johnny Johnson (Billy Dee Williams) were telegraphed by the squealing brakes of his vintage 1961 AMC Rambler. For unprepossessing urban militants like Johnny, wheeled covert activity definitely was out of the question.[81]

But if privation had its price, it also evidenced adherence to principle. The activists were noble because they were poor and poor because they were noble. On average, better educated than their outlaw counterparts, a considerable number had the specialized training and talent requisite for success in mainstream professions. Most militants, however, cared not a whit for inherited privilege or the baubles of the bourgeoisie. Energized by visions of a glorious postcapitalist future, such individuals refused to be constrained by the dictates of social class and mingled freely with more typical ghetto folk. As if to prove this point, their headquarters were "furnished cheaply" with furniture that "had seen better days" but were lined with pictures of Ho Chi Minh and other radical reformers of color.[82]

Here, in a working-class environment redolent of deliciously seedy subversiveness, could be found Cal Tech honors graduates, medal-laden military officers, former Rand Corporation researchers, and rogue CIA agents—all diligently applying their skills in unpaid tribute to the idea of a people's revolution. Fully aware that their professional status provided a possible "cover" but no guarantee of immunity from punishment should activist initiatives fail, each seemed more self-sacrificing than the next. Like Commander Daniel Smith, the Malcolm X–inspired nationalist firebrand of Fletcher Knebel's *Trespass* (1969), they were unwaivering in their commitment to black liberation. To sympathizers and underclass comrades-in-arms, these single-minded men of vision seemed "cut from the cloth of prophets."[83]

They also were built like the proverbial brick outhouse. Despite efforts to remain inconspicuous by blending into the mass of urban humanity, the revolutionaries' awe-inspiring physical presence caused them to loom head and shoulders above the crowd. Like that of other bandit heroes, their physique often was described in slack-jawed superlatives. They were, said lesser mortals, "vibrant, forceful, hard to ignore," "all muscle and three yards wide."[84]

Although by no means fully representative of the group, Julian Moreau's strapping, big-brained protagonist, Denis Jackson, established a standard of perfection to which others could aspire. The thirty-eight-year-old hero of *The Black Commandos* (1967) was five feet eight inches tall, weighed 185 pounds, and had a forty-seven-inch chest atop a compact thirty-inch waist. He could bench-press over five hundred pounds and had an equally well developed intellect. Gifted with total recall, Jackson had earned six college degrees, won patents on a half dozen discoveries and inventions, and authored texts in philosophy and psychiatry. Fluent in more than twenty-four languages, his IQ was off the chart. Truly, here was a sterling specimen of the genus *Heroicus,* one who had achieved "a peak of physical perfection no other man in all history had attained." Once seen, he was not easily forgotten. As a fellow conspirator noted in describing the ultrastrong genius, "I sometimes think the man is some sort of superior mutation."[85]

Given their uniqueness and unavoidable high visibility, it was fortunate that many such black Supermen had a Clark Kent side to their personalities. In this field, effectiveness in covert operations improved dramatically when the hero managed to maintain a low profile. Men like Dan Freeman, the bespectacled, tight-lipped subversive of the film *The Spook Who Sat by the Door* (1973), gained an upper hand on their adversaries in direct proportion to the degree to which they succeeded in convincing strangers that there was "nothing pink or radical" in their makeup. Recognizing that "a smiling black man is invisible," they sought to be perceived by whites as "a credit to [their] race"—even while remaining "black in color, black in pride, black in rage."[86] A phlegmatic manner (often described as cerebral or aloof), a calm, pliant speaking voice, and an expressionless countenance could do wonders to disguise the anger boiling within. As noted in Alan Seymour's *The Coming Self-Destruction of the United States of America* (1969), heroes of this nature tended not to shout, shunned news photographers, and revealed their "true" selves only to a select group of trusted intimates. This studied dispassion and concerted avoidance of publicity sometimes made them seem "a charismatic leader without a charisma," a "voice without a presence." But in their quietude lay strength, purpose, and total dedication to the important work at hand.[87]

Shaped more by ideological concerns and the utopian possibilities of the moment than by any serious aspiration to self-aggrandizement, the militants' worldview was grounded in three basic foundational principles. In general, they preferred revolution to reform, violence to submission, and black allies (and black women) to white. Of necessity, this idealized formulation allowed for considerable flexibility. In order to attract and maintain adherents, each activist leader was obliged to personalize the heroic—and a most effective way of doing so was to develop a unique, personally satisfying value system suitable for use in directing the destiny of the entire race.

Most militant black heroes were concerned that their followers mastered the three R's. In this context, to be properly educated meant that one was capable of distinguishing between revolt, revolution, and reform. While a revolt was defined as a brief, localized (but wholly justified) "flare-up" presaging a more expansive, more ideologically driven season of revolutionary activity, reformist approaches to societal problem solving were deemed an activist anathema.[88] As the favored political model of "phony black-help outfits, dreamed up by whites," reform was made unpalatable by its inherent timidity. Its advocates tended to settle for the piecemeal, the compromise, the half-a-loaf. For risk-taking militants, there was little virtue and no lasting satisfaction to be found in bloated civil rights oratory or Love Your Brother marches. The prospect of gradual immersion in the European-American melting pot left them cold. "Integrate into what?" they asked, eager to supply their own suitably controversial answer. "Whitey's welcome to his chrome-plated shit pile. I dig being black and the only thing I don't dig about being black is white folks messing with me." To respond otherwise was to ignore both the bloody handwriting on the wall and the big picture. It was said that to maintain firm faith in allegedly outmoded reformist principles was to "think small," an unfortunate habit of mind which virtually guaranteed that "you'll always be small" or, alternatively, that all too soon you would be dead.[89]

Far more satisfying was the prospect of joining in a large-scale, perhaps pan-African, possibly worldwide, freedom movement. This was not slated to be a polite, nonviolent, by-Robert's-Rules-type revolution. Indeed, such a blatantly reactionary concept was considered a contradiction in terms. Instead, militants forecast that the Afroworld's response to White Power's continuing impositions would be far more bloody than any previous act of ghettoite catharsis. Surely, the fire this time would do more than scorch a few white storeowners' shirttails as they beat a hasty but temporary retreat to their split-level suburban enclaves. If all went according to plan, *this* revolution would shake the white world "from top to bottom," destroying "everything that gets in its way."[90]

Should this unprecedented season of revolutionary fervor result in a significant number of "pink faced monkeys" being sent to "join their ancestors" there would be few black tears—and no feelings of guilt. As one fictional rebel's manifesto stated most unequivocally: "The white man understands and respects force. To offer him any other approach is piss in the wind." Refusing any longer to turn the other cheek, the oppressed masses would "strike to hurt, strike to maim."[91] This, of course, was not meant to infer that principled African-American warriors longed to kill for the sake of killing or that they could rest easily with "the blood of innocence" on their hands. Such terrible deeds were deemed the acts of a people who, collectively, had "tried everything else"—humble entreaties, passive resistance, economic leveraging, localized violence—only to find that "none of it worked." According to committed activists, white folk had received ample warning but had persisted in their evil ways. Now, after seizing the initiative and beginning to chart an independent course through history, heroic blacks would proceed to institute their own exacting system of revolutionary justice. By doing so, countless black lives were sure to be saved. But equally important to the long-term survival of the race was the fact that new understandings about the nature of African-American humanity would begin to circulate, informing world opinion.[92]

Fictional and theatrical militants believed that collective acts of resistance revealed their people's true substance and character. As was argued in Blyden Jackson's *Operation Burning Candle* (1973), traditional turn-the-other-cheek attitudes prevented most blacks from exhibiting a "full range of human emotions." Acceptance of the reformist program tended to stifle legitimate feelings of pain and anger—or, alternatively, to direct personal outrage toward friends or family members. However, through revolutionary struggle, black folk could effectively quash the notion that they were "less than human." Untrammeled by the nonviolent mind-set, newly empowered racial champions would strive to "answer emotion with emotion," thereby validating their multifaceted human identity. Hopefully, it was said, this "final break-through to freedom" would bring haughty white adversaries to their knees and "force them to act as humans too."[93]

Relatively few black revolutionaries conceptualized this momentous struggle as one of colorless haves versus have-nots.[94] The phrase "irrrespective of race" was not in their vocabulary. Certain basic concepts might be borrowed from, say, Mao or Marx, but more often than not, non-African-American allies were shunned, subordinated, or squeezed dry for funds needed to advance a decidedly *black* agenda. Certainly, it was one thing to purloin a proven technique or two from such notable "outsiders"; it was quite another matter to rely upon white commandos for assistance in legitimizing one's humanity.

Whether the potential ally was an "angry Jewish Communist" or a "guilty liberal Christian," white sympathizers were viewed with considerable suspicion.[95] Most were seen as trend-seeking summer soldiers high on the black urban lifestyle. Said to be confused about life in general, they were prone to carrying peace signs and hopelessly addicted to "talkin' that two-sided trash." While vowing eternal enmity to foes of the revolution, the typical white radical was privileged and protected by his pale pigmentation and daddy's fat bankroll. Unlike African-Americans, who had "nothing to drop out of," they could drop back *into* the system any time the going got tough. It was a widely shared belief that forming firm alliances with these comfortably rebellious types would dilute the strength of the black-led movement.[96] As a result, staunch nationalist organizers like D. Keith Mano's George Horn Smith not-so-politely declined the white revolutionaries' offers of long-term assistance and even bragged about eating them for breakfast.

At a rally described in *Horn* (1969), Smith's even more aggressively militant mouthpiece—strident West Indian demagogue Aylbrous Purston—pulled no punches in offering a blanket repudiation of nonblacks:

> "Do we hate white men?" screamed Purston.
> "Yeeees!" roared the crowd.
> "Do we want their segregation?"
> "Noooo!" roared the crowd.
> "Do we want their integration?"
> "Noooo!" roared the crowd.
> "Do we want our own?"
> "Yeeees!" roared the crowd.
> "Will we get it?"
> "Yeeees!" roared the crowd. "Yes! Yes! Yes!"[97]

Here, the storied inability of "concerned" whites to fathom the black mind was dealt with in an exceedingly forthright manner. Because white people couldn't seem to take a hint and had considerable difficulty accepting the fact that they weren't welcome, the black radicals' studied standoffishness some-times had to be evidenced by more than the turning of a cold shoulder. On oc-casion, it was necessary for whites (and elderly mules) to be hit square between the eyes with the truth. Only then could black revolutionaries bring the inter-lopers to understand that "our interests are the same now, but they won't always be. . . . We won't be working with [you] after the shit goes down."⁹⁸

The place of women in the black revolutionary camp constituted a related but altogether more complex policy issue. Like other social bandits, militants understood the dangers of female domination and therefore put considerable effort into developing evasive, antiemasculation strategies. Certainly, they were not about to allow the revolution to be deep-sixed by duplicitous damsels. However, far more often than their pimp-outlaw brethren, they fac-tored a racial variable into the equation.

For many activists, the nature and extent of a black man's intimate relation-ships with white women had considerable ideological importance, serving as a basic litmus test of revolutionary commitment. Claims that "I haven't met a sis-ter I can groove with" or "[t]here ain't nothin' wrong with humping whitey's wenches" were met with suspicion (or derision) by those who viewed such be-havior as hypocritical, treasonous, or just plain stupid. "I wouldn't soil my hands on a honky body," declared the self-affirming black sexual nationalist. "I think black and I sleep black." Those who felt otherwise risked being called on the carpet for sleeping with the enemy and, perhaps unwittingly, jeopardizing the entire nation-building process. In extreme cases, repeat offenders—those adjudged guilty of "constant mongrelization"—were punished severely or purged from the movement.⁹⁹

African-American women provided a useful service. Acting as "sex freak" investigators, they helped ferret out false militants who talked black but dated white. For example, in Ann Allen Shockley's short story "Is She Relevant?" (1971), a self-proclaimed "big, brassy Black revolutionary" named Flo had no qualms at all about putting preening womanizer Eli Thomas Jr. in his place. Upon learning of the dashiki-clad firebrand's long-term liaison with a win-some blue-eyed child of Freedom Summer, she literally shook with rage. "Now *you* listen here," the proud African-American woman ordered, seeking to improve Thomas's lamentably short historical memory. "It's all the Flo's who's been holding up your Black male asses for centuries. Working for you, having your babies, taking your goddam awful crap, and being your wailing wall against whitey." Then, still breathing fire, she delivered a below-the-belt coup de gras to *any* male militant who would behave in this unseemly fashion. "Damn if you all ain't thinking you're *supermen* just because you can get all the white women without getting lynched for wanting it," she railed. Finally, after nearly coming to blows with the as yet unreconstructed activist, she left the room in a controlled rage, threatening to expose Thomas and his ilk to "all the Black sisters." If Flo could have had *her* way, black men who believed that "the revolution ends at night"—in a white woman's bedroom—would forfeit their claim to leadership roles within the movement.[100]

In dramatically unfurling a red flag of doubt as to the male militants' commitment to revolution (as opposed to their ego or libido), outspoken sorts like Flo provided an informal screening device for the black heroic. But, despite their numerous contributions to the cause, few black women garnered such exalted status for themselves. Pushed aside by pop culture's rush to celebrate African-American manhood, black women possessed of heroic potential typically ended up playing second fiddle to dashing male chauvinists. This pattern of paternalistic put-downs had been perfected by black outlaws and was applied to the world of female revolutionaries after undergoing only minor modifications. In this regard, it was fortuitous—if not actually prophetic—that many high-ranking activist women either were former professional models or long-legged heartbreakers said to possess an abundance of "sullen beauty and grace."[101] If they applied themselves and worked at it hard enough, perhaps militant menfolk could work the pimps' antiemasculatory magic on *these* vixens as well.

If they were to preserve occupational distinctions, however, revolutionaries couldn't simply replicate urban outlaw behavior by treating female subservience as a money-making proposition. To be true to their activist nature, they had to couch male supremacy in ideological terms. Without question, the most manipulative of these fictional and theatrical radicals became marvelously adept at masking their reactionary and potentially harmful views with an elaborate rationale gleaned from a variety of authenticated sources. For example, in order to "even up them odds," some believed it necessary to commit to a long-term program of procreative endeavor. By doing so, the black community would counteract the effect of wrongheaded, white-sponsored "birth-control talk," thereby gaining a tactical advantage over their enemies. As babymakers of the revolution, black women's primary responsibility would be to nurture the next generation of guerrilla fighters. Others found analogues to preferred gender-based divisions of labor in nature. Committed to rearing their own personal "commando force," revolutionary black men were likened to "old Mr. lion" who spent his time "screwing and sleeping." Meanwhile, the "lady lion" presumably found great satisfaction in hustling food for her regal mate and in cleaning up after the cubs. Still others discovered useful truisms in nationalist religion. Here, holy book passages (real and imagined) depicting women as "fields" to be cultivated were said to prove that one should have sex as "often as you can get it." Few male militants contradicted such timeless wisdom.[102]

It was a most artfully accomplished antifeminist subterfuge. While agreeing wholeheartedly with the expansive affirmation that "there's nothing under the sun like a black lady, brother," black men conspired to keep female revolutionaries from getting a leg up on the culture hero career ladder. Evidencing little surprise when, as was the case in Hank Lopez's *Afro-6* (1969), female freedom fighters were among the first to surrender to the enemy, they were content to offer up a convoluted conceptualization of the revolutionary black woman as one part activist, two parts loyal and responsive bedmate. To a 1960s woman like Jeannie (Janet MacLachlan) in Jules Dassin's *Uptight,* this meant that it was wholly acceptable to demonstrate liberation by wearing one's hair in a new-style natural, and it was equally "righteous" and "together" to explain why old acquaintances no longer recognized you by sending the guileless but puzzling mixed message, "I'm off my knees now. I like my man with a gun." Militant male control freaks could—and often did—have it both ways.[103]

After mastering the ideological intricacies of the three R's and receiving invaluable instruction in racial and gender relationships, heroic revolutionaries put on their camouflage suits, packed up their Molotov cocktails, and moved out into the night. Seeking to establish a beachhead in hostile territory, most true-believing pop-culture warriors were energized by a singular vision. Against the odds, they hoped to ensure that future generations of African-Americans would be free from white economic, political, and cultural domination. Their efforts to redeem both the people and the planet (or choice parts thereof) provided real-world contemporaries with a detailed set of blueprints for radical social change.

Typically, the implementation stage of any self-respecting militant's battle plan began with a rhetoric-fueled adrenaline charge of pumped-up expectations and a fusillade of anti-institutional violence. Nevertheless, whether the immediate goal was to extract monetary reparations from white institutions, effect a withdrawl of black soldiers from Vietnam, place a soul brother on the local college's board of trustees, or end the exploitation of an inner-city neighborhood by "fat honkies who sat back in their leather office chairs dealing out death and corruption," African-American activists orchestrated their militant maneuvers so as to highlight heroism.[104] This focus on personal initiative, organizational and leadership skills, risk taking, and courage was maintained when revolutionary agendas were expanded to encompass more global concerns. Truly, here were men who knew the power of dreams.

Black field commanders understood both the big picture and the nuts and bolts of interracial struggle. Those whose concerns extended beyond the badman's preoccupation with eliminating local dope pushers and "nigger haters" were convinced that a major militant initiative required "time and patience and hard work." Rarely, they said, were successful revolutions made by "street-corner punks with headline fever." Haphazard strategizing, unclear directives, and "useless, stupid, pointless destruction" only confused—limiting the probability of success. Taking their grievances to the street only after careful planning, guerrilla leaders made sure that all involved knew their individual assignments and were in basic agreement as to the overall scope of the impending campaign of conquest.[105]

"Absolutely compulsive" about detail and discipline, these "cold, tough professionals" were revolutionary perfectionists. Demanding that their troops be "together, ready to cope with the white man," they would tolerate no slackers and were not averse to executing a careless comrade.[106] Although noticeably hesitant to share tactical information with subordinates, the most historically attuned commanders were aware that "every nigger revolt in the history of America has ended when they wasted the head nigger." To ensure survival of the movement, they selflessly encouraged leadership training and even developed futuristic "conditioning units" to inculcate loyalty to the larger cause.[107] Some, like Alan Seymour's aptly named Hero (short for Hieronymous), also pioneered special motivational techniques—"phased activity" in revolutionary parlance—to keep morale high. As a further encouragement to righteous revolutionary behavior, consumption of alcohol was forbidden when there was "work to do." As one might suspect, looting and random "kill orgies" were condemned as hooliganism—the work of "small men of narrow vision who cannot handle power."[108]

Many militant leaders conceptualized their primary mission to be the establishment of Black Camelot as a tangible political entity. Among the most ambitious military planners were those who envisioned an independent republic sprawled strategically across the southern Black Belt. With start-up funding acquired via forcefully induced federal reparations grants, the new nation would abandon the "fascistic model of the enemy" and, instead, fly the proud crimson and black flag of a "true peoples' democracy." Replete with "black mills an' black ships an' black senators and black beauties on the balconies," this rich, progressive land was to serve both as a proving ground for revolutionary principles and as a showcase for all manner of black talent.[109]

Some opted for the creation of semiautonomous city-states. Although plotted on a somewhat smaller-scale graph, these ethnic enclaves reflected their creators' adherence to a similar, deeply felt territorial nationalism. Here, a relatively compact area—say, Harlem or Manhattan—would become the "new nation conceived in blackness." Limited in size more by design than by lack of vision or will, this easily defended homeland would achieve majority rule via a permanent, forced withdrawal of all whites (but not their assets) to outlying suburbs.[110]

Other black strategists were confident that their disciplined and highly motivated troops could "take the entire country" if they so desired but feared the corrupting tendencies of centralized power. After bringing the federal government "to its knees," such leaders would be content to display their continuing influence in national political affairs through a series of major legislative initiatives. For example, one particularly detailed revolutionary agenda called for immediate implementation of a modern-day Homestead Act. The new law would guarantee every qualified African-American household $5,000, "one intermediate-sized car," and ten acres of land. Designed to promote a more equitable balance between black and white power, this updated, rehabilitated "40 acres and a mule" program would help to level the economic playing field. Presumably, once this historic feat had been accomplished, significant numbers of once poor folk would be able to achieve some semblance of the American Dream.[111]

Plans calling for even a modest amount of territorial acquisition required a precise ordering of troops and firepower. Proving themselves capable of meeting this logistical challenge, militant minds orchestrated a series of complex, large-scale military maneuvers that would have tested the mettle of a Patton, MacArthur, or Strangelove. For example, in Edwin Corley's *Siege* (1969), black liberationists seeking to create a domestic homeland in the industrial Northeast began the process of assembling a cadre of some one thousand elite revolutionary soldiers by going undercover to raid Defense Department files. Due to security concerns (and leaks), the work of setting up a dummy recruiting and data-gathering section within the Pentagon took nearly a decade to complete but resulted in the creation of a well-oiled, experienced guerrilla strike force. Supplied with arms and ammunition by sympathetic African nationals (who, in effect, were laundering U.S. economic development grants), this core group soon was supplemented with line recruits who had completed basic training at one of twelve isolated rebel camps. Each such facility was designed to look like a U.S. Special Forces base—down to the "authentic Army numbers" on the vehicles and the light-skinned, "white enough to pass" guards assigned to the main gates. So as not to appear an undisciplined mob, all troops wore uniforms with special markings based on the black nationalist flag of Marcus Garvey. These decorative patches and armbands were made in the Bahamas by Chinese seamstresses who believed they were producing logos for a professional football team.[112]

With the necessary manpower mobilized and equipped, rebel leaders attacked. Their plan was to seize Manhattan and then to trade its teeming white masses for the state of New Jersey—or "Redemption," as the new all-black land would be known. During the predawn hours of a Labor Day weekend, bridges and tunnels linking the island with the outside world were shaken by a series of devastating explosions. Guerrilla-piloted F-105 Thunderchiefs—ostensibly on a training mission—dropped live thousand-pound bombs on some of the structures. Others turned to rubble when strategically placed explosive charges were detonated by teams of black demolition experts. Access roads left open for supply purposes were mined, barricaded, and defended by machine gun emplacements. Due to meticulous military planning and a thoroughgoing infiltration of the urban crisis-response network, this opening salvo in the Afro-American War of Liberation took all of twenty-eight minutes but resonated throughout the sleepy, unsuspecting nation like the first shell burst of World War III.[113]

If unanticipated events (a raging firestorm and streets choked with terrified refugees) eventually caused this incipient East Coast revolution to fall short of stated goals, its black brain trust nevertheless emerged triumphant. The Three-Day Revolution proved that the "dark people of the world" were "losing their fear." Barely escaping defeat, white leadership elites were put on notice that they no longer could "continue down the same path to chaos." Indeed, the nation as a whole was force-fed a great deal of vital information about the nature of African-American heroism. Perhaps, even without gaining their desired territorial cession, a certain less tangible form of "Redemption" had been achieved.[114]

Given the diversity of the black militant population, their leaders' typically emblematic nature, and the universal desire of combatants to come away from every conflict victorious (in some fashion), it was to be expected that a fair number of revolutionary planners would come to view both interracial warfare and Black Camelot in symbolic terms. Without discounting the wisdom of obtaining land for black settlement or questioning the propriety of seizing white-owned property for use as bargaining chips in future negotiations, such individuals highlighted the value of violence as psychological weapon and liberator.

This school of rebel strategists found considerable satisfaction in joining traditional guerrilla tactics ("hit, run, bomb, murder and disappear before the swine know what hit them") with mental manipulation of the enemy. The implementation stage of *their* revolution might, for example, involve setting up an operations center in a symbolic "Black House" while sabotaging or tearing down hallowed monuments to white American materialism. Instead of drafting doomsday plans for all-out racial warfare, these specialists in symbolism opted for the selective assassination of, say, members of the president's cabinet or some well-known and particularly odious racist. In Chuck Stone's *King Strut* (1970), militant leaders even chose the 9 September anniversary of South Carolina's 1739 Stono slave rebellion to announce a long-awaited Day of Liberation—intensifying the intended intimidation by holding their ceremony on the porch of Nat Turner Memorial Hall, a two-story antebellum mansion painted black.[115]

Not all heavy symbolism was meant for white consumption. It was assumed that black folk, too, could take a hint and learn from these displays of revolutionary intent. Here, victories were declared when selective antiwhite violence contributed to African-American unity. As one fictional militant noted, these "collective symbolic act[s] of uprising" had considerable therapeutic value. Helping to release anger and sever mental ties with the oppressor, they promoted the psychological health and well-being of black people—and did so irrespective of territorial gain or loss. "Cleansing violence" might not, in all cases, result in a military triumph, but it had the potential to shock the downtrodden into quitting their low-down "shucking and jiving" ways. With counterproductive habits of mind altered or abandoned, these spiritually uplifted, empowered individuals could grapple with the problems of the temporal world in a much more productive fashion. Presumably, this dramatic mental transformation—the acquisition of "a whole new psychological framework"—served as a precursor and prerequisite to more tangible black victories.[116]

On the other hand, no further action was required. If the Kennedy clan could employ the Camelot device as a "personal, private symbol," it only seems right that 1960s militants would be able to declare their own symbolic achievements wholesale victories. Black Camelot, too, could be conceptualized as a state of mind and expectation. Employing a wide array of non-Kennedyesque terms, Black Power era culture heroes described it as the representation of a true and thoroughgoing racial consciousness. Although without physical boundaries or assets, this ethereal kingdom was deemed capable of supplying the needs of a generation seeking release through self-defining acts and experiences. Indeed, it was said to welcome all manner of wayfarers—"Uncle Toms," "hankerchief-heads," "museum Negroes," "half-white bushwa sonsabitches."[117] Under the guiding hand (or punishing rod) of activist reeducators, each of these pathetic souls was to be weaned from what one "Harlem street nigger" turned anarchist described as the "archaic mysticism of a psychic penitentiary called kick-my-ass-some-more." In embracing blackness, they were reborn into meaningful personhood. "Awakened, sore, angry, strong," these were just the sort of spirited fellow travelers needed to spread the militant hero's revolutionary message.[118]

Ghetto residents seemed to appreciate the rebels' determined efforts on their behalf and did what they could to further the cause of liberation. Shouting, "They're killing the honkies!" tenement-dwellers surged into the streets to welcome black brigades, provided necessary supplies and shelter, and in at least one case, contributed materially to the overall military effort by greeting white intruders with a hailstorm of pots and pans, old furniture, bricks, and pieces of lead pipe.[119] By and large, such spirited, widespread community support of revolutionary initiatives can be attributed to (1) good black leadership and (2) bad white people.

Like a bandolier-bedecked Dale Carnegie, the successful rebel hero worked hard to win the friendship and trust of the black masses. Making textbook-perfect application of effective community-organizing techniques, these heroes provided a wide range of prerevolution era public services (pro bono legal work, economic development projects, etc.) and were careful never to be disrespectful of their less well educated comrades-in-arms.[120] Most, like former U.S. congressman Lance Huggins in Warren Miller's *The Siege of Harlem* (1964), understood the historical roots of black oppression and made sure that their "finger was on the public's pulse every minute of the day and night." By applying the lessons of history even as they utilized their well-developed public relations and "people skills," such gifted individuals were able to translate the ideology of revolution into the language of the streets without breaking a sweat. Even more remarkably, they did so while maintaining a most convincing brother-on-the-block credibility. As noted by one of Huggins's awestruck acolytes awash in reverent, familial devotion, "Lance was our own, he really was, no doubt about it, he was our selfs."[121]

The rebel heroes' attractive power was matched in intensity by their adversaries' ability to repel. Prone to the use of excessive force indiscriminantly applied, white police and military leaders made few friends among those whom they sought to pacify. In most cases, the boilerplate rhetoric in which they framed their detailed "dehostilization" programs did little to obscure actual intent. To a seasoned militant, white-authored plans calling for "intense orientation and education designed to produce the self-awareness leading to voluntary correction of social deficiencies" could mean only attempted mind control—or worse.[122] Indeed, various 1960s and 1970s pop-culture scenarios posited the unseating of minority members of Congress, repeal of protective civil rights legislation, confiscation of black-owned property, and, ultimately, forced removal of the African-American population to dismal "detention centers" and "correction camps."[123]

Was the situation hopeless? Not at all. As even a devout pessimist could have anticipated, the utter perversity of these schemes only made the freedom fighters' critique of the prevailing world order more believable, their invitation to insurrection more compelling. In many cases, evil whites were among the revolutionaries' most effective recruiters. Certainly, all who hoped to secure and maintain basic human rights in a war-torn land where genocidal fascists treated every person of color as the enemy were well advised to consider carefully any and all offers of assistance tendered by Black Camelot's heroic social bandits.

Detectives

Without question, passions generated by the threat of government-sanctioned racial persecution helped determine the degree of commitment to be found among a bandit hero's compatriots. Nevertheless, during the years 1960–80, definitive decision making in such matters was made more difficult by the presence of heroic law enforcers who just happened to be black. Confirming the notion that in affairs of the heart and of popular culture the process of determining ultimate allegiances is almost always far more complicated than it seems, blaxploitation and pulp fiction lawmen (and women) of color managed to win widespread, enthusiastic, pan-racial approval with remarkable ease. In fact, they became some of the most popular, readily recognizable culture champions ever produced for the entertainment and edification of modern-day consumerist society.

By what sleight of hand did these daring detectives and protean private investigators accomplish this public relations coup, this most impressive job of spin doctoring? Having sworn allegiance to legal guidelines promulgated by "the system," weren't they supposed to be the sworn enemies of every black outlaw, revolutionary, and rabble-rouser in the land? Conversely, as outspoken, sometimes obstreperous African-Americans, wasn't their unshackled presence in the hallowed halls of white folks' justice positively guaranteed to cause considerable discomfort—if not fits of apoplexy—among self-satisfied law-and-order types? Were they racial loyalists or establishment dupes? Sly soul brothers or superhero sellouts? Indeed, what distinguished them from the badmen or the stereotypical good cops? And to what degree were they involved in either the physical or the psychological liberation of fellow blacks? Where did their ultimate loyalties reside? Since "which side are you on?" was a question asked repeatedly in a variety of confrontational contexts during these years, the nature of their collective response to such queries warrants investigation.

The most engaging detectives of film and fiction always have been something of a puzzle. From their earliest incarnation in the works of Edgar Allan Poe (French sleuth C. Auguste Dupin) and Arthur Conan Doyle (learned eccentric Sherlock Holmes), even the straightest of arrows has manifested multiple peculiarities and—on numerous occasions—a readily observable "dark side." Hard-boiled, post-Holmesian whodunit heroes are particularly quirky and prone to fits of pique. Less reliant on simple deductive logic than "classical" sleuths, twentieth-century investigators must employ firearms and fisticuffs (as well as a keen intellect and a vast array of crime-fighting gadgets) to collar the crooks. Because they deal daily with ever more reprehensible criminal acts, they must be fully capable of coping with whatever lunatics and sociopaths come their way.

Fortunately, these irreverent, tough-talking, near indefatigable knight-errants are blessed with an abundance of resourcefulness and are well schooled in the laws of survival. While most possess a basic Philip Marlowesque decency and sense of fair play, they often put as much effort into challenging authority as badmen do into resisting arrest. Some, like Mickey Spillane's Mike Hammer, seem to consider themselves above the restraints of the law. Taking the administration of justice into their own hands, they choose to shoot first and ask questions much later and at their leisure. If prone to retributive acts, such stern moralists serve as avenging angels whose chief loyalties are to themselves and to their personal, idiosyncratic vision of a just social order. At times, they are barely distinguishable from the "better sort" of social bandits. Oddly enough, this mix of attributes makes them near perfect protean heroes—well suited to the tastes of a broad spectrum of thrill-seeking armchair adventurers.[124]

Numerous variations on the basic hard-boiled theme were submitted for the approval of Black Power era pop-culture consumers. Crime and spy novels, mysteries and police procedurals, and adventure yarns of all sorts featured tough, self-directed protagonists who found great satisfaction in skillfully balancing on the thin line that separated badman from lawman. When their stories reached Hollywood, one could be certain that only the most rugged, square-jawed actors would be deemed worthy of portraying Nick Carter (Robert Conrad in NBC's *The Adventures of Nick Carter*, 1972), Philip Marlowe (James Garner in *Marlowe*, 1969), Travis McGee (Rod Taylor in *Darker than Amber*, 1970), Lew Archer (Paul Newman in *Harper*, 1966, and *The Drowning Pool*, 1975), or the Continental Op (James Coburn in CBS's 1978 miniseries *The Dain Curse*). Quick on the trigger and even quicker with a quip, these stalwarts allowed scarcely a wrong to go unrequited and took no guff from anyone. Indeed, like Robert S. Parker's caring but complex and courageous Boston private investigator, Spenser (named after Edmund Spenser, author of the English heroic poem *The Faerie Queene*, 1596), they frequently evoked the image of slightly rumpled and unruly chivalric warriors.[125]

Since the massive popularity of the genre ensured that there was enough crime-solving work for everyone, it was not surprising to find black detectives stepping up and clamoring for a piece of the action. Having served a lengthy apprenticeship as dialect-speaking domestics who went "undercover" to help solve the case of the missing white folks' wash, would-be sleuths were eager to play a more central role in the world of whodunits.[126] Indeed, before you could say "Bubber Brown and Jinx Jenkins" (aspiring Harlem p.i.'s in Rudolph Fisher's "thriller of manners" *The Conjure-Man Dies*, 1932), television and theater screens nationwide were filled with images of African-American police captains (James Earl Jones in the short-lived CBS series *Paris*, 1979–80), detectives (Harry Tenafly as played by James McEachin on the *NBC Wednesday Mystery Movie*, 1973–74), and secret agents (Bill Cosby in NBC's *I Spy*, 1965–68, and *Top Secret*, 1978). Here, they joined racial and ethnic minority group representatives such as Judge Dee, Sergeant Joe Leaphorn, and Rabbi David Small in claiming a share of the bragging rights to a noteworthy archetype.[127]

Although white he-man lawmen were a hard act to follow, black detective

types were no less capable of attracting and holding an audience or, more correctly, of appealing to several of the segmented audiences which novelists and
screenwriters routinely serviced. Here, on the main street of American popular culture, the key to drawing a crowd seemed simple enough: mix one part innovation with two parts formula, add a dash of sex and violence, mix well and
serve up to hungry consumers. The trick, of course, was to choose the ingre-
dients in such a manner as to appeal to the widest range of tastes possible—to
offer something to everyone with a dollar or two to spend. Providing a fresh,
timely "racial angle" on reassuringly familiar story lines, African-American
detective heroes of the 1960s and 1970s were well positioned for successful
mass marketing.

In casting a broad net with themselves at the center, these cagey crime-
fighters were careful to allow for variations in consumer preference—to offer
potential fans both the scintillating spice of variety and an always pleasurable
predictability. Like their social-bandit contemporaries, the rough-hewn black
lawmen were not chiseled from a single granite block. Each had a unique style
and—as much as the genre's structured expectations would allow—effectively
personalized their approach to meeting daily job-related challenges. To be
sure, incredibly hip, fabulously flashy specimens such as Richard "Super"
Spade (ex-UCLA all-American, decorated Vietnam veteran, karate and black
studies teacher, proud XKE owner) and Fred Williamson's Jesse Crowder
(black-belt champion with a $25,000 per case minimum fee; favors tight-
fitting pastel leisure suits; has a Rolls Royce as his *second* car) were the anticipated norm.[128] But the black lawman's guild also included less awe-inspiring
blokes like ebony-carving, parable-spouting pathologist Dr. Samuel Quarshie
and hotel detective Sam Kelly, a cherubic, forty-three-year-old Everyman
who favored brown pin-striped suits and straw boaters, Chopin études and
Yiddish folk songs.[129] Indeed, as frequently pointed out by snooty high-soci-
ety types, there was no accounting for taste within the popular culture—a dubious distinction which actually helped spread the influence of these diverse,
colorful African-American heroes far and wide.

Eventually, several archetypal figures separated themselves from the pack
and were replicated in both film and fiction. Joining race-specific with traditional notions of the heroic, these pivotal portrayals helped delineate a unique
but remarkably nonessentialist black worldview—one to which all fans of the
crime-fighting genre could relate. Such stories provided their readers or viewers (at least those blessed with the ability to see past superficial shadings of racial
chauvinism) with salient information about the nature of good guy/bad guy
relationships and possible models for establishing a more viable, more equitable and mutually beneficial relationship between Afro-America and the societal mainstream. Private investigators, action-adventure heroes, black

vigilantes, and several different types of detectives in public service contributed to this mixed-media movement which, in effect, targeted cultural
myopia and misunderstanding as the *real* villains.

The Private Investigator: John Shaft

The creation of white novelist-screenwriter Ernest Tidyman, Shaft appeared
in seven novels, three MGM feature films, and an eight-episode network TV
spinoff series. In his early-1970s heyday, this muscular, mustached shamus with
skin "about the color of a French-roast coffee-bean" and hands like "a five-
fingered trip-hammer" attracted a broad-based, multiethnic audience and—
unlike many blaxploitation era film heroes—was "respectable" enough to win
Tidyman an NAACP Image Award.[130] He also became a one-man marketing
megalith. With album sales of Isaac Hayes's Academy and Grammy Award–
winning soundtrack score booming, trademark leather coats, watches (his was
a wafer-thin, $4,000 emerald-studded Patek Philippe), sunglasses, nightshirts,
shaving lotion, and cologne vanished from retailers' shelves as soon as they
were displayed—a phenomenon which moved one wry media critic to predict
that "at the rate things are going, black audiences will at least be the best-
dressed, nicest-smelling film-goers anywhere."[131] If "Shaft fever" wasn't a particularly long-lived phenomenon, it was both intense and surprisingly
influential. More than two decades later, the Tidyman character—as played
with considerable flair by former Ebony Fashion Fair model Richard
Roundtree—remains a staple of Black History Month film festivals and late-
night TV.

Like earlier iconographic investigators, John Shaft cherished his independent lifestyle. Constrained by neither a permanent sidekick nor a precinct station bureaucracy, he was able to develop his heroic potential without the
hindrance of contrary opinion or due process. While Mrs. Klonsky, Shaft's
long-suffering cleaning lady, might silently curse her employer for leaving his
Greenwich Village apartment in what charitably was described as a "confused"
state, no one who took Shaft to task in a more openly confrontational fashion
escaped unscathed.[132] Either a barrage of bluster, a display of gallows humor,
or one of his flip, one-liner put-downs speedily cut them to the quick. Strong
opinions, a healthy ego, and a bountiful array of only-child idiosyncrasies conveyed the unmistakable message that he not only was unbought and unbossed
but if pressed hard enough could become aggressively protective of any personal space he happened to be occupying.

Although fond of catching a catnap while riding in the backseat of a gently
rocking taxi, the prideful p.i. took great offense at "cigar-stinking, unshaven
ragbag" cabbies' reluctance to pick up black fares. Similar slights experienced

John Shaft on soundtrack album, 1972 (author's collection)

during a hardscrabble Harlem childhood caused him to brand most Jews as chiseling, usurious "merchants of misery." White hippies, on the other hand, were considered dull and weak—"cop-outs" afraid of being tested by life.[133] The same could be said about stereotypically vain, "silly faggot[s]," who talked too much and played sissy games—such as tennis.[134] "Broads"—especially the drop-dead gorgeous types, whom Shaft had little difficulty attracting—were deemed suitable for an occasional bout of sexual gymnastics but always left him wondering, "What do you do with them after you're done with them?" Outside the bedroom, most were "a fucking nuisance." Perhaps, he mused on one occasion, they could be persuaded to tidy up the apartment before leaving.[135]

Given his independence and politically incorrect impertinence, it is ironic that Shaft often could be found mediating disputes between cops and both black and white cutthroats. How was this possible? He certainly was clever enough to pull it off—a point driven home by the movie promo tag line,

"Shaft's his name and shaft's his game."[136] Moreover, in addition to being un-burdened by establishment ties, he was privileged to lead what one film re-viewer termed "a life free of racial torment," implying that the black investigator possessed both the political and the psychological independence required for the successful completion of these difficult tasks.[137] And, finally, it must be noted that Shaft's ultravivid trash-talking decreased significantly as the years went by and he adopted increasingly decorous habits. Certainly, al-ternative, made-for-TV dialogue which substituted "granny-dodger" for "motherfucker" was far more conducive to bringing about a meeting of the minds than some of his earlier outbursts.

Whatever the sleight of hand (or show of force) employed, John Shaft was remarkably effective in making opposites attract and then convincing these an-tipodal forces to draw ever closer together. As a former ward of the state and onetime purse-snatching bad guy himself, Shaft knew all about life on the streets and understood the mind-set of those whose unfortunate upbringing or declining circumstances caused them to victimize others. He had been beaten by black cops and bore the scars of martial combat. As Tidyman noted, Shaft possessed the hardness and "edge" of all who have been baptised in the turbulent "substream" that flows beneath the city's veneer of civility. In prac-tice, this meant that he could be tough, although he was not savage or evil. While fully capable of shattering a kneecap, collapsing a larynx, or transform-ing an offending scumbag's nose into "a bloody marshmallow," he preferred fi-nesse over force and often took the most unsavory of prey alive. Such restraint, he joked, resulted from not wanting to repaint the walls. Nevertheless, Shaft's confident assertion that "there ain't anybody I ever met I couldn't take in the street" suggested a different explanation: the lawman was only a few steps removed—and often fully immersed in—the badman's world. Indeed, his responses to many types of external stimuli were indistinguishable from those of the social bandit. Therefore, it was not at all surprising that Shaft could ac-cept a retainer from noted crime boss Knocks Persons without the slightest twinge of guilt—or feel fully justified in hobnobbing with fellow risktaker and childhood-playmate-turned-revolutionary Ben Buford. Each, the bridge-building black detective understood, was a ghetto "survivor" who "had come off the same production line of the same mill."[138]

Soulmate or not, cross Shaft and you were on your way first to the emer-gency room and then to jail. Following a tour in Vietnam and an abortive at-tempt to acclimate himself to the academic environment of NYU's law school, he had apprenticed with "a big-assed nationally known agency" before opening John Shaft Investigations in a rundown office building south of Times Square. Here, he came into frequent contact with various representatives of New York's finest. Ultimately, the same individually crafted code of ethics which held that society's most conscienceless "vermin" should not be permitted to "vomit on the world without retribution" caused him to cast his lot with the forces of law and order.[139]

Shaft maintained a testy, confrontational relationship with both black and white members of the NYPD. Typically, their meetings were peppered with insults, unpleasantries, threats and counterthreats. As culture hero and cultural mediator, the black detective was nobody's fool and therefore could be no copper's tool. Theirs was destined to be a mutually beneficial, workmanlike arrangement. As partial compensation for helping solve particularly vexing cases, Shaft was recommended for lucrative private-sector jobs. He also received departmental protection whenever his roughhouse methods and borderline-legal approach to crime fighting attracted the attention of the district attorney's office. "Not really good friends, not enemies, either," savvy cops like captains Vic Anderozzi and Pete Bollin understood that both parties were playing the same game but using different editions of the playbook. Indeed, the police considered it a public service whenever their helpmeet shortened the most wanted list by one or two names on his own initiative. As the harried Anderozzi remarked on one such occasion, "There's laws and courts and prisons. There's an established order. There's rules and regulations. And there's also Shaft."[140]

But, like all truly effective mediators, the black sleuth made some powerful enemies. In addition to fictional foes, a fair number of real-world film critics seemed to have it in for Tidyman's hero. *Shaft* (1971), they said, was "a white person's Black film" featuring a homogenized version of the racial heroic. Allegedly, the big-screen trilogy more fully reflected mainstream values held by traditional white action heroes than it did the subversive, funkified philosophy of a Sweet Sweetback. Dismissed as "the usual slick, well-packaged slop," CBS's mild-mannered teleplays (which generated more heat in the press than on the tube) also were found lacking in the critical area of "blackness." Albeit a tad overstated, in this case it was justifiable for a frustrated reviewer to write that "Shaft on TV makes Barnaby Jones look like Eldridge Cleaver." After the series was canceled, coproducer William Woodfield was quoted as saying: "We knew we would get bad reviews, but we thought the American public would accept this man as a friend." So much for worthy intentions and bargain-basement high concept.[141]

Cineast nit-picking aside, it remains true that Shaft was a remarkably user-friendly hero for his day and age. In joining Black Power era impulses with widely accepted cinematic images, his handlers succeeded in updating and reinvigorating the hard-boiled detective genre. They also maximized the black investigator's potential for crossover success at the box office. As a fictional character, the self-directed Shaft was successful in mediating disputes between the forces of law and the champions of disorder largely because he had a foot in both camps. If, as Tidyman proved in the original novel, an underworld kingpin like Knocks Persons could be portrayed as "a figure standing alone on a foundation of corruption," Shaft was far too complicated to receive similar treatment. He was a black man but also "part a white man"because of what he did and where he had been. Moreover, he was "smart enough to go back and forth between black and white man."[142]

To be sure, the transition wasn't always easy. But the rewards were substantial. Some considered him "a pimp for the whores of whiteness," but Shaft could cite chapter and verse about *doing* for black people and about the many times he warned others to "stay away from black honkies."[143] If, as Richard Roundtree claimed, his theatrical alter ego was "pretty much the same type of character as Clint Eastwood plays," the black actor also considered John Shaft to be a positive, race-specific role model—a "brother"who could "hit a white man and not get killed for it. . . . a black man who is for once a winner."[144] When the no-nonsense detective defended a black U.S. senator's children against racist conspirators (*Good-bye, Mr. Shaft,* 1973), quashed a white-run slave-smuggling ring (*Shaft in Africa,* 1973), shielded the Jamaican prime minister from an assassination attempt (*Shaft's Carnival of Killers,* 1974), and sought to divert a racketeer's ill-gotten wealth to ghetto child-care projects (*Shaft's Big Score!* 1972), it was obvious that here was a race man of epic stature. More to the point, Shaft was a race man who specialized in mediational services. Ever eager for dangerous assignments, he willingly interposed himself between two warring, color-coded culture spheres in the hope of reconciling their contradictory views on the nature of black humanity and the black heroic.

The (Mostly) Good Black Cops: Coffin Ed Johnson, Grave Digger Jones, and Virgil Tibbs

Although there is nothing in his press packet to prove it, John Shaft very well could have been a close relative of at least three other black detective heroes of the 1960s and 1970s. Proximate paternity is impossible to prove, but the family resemblance is unmistakable. It was as if Chester Himes's earthy Grave Digger Jones and Coffin Ed Johnson pooled their DNA with John Ball's dignified Virgil Tibbs, had a boy child, and called him Handsome Johnny. That in later life he would reject the notion of plying his trade in the public sector did not mean that other parental traits and tendencies were as easily discarded. Many remained visible both in the fully developed Shaft character and in numerous lesser lights of the fictional crime-solving confraternity. Incestuous? Perhaps. But such eugenic data suggests that the African-American heroes' gene pool was rich in hereditary genius and possessed considerable depth, potency, and staying power.

Based on a pair of Himes's real-life tough-guy acquaintances and given additional texture by the black writer's considerable firsthand experience with both badmen and the business end of a billy club, the Harlem-based detective team of Jones and Johnson seems, at first glance, most unpromising hero material.[145] Even as they cruise the city's darkened streets in their battered, unmarked prowl car, one senses a basic lack of standard star-quality sophistication. Passing a streetlight, one could make out that both wore their hair cut short and were attired in wrinkled black alpaca suits, black cotton shirts with open collars, and well-weathered felt hats. Reminders of an early-evening pit stop at Mammy Louise's for a double order of ribs and "chicken feetsy" can be seen on their lapels. Whenever choosing to break the self-imposed silence, both employ a blunt, sometimes profane variant of standard English to recount past cases or to reminisce about the time they got thrown out of the Great Man nightclub on 125th Street for spitting watermelon seeds at strippers' behinds.

At the conclusion of their graveyard shift, daylight reveals that Coffin Ed and Grave Digger closely resemble "two hog farmers on a weekend in the Big Town."[146] Each is a large, loose-jointed, flat-footed fellow who could have been cast from the same working-stiff mold were it not for one unfortunate distinction. Jones's stubble-fringed face bore the requisite number of scars, marks, and blemishes that one would expect a veteran cop raised in Harlem during the Great Depression to have accumulated by the time he had reached his middle thirties. Johnson's grim visage, on the other hand, was said to resemble that of Frankenstein's monster or the mask of an African witch doctor. Permanently disfigured by a hoodlum's acid-throwing rampage, the black detective's ravaged countenance "was enough to scare the devil out of hell." Most associates believed that this trauma had caused him to become cynical, erratic, and prone to sudden rage—trigger-happy and "as dangerous as a blind rattlesnake." When subjected to particularly stressful situations, Coffin Ed's face twitched uncontrollably and he frequently sought out dark corners where he could hide his scarification.[147]

Thus, even after Raymond St. Jacques (Coffin Ed) and Godfrey Cambridge (Grave Digger) invested the duo with a bit more spit and polish in the big-screen versions of *Cotton Comes to Harlem* (1970) and *The Heat's On,* a.k.a. *Come Back Charleston Blue* (1972), it seemed highly unlikely that either of these somewhat seedy sleuths could aspire to superhero status. Nevertheless, it would be a mistake to underestimate the resolutely down-home Jones and Johnson. In addition to a fondness for late-night coffee and donuts, Coffin Ed and Grave Digger were endowed by their creator with a number of behavioral and personality traits which made it possible for them—in a soup-stained sort of way—to contend for a place in the urban crime-fighters' hall of fame. Himes not only situated his investigators in an environment conducive to heroic endeavor ("Harlem, where anything might happen"), but he also dropped hints throughout the eight-novel series that these men were, indeed, special cases.[148] For example, their facility with firearms seemed the stuff of legend. When drawn in anticipation of a shootout, the black detectives' oversized pistols were said to resemble "the swords of warriors of old."[149] Both cops were capable of neatly shooting the decorative chrome off a fleeing hoodlum's car or of sending an unsuspecting foe's hat dancing down the street Old West style. On occasion, they even would fire a few rounds into the ceiling to encourage attentive behavior. Rumor had it that Ed could "shoot the fat offen a cat's stomach" and once had killed a man for passing gas in his presence. Little wonder that one white homicide detective referred to Himes's dark knights as "two cowboys from the Harlem Q. ranch."[150]

However, it was the hard-boiled detective hero, not the medieval paladin or western sheriff, that Jones and Johnson most fully resembled. Earnest, visceral, and guided by an uncomplicated ethical code, Himes's protagonists were nominally police officers but in most respects acted the part of independent operatives. Although ostensibly no more than cogs in a large crime-fighting machine, they were able to exercise the discretionary freedoms of a lone-wolf investigator because (1) invariably, white cops became nervous around "wild-looking colored people," necessitating the use of ghetto-acculturated personnel to maintain order within the city's toughest black districts; (2) Grave Digger and Coffin Ed tended to do what *they* thought was right irrespective of legalities or departmental directives; and (3) *all* hard-boiled detectives behave as if dependence upon bureaucratic consent—or even reliance upon a backup team—is an emasculatory condition worse than death itself.[151] In providing his black heroes with both the gift of investigative independence and an important mediational role as in-house "interpreters" of ghetto mores for a major law-enforcing entity, Himes effectively credentialized them for work that would have tested the mettle of any number of traditional tough-guy sleuths.

Hard-boiled types hoping to succeed on Harlem's battlefront were well advised to rely less on a mastery of textbook criminology than on physical hardness and an in-depth understanding of ghetto psychology. Here, Jones and Johnson reigned supreme—the masters of all the ramshackle tenements and seedy dives they surveyed from the front seat of their trusty alligator-green sedan. Certainly, toughness was a given in this neck of the woods. Longtime residents were considered world-class experts in giving and receiving hard knocks. In this context, effective enforcement of the criminal code involved knowing who to put the screws on and when to tighten, loosen, and then unexpectedly retighten them for maximum effect. A typical day's stack of police reports ("Man kills his wife with an ax for burning his breakfast pork chop. . . . Man stabs another man for spilling beer on his new suit. . . . Woman stabs man in stomach fourteen times, no reason given") reveals that they weren't exactly dealing with choirboys or cats up a light pole.[152]

Countless confrontations with this criminal element enabled Coffin Ed and Grave Digger to perfect their investigative technique. To encourage compliance with the law, the black detectives made extensive use of "Pigeons Nest"—a windowless, soundproof basement interrogation room reputed to have hatched more stool pigeons than all the rooftop rookeries in Harlem. Here, after being ushered to a central perchlike seat upon which were focused floodlights bright enough "to make the blackest man transparent," uncooperative suspects were subjected to an intensive session of cross-examination. On any given day, this might involve threats and intimidation, good cop/bad cop psychodrama, or backhand slaps delivered with near pile driver force. The ever volatile Ed was a particularly exacting inquisitor and often needed to be reminded by Jones that "we're cops, not judges." However, neither detective was above pistol-whipping an "incestuous sister-raping thief" until the perpetrator's body "bent one-sided like a rubber man," teeth flying out sidewise "like corn popping." If, occasionally, such acts of information-gathering overkill got the deadly serious duo into hot water with the press or some civic-minded do-gooder group, they were fortunate to be able to count on support from their superiors. Those responsible for bringing law and order to Harlem understood that the methods utilized by Jones and Johnson were necessary—and often-times sufficient—for the near impossible task at hand. The sleuths, said envious departmental colleagues, were like skilled lion trainers charged with keeping a "cage of big cats" continually on their best behavior.[153]

In seeking to deflect charges of police brutality, Grave Digger and Coffin Ed disclosed the specifics of their code of conduct. A between-the-lines reading of these ghettocentric guidelines reveals the nature of their ties to the crime-plagued black community and the degree to which Jones and Johnson understood and empathized with the people whom they had sworn to protect and serve.

The first section of the code established the importance of retaining personal integrity amid corruption. They forthrightly swore to refuse all bribes—sexual, monetary, or culinary—and agonized over the widespread belief that every cop had a price. As Ed proclaimed proudly, "We may have broken some heads, but we never broke no promises."[154]

Reflecting the detectives' commitment to—and definition of—social justice, section two contained a detailed ranking of law enforcement priorities. Slated for immediate attention and speedy incarceration were violent offenders, major narcotics traffickers, and big-time confidence men—conscienceless criminals whose selfish acts "fucked-up lives." Of lesser concern were madams of orderly houses of prostitution, operators of well-run gambling establishments, and local specialists in bottle peddling, petty larceny, and the short con. "Loud-mouthed" militants and other practitioners of "unorganized violence" were, to be sure, considered something of a problem. Their culpability, however, was mitigated by the fact that they, too, were victims of poverty and white racism. Many merely were "making a statement" and only "want[ed] justice like everybody else."[155]

The third and final section of the code served as an apologia for Jones's and Johnson's hard-boiled approach to fighting urban crime. While recognizing (and frequently lamenting) that they couldn't "just light into a group of innocent people and start whipping heads until somebody talked," the detectives nevertheless made a clear case for tough talk and an even tougher walk as the best way to inspire immediate respect for lawmen and for the social and legal compact that conscientious cops were charged with enforcing. It wasn't that they actually *enjoyed* pummeling, maiming, or otherwise abusing lowlife suspects, noted Ed, somewhat unconvincingly. But the patented hard-boiled technique—a big, shiny pistol to the temple or a swift kick to the groin—did, indeed, prove effective in cutting through the troublesome red tape of by-the-book police procedures. Their goal (and life's work) was to "get down to the nitty-gritty" of a Harlem detective's raison d'être: to protect the defenseless against further victimization, thereby helping create a "decent peaceful city for people to live in."[156]

Certainly, the ace investigators had an important job to do, a vital trust to maintain. If not exactly "by any means necessary," they would go about accomplishing this most arduous series of tasks "the best way we know how."[157] Expert, two-fisted mediators between black and white, the law and social disorder, each of Himes's heroes was, in fact, good cop and bad cop all rolled up into one slightly soiled but seamless package. In struggling daily with antisocial behavior, Coffin Ed and Grave Digger revealed that they understood both the unique house rules of the hard-boiled detectives' workplace and their role in the larger, white-dominated social order. Asserting that it was white people who "commit the pointless brutality," the black sleuths disavowed any notion that they were *playing* tough. "We *are* tough," they said with a culture hero's confirmed sense of self.[158] And it was a tough love for their fellow Harlemites that Jones and Johnson passed on to John Shaft and to their other spiritual crime-fighting heirs. Entrusted with difficult assignments because of their roughhouse rapport with "the people," they remained remarkably untroubled by the knowledge that many blacks—with good reason—rejected the white, middle-class notion that "the police are your friends." They cooed reassuringly whenever attempting to pry information from reluctant, frightened witnesses, "We are all colored folks here, you can tell us the story."[159]

If Himes's colorful duo foreshadowed Shaft's rootedness in the down-home lifestyle, Pasadena-based homicide detective Virgil Tibbs most certainly was an inspiration to righteous upscale living. Whereas Digger and Ed were still mired in detective first-grade status after twelve years on the force—salaries riddled by inflation, mortgages and car loans unpaid—Edgar-winning mystery writer John Ball's heroic creation was doing quite well for himself. After committing to crime fighting following the cold-blooded murder of a seventeen-year-old black youth from his hometown in the Deep South, Tibbs tugged at his own bootstraps until he had earned a college degree, a black belt in karate, and an entry-level position as a Pasadena traffic cop. His own best affirmative action officer, the patient, goal-oriented lawman worked diligently to gain experience, earn respect, and prove himself worthy of promotion to investigator status. Eventually, along with a split-level, hillside home, a powder-blue Mustang, and a prim, attentive wife, he acquired such a wealth of expertise in the criminal sciences that other municipalities, private individuals, and even government agencies clamored for his services. Becoming, in effect, an independent operative bound to no single jurisdiction, Tibbs occasionally worked undercover in West Coast ghettos, but his sterling reputation for precise, thorough investigative work virtually mandated that much of his time would be spent on assignment elsewhere—often in exotic locales.

In one of several running jokes in the six-book series (1965–80), a character meeting the black detective for the first time remarked: "You don't look very much like Sidney Poitier."[160] Tibbs's reply was even more controlled and noncommittal than usual—perhaps because he realized that, in truth, he looked and acted almost exactly like the well-known actor who had mastered his mannerisms (or vice versa) before starring in films such as *In The Heat of the Night* (1967), *They Call Me Mister Tibbs!* (1970), and *The Organization* (1971).

An ebony saint in either entertainment medium, Tibbs/Poitier was a splendid specimen of the close-cropped, tan-trenchcoat breed: early thirties, medium height, fit as a fiddle, features "almost like a white man's" but of "pure Negro" parentage. He wrote in a "strong, precise hand" and spoke in direct, authoritative detectivese when interrogating suspects. (Sample: "One question if I may, have you been concerned because you may have personally committed an infraction?")[161] As a bachelor, Tibbs had been "overcautious to his own detriment" in matters of amour, and associates continued to marvel at his determined self-discipline in the workplace. Some thought it would be therapeutic for him to "let loose once in awhile." But early socialization in personal modesty, years of studying aikido, and a workaholic passion for the sort of peer approval one earned through nonconfrontational problem solving made him the man that he was—a highly regarded sleuth who radiated "a quiet kind of confidence, the sort you have to look for to see."[162]

This seemingly soft-boiled persona was no ruse, and the fact that he maintained the most orderly office space in detective fiction history, listened to Ravel and Debussy as well as Ellington, and preferred "Negro" to "Black" should cause no one to malign Tibbs as an overmediated Milquetoast. In truth,

Sidney Poitier—or is it Virgil
Tibbs? (*Sepia* magazine, 1968)

he was one mentally tough, self-aware dude with a lethal set of martial arts
moves. The assured, dignified walk and constantly monitored emotional output were the products of childhood trauma—privation, physical intimidation,
the humiliating taunts of bigots. In triumphing over such adversities, Tibbs
had learned to play his cards close to the vest, to maintain his composure even
in the face of "ignorant back talk," and—at all times—to demand the same
courtesies and considerations customarily accorded his pale-skinned peers.[163]
Overtly disrespectful treatment of the black lawman did not automatically result in a broken limb or trip to the morgue, but it could help earn the offending party a lengthy stay in San Quentin. A hard-nosed advocate of tough
sentencing guidelines, Tibbs had a passion for prosecution which increased
logarithmically with every affront to pride or position and with every annoyance that slowed the wheels of justice. As the committed crime-fighter noted,
by refusing to "play fast and loose with the rules," he would be doing "at least a
small part to preserve a decent society."[164]

Typically, Tibbs's investigative style was more Holmesian than hard-boiled.
Certainly, this was appropriate given his straight-arrow demeanor. With the
exception of the time he was suspended from the force for helping a group of
Third World radicals break up an international drug ring, Tibbs rarely stepped
out of line or displayed any of the baser tendencies of hard-boiled heroes.[165]

By consistently relying upon his deductive powers instead of his dukes, he developed an uncanny ability to solve cases that had left others completely baffled. As if gifted with second sight, Tibbs surveyed a crime scene with swiftness and unerring accuracy. He made mental notes of seemingly insignificant things—dust on a car hood, carpet lint clinging to the bottom of a shoe, signs of wear on a leather belt, razor nicks or suntan lines on a corpse—eventually transferring each salient piece of information to its own index card. Back at his desk, related clues were grouped together and arranged and rearranged until useful patterns emerged. Invariably, this mind-bending game of sleuthing solitaire resulted in an airtight case against a clever perpetrator whom none of his colleagues had even bothered to treat as a suspect.[166]

Although a bigoted southern lawman once offered grudging tribute to Tibbs by calling him the "smartest black I ever saw" and then graciously adding, "He oughta been a white man," the California investigator behaved as if he disagreed on both counts.[167] Ever the modest sort, he willingly shared the spotlight with colleagues and brushed aside all paeans to his own brilliance by noting that the legendary Holmes cracked even tougher cases with fewer clues. Unjaded after many years of successful sleuthing, "the excitement of a fresh scent" still made his fingertips tingle.[168]

In matters of racial identity, Tibbs could be contentious in regard to proper forms of address but was fully committed to a personal vision of African-American empowerment. "Get it through your head that I'm a black man. And I've been one a lot longer than you," he told a jeering, cop-hating mob of "professional militants" in *Johnny Get Your Gun* (1969). This "black boy with the brown nose," as their leader had the misguided temerity to label Tibbs, saw no reason why he should "go out of his way to stand on ceremony" with those of either race who disrespected his badge or the person behind it. "You're a phoney. And you're a poor excuse for a black man," he shot back, upending the terminology table. "I clawed my way up against prejudice, I licked poverty, and I earned my job. And here I'm not a black man, I'm Virgil Tibbs, a respected police officer, and nobody asks for anything more." Herein encapsulated was a definitive distillation of the detective hero's advice to all African-American strivers: abandon rhetorical approaches; authenticate your blackness by working hard ("two times harder than any white man"); help build a society committed to the irrelevancy of skin color.[169]

Tibbs didn't "especially want to be white." He wasn't color-blind. But he was color-inclusive—and optimistic enough about the course of American race relations to feel "it's getting better every day."[170] Having experienced considerable success within mainstream institutions, the veteran striver was well suited to serve as a role model for Shaft and other upwardly mobile crime-fighters. Unfettered by the nihilistic despair of those who—through self-segregation—had abandoned hope of "making it" in the larger society, such a highly motivated cohort would seek to expand upon his victories. Believing as he did that there were all too many people who "never accomplished anything because they wouldn't see it through," this vanguard group would, through competence and constant struggle, take the high road in leading a revolution of rising racial expectations.[171] Until the day of ultimate triumph, Tibbs would remain on the case. Committed to the nonessentialist tenets of his mediational methodology, he would continue to confound proponents of a color-coded social order by refusing to play by their rules. As he once noted in responding to a black youth's angry accusations of racial favoritism, "If you must look at it that way, then color me blue—I'm a policeman."[172]

The Female Crime-Fighters: Gender Mediators

John Shaft may have learned a mediational trick or two from godfathers Jones, Johnson, and Tibbs, but big sister had an important piece of wisdom to share as well: never underestimate the power of a woman (detective). By the mid-1970s, the same hiring frenzy responsible for full employment among black male sleuths enabled a select number of aspiring female crime-fighters to crack the glass ceiling of this most exclusive profession. Encouraged by both Hollywood deal makers and proponents of black women's liberation, the popular culture's dramatically increased willingness to highlight the heroism of a group more commonly depicted as either harlots or housewives was a phenomenon that had no direct analogue in the annals of social banditry.

Conceptually, black women's infiltration of the detective hero ranks was facilitated by a venerable tradition of fictional female sleuthing. Early enablers such as Agatha Christie's garrulous, bird-watching spinster, Miss Jane Marple, and teen sensation Nancy Drew paved the way for more glamorous sorts like G. G. Fickling's "sexsational private eyeful" Honey West ("Call me Honey. Call me anytime.") and tough, Baretta-packing Chicago p.i. Madge Hatchett.[173] Indeed, by the 1970s, female law enforcers were using a lot more than intuition and a talent for interpreting gossip to defend themselves in rough company. But this was equally burden and opportunity, a vexing popular-cultural conundrum made even more complicated by the otherwise refreshing presence of black women.

In a nutshell, the problem was as follows: how were novelists and screenwriters to represent such characters both as modern women and as hard-boiled heroes without straying so far from accepted norms that consumer backlash canceled out previous gains? Often the preferred solution was a jerry-built affair that brought female leads only partial relief from the onus of being conceptualized as a societal "other." Since it was believed that most fans were fixated on formula, preeminent male portrayals were allowed to define and de-limit female characterization. In hope of varying the traditional format with-out subverting tough-guy convention, overt sexuality of the male fantasy world variety was added to the list of accredited heroic traits. No longer merely adornments to the plot structure, women now were advised to employ both their fists and their feminine wiles as evidence that they, indeed, had "come a long way, baby." Without hesitation, the black women of detective film and fiction accepted this challenge, confident that eventually they would become full-fledged members of a heroic law enforcement team. In doing so, they risked becoming phallic females—odd, imperfectly hybridized beings of lim-ited complexity who were more in tune with the requirements of patriarchal portraiture than with the need to counter dominant modes of representation by reinventing themselves.

Certainly, black female sleuths of the 1970s seeking to be treated as compe-tent professionals with an equal voice in shaping genre conventions faced a daunting mediational task. Only a confirmed optimist dared maintain that the forced marriage of hard knocks and bodacious bodies would enlighten those who believed that high-level investigative work was, as in the title of P. D. James's 1972 novel, an unsuitable job for a woman. Most male detectives con-tinued to have considerable difficulty accepting the notion that women *could* measure up to their guild's exacting double standards. It was a classic Catch-22 situation, premised on wishful thinking and sustained by an insatiable need for male ego enhancement. According to this line of reasoning—here cogently expressed by Nero Wolfe's opinionated associate, Archie Goodwin—accept-able performance as a "she-dick" required a "good, thick hide," a "cold eye," and "hard nerves." Unfortunately, possession of such attributes was said to guarantee an absence of those "friendly feelings" and "nice little impulses" that attracted men to women in the first place.[174] Thus, convinced by their hor-mones that this melange of macho-man mythmaking was equally gospel and science, John Shaft, Richard Spade, and their brother chauvinists went through life behaving as if a woman's best shot at job market integration involved audi-tioning for the nightly "symphony between the sheets."[175]

Female investigators grappled with these preconceptions and prohibitions as best they could, hoping that somehow they would be able to sensitize obtuse male heroes to gender equity issues. Utilizing all available tools of the trade—and the cosmetic case—they worked diligently to develop a woman-centered worldview and to reconcile differences of opinion on key questions such as whether one had to be a man in order to maintain heroic integrity. As they did so, the feisty, short-skirted sleuths provided fans of the genre with frequent up-dates on the pan-racial battle of the sexes, expanded both the definition and the influence of the black heroic, and—once again providing a vital service as intermediaries—bridged the gap between "classical" female portrayals and the more fully emancipated, re-visioned characters created by 1980s authors such as Sue Grafton, Susan Moody, Marcia Muller, and Sara Paretsky.[176]

No single African-American woman dominated the pop-culture crime-fighting scene. In the spirit of the budding sisterhood that they foreshadowed, many different individuals contributed to the creation of a defining archetype. While offering curious culture consumers the opportunity to mix, match, or otherwise sample from a host of portrayals and story lines, these resourceful, strong-willed sleuths joined forces to champion the singular version of a modern-day female hero governed by two distinct but complementary sets of attributes: toughness, resourcefulness, and self-sufficiency; practiced, confident sexuality. Foxy Brown, Sheba Shayne, Cleopatra Jones—their very names spoke of an essential duality of characterization and spirit. Pistols drawn, shapely legs stretched wide with nosebleed-producing high heels planted firmly on both sides of this media-friendly formulation, such women believed themselves well equipped to meet whatever challenges the black heroic might bring.

To be sure, in most cases it was hard to get past external appearances. Like the executive secretary whose employment was rumored to depend more on looks than typing skills, the striking physical attributes of these female professionals made one curious to know if their credentials had been obtained through extracurricular means. Take high-priced Manhattan private investigator Angela Harpe, for example. Known in the trade as the Dark Angel (due to a penchant for affixing a decal shaped like a harp-playing member of the heavenly host to the forehead of defeated adversaries), Harpe was an ex-cop who had worked both as a high-fashion model and as a $1,000 per night call girl. Each morning, this extravagant soft-porn fantasy creation of pulp fiction writer James D. Lawrence descended from her luxury apartment in Turtle Bay Towers to confront the workaday world attired in a pricey, yet amazingly skimpy ensemble that would make RuPaul look like Jessica Fletcher. Angie accurately described herself as a "swinging single" who "swung both ways." Her lustrous black hair framed an "elegantly boned sepia face" that always was kept well glossed and shadowed. She had a pair of "breathtaking legs" which could be crossed and recrossed with disturbing effect. Some said her breasts defied containment. In short, Ms. Harpe drove men pop-eyed with lust. This was particularly noticeable when—as happened frequently—the jewelry recovery specialist was forced to flee from criminal pursuers "wearing nothing but a cryptic smile."[177]

It would be easy to underestimate the law-enforcing prowess of such a glamorous figure were it not for the fact that the typical black private investigator was preceded by a reputation for playing hardball with hoodlums. As moviegoers were warned in the theme song from *Sheba, Baby* (1975):

> Don't let her pretty smile fool ya
>
> . . . .
>
> She's a dangerous lady
> And she's well put together
> She's a dangerous lady
> Who can change like the weather
>
> . . . .
>
> You never would believe, how looks can deceive.[178]

By no means "easy," the female crime-fighters were comfortable enough with their sexuality to be feminine and flirtatious but preferred to call the shots when it came to lovemaking. They could be coy: "I know what I've got. If you want it you got to take it. What's the matter, you a faggot?"[179] Or stubborn: "If you're serious, it'll keep."[180] Even downright testy: "Don't race your motor baby. It's not leavin' the garage."[181] What they wouldn't be was sweet-talked, two-timed, or taken for granted.

Nine times out of ten, the female sleuths' sexual aggressiveness was a ploy to distract or disarm their underworld prey. In blaxploitation films such as *Coffy* (1973) and *Foxy Brown* (1974), calculated duplicity of this sort was made child's play by the hormone-driven gullibility of leading lady Pam Grier's crime-boss suitors. Finding the curvaceous undercover operative's call-girl act absolutely irresistible, these slavering thugs thought they had stumbled into some sort of Lotharian paradise—until she cracked them over the head with a bar stool, blew them away with a shotgun blast, or, in one not-to-be-forgotten instance, turned a very surprised crook into an unwilling castrato.

Certainly, with Grier in charge of come-hither strategizing, any battle of the sexes was likely to be over almost before it had begun. In anticipation of "man trouble," she carried a pearl-handled revolver tucked into the considerable expanse of her bra and, if necessary, could make effective MacGyveresque use of stray hairpins and coat hangers. Not even a trace of squeamishness was evidenced when she touched a match to a gas-soaked hoodlum or used a single-engine plane to decapitate a troublesome gangland scumbag. As Foxy Brown's brother Link knowingly remarked after finding himself on the receiving end of one of her more moderate displays of dissatisfaction with men and their low-down ways: "That's my sister, baby, and she's a whole lotta woman."[182]

In displaying a thoroughgoing mastery of numerous traditional tough-guy techniques, detective women revealed the continuing hegemonic influence that masculinist values and norms had on all popular-culture forms. But they also proved themselves to be far more than lust personified. When in a crime-fighting mode, the vivacious, statuesque beauties became door-bursting, law-bending, no-sass-taking action heroes of the first order. Some, like spider-armed karate expert Velvet Smooth, could singlehandedly rout a half dozen street thugs without getting a hair out of place.[183] Others, such as regal, fur-cloaked narcotics agent Cleopatra Jones, proved their mettle in high-speed back-alley car chases—thereby giving new meaning to the term "woman dri-ver."[184] Still others took Diana "T.N.T." Jackson's approach by utilizing stealth and advanced gymnastic skills to scale high walls and drop silently into the soon-to-be-sorry criminal's lair.[185] All seemed eager to join LAPD vice cop Christie Love in using "tough love" to rid black communities of drugs.[186] To-gether, but through separate initiatives, they worked to join oppositional im-ages of African-American women into what, for the times, was a remarkably unified whole.

If neither fully emancipated nor given their rightful due as crime-fighters, it was apparent to all but the most obtuse male chauvinist that these sexy, subver-sive women were hard to pigeonhole and even harder to dismiss. Too tough to be typecast as vacuous sexual foils and too feminine to be considered phallic fe-males, such characters more accurately can be conceptualized as liberated women in training. Convinced that they need be neither harlot nor home-maker in perpetuity, most rejected the notion that women ultimately had to make a choice between being sexual and being assertive, between earning re-spect as a professional and retaining one's dignity and personhood. Alternately seducing and pummeling naysayers into submission, they sought to close the gender gap as it related to heroism. Perhaps it was no-nonsense Chicago private investigator Sheba Shayne who most clearly represented the determination of the group as a whole when she informed skeptics: "I know you think I'm doing a man's job. But I'm not going to sit on the sidelines just because I'm a woman."[187] The firmest feminist friends of such characters hoped to utilize these striking, self-confident role models in deconstructing masculinist dis-course, identifying specifically female realms of experience, and spurring the growth of a multitalented, multidimensional cadre of liberated women who were neither the vehicles of men's fantasies nor the scapegoats of men's fears.[188]

The Action-Adventure Hero: Robert Sand, Black Samurai

The same code of fair competition that opened the ranks of the detective hero to black women also decreed that crumpet-munching, Limey tea-sippers like James Bond no longer would have a monopoly on roles involving interna-tional intrigue, martial arts mayhem, and fab futuristic crime-fighting gadgets.

Pulp fiction heroes Angela Harpe and Robert Sand (author's collection)

During the 1970s, black action-adventure heroes grabbed a major share of this lucrative market for themselves. While they didn't exactly rout Agent 007 and associates from the throne of pop-culture primacy, they made their presence felt. Indeed, by decade's end, George Lazenby—the Australian actor who played Bond in *On Her Majesty's Secret Service* (1969)—could be seen on the back lots of Hollywood, fortunate to have landed a supporting role in a bargain-basement showcase for the black heroic called *The Black Eliminator* (1978).

Among the most noteworthy of these new ethnic champions was an all-purpose righter of wrongs named Robert Sand, a.k.a. the Black Samurai. Played by a lithe but stubbornly expressionless Jim Kelly in the filmic distillation of Marc Olden's popular paperback series, Sand was described as "a one-in-a-million man, capable of fantastic achievements, and so far, unknown to most of the world." To remedy any potentially embarrassing shortfall in the notoriety department, the handsome, hardworking hero spent seven years in Japan under the tutelage of martial arts master Sensei Konuma. Gaining expertise in twenty-six different death-dealing techniques, he became the first non-Japanese samurai warrior. Thereafter, Sand devoted his time and talents to serving "moral right rather than the right made by might."[189]

Like Agent 007, the Black Samurai typically received assignments from a higher authority but exercised considerable individual decision-making power. Not wanting to put his life in the hands of others, he preferred to work alone. Sand's "M" was Mr. Gray, code name for William Baron Clarke, former U.S. president and man with a mission. As a partial "payback" to those who had supported him when in office, the wealthy Texan used his considerable assets and influence to strike down "anyone in the world who had his foot on a little guy's throat." Complementary entities, the chivalric samurai and his modern-day warlord maintained constant vigilance against all "sumbitches" bent on human exploitation and/or world domination.[190]

With this dedicated duo on the job, friends of truth, justice, and the American way had little to fear from white slavers, terrorists, or spies. No known megalomaniac could hope to match the level of concentration, commitment, or expertise which Sand had acquired through his lengthy cross-cultural education. Strict adherence to the oriental warrior's code of conduct meant that both body and mind were kept tuned to absolute perfection, permitting the always "cool," emotionally balanced, "thinking weapon" to be both "dangerous and gentle at the same time, like a sleeping tiger."[191]

If kryptonically disadvantaged and therefore unable to leap tall buildings in a single bound, the trim, muscular Sand nevertheless possessed impressive physical gifts. Whether attired in a $400 custom-made suede sports jacket or the form-fitting black leather "work" outfit which allowed him to blend effortlessly into the night, this was a man capable of doing serious damage to the mortal flesh of evildoers. He really didn't even need his prized twenty-seven-inch *tanto*. The booming "Kiaaai" which immediately preceded delivery of a series of bruising karate moves was enough to cause most crooks to get religion fast. The Black Samurai executed front-thrust kicks with the force of a speeding truck and could deliver four powerhouse punches from his "twin speeding pistons" in three seconds flat. On a good day, he could burst steel chain like a string of beads. Taught that there could be "no weakness in war," he saw nothing wrong about making an enemy's skull collapse "as though a melon had been thrown against a brick wall."[192]

More than just a bruiser, Sand was mentally tough. Konuma's training (in total darkness, hands tied, supplemented with meditation and fasting) had both sharpened his senses and taught him how to conquer fear and pain. Indeed, a battery of internal signals flashed whenever samurai instinct warned that danger was near. At least as useful in the adventure hero trade as his cannon-equipped sports car or strap-on jet flying pack, these sensory and mind-control techniques conferred the ability to (1) sniff out clues like a bloodhound, (2) read intent (malicious or otherwise) in a passing glance, (3) commit massive amounts of data to memory, and (4) remain stoic under conditions of extreme duress. In addition, Sand always made good use of plain old common sense—for example, checking into more than one room or hotel under several different assumed names when on assignment. Not surprisingly, the outwitted, outmaneuvered criminals wondered aloud whether they weren't, in fact, fighting "a handful of black smoke."[193]

If discipline and skill made Robert Sand a good samurai, it often was his race that determined specific work assignments. By virtue of his blackness, Sand maintained certain tactical advantages over melanin-deprived action-adventure heroes. It was said that societal assumptions about the relationship between skin color and mental ability led some whites to underestimate his intellect—thereby giving the black champion an important edge whenever dealing with those to whom he seemed no more than "a little colored boy just trying to get by."[194] However, possession of a somewhat dusky visage did more than make him "invisible" among bigoted white people. It also facilitated un-trammeled mobility within African-American communities and gave Sand special insight into those social factors which most tellingly influenced black criminal behavior.

Nevertheless, as befits a complex, well-traveled hero schooled in the belief that "ability has responsibility" and dedicated to a purpose beyond the self, Sand opted not to colorize his crime-fighting credo. The Black Samurai was an equal opportunity enforcer of a universally applicable morality. After escaping certain death for the umpteenth time in a single day, he might quip that "black cats have nine lives," but there would be no laxity or leniency in dealing with African-American miscreants. In fact, some of his fanciest martial arts foot-work was done to protect society-at-large from "super badass" black villains like Dessalines, mentally unstable head of a California-based terrorist organi-zation known as the Inquisition, and Pearl, pimpdom's most cold-blooded "lord of lust."[195]

Sand took considerable pleasure in bringing to justice those black social bandits who, had it been *their* movie or novel, likely would have been consid-ered heroes. This one-upsmanship was practiced neither for ego enhancement nor for purposes of professional advancement but to help resolve the issue of "whether or not anybody in the world had the right to grind anyone else's face in the dirt for their own fun and profit." He saw nothing heroic in self-aggrandizement, no ennobling challenge in causing human suffering. If, on occasion, the media were duped into treating hurtful, power-hungry black charlatans as heroic figures, a wise samurai knew better. Their false altruism, pained professions of principled activism, and "stiff third-world rhetoric" evidenced little more than studied duplicity or confused morality. It was, Sand asserted, a serious mistake to consider such conscienceless characters as anything other than "vicious and basically stupid, but still dangerous as hell."[196]

Educated in a nontraditional, multicultural environment and teamed with a wealthy member of the white establishment, Robert Sand possessed exceptional credentials in the mediational sciences. In addition to bridging the tortuous gap separating fiction and film, Olden's black-clad crime-fighter unified key mental and physical elements of classical heroic portraiture—thereby discrediting the notion that African-American protagonists were, by definition, all brawn and no brains. Moreover, in judging evil irrespective of race, he evidenced both physical courage and the courage of his expansive, life-affirming convictions. With an idealism that was both self-willed and fueled by contemporary events, Sand assumed that evenhanded enforcement of just legal codes by principled champions of color would result in a better world for all. For such a cultural mediator to believe otherwise would have seemed a coward's capitulation to the very forces of selfishness and spiritual darkness he had sworn to destroy.

The Extralegals: Vigilantes and Rogue(ish) Cops

Black police detectives, private investigators, and action-adventure heroes plied their trade in a moral shadowland. Here, on occasion, it was deemed necessary to modify or disregard established procedures lest one become hamstrung by outdated, inflexible legal codes. Black vigilantes and rogue cops took this free-form brand of crime fighting to its logical extreme. Seemingly determined to step outside the law as often as possible, some were too idealistic (or pigheaded) to be constrained by imposed guidelines of any sort. This was especially true if such rules conflicted with a personal sense of honor or obligation. Others may not necessarily have been beacons of disinterested morality but nevertheless could cite the day and hour when they first realized that white America's oft manipulated tools of governance failed to meet black needs. Thereafter, they would operate on the assumption that full and equal justice for African-Americans was never a foregone conclusion. In circumventing or short-circuiting the system, the black heroes hoped to punish both those responsible for and those who benefited from its corruptions and make manifest a more perfect justice, a more functional and fully inclusive world order. Having journeyed full circle, these fictional and theatrical representatives of the vigilante archetype knew the world of crime inside and out. They were in a perfect position to mediate the social distance between outlaw and law enforcer. Fortunately, during the 1960s and 1970s, many within their roguish ranks also found time to provide mainstream observers with a sampling of the group's largely critical, decidedly pessimistic views on the viability of American legal institutions. However unpleasant, white folks needed to have access to such information if they were to understand and appreciate the attraction of Black Camelot.

The black vigilantes of popular culture were just like your next-door neighbor—that is, if your neighbor happened to own a closet full of assault rifles, frolicked frequently with scantily clad supermodels, and was prone to issuing ultraprickly declarations such as "Kiss my ass, honkey faggot" or "*You* can eat the crap they dish out, but not *this* baby!"[197] Having no official ties to law enforcement agencies, such characters felt little need to toe the line of propriety in either jurisdictional or procedural matters. More often than not, their conscience served as ultimate guide and defender.

Drawn from the ranks of community activists, returned Vietnam veterans, ex-offenders, and plain ol' buffed-out macho dudes, vigilantes were Everymen whose life's work was to protect their black brothers from insidious and otherwise overpowering forces. Most were proactive and sought to discourage crime in black neighborhoods. Creators of the prototypical urban vigilante film, *Black Samson* (1974), even had their soft-spoken but superstrong nightclub-owner protagonist patrolling the mean streets of south central Los Angeles nightly—walking stick in hand and pet lion at the ready—to get this salient point across. Working long hours to even the odds that a corrupt, racially biased legal system had tipped in favor of evildoers, such stalwart enforcers of "the people's law" were, as argot-rich ads proclaimed, "Every Brother's Friend. Every Mother's Enemy."[198] Vigilant vigilantes put both black and white scofflaws on notice that *their* adjudication of inner-city disputes would be swift, sure, and without the slightest possibility of appeal.

But, try as they might, these self-sacrificing, socially conscious sorts never seemed able to stop local lowlifes from bumping off a favorite relative or selling overdose-inducing quantities of heroin to some little kid down at the schoolyard. Not even the sternest of warnings ("Honky, look out. Hassle a brother and the Black Six will return!") could stem the criminal tide or dissuade white hoods from asking foolish questions like "Who do you think you are, nigger?"[199] Some people just had to learn the hard way—via a powerhouse jab to the jaw, a strategically placed dynamite blast, or, as in Samson's case, a grassroots uprising in which the wrathful, newly energized citizenry joined their local hero in a celebratory subduing of neighborhood predators.

Closely related to these do-it-yourself law enforcers was a group of private eyes who had become famous for their statute-skirting approach to crime fighting. Vigilante investigators like the cigar-puffing, cognac-drinking Sam Kelly were fond of face-to-face intimidation ("I haven't killed anyone today, Carlos, and I need the practice"), but they also loved to spread nasty rumors about themselves.[200] For example, only intimates knew the real story, but it was rumored widely that J. F. Burke's fictional sleuth regularly broke the law big time in order to combat crime in his West Side, New York City, neighborhood.

On one occasion, he was said to have rescued call girls from their exploitative whoremaster by turning a gun on the creep, shoving him into a taxi on its way to Roosevelt Hospital, and working him over en route. By the time they had reached the emergency room, the cabbie had the pimp's wallet, Kelly had his satisfaction, and the unfortunate procurer had a gouged eye, a broken jaw, and a cracked spine. The cowed, crumpled criminal limped out of town shortly after an official police investigation of the incident determined that absolutely no one was willing to testify against Kelly.[201]

Then there was the time the body of a much arrested but never convicted rapist was found on the roof of a brownstone adjacent to the seedy residential hotel Sam Kelly called home. Local wags said that their neighborhood avenging angel had become increasingly frustrated by the justice system's inability to keep this particular vermin off the streets. He claimed that the cops "couldn't collar a kid for stealing apples." Therefore, instead of waiting for yet another brutal attack to occur, he decided to expedite matters by taking the case "under advisement." After spotting the man in the hotel one evening, Kelly invited him to go for a brief stroll—at gunpoint, off the roof, seventeen floors up.[202]

Whether the black detective truly was responsible for these and other acts of vigilantism remained a matter of much conjecture. But the likelihood that he was, indeed, the Needle Park Avenger caused hooligans from the Bronx, Brooklyn, and the Lower East Side to think twice about plying their trade in Kelly's bailiwick. As Burke noted, his hero's trademark straw boater always was "a welcome sight to those who had no reason to fear him." And those who had reason "learned to stay out of his way."[203]

Duly appointed law enforcers weren't particularly fond of Kelly. Neither did they have much use for no-nonsense soulmates Jesse Crowder (whose theme song contained the haunting refrain, "He just don't give an inch, not even in a pinch"), Big Bull Benson ("not an easy man to like. . . . not an easy man to push around"), or Hawk (sensitive white guy detective Spenser's freelancing "leg-breaker" assistant and proverbial "dark side"). These hard cases were famous for concealing information, carrying unregistered weapons, and consorting with known criminals. They were, said one peeved lieutenant, "no better than the scum we pull in here every day," just luckier.[204] Officers who operated by the book considered them too independent, too impudent, too inexplicably well informed. Rogue cops considered them the competition.

During the 1960s and 1970s, urban station houses served as headquarters for a number of black public servants who exhibited various bad-guy tendencies.

If not all quite as attracted to self-aggrandizement as Terence Sneed, the "certified grade-A 100 percent crooked cop" played with smart-aleck abandon by Billy Dee Williams in *The Take* (1974), such characters always seemed ready to participate in an unauthorized caper.[205] Some weren't terribly fussy about which side of the law was upheld—as long as their own needs could be met.

As was the case with community-oriented vigilantes, the motivation for this extraordinary extralegal behavior sometimes came from personal rage. In *Hit!* (1973), for example, when his teenage daughter died from a drug overdose, federal agent Nick Allen (Billy Dee Williams) pulled out all the stops. Realizing that the wheels of justice ground far too slowly, he moved the case to the fast track by recruiting his own commando team from the detritus of the ex-offender subculture. Needless to say, despite his department's discouragement of the project, the *really bad* guys were disposed of with great—and bloody—dispatch. In the end, no one complained.[206]

A marvelously quirky, colorful character created by screen- and crime-fiction writer George Baxt proved that passion and ego also could move a detective hero to bend the law to his own purposes. Considered "a bit of an enigma" by almost everyone, jive-talking Pharoah Love was a self-proclaimed "seven-day-wonder" at solving crimes. Proud to be moving through the ranks "on [his] own steam," he was eager to win accolades from his superiors so that he could be "up there with the rest of them snotty ofay detective cats." Unfortunately, Love's climb up the career ladder hit a snag when he was sent before the police review board for suppressing evidence in a murder case involving his male lover, novelist Seth Piro. Although vowing to kill anyone who tried to hurt Seth, the black detective eventually chose to switch rather than fight. After resigning from the force and undergoing a sex-change operation, he emerged as the Tara Club's saucy, masked chanteuse, Ocelot. Love's new lynx-taloned gloves and neck-to-toe ocelot leotard (with neophallic tail) was all too appropriate garb for a onetime crime-fighting wiz who elected to pervert justice when it came into conflict with his personal sexual agenda. As he once advised his protégé, a similarly insubordinate black cop named Satan Stagg, "Never go against your better judgment, cat. And follow through, regardless of what them higher-ups tell you. Once you start groveling in the face of authority, you are no longer your own man."[207]

Race—and racism—also were factors in determining a black cop's ultimate loyalties. Ed Lacy's babyfaced detective, Lee Hayes, was a particularly astute observer of these complex "internal affairs" issues. Described as an "angry young man—brown variety," the college-educated NYPD veteran was "smart and cool" but had an "absolutely fascinating sullen side, like a young tough." The warring elements of Hayes's personality were kept in near constant turmoil by the fact that he was the lone black detective in his squad. Although treated fairly by both his superior officers and his quiet, studious partner, Al Kahn, Hayes was troubled by the "forced politeness" many white liberals exhibited when interacting with "children and Negroes." He resented being selected for certain "sensitive" undercover assignments because of his race and sometimes felt that promotions would have come much more easily had he not so closely resembled the perpetrators he was duty bound to bring to the bar of justice. White people, he mused, never realized how insulting they could be.[208]

These feelings of anger and ambivalence were only made worse by his undercover work in Harlem. Reared in a predominantly white environment in Delaware, the black cop found the scene at Lenox and 129th both alien and depressing. Not unlike an out-of-town tourist, he always made "doubly sure" his car was locked when parked on the street and often remarked that he felt "more of an outsider here than Al." Made claustrophobic by the ghetto's dreary atmosphere of "misery and indifference" and taken aback by its residents' seemingly "stagnant and meaningless" lives, Hayes could not rid himself of what he termed "the fink feeling." Wasn't he simply an Uncle Tom spying on his own people?[209]

In working through these thorny matters, Hayes never resorted to unbecoming conduct. Believing retaliatory violence of any kind to be self-defeating—"a fast cop-out"—his was a more cerebral rebellion. Despite the fact that the black detective had to be taught the meaning of the three-fingered Watts "burn, baby, burn" salute, he understood the frustrations of those suffering from "ghetto fatigue." To Hayes, Black Power meant dignity and black pride, not rioting. However, when pressed on the issue, he could be downright incendiary. "They call Negroes lawless," he raged on one occasion. "Considering all the stuff we've put up with, we're so damn lawabiding it's frightening! . . . Perhaps the only way to shake up the whites is with a small taste of the same stupid violence we Negroes have been subjected to all our lives." At such times, Hayes revealed both his true colors and his mediational technique. Desperately seeking an antidote to latent Tomishness, he adopted the inclusive black "we" and assumed the persona of a roguish infiltrator of the white law enforcement community. He questioned its business-as-usual mind-set and criticized its leaders for ignoring the increasingly insistent voice of black activists. "We have a program," he said, proselytizing. "Let us decide our own destiny. In many Deep South areas whites are only a minority, yet they control their destiny. Why can't we?"[210] Other dissembling detectives may have been more flamboyant in their display of subversiveness, but Lee Hayes added depth, texture, and a sobering jolt of reality to the archetype. Rather than focusing on superficial Tomish tendencies, perhaps it would be more accurate to conceptualize this particular crime-fighter as an angry black man in blue, engaged in a dangerous caper, spying on the white establishment.

A Community of Cops and Crooks

Considered as a group, the Shafts, Coffys, Grave Diggers, Samurais, and Samsons of the 1960s and 1970s gave new meaning to the tie-dyed maxim "what goes around comes around." Influenced greatly by their times, even the most straight-laced crime-fighter could not help but reflect something of the social bandits' subversive rascality, their aversion to external constraints, and their rootedness in the community of beleaguered black folk. With remarkable ease, daring detective types made a grand display of both their psychologically liberated "race man" credentials and their commitment to bridging gaps, straightening angles, and patching cracks in the nation's popular-culture superstructure. Neither dupes nor sellouts, such characters often served as much needed mediators in the matters of race, gender, socioeconomic status, and cultural convention; between the law of the jungle and the law of the land. This fact did nothing to diminish their heroic character. Indeed, such herculean efforts only served to increase an already evident pan-racial attractiveness.

In like manner, members of theatrical and fictional social-bandit clusters revealed that they were not totally bereft of leadership skills or of desirable personality traits such as nobility, courage, compassion, and vision. Despite their contentious, turf-claiming nature, neither were they at all times averse to seeking common objectives or to serving as intermediaries between African- and European-American viewing publics. To be sure, their message was iconoclastic; their manner often insistently in-your-face. But, given the nation's history of turning a deaf ear to minority group claims and concerns, this important missive regarding black America's capacity for self-directed, heroic endeavor was a most difficult one to get across—the ultimate hard sell. As both verbal warning shot and motivational technique, straight talk developed according to accredited guidelines and delivered at attention-getting volume was wholly warranted.

Together, the two groups of pugnacious peers formed a rough-and-tumble community whose aggressively competitive nature belied an underlying agreement on fundamentals. Each, in their own way, forwarded a race-specific image of confidence, competence, and concern for community uplift. Unintimidated by White Power and blessed with oversized egos, they had little trouble conceptualizing themselves as superior to white culture heroes on all counts. Most also seemed to possess a keen historical sense and considerable training in mass-marketing stratagems. With an eye to approximating more familiar portrayals of their specific heroic archetype, African-American cops and crooks learned from Sweet Sweetback, but their creators were judicious enough to also endow them with a touch of Humphrey Bogart, a bit of John

Wayne, and a pinch of Buck Rogers. Although sometimes obscured by first-take cinematography or second-rate prose, many of these attractive, larger-than-life characters were of page-turning, theater-filling caliber. They spoke volumes about the possibilities of blackness and did so in a language that was familiar to everyone.

Undoubtedly, when the average American of the post-JFK era attended a Saturday afternoon matinee or spent an evening curled up with a detective novel, he or she anticipated nothing more than the prospect of being entertained. This is but a half-truth. While there were no recipes for tolerance building printed on the back of a box of munchies, no social-IQ enhancer in a moviehouse Coke, regular consumption of black heroic imagery could be both entertaining and enlightening. Even snack-sized portions held the potential to make one more aware of the fact that all blood and guts spill out the same and that bad eggs can come from anywhere in the carton. To those adept at reading encoded messages, the black stars of popular culture brought key bits of wisdom about the universality of heroism. Speaking to the need for improvements in the quality of cross-cultural discourse, they also suggested that opportunities existed for increased, nonadversarial interaction between the nation's segmented social constituencies. Certainly, this was valuable, supremely relevant information—and not a bad payback for the time spent with a quick read or a ninety-minute technicolor thriller. No wonder blaxploitation films and pulp fiction potboilers are considered guilty pleasures.

FIVE

Black Musical Mediators as Culture Heroes

Our purpose is to educate as well as to entertain.

CURTIS MAYFIELD OF THE IMPRESSIONS

Blacks and whites were making efforts to change things, and music
helped bridge the gaps.

MARY WILSON OF THE SUPREMES

Working in tandem with the blaxploitation and pulp fiction heroes, African-American musicians participated in a variety of pop-cultural bridge-building projects during the 1960s and 1970s—providing, as it were, a star-studded soundtrack for circumventing convention and celebrating diversity. To be sure, almost all had forgotten the words to "Dixie." The vast majority conscientiously refused to "Jump Jim Crow." But a significant number saw nothing wrong with adding versions of "Say It Loud—I'm Black and I'm Proud," "We Are Family," *and* "Let's Work Together" to their repertoire. These performers were well suited to playing the part of confident, race-conscious cultural mediators.

Equally commodity and art form, the music which this varied lot of singers and strummers created can tell us a great deal about time, place, and perception. Like most musical formulations, the black pop, soul, jazz, gospel, and blues of these years was capable of entertaining and providing release from everyday tensions, expressing ideas and emotions not normally revealed in ordinary discourse, designating class and defining (or attributing) good and evil, and either validating or critiquing prevailing social mores. As analysts of expressive cultural forms have noted, such music provides "a credible metaphor of the real"—that is, a sociocultural mirror that tuned-in scholars may then utilize to study the "audible waveband of the vibrations and signs that make up society."[1]

Like a Camelotian herald's clarion call, music also can be employed to announce imminent changes in established patterns of belief and behavior. Certainly, if some types of music are well suited to soothing savage beasts, others seem designed to create them—driving dance hall devotees to feverish frenzies of activism or rage. At such times, this normally nonthreatening form of interpersonal communication becomes decidedly political. Faster than Jumpin' Jack Flash, its cleverly encoded messages begin to stir the latent psychic energies of listeners. Such consciousness-raising may assist music lovers in formulating new identities in times of great social change. Under the right circumstances, subversive musical missives may even spur efforts to transform or overturn existing societal institutions.[2]

Clearly, music is a many splendored thing. It can wound or heal; anesthetize or invigorate; support or challenge hegemonic power; draw us together or drive us apart. As creator, facilitator, and disseminator of this dynamic cultural force, the musician's potential for leaving a recognizable mark on the contested terrain of mass culture is great—arguably far greater than most casual listeners imagine. Throughout American history, the cross-cultural, pan-oceanic range and influence of these energetic musical heroes have been nothing short of amazing. White and black alike, these heroes have repeatedly stepped up to the microphone to serenade us with seductive, personalized visions of self and society. And, like moth to flame, we come under their spell. As pop-culture conduits for the circulation of essential wisdom about our ever changing world, the sly songsters encourage their fans to sample new ideas, to expand limited horizons, and to confront deep-seated fears. Certainly, this is one of the culture heroes' time-honored tasks—to help lesser mortals grapple with matters too problematic or too painful to approach alone.

Black music's earliest heroic helpmeets were the slave "musicianers." Serving as entertainers, teachers, and transmitters of African-American folk culture, these versatile instrumentalists could be found at white dances, parties, and militia musters as well as at almost any slave quarter frolic. Fiddlers and banjoists attracted the most attention, but those skilled at "patting juba" (a syncopated hand-clapping, body-slapping, foot-tapping accompaniment to song) or playing "quills" (a collection of one-note reed flutes of various lengths bound together to form an instrument) had their devoted fans as well. If performed with sufficient artistry and alacrity, the musicianer's jigs, reels, minuets, and cotillions could earn an otherwise unexceptional field hand a reputation for improvisational excellence that extended far beyond the boundaries of his "home" plantation.[3] To cite one well-known example, violinist Solomon Northup was recognized throughout Louisiana's Red River cane-growing region as "the Ole Bull of Bayou Boeuf." Various small gratuities, greater geographic mobility, a sense of personal accomplishment, and enhanced self-esteem (which Northup revealed was essential to enduring "long years of bondage" under "a hard master") were the star instrumentalist's rewards.[4]

A slave vocalist's highest honor was to be elected to the post of "corn gen-

Slave musicianer inciting a frolic (J. Thornton Randolph, *The Cabin and Parlor; or, Slaves and Masters* [Philadelphia: T. B. Peterson, 1852])

eral." The central figures of competitive neighborhood corn-shucking jubilees throughout the plantation South, these proud cocks of the corn pile were selected by their fellow bondsmen from among those (typically) male members of the slave community who possessed a powerful voice and were known to be "original" and "amusing." Ascending to their place of preeminence atop a pile of unshucked ears, the general would lead his work team in a spirited call-and-response recitative which drew upon songs traditionally associated with the festive event. As he skillfully ordered the laborers' movements through this leader-chorus interplay, he passed the jug around and cheered them on to new corn-shucking heights with encouraging remarks such as, "That's the lick, little Ellick!" "You can beat your daddy, young York," or "Gentlemen, just look at big Frank!" Sometimes, a particularly nimble (or inebriated) general would fall to his knees while "giving out," clap his hands above his head, and sway rhythmically to the antiphony—much like an early James Brown. Then, after the corn was shucked and he had recovered from this music-induced ecstasy, the general would assemble his "army" for an equally energetic assault upon the waiting harvest table. As master of ceremonies, he might direct the servers, organize various races and games, or play the fiddle or banjo as the slaves danced far into the night. Surely, noted white observers, on such occasions, the black corn general seemed no less than "monarch of all he surveyed."[5]

In more northerly, urbanized environs, African-American musicians performed at "Pinkster" (Pentecost Sunday) festivals and strutted their stuff in colorful "Negro Election Day" parades.[6] Here, the raucous merrymaking was fueled by frenzy-inducing fiddlers like Narragansett's Polydor Gardiner and by dance-aholic drummers such as Jackey Quackenboss of Albany—who was said to have driven female spectators to distraction with his lusty thumping and the "ever-wild, though euphonic cry of 'Hi-a-bomba, bomba, bomba.'"[7] By the time of the Civil War, these earthy, amateur sensations were joined by a number of decidedly more mannered touring professionals: "The Black Swan" (ex-slave soprano Elizabeth Taylor Greenfield), "Blind Tom, the Marvellous Musical Prodigy" (Thomas Greene Bethune), and the singing Shakespearean tragedian Ira Aldridge.[8] The cross-cultural acclaim which greeted these talents, both great and small, boded well for the future of African-American musical performance.

Postbellum legatees of the early black musicians could be found crooning, swooning, and hamming it up on the minstrel and vaudeville stage. Greatly attracted to the spotlight—wherever it might shine—they thrived as Jubilee Singers, as cakewalking composers of the controversial coon songs, and as Ragtime's popular piano-tinkling "professors." Both in the cabaret and on Broadway, talented black folk contributed greatly to the development of twentieth-century musical styles such as boogie-woogie (Jimmy Yancey, Meade Lux Lewis, Cow Cow Davenport), rhythm and blues (Louis Jordan, Ray Charles, Willie Mae "Big Mama" Thornton), doo-wop (the Ravens, Orioles, Flamingos, and other avian-oriented aggregations), gospel (Thomas A. Dorsey, Mahalia Jackson), pop (Nat "King" Cole, Dinah Washington, Sam Cooke), and rock 'n' roll (Chuck Berry, Bo Diddley, Little Richard).[9]

But nowhere were black contributions to pre-1960s popular arts more evident than in the field of jazz. Rooted in and uniquely expressive of the

African-American experience, jazz—as noted by entertainment industry in-siders—"caught on with Caucasians" during the early 1920s.[10] In remarkably short order it was recognized as one of the most engaging, most marketable symbols of U.S. culture worldwide. This vital musical force with the novel rhythmic swing and penchant for spontaneous improvisation held special at-traction for those alienated from (and in revolt against) the core values of a highbrow-dominated mainstream. Within this multiracial group, black musi-cians were major players in both the sociodrama and public ritual of the day and were held up as exemplars of subversive behavior and belief, of hip talk and funky fashion statements. Paradoxically, for many they represented the deli-ciously unattainable exotic *and* provided what seemed a viable mechanism for effecting cross-cultural integration and societal change. In many respects, the colorful jazzmen and -women served as pulsing, polyrhythmic prototypes of the black musician-mediators of 1960–80.

Part of a broad continuum of African-American music that originated in slave era field hollers and spirituals, jazz journeyed north from the Storyville district of New Orleans with World War I era migrants and found a new home-away-from-home in urban clubs, theaters, and dance halls. Here, on any given evening, the tremendous attractive power of the music could be seen in the crush of cool cats and red-hot mamas streaming down Chicago's 35th Street or queued up outside Harlem's Lafayette and Apollo Theaters. Increasingly, they were supplemented by white cultural tourists, whose joyous, expectant pil-grimage to a black-and-tan dance hall or special "midnight ramble" held at an all-black club provided what one African-American commentator described as "a balm for modern ennui," a "safety valve for modern machine-ridden and convention-bound society."[11] By 1938, an estimated half a million "serious jazz fanciers" prowled these ethnic enclaves in search of invigorating, sepia-toned spectacle.[12]

If jazz (or jaz, jasz, or jass as early writers would have it) was viewed by fans as infectious, instinctive, and accessible, critics could perceive only cultural peril in the music's lightly propulsive, downbeat-driven form. It was, they said, "retrogression," a return to the "tomtom beating of savages." Dismissed as "trash" played with teeth-grating dissonance by "incompetents" wielding "lowbrow instruments," the new music was held to promote immodest dress and loose sex, to increase alcohol and drug consumption, and to create a gen-eral disregard for self-discipline, order, and authority. "Jazz," opined the de-fenders of decorum, appealed primarily to "the lover of sensuous and debasing emotions." Surely, no true connoisseur of the classics could abide its unrefined squeaks, squawks, and moans—its "savage crash and bang."[13]

Perhaps not. However, despite these determined displays of disapproval, jazz simply wouldn't go away. For some, this unnerving persistence in the face of a veritable avalanche of admonitions to "proper" taste and behavior was the jazz artists' worst offense. Having put the sin back in syncopation, these swinging sensualists seemed hell-bent on spreading their debased music and lifestyle beyond the speakeasy, over the airwaves, and into people's tidy, still Victorian homes.

For fans of the new music, the jazzmen and -women were godlike beings, wholly unrelated to the clay-footed, stick-in-the-mud provincials who were seeking to maintain the supremacy of their mannered, self-conscious, and all-too-"serious" musical entertainments. Far from being lawless spirits, they were perceived as charismatic, shamanlike mediums through whom the deity transmitted bits of infinite wisdom to humankind. Like true demigods, they often were credited with the possession of mystical knowledge, magical powers, and gargantuan appetites. Distinguished by their capacity to evoke ecstasy, a willingness to speak for the inarticulate, and the uncommon ability to radiate immediacy and glamour even while remaining inscrutably enigmatic, jazz artists provided inspirational models for transcending worldly concerns through musical flights of fancy.[14] Bathed in the supernatural aura of a King Oliver, Louis Armstrong, or Charlie Parker, admirers could, themselves, feel larger than life.

Remarkably, the musical heroes' mystical powers also enabled them to transmogrify into ordinary human beings with the greatest of ease. Indeed, had the jazz artist without flaw, fault, or blemish been asked to toss the first stone, it is likely that the sacred rock pile would have remained untouched. Fans rationalized the culture heroes' addictions and failures by noting the magnitude of their struggles against "bad luck and trouble" and by countering tales of transgressions with accounts highlighting their generous spirits and transcendent geniuses. Instead of dwelling on a musician's failings, they recalled joyous joint ventures in making the good times roll. These memorable exchanges occurred as performer and patron rubbed elbows in the dark, cozy confines of a cabaret or joined in devouring bootleg liquor and fried fish at a private, late-night rent party. Here, the intimacy of the venue combined with the music's inherent spontaneity to create an interactive, mutually supportive, and potentially liberating—if somewhat loud and smoke-filled—environment.[15] In this fashion, both jazz artists and their followers contributed to the ongoing democratization of American cultural forms.

Otherworldly, yet approachable, jazzmen were born trendsetters. Whether it was derbies, canes, and double-breasted overcoats embellished with bright silk handkerchiefs or berets, dark shades, and wide-lapeled pin-striped suits, the style of dress popularized by individual heroes was imitated widely. Curiously enough, the most slavish copycats were to be found among those who went to the greatest lengths in personalizing their appearance so as not to be mistaken for "squares." For example, when Charlie "Bird" Parker appeared in a rumpled suit, aspiring alto saxophonists did likewise. "Fellows would take their good clothes and roll them up into a ball to get them creased, because they saw Bird walking around in a suit he had long forgotten to have pressed," recalled bassist Buddy Jones. It became, he noted, quite preposterous.[16] In some cases, hard-core jazz sectarians seeking to emulate their favorites created a subculture of learned behavior that nonbelievers considered facile and faddish.

Flattery through imitation also was apparent in the utilization of the jazzman's colorfully creative (and constantly changing) in-house argot. Within hours of converting to their hero's musical faith, disciples could be overheard verbalizing hard-to-express emotions in the musician's preferred vocational idiom. To daddy-o's and chicks who were "fly" (meaning in the know), "cool" equaled "hot." "Tight" could be "tough" but rarely "uncomfortable." "Bread" was to be spent and not eaten. "Dirty" and "low-down" were deemed enviable—even supernal—states of being. Confusing matters further, advanced students of jazz-speak often opted to insinuate the all-purpose punctuation mark "like" into every third sentence.[17]

As was the case with other types of culture heroes, the jazz artists' idiosyncratic style was both enhanced and adulterated through increased contact with the entertainment mainstream. Promoters and managers made the most colorful and talented of their charges into nationally prominent personalities while phonograph records, radio, and sound motion pictures expanded the influence of jazz style far beyond the gritty urban tenderloin. But popularity had its price. As the music was packaged and marketed to a more diverse audience, tempos slowed, repertoires were broadened, and orchestras began to overshadow small bands and combos.[18] Even as they put gifted African-American performers such as Billie Holiday, Lionel Hampton, and Charlie Christian in the spotlight, white bandleaders like Benny Goodman "cleaned up" the jazz experience to make it more palatable to middle-class tastes. Before long, whites were reaping the bulk of the financial rewards garnered from extensive radio exposure and easy access to prestigious performance space. Some, like Goodman—"The King of Swing"—were accorded honorific titles which, in a perfect world, would have gone to a black pioneer like Fletcher Henderson. Posing little threat to the male bandleader's stage supremacy, distaff-side talent was thought to lack the physical stamina required for playing wind instruments. As a result, most were relegated to nonregal supporting roles as party-dressed pianists or torchy "chirpers."[19]

But be not dismayed. Black America still had its dukes, counts, and queens. And it was the privilege and burden of this musical royal family to ensure that jazz remained attractive both to its original audience and to fresh-faced newcomers. Thus, even as millions of tinny-sounding 78s were "integrating" middle-class living rooms of the 1930s, 1940s, and 1950s, African-American culture heroes were hard at work seeking to preserve the music's unique character—its essence of blackness. Whether showcased in film, fiction, art, poetry, or dance, celebratory presentations of the jazz world and its key operatives brought acclaim to the jazzmen and jazzwomen and convinced many formerly bebop-bereft Americans that both black art and black artists could compete successfully in the rapidly expanding commercial entertainment arena.

At times, it seemed as if the swingin', swayin' jazzmen were everywhere. Despite the National Association of Dancing Masters' fervent entreaties against stepping the light fantastic to "cheap jazz music," dance halls of the 1930s teemed with lindy-hopping, turkey-trotting, bunny-hugging couples frantically striving to keep pace with bandsmen who seemed to play faster and faster as the evening progressed.[20] Making good on management promises to regale patrons with "a barrage of the most electrifying spasms of entertainment ever assembled under one roof," leaders of these spirited musical aggregations snorted, stomped, and finger-popped to the Big Beat.[21] As they joined in riotous eurhythmic communion with the acrobatic dervishes assembled before their ballroom bandstand throne, jitterbugging jazzmen became central figures in a public rite which rescued countless middle-class Americans from the depths of kinesthetic and spiritual lassitude—a debilitating condition commonly found within populations subjected to a steady diet of waltzes and fox-trots.

These pied pipers of the black heroic also were well represented in the visual arts. They could be found mugging, grinning, and dancing the night away in the iconographic art of Aaron Douglas and Palmer Hayden, in James Van Der Zee photographs, and in numerous Hollywood films.[22] From 1930s Vitaphone shorts to World War II era jukebox "soundies" to musical documentaries like *Satchmo the Great* (1956), jazzmen hi-de-hoed their way into viewers' hearts with soundstage approximations of their most outrageous clubland performances. Even in cameo—or as atmospheric backdrop—the black musicians tantalized both African- and European-American audiences, leaving them with an insatiable craving for more, more, more of the magical, mystical, musical exotica.

The jazzmen and jazzwomen were equally charismatic on paper. Literary and poetic depictions of big-city club life interpreted and extended the musical idiom, thereby revealing this diverse, performance-oriented community's characteristic complexity. Some were visionaries and dreamers whose job it was to impose order on "the roar rising from the void . . . as it hits the air." Others seemed more like improvisational gamblers who were willing to risk all so that the "unnamable truth of music . . . might happen."[23] Among their number were young men with brassy, phallic horns and "patent-leathered" hair whose remarkable talents led them "right up to the place where genius and madness grapple before going their separate ways";[24] cigar-smoking "Wahoo wildhouse Piany" players who walloped the ivories with such force and abandon that observers couldn't help but liken them to the "furtive madman" of far saner times;[25] "barbaric, yet beautiful" songbirds known to be equally adept at charming male fans and at holding their own in knock-down drag-out fights with jealous wives and girlfriends;[26] lanky, sax-toting rebels with pencil-thin moustaches and suede shoes who possessed the rare ability to "stir the imagination deeply and uncomfortably";[27] and a multitude of others, both old and young, sharp-dressed and soup-stained, whose "marvelous, frightening" stage presence dropped jaws, loosened ties, and set arms and legs flailing in imperfect but enthusiastic emulation of their heroes.[28] Individually and collectively, they battled heroin, hard liquor, clinging camp followers, and white patrons eager to call "certain Negroes" their friends. Gifted with the "intense emotional energy so peculiar to his race," a skilled jazzman was deemed capable of convincing even the most cloistered, bookish literati to "revel in colour and noise and rhythm"—to abandon themselves totally and enter into an amatory state of transcendence over all that was mundane in modern American life.[29]

If still a tad too worldly-wise for some, by the 1960s, jazzmen were well known for the manner in which their life-enhancing musical constructions nourished what poet Langston Hughes termed the "shining rivers of the soul."[30] During that decade and the one which followed, hipster heroes expanded their agenda by addressing issues of political, as well as spiritual, liberation. An abrasive counterpoint to jazz classicism and the canonical constraints of harmony, time signature, and song form, the shrieks, squawks, wails, and gurgles of "free-jazz" stylists such as Ornette Coleman and Cecil Taylor mirrored societal discontent with the race relations status quo. Conceptualizing their densely textured compositions both as a form of social protest and as a mechanism for the enhancement of black self-awareness, this black musical avant-garde sought to "take the music away from the people who control it."[31] They launched spirited protests to get more jazz played on network TV, memorialized black nationalist heroes in song, and dismissed the contributions of white "imitators" as lacking in creativity. Self-proclaimed "angry young men," the black musicians told all who would listen that music was a tool of liberation and that it was the jazzman's destiny to free America "aesthetically and socially from its inhumanity."[32]

Unfortunately, theirs was a music of limited appeal. More often heard in coffeehouses, small theaters, and art galleries than on the radio, free jazz lacked the broad-based constituency of earlier, more swinging (if less socially conscious) variants. Moreover, proponents of "freedom music" had the great misfortune to be competing for airplay in the midst of a power-chord-fueled boom in the popularity of rock 'n' roll. Ultimately, few jazzmen other than Miles Davis and

Jazz royalty Edward Kennedy "Duke" Ellington receives the Medal of Freedom from
President Richard Nixon, 1969 (Library of Congress)

Herbie Hancock succeeded in convincing the masses that jazz-rock fusion was
an innovation worthy of serious consideration. Thus, while this potent, improvisational music generated its own mystique and developed its own pantheon of
heroes, other forms of African-American musical expression had to assist in
carrying free jazz's vinyl-clad messages of cultural and social transformation beyond the turntables of the already-converted. Throughout the 1960s and
1970s, black blues and soul artists shouldered the burden of bridging musical
worlds and of encapsulating liberationist messages in more accessible song
structures. Like jazzman-extraordinaire John Coltrane, many had faith in the
power of black artistry and hoped somehow to "create the initial thought
patterns that can change the thinking of the people."[33]

To many, blues is a simple, sad, limited music spawned in the backwater
burgs of the Mississippi Delta and brought to the attention of curious outsiders
by an entrepreneurial traveling bandleader named W. C. Handy. According to
legend, a "lean, loose-jointed Negro" playing what was described as "the
weirdest music I . . . ever heard" had the good fortune to serenade Handy at the
Tutwiler, Mississippi, railway station one evening in 1903.[34] With Handy's

help, the anguished declamations of rural black folk on the subject of life as a lonely walk and a low-down dirty shame caught the fancy of urbanites in dire need of what one modern-day blues scholar has termed quite grandly "a phylogenetic recapitulation—a nonlinear, freely associative, nonsequential meditation—of species experience."[35] The rest, as they say, is history. Not very good history, but serviceable nonetheless. In truth, the story—like the music—is far more complex and upbeat.

Blues—Delta blues—did, indeed, rise out of the cotton fields and labor camps of the nineteenth-century South as a musical synthesis combining elements of traditional work songs and field hollers, group seculars and sacred harmonies, folkloric proverbs and political commentary, rough-hewn humor and elegiac lament. Nevertheless, contrary to the beliefs of both the uninformed and the musicological purists, engagingly "authentic" blues music was performed regularly north of Memphis and long after the tormented Robert Johnson bid farewell to his last hellhound in 1938. If its deepest waters were located somewhere in the vicinity of Belzoni, Yazoo City, and Lake Cormorant, the blues stream wound its way to both coasts and had a major tributary in the Windy City. In these locales, the rough, heavy, unamplified sound of the Delta was bent and squeezed to fit personal styles and particular audiences. Brass and keyboards were added. Tempos increased. The bluesman's storied repertoire of downcast ditties about contrary women and bad boss men was leavened with a variety of tunes that were eminently danceable—and sometimes mocking or risqué. Now, more easily than before, perceptive observers could see that this was—and, in truth, always had been—a music of both agony and ecstasy; of pain but also of release, exhilaration, and renewal; of endurance in the face of mistreatment and heartbreak.

Paradoxical, but not unfathomable, the blues—wherever it was performed—constituted an oral art of considerable depth and texture. Seldom divorced from the concerns and emotions of ordinary people, the music's foundational sense of melancholy often was relieved by assertions of black self-love and by wry, sometimes caustic, commentary on the absurdities of life in a caste-based society. Certainly, the blues was about more than victimization. By articulating what was wrong with the world, blues musicians—and their audience—distanced themselves from immediate troubles and thereby effected a certain degree of transcendence over them. In displaying open wounds and detailing personal tragedies, they created emotional forms of reference that were conducive to group unity and well-being. Indeed, the blues artists' compelling exposition of Afro-America's journey in search of better times affirmed both the humanity and the heroism of a beleaguered but never defeated racial community. In the process of doing so—of evidencing fortitude amid desolation—they earned their stripes as culture heroes.

Lauded more for their honest, down-home expression of human emotion than for any other trait, blues artists have had a far-reaching influence on twentieth-century American cultural expression. Some intellectuals and creative artists contend that one should conceptualize the blues as an overarching cultural ethos or aesthetic.[36] Others seem content to reference the music primarily to identify stylistic elements that are intrinsically African-American. In either case, those with an affinity for the form often utilize it to make personal statements which echo those of their musical reference points. Poets memorialize blues greats and attempt to capture something of the musicians' elemental but compelling imagery in their own verse.[37] Dramatists and filmmakers employ the rhythms and meanings of the blues to create a specific ambience or to illustrate a desired mood.[38] Novelists weave strands of the blues artists' experience into the fabric of their work through characterization, dialogue, and emulation of a particular rhythmic style.[39] Even if flawed in terms of execution, such attempts to partake of the blues experience are wonderfully revealing. In helping others to appreciate the timeless wisdom and keen observational skills of unschooled songster sages, modern-day artists honor their mentors both as conservators and as shapers of a living tradition. Having learned a great deal from the musicians, they, too, alternate between the autobiographical and the universal in their artistic expressions of black reality. Some emulate their role models by voicing sentiments, longings, and impulses which typically must be repressed in everyday life. The most perceptive see the blues artists for what they are: equally survivors and liberators; helpmeets and valued advisors in the continuing struggle against life's adversities.

But the blues can repel as well as attract. Historically, much of this countervailing tendency can be traced to a long-standing in-house dispute over the primacy of the sacred versus the secular in African-American life and cultural expression. Critics often portray the bluesman as a bad influence on the community: sensual, materialistic, individualistic; frequent visitor to establishments of ill-repute; the patron saint of idlers, womanizers, and wine bibbers. For such individuals, living right, praising the Lord, and looking forward to a better day in the afterlife seemed to hold little attraction. Their behavior suggested the existence of a continuous present in which sorrow and joy, reward and punishment, were immediate, decidedly nonexistential concerns.

Was this a fair encapsulation of the blues artist's character and worldview? Is the sacred/secular dichotomy more than a matter of musical taste—of eight- or sixteen- as opposed to twelve-bar patterns? Were these oft-recounted tensions rooted in reality or cliché? Over the years bluesmen have regaled interviewers with numerous stories of their epic internal struggles over whether to serve God or play "the devil's music." Some claim to have been disowned by family members or expelled from their church homes for making the wrong choice.[40] Others somehow hoped to disguise the fact that their repertoire included blues tunes.[41] Still others have attempted to salve troubled consciences and to avoid "playin' with God" by keeping the sacred and secular forms strictly separated or by opening their sets with gospel tributes.[42] Indeed, during the 1930s, one such performer tried to cover all the bases by recording both as "The Singing Christian" and as "Pinewood Tom and His Blues Hounds"—sometimes back-to-back on the same record.[43]

The last case suggests that bluesmen saw fewer contradictions between the sacred and the secular spheres than did their detractors. Many said as much. They attributed special musical gifts to God; claimed to like the "church songs" they composed and performed "better than the blues"; and asserted that both sacred and secular forms of musical expression were capable of "grasping . . . the heart," thereby providing consolation and uplift in troubled times.[44] As St. Louis bluesman Henry Townsend told folklore researcher Barry Lee Pearson, bigoted naysayers would be well advised to forsake the notion that at the end of one's days the blues "will send you anyplace different from gospel." Both were held to convey important wisdom about the human condition—one truth no greater than the other. Blues tunes, he said, couldn't possibly be the "devil's music," because it was well known that Satan put little stock in truthfulness. Besides, added Beale Street keyboardist John Williams (Piano Red) in support of Townsend's plea for evenhandedness, "some of those church people can make a pure monkey out of you in drinking."[45]

Sounding for all the world like a modern-day rap artist seeking to distance himself from a drive-by shooting, such bluesmen sometimes protested a bit too strenuously to be believed. To be sure there were those who did an admirable job of acting out the verse in T-Bone Walker's "Stormy Monday" that describes a bluesman's guilt-free meanderings betwixt the sacred and the secular ("The eagle flies on Friday, and Saturday I go out to play / Sunday I go to church, then I kneel down and pray").[46] Like the legendary Son House, for a time they succeeded in "preachin' the blues"—skillfully juggling sacred and secular beliefs and lifestyles. Some musicians, however, either were uneasy about transmitting a "mixed message" or were incapable of pulling it off. Gary Davis, Skip James, Moody Jones, Rubin Lacy, Gatemouth Moore, and Johnny Williams, among others, left the blues circuit for the ministry. According to bluesman-turned-clergyman Reverend Robert Wilkins, there *was* an important distinction to be made between singing the blues and offering up hymns of praise to God. "You can only sing one and not the other," he claimed. "See, your body is the temple of the spirit of God, and ain't but one spirit can dwell in that body at a time. That is the good spirit or the evil spirit. . . . Blues are songs of the evil spirit."[47]

So which self-penned portrait was closer to the truth—Townsend's or

Wilkins's? Was it true that the blues stream always ran parallel to the gospel road, never intersecting or allowing for a partial synthesis of competing world-views? Were the bluesmen obliged to become *either* reprobates *or* saints in or-der to resolve troublesome internal conflicts? Did they expect to meet God or the devil at the end of life's long, lonesome journey? And, to personalize these matters further, who was the *real* Thomas A. Dorsey: the good deacon of gos-pel music who penned sacred classics such as "Peace in the Valley" and "Take My Hand Precious Lord" or the secular musician known as Georgia Tom, pur-veyor of some of the filthiest double-entendre blues tunes of the 1920s?

Certainly, these are important questions. But, ultimately, they mislead. In truth, the sacred/secular dichotomy is a European, not an African, conceptu-alization. This is not to say that the model has no basis in reality, only that other models must be considered—including those derived from West Africa's more holistic indigenous cosmologies. Compared to Western Christians' typically bifurcated, more neatly compartmentalized worldview, these peoples tended to blur the sacred and the secular in a manner which, in a diaspora context, tends to support Henry Townsend's belief in the irrelevancy of the term "devil's music."[48] Blues and spirituals reflect different elements of the same foundational experiences and are equally valid forms of group cultural expres-sion. In this view, the blues is held to possess what musicologists call "synchro-nous duplicity." Simply stated, a blues tune is both sacred and profane—a secular spiritual, if you will.[49] Indeed, the ever present tension between the two elements is part of the music's—and the performer's—historical appeal. That critics think otherwise does not change this fact. Nor does their disap-proval carry sufficient weight to convince the Henry Townsends of the world to abandon what is perceived as a noble calling—a lifetime gig fit for a hero.

Blues artists can be said to approach the sacred whenever they (1) utilize vo-cal techniques (melisma) and interjections ("Lord have mercy") derived from black-church styles; (2) attempt to universalize the spirituals' time-honored message of endurance; (3) spur hope by employing the language of liberation (Babylons to flee, rivers to cross, a Promised Land to be reached); and (4) pre-cipitate release from routine cares via up-tempo dance numbers—whether the words to such songs are perfectly "clean" or not. Indeed, in an important sense, the blues artist and the down-home preacher are analogues of one another. As joint solicitors of human emotional response, both dig deeply into their im-provisational bag of tricks for just the right words and the perfect tone and tempo that will reveal ways to circumvent the "stones" that Robert Johnson said are in all of life's "passways."[50]

On the other hand, irrespective of whatever superficial similarities one might find when comparing a red-hot blues performance with a sanctified church service, the fact remains that juke joints were not places of worship. To be sure, both were popular community institutions, but the far more "worldly" juke sensualized rather than sanctified. Here, to paraphrase Sonny Boy Williamson, the sexual power of a beautiful woman—not the healing of the Holy Spirit—was said to bring "eyesight to the blind." Here, as noted by Koko Taylor, backslidden types like "Automatic Slim," "Razor Totin' Jim," "Butcher-Knife Totin' Annie," and "Fast-Talkin' Fannie" always seemed eager to "romp and stomp 'til midnight / ... fuss and fight 'til daylight." Having little immediate concern over the perilous state of their spiritual well-being, they would "pitch a Wang Dang Doodle" all night long. More often than not, it was the bluesman who led this irreverent musical aggregation down the gin-soaked road to perdition.[51]

Vital elements of the blues musicians' heroic persona—as well as much of their unfavorable reputation in church circles—derived from this leadership role. To detractors, bluesmen were pied pipers of the damned and seemed ever willing to provide proof in support of such claims. Often containing purplish prose, their songs gave the distinct impression that the singers were, themselves, the black badmen of legend. Revived, rejuvenated, and returned to contemporary life with a song in their hearts, lust in their loins, and nimble fingers itching for "action" of an unspecified sort, musicians claiming to be "bad like Jesse James" bragged openly that they were "just as evil as a man can be." "Smokin' dynamite" and "drinkin' TNT," they acted the part of their rough-and-ready folkloric counterparts—"walk[ing] the streets all night" just hoping some "screwball [would] start a fight."[52] Many claimed to spend their off-hours at too tight parties and shake-me-downs; risked their weekly earnings on games of five-card stud, coon-can, and Georgia skin; and engaged in spirited barrelhouse tussles with similarly disposed hard cases. Troubling, too, was the fact that singers of both sexes were absolutely shameless in waxing rhapsodic about black snakes, spike drivers, meat grinders, honey drippers, little red roosters, and bumblebees with stingers as long as your arm. Frequently, riotous tunes reflective of male braggadocio like Bo Carter's "Ram Rod Daddy," "Please Warm My Wiener," and "Don't Mash My Digger So Deep" were answered by coarse, distaff-side missives such as Bessie Smith's innuendo-filled "Nobody in Town Can Bake a Sweet Jelly Roll like Mine" and Lil Johnson's "My Stove's in Good Condition."[53] The fact that numerous noteworthy blues figures imbibed heavily, swore often, served jail time, and sported violence-prone dispositions in real life only added additional detail to the overall picture.

The blues performers' spiritual walk—or lack thereof—also distanced them from well-churched African-Americans. In both song and deed, many seemed hell-bent on thumbing their noses at behavioral and theological guidelines set forth by the Almighty. They ridiculed the divinely sanctioned institution of marriage ("Why should I bother getting a wife when the man next door got

one just as good?"—Furry Lewis); either questioned the existence of an afterlife ("Ain't no heaven, ain't no burnin' hell. . . . / Where I die, where I go, nobody tell"—John Lee Hooker) or reshaped it to meet their own needs ("I'm
gonna build me a heaven, have a kingdom of my own, / Where these brown-
skin women can cluster round my throne"—Texas Alexander); skewered the
clergy ("Now some folks say a preacher won't steal, / I caught three in my
cornfield"—Kansas Joe McCoy); and doubted God ("You know this must've
been the Devil I'm servin', I know it ain't Jesus Christ, / All I ask Him is to save
me, and look like He's tryin' to take my life."—J. T. "Funny Paper" Smith).[54]

Some, of course, claimed that the bluesmen *were* serving Satan. Robert
Johnson, Tommy Johnson, and Howlin' Wolf, among others, were said to have
bartered their souls for the acquisition of musical skills.[55] Such tales of dead-
of-night crossroads commerce increased markedly in believability whenever
supporting evidence (mythic or otherwise) could be found. Were there bluesmen who asserted that they had learned to play their instruments through
"dreams"? Yes—Mississippi John Hurt and Jimmy Spruill did.[56] Could they
see spirits because they had been born with a "veil" (placenta) over the face?
Yes—Eddie Kirkland claimed as much.[57] Did they believe in or practice
voodoo? Yes—Big Joe Williams, Mance Lipscomb, and Lillie May Glover (Big
Mama Blues) couldn't deny the fact.[58] Did they suddenly disappear from the
pages of blues history under mysterious circumstances or without leaving so
much as a trace of black cat bone as a clue? Yes—Blind Blake, Casey Bill Weldon, and Robert Johnson did, prompting suspicion that their vanishing acts
may have been tied to an earlier black arts bargain. Well enough. As the Muddy
Waters song warned, these musically gifted hoochie coochie men (and
women) did, indeed, seem to be in league with powerful and little-understood
forces. If riled, they very likely would consider putting the whammy on you.[59]

All of this was a bit foreboding but also the stuff of legend. Like many well-
churched and better-mannered culture heroes, blues artists enjoyed stirring
the calm waters of orthodoxy. They found considerable pleasure in tipping as
many sacred cows as possible. Part of their burden and part of their charm, the
musicians' prominent "dark side" made it seem obvious that they were "bad."
Nevertheless, as those schooled in the African-American vernacular tradition
well understood, "bad" could be used to describe something that was extremely good. When playing the hero role in a world where Du Boisian dualities still had considerable relevance, the blues artist had to be considered both
"bad" *and* "good"—a most subversively attractive, even mythic, figure. As if in
agreement with this conceptualization as it related to blues fandom, an admirer
of the late slide guitar wiz Elmore James once remarked: "That man was a
myth. He was always doin' somethin'. There wasn't a day passed that Elmore
wasn't gonna do somethin' excitin'."[60] And, true to form, in 1963 James died

suddenly and before his time after recording for only eleven years. No one knows for sure, but it is possible that he once had visited the legendary cross-roads and now was paying the price of heroism.

By 1960, blues was an established musical form with a long and storied history. But for many youthful blacks, it was too "traditional"—an "old-timey" music that one's parents played when they rolled back the rug in search of fading memories and half-forgotten dance steps. The numerous demographic and political changes which had begun to alter the map of black America created an insatiable demand for whatever was new under the sun. And as the Black Power years approached, soul music seemed like dawn's early light.

An engaging synthesis of gospel and blues with additional elements borrowed from a variety of musical styles often lumped together and labeled "race music" or "R & B" (rhythm and blues), "soul" was a media-friendly catchall term which could be used to describe the driving dance sound of a James Brown, the sophisticated stylings of a Roberta Flack, *and* the pop-oriented performances of vocal groups like the Supremes and the Jackson 5. Boosted by heavy airplay from ultrahip "Soul Brother" disc jockeys, the new, infectious music became a national pan-racial passion during the Black Power years. Both brown- and blue-eyed groups (Soul Children, Soul Clan, Soul Survivors) sang about the joys of listening to a "Soul Serenade" while doing the "Soul Limbo" at a "Stoned Soul Picnic." They offered up tuneful tributes to "Soul Power" and to the men and women ("Soul Brother, Soul Sister") most visibly infused with "Soul Pride." Indeed, as acknowledged in a song by Marvin L. Sims, it seemed that just about everyone with any interest in perfecting their make-out moves or acquiring a favorable dance hall reputation was "talkin' 'bout soul."[61]

Those who listened carefully to these multitracked paeans to soulfulness were provided with (1) a lexicon of contemporary street talk and slang, (2) a guide to the shared understandings and concerns of black youth, (3) a running commentary on various aspects of the 1960s and 1970s social revolution, and (4) the script for yet another round of debate over whether Black America's culture heroes populated a moral universe grounded in the sacred or in the profane. For devoted fans, soul music became a supernal all-purpose panacea that was capable of conveying the concepts of salvation and transcendence to a secular audience far more effectively than any droning blues ode. As one versifier of the day put it, by digging "deep down . . . into the depths of the gospel roll," the creators of soul were transformed into sanctified musical enablers.[62] Offering up a "message music" which preached the ideal of black unity, they seemed determined to put an end to the most ancient blues/gospel-based divisions plaguing African-American musical culture. In truth, by the end of the 1970s, the soulsters had accomplished much of this monumental task. Walking the epistemological and emotional tightrope separating sensualist and spiritualist, they came down on the side of the gods often enough to quiet any lingering doubt that black secular-music heroes possessed sufficient moral agency and authority to be deemed worthy of an upright devotee's passion.

Certainly, not all members of the soul crowd could be considered saints. The streetwise James Brown, for example, admitted to the youthful indiscretion of pilfering "everything that wasn't nailed down" and "redistributing the wealth" among his friends.[63] Some of heroin-addicted O. V. Wright's best work was released by his record label while the deep soul balladeer was serving a three-year federal prison term for dealing drugs.[64] Even silky-voiced Al Green—future pastor of Memphis's Church of the Full Gospel Tabernacle—once was dismissed from his father's gospel group for listening to the "worldly" music of Jackie Wilson.[65] For that matter, who among late-1960s soul fans actually believed that Sam Moore and Dave Prater's hit "Hold on, I'm Comin'" had deep spiritual connotations that transcended the ejaculatory?[66]

Nevertheless, a strong case can be made for the claim that soul music borrowed a great deal more from the traditional gospel songbook than its name. The two musical forms shared both performance style and, for a time, the performers themselves. Having apprenticed in church choirs from an early age, many soulsters found it both appropriate and natural to incorporate gospel elements into their commercial recordings. Falsetto screams, broken cries of ecstasy, and barely controlled bouts of stuttering were joined to familiar gospel chord progressions and call-and-response patterns of vocal interplay as the fervent devotional energy of African-American church music was redirected and used to energize secular sermons. Hand claps and tambourine taps, rhythmic grunts, and frequent interjections of "ha" and "good God" enlivened the heavenly harmonizing of the most impassioned soulsters, providing a direct link to the black-church tradition.

As a result of this musicological acculturation, the soulsters' songs often contained themes and imagery drawn from gospel roots. Without question, "message" songs like the Staple Singers' "Respect Yourself" and James Carr's "Freedom Train" reflected the political activism of the day.[67] But, in truth, these soulful homilies were even more fully grounded in music the artists had heard as youngsters growing up in the black church, had performed as members of gospel groups such as the Dixie Nightingales (David Ruffin), the Northern Jubilee Gospel Singers (Jerry Butler and Curtis Mayfield), and the Soul Stirrers (Sam Cooke and Johnnie Taylor), or—as in the case of nine-year-old "Wonder Boy Preacher" Solomon Burke—had directed their own congregations to sing. For many, including soul's "godfather," James Brown, this gospel music experience was relevant—even essential—to a successful career in soul. In addition to the sort of technical instruction in composition and instrumentation which could be applied to other musical formats, a background in sacred music made budding soulsters aware that a "spirit-filled" performance which facilitated honest, person-to-person contact was every artist's holy grail. An effective musical enabler not only had to "let people be themselves and *see* themselves" and their lives reflected in song but also had to make the audience realize "you are there to lift 'em up." To Brown, this was the key to a winning act—an essential piece of wisdom which, he noted, "came from my church."[68]

If songs like Aretha Franklin's "Spirit in the Dark" or Marvin Gaye's "Let's Get It On" made ambiguous use of concepts like "spiritual" and "sanctified"— blurring distinctions between the sacred and the secular—much of the soulster's repertoire provided an essential counterpoint to the bluesman's hard-to-shake reputation as a rake and a reprobate. Endowed with the gospel musicians' fervor and future-oriented, this-is-the-way-the-world-should-be philosophy, soul artists typically made many more "joyful noises" than did performers steeped in the Delta blues tradition. When some, like Smokey Robinson and the Miracles, said they had to "dance to keep from crying," one could rest assured that there would be no shortage of funky, danceable music to uplift the spirits. Seldom given to expressions of unrelieved sorrow, they employed past personal defeats as reference points and as an encouragement to "keep on pushin'."[69] When they did move on, it often was as a member of a fast-paced, well-choreographed soul revue—not as a romanticized individualist strumming alone somewhere in the lonesome pines. Collectively, soul musicians possessed more than enough charisma, spunk, creative vision, and high moral character to see them safely through any reasonably fair competition with other types of American culture heroes.

During the years 1960–80, blues and soul artists contributed a variety of compelling musical selections to the soundtrack of an epic societal passion play. Each cohort adopted a somewhat different worldview and maintained a distinctive approach to problem solving, but both offered their audiences emotional release and renewal. Many blues artists did so by articulating what it was like to endure—and to survive—tough times. Most soulsters accomplished their goal by leading in the celebration of good times. Broadly appealing, the two groups composed the yin and yang of a race-specific moral universe. Here, even the most morally suspect of musicians could compensate for perceived shortcomings and become a living legend, either through a character reevaluation based upon conceptualizations derived from Africa's "sacred cosmos" or by drawing upon soul's abundant storehouse of accredited "New World" religious values. Spared what W. E. B. Du Bois had described as the "moral obtuseness and refined brutality" of white culture heroes, blues and soul musicians were seen by many as "the spiritual hope of this land."[70] Blacks who were willing to forgive minor behavioral flaws came to cherish such figures while like-minded whites sought to emulate them or to claim them as their own creations.

Buoyed by the belief that both their emotive skills and their moral underpinnings were superior to anything the competition could offer, African-American blues and soul musicians proceeded to get down to the important business of getting *down*. Was this a good thing? Here, again, black vernacular usage could confuse. But what is certain is that these skillful cultural interpreters had experienced the condition in both a positive and a negative sense and could distinguish "down" from "up" at least as well as their fans. Like jazz world counterparts, these were black men and women who understood what it was like to be exploited both as black persons and as entertainment world commodities. Typically, they resented being "used like a doggone tool" but gained both comfort and strength from the realization that they weren't "just all alone, there is others too."[71]

Performing artists have always complained about the deceptions and abuses of business agents and record label executives. Black artists were no different in this respect. They continually bewailed their victimization by arrogant, calculating industry overlords. Bluesmen told of being lured to recording studios or concert halls with promises of checks that always seemed to be "in the mail." Soulsters complained about crooked promoters, sales undercounts, and copyright theft. Some worked for salary alone or found themselves burdened with contracts in which everything but the kitchen sink (studio and instrument rental, salaries of backup musicians, cost of tapes and album cover artwork) was charged against their royalty earnings. When the Supremes first signed with Motown Records, the group received 3 percent of 90 percent of the suggested retail price for each record sold—less taxes, packaging, and related costs. For each Supreme, this amounted to about half a cent per single, or $5,000 per million sold. Terms were somewhat more favorable for experienced artists, but as late as 1975—after placing more than a dozen hits on the *Billboard* charts—the Jackson 5's contract with Motown called for them to receive 2.7%, or $0.16, per $5.98 album.[72]

Certainly, adversity was no stranger to the performing artist. Since childhood black performers had been forced to cope with the same racial, class, and gender-based discriminations that plagued less musically gifted African-Americans. Irrespective of occupation or locale, all members of this racially defined community of sufferers and survivors understood the nature of "shattered dreams" and what it meant to have enemies who were always "trying to keep you down." They, too, sought release from the "chains and things" that threatened devastation and despair. Sometimes, their only solace was the knowledge that "you can't spend what you ain't got / You can't lose what you ain't never had."[73]

Raised in a rural southland governed by medieval notions of social justice and a color-coded system of racial etiquette, musicians such as Mance Lipscomb, Big Joe Williams, and Muddy Waters acquired considerable firsthand experience in chopping cotton and pulling corn from "Caint ta Caint" (dawn to dusk); in working for sub-subsistence wages under brutal bosses who "beat you if you tried to rest a bit"; and in coping with the gut-wrenching loss of loved ones who were savaged or murdered by nightriders. They knew what it was like to live in fear, to be treated with less respect than "a dog or sumpm," to pay their "dues."[74]

Other performers experienced privation and discrimination in more urbanized settings. As a youngster, New Orleans bluesman "Cousin Joe" Joseph subsisted on a regular diet of "watered coffee and a little cow's milk," red beans, and meat scraps. James Brown danced for tips on the street corners of Augusta, Georgia, and was so poor that on several occasions his elementary school principal sent him home for having "insufficient clothes." Otis Redding's struggling family lived in a housing project in West Macon that was known officially as Belleview but that was so tough that residents more accurately called it "Hellview." And in Washington, D.C., future Motown hitmaker Marvin Gaye was privileged to gaze upon the majestic Capitol dome from the windows of his junior high school but was forbidden to enter "whites only" public playgrounds.[75]

These harsh early-life experiences prepared future culture heroes for the discourtesies and inconveniences that were to come their way as touring professionals in the all-too-slowly desegregating South of the 1960s.[76] Whether raised on a "concrete reservation" or in a "one-room country shack," members of this musical vanguard were socialized to stand shoulder to shoulder with their long-suffering black fans in support of group empowerment.[77] According to Memphis-born, Chicago-based bluesman Johnny Shines, it was the black performers' duty and privilege to preserve this down-home spirit of community and commonality against the many countervailing tendencies of modern life—to "remind people, black people especially, [that] if you forget your beginnings you can't do much with the future."[78]

If the musicians were country cousins to the average African-American, what made them seem special—and heroic? Was it the way they evoked, embodied, and transmitted the warmth, wit, pathos, and funkiness of group folklife? Could it be attributed to their bold negation of racism's ability to stifle creativity? Did it have something to do with the universal human attraction to success, however acquired and defined? Certainly, it is conceivable that one or more of these definitional elements might come into play whenever a member of the black extended family was considered for elevation to the status of culture hero. Nevertheless, beyond these factors lay the simple truth that most black musical heroes were only part-time Everymen and Everywomen. When placed on public display—which for many constituted a significant block of time—they ballooned to larger-than-life size and proceeded to conduct themselves in a manner befitting those who are transparently extraordinary. This, of course, approximated the modus operandi of many other world-class hero prototypes. However, the black musicians had their own ways of expressing uniqueness.

The most splendid of the soul and blues champions strived mightily to avoid faint praise, still waters, and managers who wanted them to be black without being overly colorful about it or no more than simple, unassuming agents of an unchanging folk tradition. Instead, they sought to project a personalized, commodified "difference" that was palpable, praiseworthy, and capable of effecting spontaneous concert hall combustion within minutes. Some came by these qualities quite naturally, but even masters of the soulful, funkified arts had to work hard. Indeed, during the mid-1960s, James Brown claimed that he logged some 80 hours onstage, performed over 900 songs, sweat through 120 suits, and distributed 1,000 pairs of cuff links and 5,000 photos to loyal fans *each month*.[79] In return, popular performers acquired the financial resources needed to create show business magic.

Some hopeful culture heroes sought to convey the notion that they were, like Brown, "bigger than life, broader than the average person," by altering their names to fit new, more resplendent stage personas.[80] It was for this reason that Sam Cook, Dionne Warwick, and Marvin Gay added a distinguishing *e* to their family names; that Chester Arthur Burnett became Howlin' Wolf; and that young Steveland Judkins Morris rechristened himself Little Stevie Wonder. Here, also, one discovers method in the mad scramble to acquire a suitably regal (King Curtis, the Duke of Earl, the 5 Royales, the Queen of Soul) or size-enhanced (Big Mama Thornton, Big Chief Ellis, Arthur "Big Boy" Crudup, Johnny "Big Moose" Walker) moniker. Unlike average folk, some musicians (John Lee Hooker, Alberta Hunter) even could get away with using pseudonyms (to sidestep "exclusivity" clauses in their recording contracts). But the all-time crown prince of confusion had to be Aleck "Rice" Miller, a.k.a. Willie Williamson. Best known as Sonny Boy Williamson (no. 2), the harmonicist not only adopted another famous bluesman's name and cited several different birth dates but always insisted he was the *real* Sonny Boy. When challenged by critics of his usurpatious behavior, the dapper musician was said to have favored the response, "Ah, hell, it ain't none of their business."[81] Certainly, true culture heroes were above such mundane concerns and saw no need to stick to a fixed identity.

Like musical contemporary Frank Zappa, the black stars also believed that brown shoes don't make it.[82] Soulsters, in particular, were concerned that their wardrobe set them apart from the mainstream. While there were many differ-

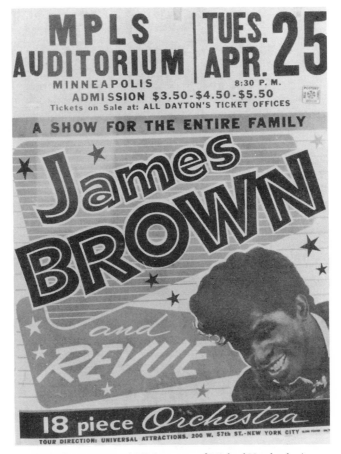

James Brown poster, 1968 (courtesy of Michael Haralambos)

ent approaches to sartorial distinction, all were aimed at making the performer "look like somebody you would pay to see."[83] Hoping to provide fans with a brief, but refreshing respite from the deadening conformity of convention, 1970s funkmeister George Clinton and designer Larry LeGaspi developed a series of outlandish, otherworldly, often downright comical costumes for Clinton's Parliament/Funkadelic concert tours. Included in this bizarre collection were fish with huge, Day-Glo lips; fur-covered football helmets sporting TV antennas and fox tails; gray leather pants with white toenails at the feet and an elephant's head and trunk swinging back and forth between the legs; and soft-sculpture bulldog shoes with extralong laces that made it look like the performer was walking his "dogs" as he crossed the stage. Somewhat less elaborate but no less eye-catching were Rufus Thomas's hot pants and Funky Penguin suits, Solomon ("King of Rock and Soul") Burke's "crown jewels" and ermine-trimmed cape, and Isaac Hayes's gold and silver chain-mail suits. Even the relatively sedate haute couture of the Temptations (brightly colored, sequined trousers with flames licking up the legs) and the Supremes (who wore body padding and three pairs of false lashes bonded together with Eye Lure, the Crazy Glue of the cosmetics industry) transmitted the unmistakable visual message that these were black folk who wouldn't settle for drab.[84]

Glamorous, larger-than-life figures such as these tended to sport other trappings of success and material well-being which served to complement their unique wardrobes. In this regard, it is scarcely surprising to learn that Flo Ballard, Mary Wilson, and Diana Ross of the Supremes resided in a picture-

The resplendent Isley Brothers (*Sepia* magazine, 1969)

Aretha Franklin (*Sepia* magazine, 1970)

postcard neighborhood of brick, Tudor-style homes with green canvas awnings, stained-glass windows, seventeen-foot sofas, and marbled end tables that hung down from the ceiling on gold chains. Neither did it seem out of character for James Brown to travel in his own Learjet with "Out of Sight" painted on the fuselage or to own a chain of radio stations (including Augusta's WRDW, on whose front steps he once had shined shoes). Certainly, it was only fitting for Otis Redding to live on the 300-acre "Big O Ranch" near Macon and for Aretha Franklin to be accompanied by two dozen attendants as she walked down the aisle of her father's Detroit church to wed actor Glynn Turman. Indeed, Lady Soul's mink-trimmed silk gown with its fine lace appliqués, 17,500 seed pearls, and seven-foot train seemed wholly appropriate to the magnitude of the occasion and the celebrity of its participants.[85]

Less fully anticipated were the lifestyle flourishes of the more prosperous blues singers. To be sure, most still struggled mightily, eking out a meager existence by toting their own equipment from town to town and playing what Albert King called "them *small* joints," the ones where "folks be callin' each other bad names from way 'cross the room and someone like to throw a wine bottle at you."[86] But, by the end of the 1970s, a major star like B. B. King could seek temporary refuge from the rigors of touring by retiring to a plush, thirteen-room home in Las Vegas. Here, far removed from the steamy one-room jukes of his early career, a staff of three provided the former singing DJ with at least as much comfort as Pep-Ti-Kon—the alcohol-rich painkiller he'd hawked on Memphis radio station WDIA during the late 1940s.[87]

On occasion, increased public acceptance caused such performers to wax nostalgic about the days when they played "places so hot the moisture in the air condensed on our instruments; so cold we'd have to thaw out our hands with matches before we could play."[88] They did not, however, seek to disavow their newfound riches. Neither did they make a show of feeling guilty about reaping hard-earned rewards. Instead, suggesting that the blues could mediate creativity and commerce, these African-American strivers proceeded to distance themselves from unflattering stereotypes of the black musician as "some ignorant lush moaning in a gutter some place." There was absolutely no reason, said King, "why a man can't sing blues as a profession and still be a gentleman."[89] Most assuredly, added fellow success story Muddy Waters, not all who continued to play in the down-home style were "half slouching," "raggedy," and "loud." "I was never that type of man who'd have a great big quart of wine laying back of the amplifier," he bragged. "I am an intelligent blues singer. I sing deep, Deep South blues, straight out of the bottom. But I made myself classy with it. . . . When I wanted a drink it was Chivas Regal. . . . I'm sharp. I've got my mohair." Fortunately, fans wondering how poverty could be transformed into such abundance without there being a corresponding decline in the "authenticity" of the music were offered immediate reassurance. When, for example, Waters was asked by an interviewer how he could put the same rough-edged, roadhouse-flavored feeling into his music after he had become "successful and comfortable," the bluesman spoke for many when he responded tersely: "I've got a long memory."[90]

He also could have credited the musical acumen of his chief music business rivals. Indeed, both blues and soul musicians spoke often of how the profession's competitive nature kept them on their toes, skills sharp and sensibilities unspoiled by bright lights and big cities. Cutting contests and cleverly orchestrated "battles" between vocal groups were only the most visible manifestations of this phenomenon. As Motown's Smokey Robinson noted, the recording industry of the 1960s and 1970s was a "hotbed of competition" where "no one wanted to lose."[91] Here, one could find hard-driving performers lobbying for top billing on package tours and complaining to marketing directors about getting insufficient airplay vis-à-vis their labelmates. They constantly developed new instrumental and vocal techniques to set themselves apart from the crowd and worried that either their latest contract, their "sound," or their stage moves would be topped by some flashy upstart. On occasion, established culture heroes like the curmudgeonly Howlin' Wolf went to extremes to ensure continued supremacy: turning down a competitor's mike, stretching out their own sets to limit the stage time available to other acts, or firing band members said to have designs on the spotlight.[92] Although these juvenile antics often were described as "friendly competition," all interested parties understood that the stakes were high. "Stars, you see, are merely leaping from hit to hit," explained soulster Marvin Gaye. "Below us, the public watches and waits for us to fall on our ass. But if we don't keep leaping, we fade and die."[93] The pressure to stay at the head of the pack—to avoid becoming what B. B. King referred to as a "petrified forest"—could be incredibly intense. According to King and Muddy Waters, all those who wished to stay in the race—to remain "a known person"—had to "scuffle" *and* to maintain appearances.[94] Each was deemed essential to a musician's survival. Both considerations served as rationale and justification for the star's consumerist excesses.

If the competitive dynamics of the recording industry could be credited with creating numerous highly motivated and splendidly outfitted Horatio Algers, it also spawned a fair number of arrogant jackanapes. At least they would appear as such in a more traditional setting. Some stars seemed to cultivate aloofness, arriving at performance venues hours late, keeping stage banter and eye contact to an absolute minimum, and refusing interviews or autographs. Through egocentric unpredictability and self-absorption, such culture heroes created an atmosphere of anticipation—whetting fans' appetites for more, more, more of a good thing with their aura of personal mystery. Other black heroes worked the opposite side of the street, constantly seeking to forward and reconfirm their headliner status by making themselves ever available to the media. Typically, a major goal of these publicity hounds was to have their names on everyone's lips and a flattering publicity photo in every major teen magazine in the land. Supported in this noble quest by a veritable king's court of gofers, sycophants, and starry-eyed wanna-bes, they carried themselves like royalty and stopped frequently to bask in their own regal glory.

At times, vanity levels could skyrocket. Certainly, near record readings were recorded whenever the Supremes, trailed by three or more package-bearing porters, exited a department store after engaging in one of their frequent price-is-no-object shopping sprees;[95] on the afternoon that blues diva Alberta Hunter turned down an invitation to give a Sunday concert in the White House rose garden because "it was my day off";[96] and when Marvin Gaye opted to be depicted as a cartoon-style Man of Steel on the cover of his *Super Hits* (1970) album.[97] Obviously, these performers knew a great deal about both artistry and showmanship. They understood the importance of making passersby stop dead in their tracks to stare awestruck at the grand extravagance of a consummate culture hero in full stride. Declaring themselves "king of all snakes," they seemed pleased when fans went the extra mile to grant their every wish.[98] Nevertheless, they tried not to let on and acted as if such indulgences were *expected* of loyal supplicants. Perhaps, as nonfans sometimes grumbled, they *were* arrogant, unbridled show-offs who put too much stock in the creative effusions of their own publicity agents. But it was all purposeful and, ostensibly, for a good cause. As showbiz sage James Brown once observed, "It doesn't just happen. You have to *make* it happen."[99] And, far more often than not, megastars like Brown made it seem that a great deal was "happening"—both in their own and in their fans' daily lives. Possessed of considerably more than the average person's share of glitz and glamour, black musical culture heroes were the sort of iconic figures around whom common folk tended to rally in the hope of receiving random words of encouragement and bluesy, soulful visions of an extraordinary future. Over time, empowering legends accumulated around these musically gifted denizens of Black Camelot for the simple reason that their own considerable personal investment in the legends made them ring true.

Viewed in this light, established entertainers can be conceptualized as master teachers, role models, and enablers. Many provided promising neophyte musicians with direct, hands-on instruction. These informal tutorials in vocal and instrumental technique, song arranging, and staging were greatly appreciated and long remembered. "He'd give you plenty of tips. He didn't care who you were," West Coast bluesman Lowell Fulson recalled, offering a fond tribute to his distinguished mentor T-Bone Walker. "He'd say, 'It goes like this.' Then he'd tell me: 'Swing the blues a little more. Put in a little life, a little pep. Rock into it, tap your foot off of what you're doing.'"[100] Invariably, fatherly advice of this sort was accompanied by less technical but equally essential instruction in successful, self-directed living ("Don't nobody owe you nothin'. You owe your own self somethin'." "Do not disrespect the public." "Just go out and do it.") and was reinforced whenever the budding talent was called upon to perform a guest spot during one of the headliner's shows.[101] This arrangement seemed satisfactory to both parties and was perceived as being mutually beneficial. As noted by Muddy Waters, whose band nurtured such talents as James Cotton, Little Walter, Otis Spann, and Junior Wells, "I'm the old grandfather of 'em. I set the pattern for 'em. They got a little of me, then advanced out and picked up other stuff, but I'm in there somewhere."[102] The stature of a veteran performer was enhanced whenever worthy apprentices or sidemen left the nest to begin their own hero's journey.

Highly contagious, inspiration seldom stopped at the edge of the bandstand. Fans, too, were caught up in the "educational" process and regularly sought a star's guidance on a variety of topics. As was to be expected, matters of dress, demeanor, and male-female relationships usually topped the study list.

Both in verse and through between-song patter, the stars shared key bits of wisdom on these matters, thereby making audience members feel as if someone understood and cared about their problems. Seeking to facilitate higher learning by putting their "students" at ease and making them active collaborators in the evening's show, master teachers like B. B. King began their sets in a conversational mode, stopped occasionally to recount a shaggy-dog story or two, and sometimes even revealed minor personal foibles or played the clown in order to draw the crowd into their world. "I'd like to tell you a little story now," they might say, easing into the lesson at hand. "Ladies, if you got a man, husband, or whatever you want to call him, and he don't do exactly like you think he should, don't cut him, because you can't raise him over again you know. Don't hurt him. Treat him nice." A few random guitar chords and some minor throat-clearing would follow, adding emphasis and allowing the message to sink in. Then, it was time for the other half of the "class" to receive instruction. "Fellas," the culture hero continued, "I want to say to you, if you got a wife, a woman, or whatever you want to call her, and she don't do like you think she should, don't go up side her head. That don't do but one thing: that'll make her a little smarter, and she won't let you catch her the next time." Before they realized it, attentive listeners found themselves awash in slyly sage advice about working hard, saving money, getting a good education, and respecting their elders.[103] Sometimes there was too much material to be absorbed at one sitting, necessitating repeat visits to the black "educator's" show. Rarely did truancy or tardiness become a problem.

The most studious audience members took these admonitions to heart immediately. Later, some would write to thank the all-wise culture hero for helping them get their lives "back on the track."[104] For others, the instruction seemed almost subliminal—conveyed from teacher to student more by example than by precept. Here, quantifiable data fails, but important questions related to the culture hero's pedagogical effectiveness tantalize nonetheless. For example, one wonders how many self-conscious young women with a "weight problem" felt better about themselves when the Supremes' Flo Ballard (a well-rounded size 10/11) responded to petite (size 4) Diana Ross's assertion that "thin is in" with the humorous stage retort, "Yeah, but fat is where it's at." Did large numbers of very dark skinned African-American men (with or without prison records) seek to emulate the ultraproud, ultrasuccessful James Brown or adopt him as a substitute father figure? Indeed, were there visually handicapped fans of Stevie Wonder who took the sightless star's advice and refused to be "preoccupied" with blindness? If so, these black musician-heroes had done far more than required of them as "entertainers."[105]

According to James Brown's sax player, Maceo Parker, high-profile role models had "real control, real rapport with people's emotions."[106] After estab-

Bluesmen at Chicago's Regal Theatre, 1968 (courtesy of Michael Haralambos)

lishing a suitably groovy vibe, the skillful performer could—and did—choose to utilize this awesome power for the group good. Drenched in sweat, spangles, and spotlights, experienced practitioners of the soulful arts bonded with the romping, stomping crowd in a ritual exorcism of excessive self-pity and subpar self-esteem. Going beyond the standard contractual promise to "work hard for you, baby," they urged each and every member of this musical mutual support network to "get off your seat, / And get your arms together and your hands together, / And give me some of that old soul clappin'"[107] In response, committed fans testified loudly as to the wisdom spoken by their heroes. Amid pyrotechnical outbursts from raging horn sections and out-of-control electric guitars, they were given release and made whole.

By the mid-1960s, this glorious communal cacophony had begun to sound like the roar of lions. For many, it was a familiar sound, rooted in the black lib-

eration struggle of bygone days. Updated and electronically enhanced, yet reso-
nant with the protest ethic which coursed through slave era work songs and
abolitionist odes, black music of the 1960s and 1970s served as a stereophonic
summons to societal change. "No more slavery chains for me," said the bluesmen and soulsters as they renewed their commitment to purposeful activism.
Utilizing the power inherent in African-American musical expression, they
vowed to denounce injustice, to heighten racial self-awareness, and to issue pe-
riodic calls to arms. As role models that were both similar (cultural and socioeconomic background) and different (acquired status and wealth) from the
masses who idolized them, black musical culture heroes both personified and
strengthened their audience's desire to quicken the pace of Afro-America's
journey down freedom's road.

Black performers relished this task. Indeed, many hoped to transform the
bandstand into a bully pulpit of empowerment. There was nothing improper in
this, they said. Only good could come from their determined efforts to facilitate
black psychological liberation. The "painless preaching" of a well-known ac-
tivist-musician would speed the pulse, elevate the consciousness, and—if all
went well—move attentive listeners to question received wisdom and to believe themselves capable of greatness. After accepting the star's empowering
message, they, too, could become "somebody."[108] As Curtis Mayfield of the
Impressions noted in lending his support to this militant musicological endeavor, the most compelling music of the day was that which went beyond the
preoccupations of traditional romantic balladry to influence opinion on affairs
more weighty than those of the heart. In tune with the spirit of the times, he
considered it far more satisfying to sing of self-pride—as in "We're a Winner"—
than to urge listeners to party down and "do the Boo-ga-loo."[109] Here, the
beauty of black music was that it educated as well as entertained.

Whereas certain of the more visionary free jazz improvisationists seemed
intent upon subverting Western musical conventions by creating an elaborate
"hidden language" which excluded whites, most of the race-conscious sentiments expressed by blues and soul artists were suitably clear to all but the most
obtuse. If not specifically directed to nonblack listeners, many of these musical
offerings gained their attention by "talkin' about a change" that would be
"more than just Evolution."[110] Cross-cultural transmission of these politicized points of view occurred in a variety of performance venues, but none
more accommodating than the urban coffeehouses of the early 1960s.

Before they all packed their bags, moved to San Francisco, and put flowers in
their hair, fresh-faced urban youth clad in navy surplus peacoats, blue work
shirts, rumpled corduroy pants, and Fred Braun sandals congregated at establishments like Greenwich Village's Cafe Wha? and Gerdes's Folk City. Here,
they rubbed chambrayed elbows with representatives of a rising generation of

idealistic, middle-class white social activists whose passion in life was to identify with the socially oppressed. Finding an integrity and lack of pretense in
old-timey folk ballads and finger-picked blues tunes that seemed in short supply elsewhere, they made heroes of those whose nonconformity and aversion
to materialism provided evidence of a pure heart. For a brief time, spiritual
heirs of Woody Guthrie such as Phil Ochs, Joan Baez, and Peter, Paul, and
Mary sated this raging demand for "protest singers" of topical songs. Nevertheless, before long, folkies returning from forays into the civil rights era South
made it known that this would not do. These white "witnesses for freedom" recognized that the times were a-changin' and opted to receive instruction in contemporary race relations from artists who could recount stories of struggle from
an informed, firsthand perspective. Many no longer would settle for Bob Dylan
pining over "The Lonesome Death of Hattie Carroll."[111] They wanted a "Hattie" alive and onstage. If this couldn't be arranged, they would accept Odetta or
Elizabeth Cotten as a substitute. Eventually, supply and demand were adjusted,
and music lovers everywhere could receive "authentic," socially conscious messages from a variety of African-American performer-proselytizers.[112]

White folkies in impromptu jug band performance at Brooklyn College, 1963 (courtesy of
Diane Sommers)

Socialized in the black-church tradition, soul singers seemed ready-made for the job of adapting traditional gospel themes and imagery to the cause of temporal liberation. Certainly, the sacred influence was everywhere apparent in the songs of the southern freedom movement ("Go Tell It on the Mountain," "Up above My Head").[113] Soon, echoes of inspirational movement mainstays like "Freedom Is a Constant Struggle" could be heard in soulful anthems such as the Chi-Lites' "(For God's Sake) Give More Power to the People" and Willie Hightower's ode to the rebirth of black pride, "Time Has Brought about a Change." Like Old Testament prophets, the creators of this activist-oriented music claimed the ability to "see the face of things to come" and some predicted that it "won't be water but fire next time."[114]

Thus, with their gazes fixed on the Promised Land and fingers snapping to the beat, soulsters moved into the Black Power era in a spirit-filled but somewhat less than devotional mood. Having added a political dimension to gospel's liberationist message, they proceeded to compile a list of demands which white elites could ignore at their own risk. Typically, tunefully acerbic social commentary communicated shared racial experiences and promoted black solidarity far better than socially conscious—sometimes self-conscious—white pop songs like "In the Ghetto," "Abraham, Martin and John," and "People Got to Be Free."[115]

The soul singers rejected pity, demanded respect, and proclaimed their people "winners" who were taking advantage of every opportunity and "moving on up." Preferring "true communication" to token integration, they delivered separate messages to blacks ("Be What You Are"; "Get Up, Get into It, Get Involved"; "Fight the Power") and to whites ("We'd rather die on our feet / Than keep living on our knees"; "Move over, son, 'cause I'm comin' through"). With music their "only weapon," some called on government leaders to "stop the war now" and "bring the boys home." Claiming that the "inner city blues" made them "wanna holler," others recounted horrific tales of families living on dogfood and "babies [who] die before they're born / Infected by the grief." All was laid at the feet of the Man, who was told in no uncertain terms to "give the people what they want" (i.e., freedom, justice, and equality) before cries of "burn, baby, burn" rang out across the land.[116]

On occasion, as in Marvin Gaye's multithematic *What's Going On* (1971) LP, these urgent messages were wafted through the airwaves to the accompaniment of angelic strings, gospel-like vocal flourishes, and bubbly Third World rhythms. Like the gently loping but insistent protest music of Jamaican reggae warriors Bob Marley and Peter Tosh, the black musicians' critiques of Babylon seemed to celebrate life even as they embodied struggle, serving as both personal meditation and societal warning shot.[117]

Elsewhere, the music lashed rather than lilted. Abrasive, doomsday-droning

recitations by New York's streetwise improvisation-oriented ensemble the
Last Poets warned listeners that "time is running out on bullshit changes." As
they saw it, the creative artists' role was to "turn people on, to wake people up,"
before black folk found themselves "drowning in a puddle of the white man's
spit." In time, they said, African-Americans—the first people—would be the
last. Until this was accomplished, the Poets vowed to continue their assault
upon the ears and conscience of the record-buying public. Harassing, threatening, and shaming all who were "scared of revolution" or too comfortable or
complacent to believe that white-sponsored genocide was possible, they
joined with confrontational artists such as the Watts Prophets and Gil Scott-
Heron in serving as musicological harbingers of the day white power would
turn to black.[118]

Even blues artists got into the act. Tapping into the music's aesthetically sub-
versive core, they displayed their cantankerous nature by baiting Whitey and
complaining endlessly about the vicissitudes of modern life. In the tradition of
Leadbelly's "Scottsboro Boys" and Big Bill Broonzy's "When Do I Get to Be
Called a Man," the songs of outspoken tunesmiths like J. B. Lenoir, Iverson
Minter (Louisiana Red), and Weldon "Juke Boy" Bonner revealed a younger

The Last Poets, 1970 (courtesy of John T. Matarazzo)

generation's openly defiant attitude toward the repressive norms of an exploitative social order.[119] If some performers still masked their anger by referring to powerful enemies as "they" or "rich people," others abandoned code words, circumspection, and commercial considerations in order to spell out exactly what had given them a case of the "Birmingham Blues" (a fatal 1963 church bombing) or forced them to "Struggle Here in Houston" ("some cat that'll bump you off just to hear his pistol bark"). Described as "semi–folk song[s] and protest" by Windy City blues guitarist Eddy Clearwater, these updated, politicized compositions may have *sounded* like traditional rural blues, but the lyrics reflected changing times and sensibilities.[120] Certainly, no one who listened carefully to the words of Minter's "Red's Dream" could feel that black political empowerment was more than a rollin' stone's throw away. Instead of getting into a blue funk about unspecified wrongs committed by unnamed evildoers, Red put down his harmonica, puffed up his chest, and offered the nation's chief executive specific advice on how to improve his Oval Office job performance:

> You run the country, I'm gonna run the Senate.
> I'm gonna make a few changes, [put] a few soul brothers in it.
> Ray Charles and Lightnin' Hopkins, a guy like Jimmy Reed,
> Bo Diddley and Big Maybelle, all I need.[121]

Clearly, the bluesmen had hit the campaign trail and there was no turning back.

Outside the recording studio, all manner of musicians could be found forwarding oppositional truths and working overtime to transform Red's visionary soundscape into reality. During the civil rights and Black Power years, black culture heroes played benefit concerts for activist causes, lauded the "strength and truth-telling" of marchers and militants, and offered themselves as "living examples of the slogan 'black is beautiful.'"[122] As they urged fans "to organize and become involved and unified," many instituted personal stylistic changes. Given the politically charged atmosphere, these often were interpreted as broad political statements: James Brown sacrificed his highly prized processed pompadour for the movement. Marvin Gaye grew a beard to counter the notion that African-American men shouldn't appear "overtly masculine." Aretha Franklin made a point of being photographed in African-style dress for her album covers. Proudly presenting themselves "just as we are," the black recording stars both mirrored and helped shape cultural norms.[123] The most outspoken would "seize the time" by validating the ethic of social struggle and popularizing freshly minted models of attitude and behavior.[124]

But how did the activists' act play in Peoria? It seemed certain that the musician-as-militant was capable of promoting black self-esteem. Remaining problematic was the question of whether by doing so they risked alienating a significant portion of their interracial audience. To be sure, many musicians (assisted by image-conscious publicists and record label executives) did their best to moderate tensions created by the music's more aggressively anti-institutional tendencies. During the 1968 riots, James Brown broadcast soulful but soothing messages over his radio stations in Baltimore and Knoxville and on live TV in the nation's capital: "Don't terrorize. Organize. Don't burn. Give kids a chance to learn." Claiming to be a humanitarian, not a politician, he noted the illogic of destroying black-owned businesses and urged his fans not to dishonor Dr. King's memory with their blood and rage.[125] Even more conducive to calm was the saccharine civil rights monologue that the Supremes inserted into their nightclub act during the late 1960s. "There's a place for us. A place for all of us," Diana Ross would intone breathlessly during the singing of the *West Side Story* showstopper "Somewhere." "Black and white, Jew and Gentile, Catholic and Protestant. So was the world of Martin Luther King and his idea. If we keep this in mind, then we can carry on his work."[126] Socially conscious high rollers and lounge lizards ate it up and went home inspired. Other Motown acts shunned "message" songs altogether, claiming to be proud of their blackness but refusing to disguise a "lecture" as entertainment. Careful to distinguish between black pride and Black Power, such artists became agitated whenever a "cute teen song" was misinterpreted as a crusading countercultural "statement." Typically, they kept their "political thoughts" to themselves and substituted financial contributions for direct involvement in controversial activist initiatives.[127]

Perhaps this cautious backpedaling was unnecessary. As correctly forecast by prescient Greenwich Village trendsetters, throughout the late 1960s and early 1970s young white folk went positively gaga over black music. With great relish, they sent unbleached nuggets of pure southern soulfulness like Percy Sledge's "When a Man Loves a Woman" to the top of the pop charts and crowded festival stages nationwide in anticipation of receiving life-transforming missives from the mouths of craggy ex–Mississippi sharecroppers or authentic dyed-in-the-'hood blues brothers.[128] In the context of the times, these were remarkable occurrences. This burgeoning musicological multiculturalism suggested that white people either were wising up and acting responsibly in the hope of staving off a predicted racial firestorm or temporarily abandoning their segregated cultural enclaves in search of colorful alternatives to the white-bread entertainments of Bobby Vinton and Petula Clark. Was the troubled land to be free at last or simply free of Frankie Valli and the Four Seasons?

Before this line of inquiry could be explored fully, black conservators of the racial heritage identified a potentially disturbing trend. In the absence of sufficient supplies of suitably aged black blues singers and genuinely groovy soul

brothers and sisters, white "interpreters" were popping up right and left. Indeed, some were turning out surprisingly accurate approximations of black
musical styles—and having hit records with them. Were these rhythmic renderings of a one-time "race music" to be considered high praise or highway
robbery? Emulation or exploitation? Samples of both informed and inflamed
opinion on these issues were plentiful and given out freely. Indeed, lines
formed early at the culture hero's door as perplexed fans sought expert advice
in choosing up sides for what promised to be a fight to the finish over the viability of black cultural distinctions.

Skeptical of white folks' good intentions, champions of the African-
American heroic suggested that imitation was less a form of flattery than an
unnecessary duplication of effort. In support of this viewpoint, they marshaled
considerable evidence from the American musical past which reflected poorly
on the motivations of white artists. Antebellum minstrels, early white bluesmen, rock 'n' rollers, and blue-eyed soulsters were adjudged guilty of traffick-
ing in and profiting from someone else's genius. They had crossed the fine line
distinguishing appropriation from appreciation. All were believed capable of
commiting musicological genocide. In search of fame and fortune, they would
separate black music from its source of inspiration, consign its creators to
opening-act status, and claim credit for any beauty, insight, or vitality that
managed to survive intimate contact with their clammy touch.[129]

Early attempts at black cultural co-optation and commodification were said
to have ranged from the ridiculous to the pathetic, never even approaching the
sublime. In addition to being altogether graceless, banjo-plucking blackface
minstrels' delineations of African polyrhythms were made morally repugnant
by the fact that many of these musical counterfeits were fashioned to racist
ends.[130] Similarly distasteful were the country blues expropriations of Frank
Hutchison, Cliff Carlisle, and Larry Hensley. Here, during the 1920s and
1930s, financial injury and racial insult were added to musicological affront
whenever a nonblack artist made a bundle by successfully "covering" an
African-American composition or, as in the case of pianist Frank Melrose,
when whites chose to record under ludicrous pseudonyms like "Broadway
Rastus."[131] Little wonder, then, that in the mid-1950s, Elvis Presley and other
white rockers would attempt to garner mainstream success with material "borrowed" from black musicians, such as Arthur Crudup, or that a decade later
pale-skinned soul men would seek to pass for the real thing as far away as
Poland, Japan, and Spain. Los Pop Tops, indeed![132]

Thus, if distasteful, the sight of outsiders growing rich through the marketing
of reconstituted black cultural forms was both familiar and anticipated. As noted
by a sarcastic LeRoi Jones in 1968, "the more intelligent the white, the more the
realization he has to steal from niggers." According to this view, most mainstream

music was so lacking in imagination and spontaneity it was imperative that *something* be done, even if it involved pillaging black culture. Fortunately, said race-conscious critics, the imitators continued to be wholly unconvincing. More concerned with swag than with swing and sway, they rarely advanced beyond a superficial understanding of the African-American musical aesthetic. Certainly, this was the white performers' historical burden. "Minstrels," observed Jones, "never convinced anybody they were Black either."[133]

During the Black Power years, this unflattering indictment most often was laid at the feet of white blues-based musicians. The vast majority were deemed noisome hangers-on. Hooked on the blues and infatuated with the "looseness" of black lifestyles, they seemed to spend an inordinate amount of time cruising the clubs and working on developing an appropriately bluesy persona. "If the Elvis-type guy was a wild and crazy guy, you know, then the blues guys were even cooler," asserted white guitarist Michael Bloomfield, confirming black fears. "They were the epitome of what I'd like to be, that sort of attitude." Although talented musicians like Bloomfield eventually developed their own blues forms and utilized the music to articulate personal, political, and generational frustrations, these initial forays into black cultural strongholds rankled. No matter how often whites claimed to be "honoring" African-American musical pioneers by "carrying on the tradition," they would be considered an annoyance until they learned to play their own songs, not just those of Jimmy Reed and Muddy Waters.[134]

Even after personalizing their styles, white blues singers of the 1960s and 1970s were said to owe more to modern audio technology than to deeply felt human emotion. Substituting "artificial, simulated, canned musical pollutants" for naturally soulful expression, they often employed ear-piercing amplification and a variety of "visual-electronic novelty effects" to approximate the "electricity and power of *human* magnetism" generated by skilled black practitioners of the art. Allegedly, most of those who in some fashion managed to duplicate the gut-wrenching intensity of an authentic blues singer's performance could accomplish this feat only with their guitars—and then only when they were under the influence of psychedelic drugs. White vocalists' attempts to mimic the speech patterns and inflections of African-American blues shouters, plantation field hands, or ghetto hipsters typically were dismissed as awkward, insulting, or totally laughable.[135] They most definitely made inferior culture heroes.

By adopting and promoting these views, supporters of the black heroic risked being tagged as chauvinistic racial essentialists. They did so willingly—with shoulders thrown back and chins thrust forward. Under the influence of Black Power and cultural nationalism, many African-Americans were beginning to consider themselves an exceptional people. Why, they asked, should their musical productions be any different? Contemporary black music was said to be derived from tonal and rhythmic values that were part of an African cultural continuum. In the New World, traditional forms were filtered through unique historical experiences. Over time, these musical expressions became the exclusive aesthetic property of the oppressed black masses—an indigenous, spontaneous expression of the collective African-American experience to which no outsider could lay legitimate claim.[136] "We got more soul," boasted the soul brother. "Ain't no white man yet that can sing the blues like the colored guy," added the strutting country bluesman. In this manner, black performers and fans made their most determined, most joyous stand against the white usurpers. Their weapon of choice was a proud particularism which held that nonblacks could attempt to *play* the music but lacked the experiential prerequisites needed to *feel* it deeply or to *become* a true blues or soul artist. "I *am* the blues," they said, daring envious white folks to prove otherwise.[137]

Some would say that this mind-set was alienating and exclusive, that it reinforced racial differences and inhibited cross-cultural communication, that it either unduly burdened black artists with preserving "authenticity" or endowed them with mythic powers. These are only partial truths. During the years 1960–80, black music united blacks *and* facilitated interracial understanding. If this became a burden to the black performers, they seldom complained, perhaps because they were so caught up in the business of behaving like culture heroes. For such individuals, both music and myth served as pop-culture pathways to fame.

As the era progressed, an arresting array of unlikely allies assembled to cheer the black champions on to greater glories. White emulators, both domestic and imported, joined with record industry kingpins and the culture heroes themselves to shape an image of "blackness" which captivated all manner of fans. If each contingent had its own reasons for participating in this endeavor—not all of which were by any means altruistic—they nevertheless put on a spectacular display of multiethnic cooperation in support of the black heroic. It was a show for the ages which no overtly "political" figure—perhaps not even the wonder-working JFK himself—could have staged to such effect.

Refusing to abandon their quest for the soul-satisfying wellspring of wisdom that was said to lie at the headwaters of the black musical stream, white musicians struggled mightily to dodge the slings and arrows of essentialist presumption. While some had more success than others in removing critical barbs from their denim-clad posteriors, even the most hapless wanna-bes helped draw attention to the scope and richness of the African-American musical tradition, to the wisdom and skill of its contemporary practitioners, and to the ability of popular music to transmit messages of liberation and empowerment across the color line.

British bluesmen were particularly enamored with their black American counterparts. What critics interpreted as co-optive copying was to many of these youthful musicians no more than harmless hero worship. Caught up in the worldwide revolt against mainstream conformity, they rejected the reigning pop balladeers of the early 1960s as "plastic," "bland," and "tired." A correspondingly high value was placed on "direct and down to earth" music performed by artists who refused to be "tricked up with million dollar suits." As noted by a young Eric Clapton, it seemed that everything had "been done better, years before, in America by Negroes." For such individuals, respectful emulation appeared the best—perhaps only—way to relate to these exotic ethnic Americans and their "raw, primitive, . . . incredibly personal" music.[138]

Unsolicited testimonials from members of the most important British blues bands of the day (Spencer Davis Group, Savoy Brown, Pretty Things, John Mayall's Bluesbreakers, and the Yardbirds) magnified the black bluesman's mythic aura and encouraged record buyers on both sides of the Atlantic to sample the black culture hero's wares. In some cases, these musicological missionary efforts were undertaken with evangelical fervor. "We had this sort of obsession about pushing rhythm 'n' blues across to a wide public here," recalled the Rolling Stones' Brian Jones. "We wanted *our* idols to be idolized by everybody else. We didn't have the money to buy a banner and cart it through the streets, but if we had we would have done just that." At least in the beginning, "cashing in" on a new trend was said to be the furthest thing from their minds. "If we can play a [Bo] Diddley number, and interest a few more people in him and his stuff, then I reckon we're doing a good job," said Jones's bandmate Mick Jagger. "If we thought we were conning people out of their money, we'd soon shut up and pack up. . . . We *are* fans ourselves. Not just clumsy hangers-on."[139]

To prove their good intentions, British musicians named their bands after black songs and performers (the Groundhogs, after a John Lee Hooker song; Pink Floyd, after Carolina bluesmen Pink Anderson and Floyd Council), adapted the Americans' repertoire and subculture argot to English music hall tastes and dialectical peculiarities, and invited these "living legends" to tour with them throughout Europe as "fathers and sons."[140] On one such occasion in 1965, future Led Zeppelin vocalist Robert Plant was so taken with harpist Sonny Boy Williamson that he stole backstage and pocketed one of the elderly bluesman's instruments. This act of thievery put him into physical contact with his idol and motivated the seventeen-year-old to join a blues band—the Crawling King Snakes, memorializing yet another Hooker tune—later that year.[141] In such cases, established British acts proved themselves more than mere "interpreters" of the black American subculture and its values. They served as enablers—offering black artists who may have been underappreciated in the United States a chance to bask in the spotlight overseas. By doing so, they also provided English teens with an opportunity to learn from the masters firsthand. Many such students came to conceptualize the music as an art form which spoke of both race-specific and universal struggles against economic and emotional poverty.

For the most part, the black heroes seemed to thrive on this unanticipated attention—especially when they were paid regularly and given credit for their contributions to the field. The most worldly-wise among them understood that British guitar slingers had pumped new life into traditional blues forms and that a stamp of approval from, say, one of the Rolling Stones, Animals, or Fleetwood Mac was as good as money in the bank. According to B. B. King, being "discovered" and having one's achievements recognized was "like riding in the front of the bus for the first time."[142]

Some returned the favor by inviting their hip young friends to the States. As the post-Beatles "British invasion" of the midsixties picked up steam, many accepted the kind invitation. During their tour of the colonies, mop-topped delegations performed on *American Bandstand, Shindig!* and *Hullabaloo,* thereby enlightening those who as yet hadn't heard diddly about Bo. As noted by Muddy Waters, this phenomenon of lads from Liverpool and Newcastle taking "coals" to Philadelphia and New York was "a funny damn thing." If good for the black musician's pocketbook and ego, it did somehow seem strange that it took "somebody from out of another country" to provide ill-informed American youth with proper instruction in hero worship. "They're crying for bread," said Waters, "and got it in their backyard."[143]

To make sure that their primacy in the field remained unquestioned, veterans sometimes made life difficult for newcomers, foreign or domestic. The most prickly of the old guard didn't seem terribly impressed by the number of blues LPs an aspiring white bluesman had mail-ordered and memorized. They expected improvisational perfection. As a result, for some white players, the price paid for the privilege of taking the stage with their idols was total embarrassment. "He would turn round to the band, and say 'this ones in E,'" recalled Sonny Boy Williamson sideman Tom McGuinness, "and he would then deliberately start playing in C, or anything but E. Then he'd stop the band and say to the audience, 'You see, these white boys can't play the blues!'"[144]

Even the most studious and highly regarded of the "sons" came in for harsh, unfatherly-like treatment. On one occasion, an angry T-Bone Walker backed Eric Clapton up to a dressing-room wall and, chin to chin, informed him that johnny-come-latelies were to be on their best behavior—and suitably respectful—when in the presence of the "original . . . main man" of blues guitar. In another heated backstage confrontation, Nina Simone and her husband berated the Animals' Eric Burdon for daring to have a big international hit with a cover version of her song "Don't Let Me Be Misunderstood." In the end, all parted amicably, but not before the "nerv[y] . . . little honky" was dressed down for "stealing" Simone's music and recording "the worst rendition of that song I ever heard." Overall, noted Burdon—who once hitchhiked from England to Antibes in the South of France just to see Ray Charles perform—it was a most unforgettable evening.[145]

But black heroes didn't have to be rude or haughty to prove their greatness. They simply had to be themselves and let fans engage in comparative shopping. Some seemed oblivious to the pop music world of their legatees, claiming never to have listened to any of their white emulators' albums. As blues world elder statesman Bukka White remarked after being favored with a backstage performance of "Dust My Broom" by members of the well-established Rolling Stones, "That's good. These boys is *good*. Has you ever made any records?" When informed by Keith Richards that the band had, indeed, sold a few platters, White seemed pleased—and not at all jealous. "This a star, here," he announced, holding his open hand over the white guitarist's head as would a king about to knight a loyal subject. "This a Hollywood Star. If I'm lyin', I'm dyin'."[146] Such confident culture heroes had nothing to fear from the competition.

Other rustic-but-regal types communicated this important message to a newly attentive generation by allowing themselves to be "rediscovered" and field-recorded by folklore researchers. After being flushed from their rural southern lairs, these long-retired former talents were presented in all their unaffected authenticity to college-age audiences whose socialization in the blues had come primarily from overseas or from white artists like Bonnie Raitt or Canned Heat. Many who found themselves the darlings of young hippie America during the 1960s and 1970s hadn't performed professionally or, as noted by Alberta Hunter, hadn't even "hummed a tune" in the bathtub for years.[147]

Nevertheless, proving themselves able self-promoters, the elderly musicians rose to the challenge. The bluesmen's remarkable ability to adapt to changing times and environments was an inspiration to all. Certainly, their willingness to share hard-to-acquire insights with youthful audiences eager to celebrate African-American traditions was evidence of a firm faith placed in the alternative consciousness encapsulated by the black heroic. No wonder white blues aspirants said they felt "far behind" when asked to compare their own proficiency to that of these rejuvenated elder statesmen.[148]

Of course, professional promotion was a part of the cagey culture hero's game plan as well. It couldn't be avoided. In the blues world, bookish folklorist/discoverers transmogrified into aggressive agent/managers with remarkable alacrity. Nor was it unheard of for established blues artists to take their record label's advice and try to expand their audience base by recording potential "crossover" material like Junior Parker's *You Don't Have to Be Black to*

Love the Blues (1973).[149] Some were encouraged to practice what linguists call "code switching," that is, adapting performance style to perceived fan taste. In such instances, a skillful sultan of the switcheroo like John Lee Hooker would play smoothly swinging jazz or soul-tinged urban blues with electric guitar and backup combo in black clubs. For an audience of white folkies, he would dress down, break out the acoustic guitar, and sing solo country blues. The prolific Hooker claimed that he even could do "hillbilly stuff" if necessary.[150]

Soul stylists were somewhat more dependent on outside advisors for assistance in communicating with this diversified clientele. Since they already had the African-American radio-listening and record-buying public in their pocket, the bulk of the professional advice received by soulsters centered on how to improve their demographics among white teens. It seemed that every act desperately wanted a crossover hit. Most were willing to play an occasional open-air pop festival or to be booked as an opening act for the acid brigade's flavor of the month in pursuit of this tantalizing goal. The sight of Joe Tex fronting a band composed of half soul, half country and western musicians or of James Brown—in sequined sweater, stretch pants, and Cuban heels—singing "I Got You (I Feel Good)" to a bevy of frugging alpine lasses in the Frankie Avalon film *Ski Party* may have seemed odd, but there definitely was method in the black performers' seeming madness.[151] As noted by ex-DJ Al Bell, an executive with Stax Records during the late 1960s, the maximum sales an artist could muster with a single that appealed only to a black audience was 300,000—a half million tops. Anything over 250,000 copies sold meant that the record company had succeeded in "getting to the white consumer's ears." A million-seller was deemed impossible without strong biracial appeal.[152]

In search of sales, the industry experimented with numerous marketing techniques and a plethora of gimmicks. The singing chipmunks and novelty "break-in" records of the 1950s were nothing compared to the creation of a frizzy-haired white female singer (Janis Joplin) who idolized Bessie Smith, dressed like a Haight-Ashbury thrift shop, and presented her arm-grabbing brand of "kozmic blues" in the pained, gin-soaked rasp of a down-and-out black barroom queen from Memphis.[153] Hoping to have it both ways, Jimi Hendrix's record company spent considerable time and money marketing an expatriate artist whose Statocaster-served-flambé solos revealed the many artistic and commercial possibilities open to those skilled in borrowing from whites who had stolen from blacks. As one perceptive observer noted, "Hendrix plays Delta blues for sure—only the Delta may have been on Mars."[154] Together, the two flamboyant musicians made a dynamite duo. Gifted with considerable crossover appeal, they were responsible for introducing numerous holdouts and stragglers to the stellar body of work compiled by more traditional blues practitioners.

Even so, no promoters of the cross-cultural ethic were more successful than Berry Gordy and his stable of Tamla/Motown miracle workers. If, initially, this enterprising former featherweight boxer and Detroit auto plant worker entered the record business in order to "capture the feeling of my roots" or to preserve the "down-home quality of warm, soulful country-hearted people I grew up around," he quickly discovered that soul music possessed the potential to generate both pride and profit while conveying a wide range of universally applicable wisdom to a multicultural public. To Motown acts of the early 1960s, the necessity of expanding one's popularity to every conceivable age group, region, and color became a definite given: "Pop meant selling whites, and R & B or soul meant selling the sisters and brothers back in the neighborhood," observed the matter-of-fact Marvin Gaye. "Everyone wanted to sell whites 'cause whites got the most money. Our attitude was—give us some. It's that simple."[155]

While easily fathomed, accomplishment of this task was a complex undertaking involving a host of skilled professional image shapers. The major administrative divisions of this enterprise and their assigned tasks were as follows.

Artist Development. Detroit finishing-school operator Maxine Powell, assisted by staff choreographer Cholly Atkins and musical director Maurice King, taught their starry-eyed charges from the projects all about social graces and graceful moves. Their students learned to sit, stand, shake hands, and gesture properly; the best way to conduct a totally inoffensive interview; and how to kick their youthful gum-snapping, eye-averting, shoulder-slouching habits. Powell and her assistants doubled as road tour chaperones, and it was undoubtedly pressure from this division that convinced Gordy to nix Mary Wilson's plan to install mirrors on her bedroom ceiling. It wouldn't "sound right" if the press found out and violated the Dale Carnegiesque artist development motto: "Your best friend is your self-image."

Songwriting and Production. Employing the wildly successful K.I.S.S. (Keep It Simple Stupid) formula, in-house tunesmiths made sure that even the most out-of-the-loop Caucasians could catch all the words to a Motown song. Merging a booming funk beat with string and horn arrangements performed by members of the Detroit Symphony, this division's masterful knob-twisters created a unique sound. Energetic and primal, yet lush and sophisticated, it was black in ways that appealed to whites and made just about everyone want to do the watusi.

Booking. Major Motown acts were among the most well traveled in the business. They helped open overseas markets for soul music, toured the States with the Rolling Stones and with Dick Clark's Caravan of Stars, and performed at prestigious upscale clubs coast to coast. In late 1964, the Supremes made their first appearance on *The Ed Sullivan Show,* along with the folksy

Serendipity Singers, comedian Frank Gorshin, and Iceland's national basketball team. Numerous TV specials, typically tied to record release dates, followed. Berry Gordy even managed to get his franchise act a guest shot on the weekly *Tarzan* series, where they played nuns and sang "The Lord Helps Those Who Help Themselves." Surely, they knew of what they spoke.

Sales and Promotion. According to Gordy, one had to cope with many unpleasant but unavoidable aspects of the record business when attempting to penetrate mainstream markets. One was that you had to "deal with people's prejudices."[156] Before the music's popularity made such considerations unnecessary, Motown record jackets featured cartoon characters or glamorous white models almost as often as they did photos of the black singers. The Marvelettes' *Please Mr. Postman* (1961) featured a picture of a mailbox; Mary Wells's *Bye Bye Baby* (1961), a love letter.[157] All were promoted by a sales department

The Supremes (*Sepia* magazine, 1969)

which lobbied aggressively to ensure that Motown artists were played on pop radio stations and that their records registered on both the pop and R & B sales charts.[158]

Whether they recorded for Motown or Atlantic, Chess or Stax, most black blues and soul musicians of the years 1960–80 came into contact with some variant of Gordy's cross-cultural star-making machinery. If a few complained about being molded into something they weren't, many others expressed gratitude for the splendid makeover and the once-in-a-lifetime opportunity to vault across the chasm which separated raw talent from large-scale commercial success.

As they worked to perfect their art (and science), many came to understand that both a white musician's emulation of African-American style and a black musician's purposeful efforts to garner mainstream acclaim were significant acts of cultural mediation. The most perceptive recognized that the entire music-making process was grounded in bridge building; that cultural forms often retained their vitality through selective borrowing; and that eyes-only, in-house messages inevitably were "leaked" to surrounding cultural communities, where they provided fodder for both debate and dance. Surely, the early African-American blues singers understood this when they added country, white pop, and English folk ballads to their repertoires. So did modern-day practitioners Eddie Kirkland and Byther Smith. Both freely cited white artists (Jimmie Rodgers, Roy Buchanan) as major stylistic influences, as did many successful southern soulsters whose "sound" was developed in tandem with white songwriter-sidemen such as Steve Cropper, Dan Penn, and Spooner Oldham.[159] As Motown's Smokey Robinson once noted, black music "reached out to everyone." It was in its nature to be both innovative and inclusive.[160] If narrowly political or determinedly academic types considered the black musicians' more "commercial" renderings formulaic or lacking in authenticity, creative artists like Robinson could take satisfaction in the following musicological fact of life: in all eras, there have been those who have labeled as "inauthentic" the very music that most black folk were listening to at the time.[161]

CONCLUSION

Black Camelot Found and Lost

Don't let it be forgot,
That once there was a spot,
For one brief shining moment
That was known as Camelot

ALAN JAY LERNER AND FREDERICK LOEWE

It is a well-known fact that record producers often sweeten their recorded sound by ordering an additional take or by grafting a chorus or horn break onto a previously recorded album track. Hollywood directors frequently alter the endings of their films after less-than-ecstatic test screenings. In sports, the "second season," return bout, or overtime period can transform failed expectations and doused hopes into spirit-lifting, against-the-odds triumphs. Unfortunately, cultural historians must work with a national past that is far less malleable. History may reflect the progressive enlightenment of humankind, but not with any degree of regularity or predictability. There are no guaranteed happy endings in everyday life. Thus, readers who are fond of come-from-behind victories and wholly upbeat conclusions may be well advised to put this book aside until such time as they are emotionally prepared to cope with a mixed review of post-1970s Camelotian prospects.

To be sure, by 1980 the African-American heroes had succeeded in establishing a pop-culture homeland where individuals such as themselves could be universally respected—even revered—while remaining uniquely black and proud. Their Black Camelot stood at the intersection of John F. Kennedy Avenue and W. E. B. Du Bois Boulevard. Both a visionary resolution of Du Boisian duality and a variant of JFK's seamless melding of politics and culture, this unique polity joined aesthetics and commerce, myth and reality, and black and white representational identity in ways previous generations never imagined possible. Certainly, black sports figures, musicians, and action-adventure heroes had worked hard to accomplish this most difficult feat. During the previous twenty years, they had combined talents, strategized carefully, and then aimed their Black Power–fueled Trojan horse smack dab at the living rooms of white, middle-class America. In dire need of a spiritual boost following Kennedy's assassination, nonblacks seemed eager to let these historically maligned "barbarians" breach sacred gates. Before anyone knew it, this cloistered world was alive with messages of both universal and race-specific liberation.

Serving as an integrative social force, black culture heroes sought to bring the troubled land to the cusp of a new era—one in which a significant segment of the majority population at last would admit to a societal diversity it long had feared and refused to acknowledge. Indeed, with both the national will and minority-group aspirations in sync, the time seemed right for these courageous mediators to lead their followers into a multicultural Promised Land. Here, it was believed, significant revolutions of the mind would be accompanied by tangible economic and political gains as former black cultural counterpoints became majoritarian understandings. To steal a line from rhythm-and-blues great Screamin' Jay Hawkins, these developments wouldn't "put pretty hair on grandma's bald head" (i.e., solve all the nation's race-related problems), but they definitely would mark an important milestone in Afro-America's historical struggle against adversity.[1] Perhaps Du Bois's heroic vision *could* serve as a model for a universally expressed humanism. Perhaps Kennedy's short-lived Camelot, replete with an array of African-American dignitaries, *could* be resurrected. For a time, the possibilities seemed endless.

Sadly, however, long before the vast majority of ordinary humans were able to join their heroic role models within Black Camelot's protective walls, the narrow drawbridge connecting black and white cultural communities was raised in response to what has been termed the "Reagan Revolution" of the 1980s. If more a nostalgic reaffirmation of midcentury bourgeois normalcy than a true revolution, the Reagan ascendancy altered the course of history. The "Great Communicator's" stunning electoral victory (489 to 49) over a beleaguered Jimmy Carter provided legions of long-exiled conservative loyalists with a heroic symbol for a disengaged age. Serving as a rallying point for all who were tired of conflict, hard questions, and the relentlessness of change, Reagan proved himself a master of conjuring up visions of the truly needy and the truly greedy—and then blurring the distinction between them. He placed foxes in regulatory henhouses, privileged individual aggrandizement over the quest for community, and effected a strategic withdrawal from social policies that had attempted to address the complex problems facing black and poor people. The administration's opposition to affirmative action and public-school busing served to weaken national social consciousness, thereby making racism both more palatable and increasingly potent politically. To blacks and others excluded from the shaping of this ambitious agenda, the Reagan Revolution was no benign celebration of a prelapsarian "don't worry, be happy," world where non-Kennedyesque dreams at long last came true. It was an unconscionable squandering of a once-in-a-lifetime opportunity to put America's house in order, a turning away from the nation's emerging multicultural future.[2]

Both pathos and irony were involved in these developments. Jack Kennedy was a politician who became a movie-star-quality cultural icon. The new Republican president was a retired Hollywood actor and television host turned successful politician. When addressing policy matters central to the continuation of the American saga, each worked from his own script and employed a different cast of supporting characters. Since little of JFK's scene-stealing charisma seemed to have rubbed off on brother Ted and the other leading Democrats of the day, it was the beginning of a proverbial dark night of the soul for those who had found the possibilities of a peaceable, progressive, united Camelotian republic so magical and inspiring.

To many, it now seemed certain that the societal pendulum would return to its more customary right-of-centrist position. The purely pragmatic pointed out that it had been drifting in that direction for some time. Those who preferred to view the world in the harsh, unforgiving light of day—rather than through rose-colored Aquarian glasses—claimed that there were far more roadblocks on the pathway to Black Camelot than the combined might of culture heroes could dismantle in several lifetimes. As with King Arthur's Camelot, some began to question whether the black domain existed at all, for any dark-skinned person, hero or otherwise.

Even hopeful idealists and those who traditionally placed more faith in culture than in politics recognized that a long shot had become far longer. The possibility of realizing the improbable became ever more fanciful. Everywhere, earlier activist initiatives were being disparaged by nostalgic knights in rusty armor. Black Power was out and Buppies in. Young Republicans stepped lively while aging militants lay low, licking their wounds and growing cynical. Worse yet, 1960s styles were being mothballed. Soul was consumed by the disco inferno of the late 1970s, which in turn was snuffed out in the 1980s by a rap attack of major proportions.[3] In Hollywood, a megamedia conglomerate-sponsored "cinema of recuperation" substituted the *Star Wars* trilogy and Sylvester Stallone's *Rocky* series for *Shaft* and *Super Fly*.[4] Before long, even Sweet Sweetback (Melvin Van Peebles) seemed to realize that the day of the baadasssss had passed. During the 1980s, he emerged from the blaxploitation jungle as a Wall Street floor trader and author of *Bold Money: How to Get Rich in the Options Market*.[5] Gone, it seemed, were the head-turning, mind-changing cultural visions of yesteryear.

As one would expect, nasty rumors about JFK's Camelot circulated widely in this changed environment. These recyled tales of Kennedy's extramarital affairs and other déclassé deeds cast an ominous shadow upon "New Frontier" conceptualizations and initiatives.[6] But the former president wasn't the only one to receive such a "reappraisal." In the last two decades of the millennium, all manner of culture heroes have come under intense scrutiny—their every weakness probed and flaw magnified. Seemingly, it wasn't bad enough that *Shaft's* once mighty Richard Roundtree was acting in summer stock or that *Cleopatra Jones's* Tamara Dobson had been reduced to doing German-made women's prison flicks.[7] Insults to the superstars' image and dignity began to come from previously "friendly" sources, even from blood relatives. In one of the best-known examples of this trend, what impressionable Jackson 5 fans once had been led to believe was a group of "regular kids," leading a "surprisingly normal family life," turned out to be a "not-so-typical but classic dysfunctional family. . . . poisoned by emotional and physical abuse, duplicity, and denial." These revelations by Jackson sister LaToya cast the bubble-gum soulsters in a newly unfavorable light and foreshadowed even more disturbing revelations about brother Michael. Was it all, as Ms. Jackson and disaffected stargazers claimed, a "charade" and a "lie"?[8] Would the authors of hero-debunking "tell-all" exposés have the final word on the import and character of the 1960s and 1970s culture heroes? Had we entered a postheroic age?

According to some observers, whatever once was considered special or glamorous about the star-making process now had become routine, even mechanical. "Everybody knows how it happens, everybody knows what toll it takes," remarked one world-weary entertainment industry insider in 1994. "The magic isn't in the rise, the magic is in the disintegration."[9] The tragic fall of once ascendant recording stars such as Jimi Hendrix and Janis Joplin, as well as a variety of public opinion polls showing a relative decline in belief in heroes, gave credence to this downbeat conclusion.[10]

Nevertheless, not all was lost. Gloom and doom might occasionally occlude, but they could not obliterate the culture hero's resplendent visage. Hero bashing—while on the rise—was not destined to become the national pastime. Despite recession and Reaganomics, Watergate and Whitewater, the heroic continues to have an abundance of supporters. Today, an estimated 3,500 fan clubs (450 for Elvis Presley alone) keep the flames of fandom alive.[11] Supported by less celebrity-oriented ventures such as the Pittsburgh-based Carnegie Hero Fund Commission and the Giraffe Project of Langley, Washington (both of which honor nonfamous heroes who "stick their necks out and stand tall for what they believe in"), these lobbyists for the larger-than-life are constantly searching for fresh faces and courageous constitutions.[12] They also respect past champions and their heirs—as was evidenced upon the passing of Jackie Kennedy Onassis in 1994 and by the media's designation of John Jr. as a modern-day Prince Charming.[13] Certainly, filmmaker Oliver Stone understood the power and undying attraction of major national heroes when, in *Nixon* (1995), he had the tired, disgraced chief executive pour out his soul to a portrait of the forever youthful JFK. "When they look at you, they see what they want to be," he mused. "When they look at me, they see what they are."[14] Herein lies the key to the remarkable staying power of culture heroes.

During the past twenty years, black heroes have shown that they, too, operate on this informed understanding of pop culture's unique interface with the real world. If they have been unable to effect the type of "political" liberation forecast during the Black Power years, most maintain an active interest in the closely related area of spiritual rejuvenation. Although the raging floods of the Reagan era severely damaged the bridge upon which the long-suffering pilgrims were to cross over into Camelot, it nevertheless is heartening to learn that new hero/bridge builders are being apprenticed daily. Some sound remarkably like the most boisterous barricade busters of old—talking tough to Whitey while digitally sampling 1960s tunes and ideologies in their gritty rap re-creations of urban reality.[15] Others pay homage to the big-screen heroes of the 1970s through their hard-boiled Hollywood homeboy personas.[16] Still others re-create themselves while formulating new myths for the 1990s, for example, soccer great Pelé's claiming the ability to cure children of cancer and pro hoops legend Wilt Chamberlain's boasting about having had sex with 20,000 women.[17] It is a diverse lot. Collectively, they serve as a vivid metaphorical representation of a defiantly nonstereotypical population.

In building on past styles and achievements, today's heroes make us aware that the nation as a whole has drawn somewhat closer to Camelot's borders over the years. While still deeply troubled by difference, we have not totally abandoned the search for common ground. If, in the future, Black Camelot is to be more than an ideal, all prospective citizens will need a measure of Job's patience and Solomon's wisdom—and the good sense to avail themselves of the many proactive services provided by African-American culture heroes. Past experiences on the road to Camelot suggest that the heroes are invaluable allies. Without their empowering protest ethic and advanced intergroup mediational skills, it is unlikely that our weak wills and flabby moral characters can be strengthened sufficiently to make the final leg of this epic pilgrimage. By maintaining the viability of the heroic tradition, black culture heroes provide hope that their Camelot will someday be a thriving concern populated by millions of self-directed, liberty-loving folk—a multicultural collective of individuals who have succeeded in having their "star" potential recognized, unequivocally, by all.

NOTES

Introduction

1. Thomas Carlyle, *On Heroes, Hero-Worship, and the Heroic in History* (1841; reprint, London: Oxford University Press, 1968), 1.

2. Lee R. Edwards, *Psyche as Hero: Female Heroism and Fictional Form* (Middletown, Conn.: Wesleyan University Press, 1984), 4; Marshall W. Fishwick, *American Heroes: Myth and Reality* (Washington, D.C.: Public Affairs Press, 1954), 3; Marshall Fishwick, *The Hero, American Style* (New York: David McKay, 1969), 25; Dixon Wecter, *The Hero in America: A Chronicle of Hero-Worship* (New York: Charles Scribner's Sons, 1941), 476, 486, 488; James D. Wilson, *The Romantic Heroic Ideal* (Baton Rouge: Louisiana State University Press, 1982), 15.

3. Marshall W. Fishwick, *Seven Pillars of Popular Culture* (Westport, Conn.: Greenwood, 1985), 61.

4. Daniel J. Boorstin, *The Image: A Guide to Pseudo-Events in America* (New York: Harper & Row, 1964), 45–76; Joseph Campbell, *The Power of Myth* (New York: Doubleday, 1988), 132; Mark Gerzon, *A Choice of Heroes: The Changing Faces of American Manhood* (Boston: Houghton Mifflin, 1982), 233; Orrin E. Klapp, *Heroes, Villains, and Fools: The Changing American Character* (Englewood Cliffs, N.J.: Prentice-Hall, 1962), 123, 143–44; Deyan Sudjic, *Cult Heroes: How to Be Famous for More than Fifteen Minutes* (New York: W. W. Norton, 1990), 10, 14.

5. Kenneth A. Bruffee, *Elegiac Romance: Cultural Change and Loss of the Hero in Modern Fiction* (Ithaca: Cornell University Press, 1983), 15, 54; Theodore L. Gross, *The Heroic Ideal in American Literature* (New York: Free Press, 1971), 193–95, 294; Joe McGinniss, *Heroes* (New York: Viking, 1976), 16–18, 26; Arthur M. Schlesinger Jr., "The Decline of Greatness," *Saturday Evening Post,* 1 November 1958, 25, 68, 70–71.

6. Ray B. Browne, "Hero with 2,000 Faces," in *The Hero in Transition,* ed. Ray B. Browne and Marshall W. Fishwick (Bowling Green: Bowling Green University Popular Press, 1983), 92–94.

7. William Manchester, *Portrait of a President: John F. Kennedy in Profile* (1964; reprint, New York: Macfadden-Bartell, 1967), 46, 67, 82; Mary Barelli Gallagher, *My Life with Jacqueline Kennedy* (New York: Paperback Library, 1970), 151.

8. Jim Bishop, *A Day in the Life of President Kennedy* (New York: Bantam, 1964), 89.

9. On Kennedy's medical history, see Joan Blair and Clay Blair Jr., *The Search for JFK* (New York: Berkley, 1976).

10. Bishop, *Day in the Life,* 10; Hugh Sidey, *John F. Kennedy, President* (Greenwich, Conn.: Fawcett, 1964), 205, 354.

11. Theodore C. Sorensen, *Kennedy* (New York: Bantam, 1966), 412.

12. Kenneth P. O'Donnell, David F. Powers, and Joe McCarthy, *"Johnny, We Hardly Knew Ye": Memories of John Fitzgerald Kennedy* (New York: Pocket Books, 1973), 418.

13. Bill Adler, ed., *The Complete Kennedy Wit* (New York: Citadel, 1967), 63.

14. Sorensen, *Kennedy,* 429; Gene Wortsman, *The New Frontier Joke Book* (New York: Macfadden, 1963), 31, 59, 81.

15. Anne H. Lincoln, *The Kennedy White House Parties* (New York: Viking, 1967), 50, 118, 138, 152; Thomas Brown, *JFK: History of an Image* (Bloomington: Indiana University Press, 1988), 13–15.

16. Sidey, *Kennedy,* 336–37.

17. Manchester, *Portrait,* 73, 75–76.

18. Robert J. Donovan, *PT 109: John F. Kennedy in World War II* (Greenwich, Conn.: Fawcett, 1962); Jimmy Dean, "PT 109," Columbia 42338, 1962; *PT 109* (Warner Brothers, 1963).

19. O'Donnell, Powers, and McCarthy, *Memories,* 73; Gallagher, *My Life,* 173; Donovan, *PT 109,* 155.

20. Sorensen, *Kennedy,* 840.

21. Ibid., 55, 115, 529.

22. William H. A. Carr, *JFK: The Life and Death of a President* (New York: Lancer, 1963), 106.

23. Carl M. Brauer, *John F. Kennedy and the Second Reconstruction* (New York: Columbia University Press, 1977), 46.

24. Harry Golden, *Mr. Kennedy and the Negroes* (Greenwich, Conn.: Fawcett, 1964), 114.

25. Brauer, *Reconstruction,* 68–69, 84, 319; Sorensen, *Kennedy,* 536; Robert E. Gilbert, "John F. Kennedy and Civil Rights for Black Americans," *Presidential Studies Quarterly* 12 (summer 1982): 386–88.

26. Irving Bernstein, *Promises Kept: John F. Kennedy's New Frontier* (New York: Oxford University Press, 1991), 296; Hugh Davis Graham, *The Civil Rights Era: Origins and Development of National Policy, 1960–1972* (New York: Oxford University Press, 1990), 74–99, 125–34.

27. Brauer, *Reconstruction,* 75; Taylor Branch, *Parting the Waters: America in the King Years, 1954–63* (New York: Simon & Schuster, 1988), 656–72, 821–24; Golden, *Mr. Kennedy and the Negroes,* 121.

28. Thomas C. Reeves, *A Question of Character: A Life of John F. Kennedy* (New York: Free Press, 1991), 348; Golden, *Mr. Kennedy and the Negroes,* 120–21.

29. Theodore H. White, *In Search of History: A Personal Adventure* (New York: Harper & Row, 1978), 472; Reeves, *Question of Character,* 211.

30. John F. Kennedy, *Profiles in Courage* (New York: Pocket Books, 1957), 203–6, 209; Sorensen, *Kennedy,* 852.

31. George H. Gallup, *The Gallup Poll: Public Opinion, 1935–1971,* vol. 3, *1959–1971* (New York: Random House, 1972), 1717, 1850.

32. For a detailed account of the funeral, see William Manchester, *The Death of a President: November 20–November 25, 1963* (New York: Harper & Row, 1967). On media coverage of Kennedy's death, see Barbie Zelizer, *Covering the Body: The Kennedy Assassination, the Media, and the Shaping of Collective Memory* (Chicago: University of Chicago Press, 1992).

33. Gallagher, *My Life,* 341; William G. Walsh, *Children Write about John F. Kennedy* (Brownsville, Tex.: Springman-King, 1964), 1, 6–8, 10, 33, 57.

34. Anne Chamberlin, "The Commercialization of J.F.K.," *Saturday Evening Post,* 21 November 1964, 20–21; Herbert Kupferberg, "Kennedy Memorial Albums," *Atlantic* 213 (April 1964): 134, 136–37; "Memorial Boom," *Newsweek,* 30 December 1963, 49–50; Edward C. Rochette, *The Medallic Portraits of John F. Kennedy* (Iola, Wis.: Krause, 1966). For a

sampling of blues-based musical tributes, see the compilation CD *Can't Keep from Crying,*
Testament 5007.

35. "A Compendium of Curious Coincidences," *Time,* 21 August 1964, 19; Eyal J.
Naveh, *Crown of Thorns: Political Martyrdom in America from Abraham Lincoln to Martin Luther
King, Jr.* (New York: New York University Press, 1990), 174; Vincent L. Toscano, *Since Dallas: Images of John F. Kennedy in Popular and Scholarly Literature, 1963–1973* (San Francisco:
R & E Research Associates, 1978), 3.

36. Bruce A. Rosenberg, "Kennedy in Camelot: The Arthurian Legend in America,"
Western Folklore 35 (January 1976): 52–59; "Ari Bought Jackie the Island of Scorpios," *National Enquirer,* 2 July 1970, 1, 8–9.

37. For a paradigmatic portrayal of JFK's life as a classical heroic saga, see Fishwick, *Hero,*
11–12.

38. White, *In Search of History,* 523.

39. Rose Fitzgerald Kennedy, *Times to Remember* (Garden City, N.Y.: Doubleday, 1974),
112.

40. Henry Fairlie, *The Kennedy Promise: The Politics of Expectation* (New York: Dell, 1974),
7, 123, 151, 257, 292.

41. Reeves, *A Question of Character,* 414–15; Nancy Gager Clinch, *The Kennedy Neurosis*
(New York: Grosset & Dunlap, 1973), 19; Richard J. Barnet, *Intervention and Revolution: The
United States in the Third World* (New York: World, 1968), 208–12; William L. O'Neill, *Coming Apart: An Informal History of America in the 1960's* (Chicago: Quadrangle, 1971), 76–83,
91–92, 135; Kent M. Beck, "The Kennedy Image: Politics, Camelot, and Vietnam," *Wisconsin Magazine of History* 58 (autumn 1974): 50–55; Noam Chomsky, *Rethinking Camelot:
JFK, the Vietnam War, and U.S. Political Culture* (Boston: South End, 1993), 49–83.

42. Brauer, *Reconstruction,* 11, 13–14, 29; Harvard Sitkoff, *The Struggle for Black Equality,
1954–1980* (New York: Hill & Wang, 1981), 106–7, 124–25, 128, 138.

43. Victor Lasky, *J.F.K.: The Man and the Myth* (New York: Macmillan, 1963), 251; Brauer,
Reconstruction, 87–88, 165, 167; Clayborne Carson, *In Struggle: SNCC and the Black Awakening of the 1960s* (Cambridge: Harvard University Press, 1981), 83–95; Manning Marable, *Race,
Reform, and Rebellion: The Second Reconstruction in Black America, 1945–1982* (Jackson: University Press of Mississippi, 1984), 79–83; Jack M. Bloom, *Class, Race, and the Civil Rights
Movement* (Bloomington: Indiana University Press, 1987), 165–68; Brown, *JFK: History of an
Image,* 58–59; Reeves, *A Question of Character,* 336, 338; Mark Stern, *Calculating Visions:
Kennedy, Johnson, and Civil Rights* (New Brunswick: Rutgers University Press, 1992), 63–112.

44. Fairlie, *Kennedy Promise,* 202–6; Simeon Booker, *Black Man's America* (Englewood
Cliffs, N.J.: Prentice-Hall, 1964), 32; Martin Luther King Jr., "Fumbling on the New Frontier," *Nation,* 3 March 1962, 191; Victor S. Navasky, *Kennedy Justice* (New York: Atheneum,
1971), 97–99, 243–76.

45. Kitty Kelley, *Jackie Oh!* (New York: Ballantine, 1979), 122–24; Stephen Dunleavy and
Peter Brennan, *Those Wild, Wild Kennedy Boys* (New York: Pinnacle, 1976), 68–70; "Jack
Kennedy's Other Women," *Time,* 29 December 1975, 11–12; Judith Exner, *My Story* (New
York: Grove, 1977), 89–105, 131–35, 164–66, 176–78, 205, 218–22, 238–48; Traphes
Bryant and Frances Spatz Leighton, *Dog Days at the White House: The Outrageous Memoirs of
the Presidential Kennel Keeper* (New York: Macmillan, 1975), 37–40; Maxine Cheshire and
John Greenya, *Maxine Cheshire, Reporter* (Boston: Houghton Mifflin, 1978), 54–59, 114;
Nancy Dickerson, *Among Those Present: A Reporter's View of Twenty-five Years in Washington*
(New York: Random House, 1976), 66–67; Herbert S. Parmet, *JFK: The Presidency of John F.
Kennedy* (New York: Dial, 1983), 111–12, 304–7.

46. Dunleavy and Brennan, *Kennedy Boys,* 85, 104–5; Kelley, *Jackie Oh!* 132, 134–35.

47. Tristram Potter Coffin and Hennig Cohen, eds., *The Parade of Heroes: Legendary Figures in American Lore* (Garden City, N.Y.: Anchor/Doubleday, 1978), 365.

48. A *Newsweek* poll conducted in October 1983 revealed that three-quarters of those interviewed rated the Kennedy presidency as good to great. Thirty percent wished that JFK was still president. "Kennedy Remembered: After 20 Years, A Man Lost in His Legend," *Newsweek,* 28 November 1983, 64. See also Louis Harris, *The Anguish of Change* (New York: W. W. Norton, 1973), 201.

49. On this point, see Paul R. Henggeler, *In His Steps: Lyndon Johnson and the Kennedy Mystique* (Chicago: Ivan R. Dee, 1991).

Chapter One

1. Henry Cabot Lodge and Theodore Roosevelt, *Hero Tales from American History* (New York: Century, 1895), 2–3.

2. Ibid., 4–5, 7–8.

3. Ibid., 11–14. For evaluations of Washington's heroic image in other American-history books, see Ruth Miller Elson, *Guardians of Tradition: American Schoolbooks of the Nineteenth Century* (Lincoln: University of Nebraska Press, 1964), 194–203; William Alfred Bryan, *George Washington in American Literature, 1775–1865* (New York: Columbia University Press, 1952), 86–120; Barry Schwartz, *George Washington: The Making of an American Symbol* (New York: Free Press, 1987), 107–18, 193–207.

4. M. A. DeWolfe Howe, *James Ford Rhodes: American Historian* (New York: D. Appleton, 1929), 120. On Roosevelt's racial ideology, see Thomas G. Dyer, *Theodore Roosevelt and the Idea of Race* (Baton Rouge: Louisiana State University Press, 1980).

5. For commentary on racism and Teutonism in the American historical profession of the era, see I. A. Newby, *Jim Crow's Defense: Anti-Negro Thought in America, 1900–1930* (Baton Rouge: Louisiana State University Press, 1965), 52–82; John David Smith, *An Old Creed for the New South: Proslavery Ideology and Historiography, 1865–1918* (Westport, Conn.: Greenwood, 1985), 103–96.

6. For biographical treatments of Du Bois's multifaceted career, see Arnold Rampersad, *The Art and Imagination of W. E. B. Du Bois* (Cambridge: Harvard University Press, 1976); Manning Marable, *W. E. B. Du Bois: Black Radical Democrat* (Boston: Twayne, 1986); David Levering Lewis, *W. E. B. Du Bois: Biography of a Race, 1868–1919* (New York: Henry Holt, 1993).

7. W. E. Burghardt Du Bois, *The Souls of Black Folk* (1903; reprint, Greenwich, Conn.: Fawcett, 1961), 17. For contemporary interpretations and applications of Du Bois's ideas about the dualities in black self-perception which result from being both "a Negro and an American," see Gerald Early, ed., *Lure and Loathing: Essays on Race, Identity, and the Ambivalence of Assimilation* (New York: Penguin, 1993).

8. For commentary on the shaping of Du Bois's views regarding racial characteristics, see Wilson Jeremiah Moses, *Black Messiahs and Uncle Toms: Social and Literary Manipulations of a Religious Myth* (University Park: Pennsylvania State University Press, 1982), 171–75; Wilson Jeremiah Moses, *The Golden Age of Black Nationalism, 1850–1925* (Hamden, Conn.: Archon, 1978), 133–36, 159–69; Sterling Stuckey, *Slave Culture: Nationalist Theory and the Foundations of Black America* (New York: Oxford University Press, 1987), 263–76; Vincent Harding, "W. E. B. Du Bois and the Black Messianic Vision," *Freedomways* 9 (winter 1969): 44–58.

9. Du Bois, *Souls,* 16, 22; W. E. Burghardt Du Bois, *The Gift of Black Folk: The Negroes in*

the *Making of America* (1924; reprint, New York: Washington Square, 1970), 158, 178, 189–90; W. E. Burghardt Du Bois, *Dusk of Dawn: An Essay toward an Autobiography of a Race Concept* (1940; reprint, New York: Schocken, 1968), 147–48, 150–51; W. E. B. Du Bois, "The Shadow of Years," *Crisis* 15 (February 1918): 167.

10. Du Bois, "Shadow," 168; W. E. Burghardt Du Bois, "Criteria of Negro Art," *Crisis* 32 (October 1926): 292; W. E. B. Du Bois, *Darkwater: Voices from within the Veil* (1920; reprint, New York: Schocken, 1969), 46; Du Bois, *Dusk,* 148–49; W. E. Burghardt Du Bois, *The World and Africa: An Inquiry into the Part Which Africa Has Played in World History* (1947; reprint, New York: International, 1965), 23; W. E. B. Du Bois, "Jefferson Davis as a Representative of Civilization" (1890), in *Writings,* ed. Nathan I. Huggins (New York: Library of America, 1986), 812; W. E. B. Du Bois, "The Burden of Black Women," *Crisis* 9 (November 1914): 31.

11. Du Bois, *World,* 24; Du Bois, "Jefferson Davis," 811–13; Nathan I. Huggins, "W. E. B. Du Bois and Heroes," *Amerikastudien/American Studies* 34, no. 2 (1989): 167–74. For Du Bois's views on the relative virtues of the slaveholding George Washington, the black American military heroes of the Revolutionary War, and Toussaint-L'Ouverture, see W. E. B. Du Bois, "George Washington and Black Folk: A Pageant for the Bicentenary, 1732–1932," *Crisis* 39 (April 1932): 121–24.

12. Du Bois, "Jefferson Davis," 813; Du Bois, *Souls,* 17; Du Bois, *Gift,* 189–90.

13. W. E. B. Du Bois, "The Song of the Smoke," *Horizon* 1 (February 1907): 5; Du Bois, *Dusk,* 148, 153; W. E. B. Du Bois, "The Conservation of Races" (1897), in *Writings,* 822.

14. Du Bois, *Dusk,* 97, 149.

15. For an introduction to the resources available for the study of black imagery in American popular culture, see Jessie Carney Smith, ed., *Images of Blacks in American Culture: A Reference Guide to Information Sources* (Westport, Conn.: Greenwood, 1988). Broadbased interpretive studies based on these materials include Catherine Silk and John Silk, *Racism and Anti- racism in American Popular Culture: Portrayals of African-Americans in Fiction and Film* (Manchester: Manchester University Press, 1990); and William L. Van Deburg, *Slavery and Race in American Popular Culture* (Madison: University of Wisconsin Press, 1984).

16. Aphra Behn, *Oroonoko; or, the Royal Slave* (1688; reprint, New York: W. W. Norton, 1973). For other British models of tragic Africans, see Thomas George Street, *Aura; or, The Slave* (London: J. Stevenson, 1788); Anna Maria Mackenzie, *Slavery; or, The Times* (London: G. G. J. and J. Robinsons and J. Dennis, 1792).

17. Thomas Branagan, *The Penitential Tyrant* (Philadelphia: privately printed, 1805), 77. For other early fictional treatments of slave suicide and death, see "The Desperate Negroe," *Massachusetts Magazine* 5 (October 1793): 583–84; L. B., "Nico—A Fragment," *New-York Weekly Magazine,* 27 January 1796, 239; "Extraordinary Friendship of Two Negroes," *Philadelphia Minerva,* 16 December 1797, 3.

18. Dion Boucicault, *The Octoroon; or, Life in Louisiana* (1859; reprint, Upper Saddle River, N.J.: Literature House/Gregg, 1970), 16–17. For other examples of the tragic mulatto archetype, see John Townsend Trowbridge, *Neighbor Jackwood* (Boston: Phillips, Sampson, 1857); Joseph Holt Ingraham, *The Quadroone; or, St. Michael's Day* (London: Richard Bentley, 1840); Henry Wadsworth Longfellow, "The Quadroon Girl," in *Poems on Slavery* (Cambridge: J. Owen, 1842); Mayne Reid, *The Quadroon; or, A Lover's Adventures in Louisiana* (New York: R. M. DeWitt, 1856); H. L. Hosmer, *Adela, the Octoroon* (Columbus, Ohio: Follett, Foster, 1860). See also Judith R. Berzon, *Neither White nor Black: The Mulatto Character in American Fiction* (New York: New York University Press, 1978).

19. For material-culture artifacts depicting this archetype, see Robbin Henderson, Pamela Fabry, and Adam David Miller, eds., *Ethnic Notions: Black Images in the White Mind* (Berkeley: Berkeley Art Center Association, 1982); Jackie Young, *Black Collectibles: Mammy and Her Friends* (West Chester, Pa.: Schiffer, 1988); Dawn E. Reno, *Collecting Black Americana* (New York: Crown, 1986); P. J. Gibbs, *Black Collectibles Sold in America* (Paducah, Ky.: Collector, 1987); Kenneth W. Goings, *Mammy and Uncle Mose: Black Collectibles and American Stereotyping* (Bloomington: Indiana University Press, 1994); Patricia A. Turner, *Ceramic Uncles and Celluloid Mammies: Black Images and Their Influence on Culture* (New York: Anchor, 1994). Lyrics to the late 1920s–early 1930s songs cited may be found in Sam Dennison, *Scandalize My Name: Black Imagery in American Popular Music* (New York: Garland, 1982), 458, 463, 467–68. In operation from 1924 through the early 1950s, Coon Chicken Inns could be recognized by the large, smiling black porter's face that adorned the front of each restaurant. Patrons entered through his mouth.

20. Thomas Cripps, *Slow Fade to Black: The Negro in American Film, 1900–1942* (New York: Oxford University Press, 1977), 28–29.

21. A. C. Gordon and Thomas Nelson Page, *Befo' de War: Echoes in Negro Dialect* (New York: Charles Scribner's Sons, 1888), 118.

22. John Spencer Bassett, *Slavery and Servitude in the Colony of North Carolina* (Baltimore: Johns Hopkins Press, 1896), 11.

23. Jim Haskins and N. R. Mitgang, *Mr. Bojangles: The Biography of Bill Robinson* (New York: William Morrow, 1988), 44.

24. On the early minstrel-style radio comics, see Joseph Boskin, *Sambo: The Rise and Demise of an American Jester* (New York: Oxford University Press, 1986), 164–97; Arthur Frank Wertheim, *Radio Comedy* (New York: Oxford University Press, 1979), 18–58; J. Fred MacDonald, *Don't Touch That Dial! Radio Programming in American Life, 1920–1960* (Chicago: Nelson-Hall, 1979), 331, 336–37, 340–45, 350–51; William Barlow, "Commercial and Noncommercial Radio," in *Split Image: African Americans in the Mass Media,* ed. Jannette L. Dates and William Barlow (Washington, D.C.: Howard University Press, 1990), 175–89.

25. "Over the Mountain," in *The Ethiopian Glee Book,* by Elias Howe [Gumbo Chaff] (Boston: Elias Howe, 1848), 31; Dan Myers and Silas S. Steele, "Dandy Jim O'Caroline," in Howe, *Glee Book,* 7; "Black Sam," in *Christy's Panorama Songster* (New York: William H. Murphy, 1860), 134; Boskin, *Sambo,* 166.

26. Melvin Patrick Ely, *The Adventures of Amos 'n' Andy: A Social History of an American Phenomenon* (New York: Free Press, 1991), 79, 119–24; Boskin, *Sambo,* 143, 181.

27. Bart Andrews and Ahrgus Juilliard, *Holy Mackerel! The Amos 'n' Andy Story* (New York: E. P. Dutton, 1986), 38.

28. James Fenimore Cooper, *The Spy: A Tale of the Neutral Ground* (1821; reprint, New York: Dodd, Mead, 1946), 100, 104, 201; Alfonso Sherman, "The Diversity of Treatment of the Negro Character in American Drama prior to 1860" (Ph.D. diss., Indiana University, 1964), 84, 156; Ely, *Amos 'n' Andy,* 77–78.

29. James H. Fairchild, *The Underground Railroad* (Cleveland: Western Reserve Historical Society, 1895), 94; Eber M. Pettit, *Sketches in the History of the Underground Railroad* (Fredonia, N.Y.: W. McKinstry, 1879), 90; Wilbur H. Siebert, *The Underground Railroad from Slavery to Freedom* (New York: Macmillan, 1898), 87; John Spencer Bassett, *A Short History of the United States* (New York: Macmillan, 1913), 470.

30. J. H. Collins and Frank Sulzner, "The Slave's Return" (New York: William Hall, 1851); Charles White, *Uncle Eph's Dream* (1874), in *This Grotesque Essence: Plays from the*

American Minstrel Stage, ed. Gary D. Engle (Baton Rouge: Louisiana State University Press, 1978), 57; Dan Emmett, "I'm Going Home to Dixie" (1861), in *Dan Emmett and the Rise of Early Negro Minstrelsy,* by Hans Nathan (Norman: University of Oklahoma Press, 1962), 351–53.

31. Ulrich B. Phillips, *Life and Labor in the Old South* (1929; reprint, Boston: Little, Brown, 1963), 196.

32. Wertheim, *Radio Comedy,* 41.

33. A. C. D. Sandie, "Ole Uncle Abrum's Comin'" (ca. 1862), in *The Singing Sixties: The Spirit of Civil War Days Drawn from the Music of the Times,* by Willard A. Heaps and Porter W. Heaps (Norman: University of Oklahoma Press, 1960), 270; Dan Emmett, "The Black Brigade" (New York: William A. Pond, 1863); William Shakespeare Hays, "Nigger Will Be Nigger" (Louisville: Louis Tripp, 1864).

34. On the black literary primitives of twentieth-century fiction, see John R. Cooley, *Savages and Naturals: Black Portraits by White Writers in Modern American Literature* (Newark: University of Delaware Press, 1982). On the demeaning ethnological exhibits, see Robert W. Rydell, *All the World's a Fair: Visions of Empire at American International Expositions, 1876–1916* (Chicago: University of Chicago Press, 1984), 28–29, 31–32, 65–66, 87–88, 119, 145–47, 179–80, 228; Phillips Verner Bradford and Harvey Blume, *Ota Benga: The Pygmy in the Zoo* (New York: St. Martin's, 1992), 113–26. On the "Tarzan" image of Africans, see Michael McCarthy, *Dark Continent: Africa as Seen by Americans* (Westport, Conn.: Greenwood, 1983); Jan Nederveen Pieterse, *White on Black: Images of Africa and Blacks in Western Popular Culture* (New Haven: Yale University Press, 1992); Alfred E. Opubur and Adebayo Ogunbi, "Ooga Booga: The African Image in American Films," in *Other Voices, Other Views: An International Collection of Essays from the Bicentennial,* ed. Robin W. Winks (Westport, Conn.: Greenwood, 1978), 343–75. On racial stereotypes in toys, see Doris Yvonne Wilkinson, "Racial Socialization through Children's Toys: A Sociohistorical Examination," *Journal of Black Studies* 5 (September 1974): 96–109; Doris Y. Wilkinson, "Play Objects as Tools of Propaganda: Characterizations of the African American Male," *Journal of Black Psychology* 7 (August 1980): 1–16.

35. J. T. Trowbridge, *Cudjo's Cave* (1863; reprint, Boston: Lothrup, Lee & Shepard, 1891), 120, 272.

36. On the film adaptation of Stark Young's 1934 novel, see Arthur Draper, "Uncle Tom Will Never Die!" in *Black Films and Film-Makers: A Comprehensive Anthology from Stereotype to Superhero,* ed. Lindsay Patterson (New York: Dodd, Mead, 1975), 30–35.

37. Hamilton W. Mabie and Marshal H. Bright, *The Memorial Story of America* (Philadelphia: John C. Winston, 1892), 291.

38. Harriet Beecher Stowe, *Uncle Tom's Cabin* (1852; reprint, New York: Washington Square, 1966), 353–54, 361, 366.

39. On the lecherous brutes of Griffith's 1915 epic *The Birth of a Nation,* see Brian Gallagher, "Racist Ideology and Black Abnormality in *The Birth of a Nation,*" *Phylon* 43 (March 1982): 68–76; Joan L. Sherman, "*The Birth of a Nation:* Prohibition Propaganda," *Southern Quarterly* 19 (spring–summer 1981): 23–30. On Elkins's controversial 1959 book, *Slavery: A Problem in American Institutional and Intellectual Life,* see Ann J. Lane, ed., *The Debate over Slavery: Stanley Elkins and His Critics* (Urbana: University of Illinois Press, 1971).

40. Du Bois, *Souls,* 23.

41. On these early developments in black studies, see Benjamin Quarles, "Black History's Antebellum Origins," *Proceedings of the American Antiquarian Society* 89 (April 1979): 89–122; James G. Spady, "The Afro-American Historical Society: The Nucleus of Black Biblio-

philes, 1897–1923," *Negro History Bulletin* 37 (June–July 1974): 254–57; Alfred A. Moss Jr., *The American Negro Academy: Voice of the Talented Tenth* (Baton Rouge: Louisiana State University Press, 1981); Lawrence Crouchett, "Early Black Studies Movements," *Journal of Black Studies* 2 (December 1971): 189–200; William L. Van Deburg, "The Development of Black Historical Studies in American Higher Education," *Canadian Review of American Studies* 11 (fall 1980): 175–91; August Meier and Elliott Rudwick, *Black History and the Historical Profession, 1915–1980* (Urbana: University of Illinois Press, 1986), 1–71; Jacqueline Goggin, "Carter G. Woodson and the Collection of Source Materials for Afro-American History," *American Archivist* 48 (summer 1985): 261–71; Tony Martin, "Bibliophiles, Activists, and Race Men," in *Black Bibliophiles and Collectors: Preservers of Black History,* ed. Elinor Des Verney Sinnette, W. Paul Coates, and Thomas C. Battle (Washington, D.C.: Howard University Press, 1990), 23–34.

42. Carter G. Woodson, "Ten Years of Collecting and Publishing the Records of the Negro," *Journal of Negro History* 10 (October 1925): 600.

43. Paul W. L. Jones, "Negro Biography," *Journal of Negro History* 8 (April 1923): 129–30.

44. Arthur A. Schomburg, "The Negro Digs up His Past," in *The New Negro,* ed. Alain Locke (1925; reprint, New York: Atheneum, 1968), 231.

45. Lawrence D. Reddick, "Racial Attitudes in American History Textbooks of the South," *Journal of Negro History* 19 (July 1934): 234–35, 264.

46. See, e.g., J. A. Rogers, *Africa's Gift to America: The Afro-American in the Making and Saving of the United States* (New York: Futuro, 1959), 3; J. A. Rogers, "The Suppression of Negro History," *Crisis* 47 (May 1940): 136–37, 146; W. M. Brewer, "Acquainting the Negro with History," *Negro History Bulletin* 8 (December 1944): 53–54, 67–68; Charles H. Wesley, "The Reconstruction of History," *Journal of Negro History* 20 (October 1935): 411–27; John Hope Franklin, "The New Negro History," *Crisis* 64 (February 1957): 69–75.

47. On the stereotypical portrayal of blacks in the white pageants, see David Glassberg, *American Historical Pageantry: The Uses of Tradition in the Early Twentieth Century* (Chapel Hill: University of North Carolina Press, 1990), 23, 132, 254–55.

48. W. E. B. Du Bois, "The Spirit of Modern Europe" (ca 1900), in *Against Racism: Unpublished Essays, Papers, Addresses, 1887–1961,* ed. Herbert Aptheker (Amherst: University of Massachusetts Press, 1985), 56.

49. W. E. B. Du Bois, "The National Emancipation Exposition," *Crisis* 7 (November 1913): 339–41.

50. W. E. B. Du Bois to S. L. Smith, 10 May 1932, in *The Correspondence of W. E. B. Du Bois,* ed. Herbert Aptheker (Amherst: University of Massachusetts Press, 1973), 1:457.

51. Dorothy C. Guinn, *Out of the Dark* (1924), in *Plays and Pageants from the Life of the Negro,* ed. Willis Richardson (Washington, D.C.: Associated, 1930), 316. On the freedom celebration pageants, see William H. Wiggins Jr., *O Freedom! Afro-American Emancipation Celebrations* (Knoxville: University of Tennessee Press, 1987), 49–59, 71–78.

52. In 1937, *Time* estimated that Father Divine had 50,000 followers, a number still deemed plausible by his most recent biographers ("Messiah's Troubles," *Time,* 3 May 1937, 61).

53. Sara Harris, *Father Divine* (1953; reprint, New York: Collier, 1971), 23, 67; Robert Weisbrot, *Father Divine* (Boston: Beacon, 1984), 62–63.

54. Jill Watts, *God, Harlem U.S.A.: The Father Divine Story* (Berkeley: University of California Press, 1992), 55.

55. Harris, *Father Divine,* 175–76, 187–88.

56. Watts, *God,* 40, 81, 118, 171.

57. Weisbrot, *Father Divine,* 110–12.

58. Harris, *Father Divine,* 1–3, 23, 117–18; Watts, *God,* 130; Weisbrot, *Father Divine,* 86.

59. Harris, *Father Divine,* 11, 164.

60. Chappy Gardner, "Man of Mystery Walks out Free—Very Cheerful," *Negro World,* 2 July 1932, 2.

61. Watts, *God,* 116–17.

62. *Father Divine: His Words of Spirit, Life, and Hope,* ed. St. John Evangelist and James Hope (Philadelphia: New Day, 1961), 58.

63. Tony Martin, *Race First: The Ideological and Organizational Struggles of Marcus Garvey and the Universal Negro Improvement Association* (Westport, Conn.: Greenwood, 1976), 68–69, 75; Moses, *Black Messiahs,* 123.

64. Claude McKay, *Harlem: Negro Metropolis* (1940; reprint, New York: Harcourt Brace Jovanovich, 1968), 151.

65. Harris, *Father Divine,* 4; Kenneth E. Burnham, "Father Divine and the Peace Mission Movement," in *Black Apostles: Afro-American Clergy Confront the Twentieth Century,* ed. Randall K. Burkett and Richard Newman (Boston: G. K. Hall, 1978), 28.

66. Amy Jacques Garvey, *Garvey and Garveyism* (1963; reprint, London: Collier-Macmillan, 1970), 2.

67. Amy Jacques Garvey, "The Early Years of Marcus Garvey," in *Marcus Garvey and the Vision of Africa,* ed. John Henrik Clarke (New York: Vintage, 1974), 31.

68. *Philosophy and Opinions of Marcus Gravey,* ed. Amy Jacques-Garvey (1925; reprint, New York: Atheneum, 1974), 2:124.

69. Marcus Garvey to Robert Russa Moton, 29 February 1916, in "Marcus Garvey Writes from Jamaica on the Mulatto Escape Hatch," ed. Carl S. Matthews, *Journal of Negro History* 59 (April 1974): 173.

70. *Philosophy and Opinions,* 2:126.

71. Ibid.

72. Ibid., 305–6. After studying contribution lists, branch reports, and contemporary press estimates, historian Theodore Vincent concluded that the UNIA probably had attracted about three-quarters of a million members during the early 1920s and that well over a million blacks paid dues to the organization at one time or another. Nonpaying followers likely added another one to two million to the total (Theodore G. Vincent, *Black Power and the Garvey Movement* [Berkeley: Ramparts, 1971], 151).

73. Randall K. Burkett, *Black Redemption: Churchmen Speak for the Garvey Movement* (Philadelphia: Temple University Press, 1978), 83.

74. Tony Martin, *Literary Garveyism: Garvey, Black Arts, and the Harlem Renaissance* (Dover, Mass.: Majority, 1983), 45–46.

75. James H. Robinson, "Wilderness Leader," *Christian Century,* 8 June 1955, 684.

76. E. Franklin Frazier, "The Garvey Movement," *Opportunity* 4 (November 1926): 347.

77. Paul Robeson, *Here I Stand* (Boston: Beacon, 1958), 1.

78. On the animal trickster tales, see John W. Roberts, *From Trickster to Badman: The Black Folk Hero in Slavery and Freedom* (Philadelphia: University of Pennsylvania Press, 1989), 17–48; Lawrence W. Levine, *Black Culture and Black Consciousness: Afro-American Folk Thought from Slavery to Freedom* (New York: Oxford University Press, 1977), 102–21. On the West African tales, see Robert D. Pelton, *The Trickster in West Africa: A Study of Mythic Irony and Sacred Delight* (Berkeley: University of California Press, 1980).

79. "Ole Pete," in *American Negro Folklore,* ed. J. Mason Brewer (Chicago: Quadrangle, 1968), 30–31; Levine, *Black Culture,* 403.

80. For a listing and evaluation of this material, see Brett Williams, *John Henry: A Bio-Bibliography* (Westport, Conn.: Greenwood, 1983); Richard M. Dorson, "The Career of 'John Henry,'" *Western Folklore* 24 (July 1965): 155–63.

81. Louis W. Chappell, *John Henry: A Folk-Lore Study* (1933; reprint, Port Washington, N.Y.: Kennikat, 1968), 38, 48; John Harrington Cox, "John Hardy," *Journal of American Folklore* 32 (October–December 1919): 505.

82. Roark Bradford, *John Henry: A Play* (New York: Harper & Brothers, 1939), 5; Chappell, *John Henry,* 33, 38, 48; "John Henry and the Cape of Fear," in *Bundle of Trouble and Other Tarheel Tales,* ed. W. C. Hendricks (Durham: Duke University Press, 1943), 42.

83. Roark Bradford, *John Henry* (New York: Harper & Brothers, 1931), 64, 98, 132.

84. Ibid., 3–4.

85. Guy B. Johnson, *John Henry: Tracking down a Negro Legend* (Chapel Hill: University of North Carolina Press, 1929), 144–45.

86. Ibid., 143; Bradford, *John Henry,* 130, 144; Chappell, *John Henry,* 32; Frank Shay, *Here's Audacity! American Legendary Heroes* (New York: Macaulay, 1930), 249; Williams, *John Henry,* 97.

87. William Wells Brown, *Clotel; or, The President's Daughter: A Narrative of Slave Life in the United States* (1853; reprint, New York: Collier, 1970), 107–8.

88. "The Horsefly," in *A Treasury of Afro-American Folklore,* ed. Harold Courlander (New York: Crown, 1976), 440–41.

89. Zora Neale Hurston, *Mules and Men* (1935; reprint, Bloomington: Indiana University Press, 1978), 84–85. For additional commentary on the slave trickster tales, see Bruce D. Dickson Jr., "The 'John and Old Master' Stories and the World of Slavery: A Study in Folktales and History," *Phylon* 35 (December 1974): 418–29; Levine, *Black Culture,* 121–33.

90. Kathryn L. Morgan, "Caddy Buffers: Legends of a Middle Class Negro Family in Philadelphia," *Keystone Folklore Quarterly* 11 (summer 1966): 73. See also Kathryn L. Morgan, *Children of Strangers: The Stories of a Black Family* (Philadelphia: Temple University Press, 1980).

91. Morgan, "Caddy Buffers," 79.

92. Ibid., 68–69, 72.

93. James Madison Bell, "The Day and the War" (1864), in *The Poetical Works of James Madison Bell* (Lansing: Wynkoop Hallenbeck Crawford, 1901), 57; Paul Laurence Dunbar, "Lincoln" (1903), in *The Complete Poems of Paul Laurence Dunbar* (New York: Dodd, Mead, 1913), 184.

94. On the place of biblical heroes in African-American folklore, see Roberts, *Trickster,* 147–66; Levine, *Black Culture,* 37–53.

95. Harold Courlander, *Negro Folk Music, U.S.A.* (New York: Columbia University Press, 1963), 184–86.

96. Paul Laurence Dunbar, "Harriet Beecher Stowe" (1899), in *Complete Poems,* 119.

97. Arna Bontemps, *Black Thunder* (1936; reprint, Boston: Beacon, 1968), 159.

98. Robert E. Hayden, "Gabriel," *Opportunity* 17 (October 1939): 300.

99. Sterling Brown, "Remembering Nat Turner," *Crisis* 46 (February 1939): 48.

100. Randolph Edmonds, *Nat Turner,* in *Six Plays for a Negro Theatre* (Boston: Walter H. Baker, 1934), 71.

101. John Henrik Clarke, "Sing Me a New Song" (1948), in *The Poetry of Black America: Anthology of the Twentieth Century,* ed. Arnold Adoff (New York: Harper & Row, 1973), 143.

102. Georgia Douglas Johnson, *Frederick Douglass,* in *Negro History in Thirteen Plays,* ed. Willis Richardson and May Miller (Washington, D.C.: Associated, 1935), 147, 152.

103. Guinn, *Out of the Dark,* 313.

104. May Miller, *Harriet Tubman* (1935), in *Black Heroes: Seven Plays,* ed. Errol Hill (New York: Applause Theatre Books, 1989), 105, 111; Margaret Walker, "Harriet Tubman" (ca. 1942), in *The Poetry of the Negro, 1746–1970,* ed. Langston Hughes and Arna Bontemps (Garden City, N.Y.: Doubleday, 1970), 320; Richard Durham, *Railway to Freedom* (1948), in *Richard Durham's Destination Freedom: Scripts from Radio's Black Legacy, 1948–50,* ed. J. Fred MacDonald (New York: Praeger, 1989), 68.

105. May Miller, *Sojourner Truth* (1935), in Richardson and Miller, *Thirteen Plays,* 316.

106. Langston Hughes, "The Negro Mother" (1931), in *The Negro Mother and Other Dramatic Recitations* (Freeport, N.Y.: Books for Libraries, 1971), 17.

107. John Wesley Holloway, "Black Mammies," in *From the Desert* (New York: Neale, 1919), 97.

108. Ibid., 98–99.

109. Ibid., 97–98.

110. See William C. Nell, *The Colored Patriots of the American Revolution* (Boston: Robert F. Wallcut, 1855), 5.

111. See, e.g., John Murdock, *The Politicians; or, A State of Things* (Philadelphia: privately printed, 1798), 19–20, 30; John Murdock, *The Triumphs of Love; or, Happy Reconciliation* (Philadelphia: R. Folwell, 1795), 19, 51.

112. See Sherley Anne Williams, *Give Birth to Brightness: A Thematic Study in Neo-Black Literature* (New York: Dial, 1972), 53–57.

113. See Richard Yarborough, "Race, Violence, and Manhood: The Masculine Ideal in Frederick Douglass's 'The Heroic Slave,'" in *Frederick Douglass: New Literary and Historical Essays,* ed. Eric J. Sundquist (Cambridge: Cambridge University Press, 1990), 168–69.

114. Henry Highland Garnet, "The Past and the Present Condition and the Destiny of the Colored Race" (1848), in *"Let Your Motto Be Resistance": The Life and Thought of Henry Highland Garnet,* by Earl Ofari (Boston: Beacon, 1972), 166; Hosea Easton, *A Treatise on the Intellectual Character, and Civil and Political Condition of the Colored People of the U. States; and the Prejudice Exercised Towards Them* (Boston: Isaac Knapp, 1837), 19; William Wells Brown, *The Black Man: His Antecedents, His Genius, and His Achievements* (Boston: Robert F. Wallcut, 1865), 34.

115. Rogers, *Africa's Gift,* 31, 33; Garnet, "Past and Present," 166; Easton, *Treatise,* 18.

116. Booker T. Washington, *The Story of the Negro* (New York: Doubleday, Page, 1909), 1:12; Benjamin Brawley, *The Negro Genius* (New York: Dodd, Mead, 1937), 1–2, 8–9, 15; Benjamin Brawley, *A Social History of the American Negro* (1921; reprint, New York: Collier, 1970), 381, 384–85.

117. Brawley, *Negro Genius,* 1.

118. See Ann Charters, *Nobody: The Story of Bert Williams* (New York: Macmillan, 1970), 27, 96; J. B., "Bert Williams," *The Soil* 1 (December 1916): 19.

119. MacDonald, *Destination Freedom,* 2.

120. Richard Durham, *Dark Explorers* (1948), in MacDonald, *Destination Freedom,* 16, 17, 25, 26.

121. Ibid., 25–29.

122. See, e.g., Willis Richardson, *Attucks, the Martyr* (1935), in Richardson and Miller, *Thirteen Plays,* 29–61.

123. Bradford, *John Henry: A Play,* 17; Leon R. Harris, "That Steel Drivin' Man," *Phylon* 18 (winter 1957): 404.

124. Melvin B. Tolson, "Dark Symphony," *Atlantic Monthly* 168 (September 1941): 316.

Chapter Two

1. For overviews of 1960s popular culture and its heroes, see Joel Makower, *Boom! Talkin' about Our Generation* (Chicago: Contemporary, 1985); John Javna and Gordon Javna, *60s!* (New York: St. Martin's, 1983); Andrew J. Edelstein, *The Pop Sixties* (New York: World Almanac, 1985); Jane Stern and Michael Stern, *Sixties People* (New York: Alfred A. Knopf, 1990).

2. William Hamilton, *Address to the Fourth Annual Convention of the Free People of Color of the United States* (New York: S. W. Benedict, 1834), 4.

3. Howard H. Bell, "Expressions of Negro Militancy in the North, 1840–1860," *Journal of Negro History* 45 (January 1960): 11.

4. On pre–Civil War pan-Africanism, see Floyd J. Miller, *The Search for a Black Nationality: Black Emigration and Colonization, 1787–1863* (Urbana: University of Illinois Press, 1975); Cyril E. Griffith, *The African Dream: Martin R. Delany and the Emergence of Pan-African Thought* (University Park: Pennsylvania State University Press, 1975); Joel Schor, *Henry Highland Garnet: A Voice of Black Radicalism in the Nineteenth Century* (Westport, Conn.: Greenwood, 1977). On Turner, see Edwin S. Redkey, *Black Exodus: Black Nationalist Movements, 1890–1910* (New Haven: Yale University Press, 1969). On Garvey, see Tony Martin, *Race First: The Ideological and Organizational Struggles of Marcus Garvey and the Universal Negro Improvement Association* (Westport, Conn.: Greenwood, 1976).

5. On black emigration to the Plains states, see Nell Irvin Painter, *Exodusters: Black Migration to Kansas after Reconstruction* (New York: Alfred A. Knopf, 1976); Kenneth Marvin Hamilton, *Black Towns and Profit: Promotion and Development in the Trans-Appalachian West, 1877–1915* (Urbana: University of Illinois Press, 1991). On Briggs and the pan-Africanist-oriented African Blood Brotherhood, see "Racial and Radical: Cyril V. Briggs, the *Crusader* Magazine, and the African Blood Brotherhood, 1918–1922," in *The Crusader,* ed. Robert A. Hill (New York: Garland, 1987), 1:v–lxvi. On the National Movement for the Establishment of a Forty-ninth State, see Raymond L. Hall, *Black Separatism in the United States* (Hanover, N.H.: University Press of New England, 1978), 86. On the Nation of Islam, see E. U. Essien-Udom, *Black Nationalism: A Search for an Identity in America* (Chicago: University of Chicago Press, 1962); C. Eric Lincoln, *The Black Muslims in America* (Boston: Beacon, 1961).

6. Elijah Muhammad, "What Do the Muslims Want?" in *Black Nationalism in America,* ed. John H. Bracey Jr., August Meier, and Elliott Rudwick (Indianapolis: Bobbs-Merrill, 1970), 404.

7. Martin Robison Delany, *The Condition, Elevation, Emigration, and Destiny of the Colored People of the United States* (1852; reprint, New York: Arno Press and the New York Times, 1969), 10.

8. On this form of self-definition, see Lerone Bennett Jr., "What's in a Name? Negro vs. Afro-American vs. Black," *Ebony* 23 (November 1967): 46–54; Donald L. Grant and Mildred Bricker Grant, "Some Notes on the Capital 'N,'" *Phylon* 36 (December 1975): 435–43; Sterling Stuckey, *Slave Culture: Nationalist Theory and the Foundations of Black America* (New York: Oxford University Press, 1987), 193–244; Ben L. Martin, "From Negro to Black to African American: The Power of Names and Naming," *Political Science Quarterly* 106 (spring 1991): 83–107; Geneva Smitherman, "What Is Africa to Me? Language, Ideology, and African American," *American Speech* 66 (summer 1991): 115–32.

9. "The Boston Massacre, March 5, 1770: Commemorative Festival in Faneuil Hall," *Liberator,* 12 March 1858, 42.

10. Langston Hughes, *Don't You Want to Be Free?* in *Black Theater, U.S.A.: Forty-Five Plays by Black Americans, 1847–1974,* ed. James V. Hatch and Ted Shine (New York: Free Press, 1974), 263.

11. John Hope Franklin, *From Slavery to Freedom: A History of Negro Americans* (New York: Alfred A. Knopf, 1980), 481, 484–85, 487; August Meier and Elliott Rudwick, *From Plantation to Ghetto* (New York: Hill & Wang, 1976), 287, 294–95, 298, 300, 304–5, 308; Benjamin Quarles, *The Negro in the Making of America* (New York: Macmillan, 1987), 273; Mary Frances Berry and John W. Blassingame, *Long Memory: The Black Experience in America* (New York: Oxford University Press, 1982), 384–85, 387, 418.

12. John O. Killens et al., "Black Power: Its Meaning and Measure," *Negro Digest* 16 (November 1966): 92; Donald Jackson, "Unite or Perish," *Liberator* 7 (February 1967): 17; Stokely Carmichael, *Stokely Speaks: Black Power Back to Pan-Africanism* (New York: Vintage, 1971), 57; Nathan Hare, "How White Power Whitewashes Black Power," in *The Black Power Revolt,* ed. Floyd B. Barbour (Boston: Porter Sargent, 1968), 183.

13. See, e.g., Joel D. Aberbach and Jack L. Walker, "The Meanings of Black Power: A Comparison of White and Black Interpretations of a Political Slogan," *American Political Science Review* 64 (June 1970): 367–88; Joyce Ladner, "What 'Black Power' Means to Negroes in Mississippi," *Trans-action* 5 (November 1967): 7–15; Solomon P. Gethers, "Black Power: Three Years Later," *Negro Digest* 19 (December 1969): 4–10, 69–81.

14. Marcus Garvey, "The Negro's Greatest Enemy," *Current History* 18 (September 1923): 957.

15. Huey P. Newton, *To Die for the People: The Writings of Huey P. Newton* (New York: Vintage, 1972), 101; "Huey Newton Talks to the Movement about the Black Panther Party, Cultural Nationalism, SNCC, Liberals, and White Revolutionaries," in *The Black Panthers Speak,* ed. Philip S. Foner (Philadelphia: J. B. Lippincott, 1970), 61.

16. Ronald Walters, "African-American Nationalism: A Unifying Ideology," *Black World* 22 (October 1973): 26; Stokely Carmichael and Charles V. Hamilton, *Black Power: The Politics of Liberation in America* (New York: Random House, 1967), 37–38; *Eldridge Cleaver: Postprison Writings and Speeches,* ed. Robert Scheer (New York: Random House, 1969), 54–56; Julius Lester, *Look Out, Whitey! Black Power's Gon' Get Your Mama!* (New York: Grove, 1969), 100; Robert S. Browne, "The Case for Two Americas—One Black, One White," *New York Times Magazine,* 11 August 1968, 50.

17. For conceptualizations of the "conversion experience," see William E. Cross Jr., "The Negro-to-Black Conversion Experience: Toward a Psychology of Black Liberation," *Black World* 20 (July 1971): 13–27; William S. Hall, William E. Cross Jr., and Roy Freedle, "Stages in the Development of Black Awareness: An Exploratory Investigation," in *Black Psychology,* ed. Reginald L. Jones (New York: Harper & Row, 1972), 156–65; Charles W. Thomas and Shirley W. Thomas, "Something Borrowed, Something Black," in *Boys No More: A Black Psychologist's View of Community,* ed. Charles W. Thomas (Beverly Hills: Glencoe, 1971), 113–14; JoAnn E. Gardner and Charles W. Thomas, "Different Strokes for Different Folks," *Psychology Today* 4 (September 1970): 78; William E. Cross Jr., "The Thomas and Cross Models of Psychological Nigrescence: A Review," *Journal of Black Psychology* 5 (August 1978): 13–31.

18. Doris P. Mosby, "Toward a Theory of the Unique Personality of Blacks—A Psychocultural Assessment," in Jones, *Black Psychology,* 132.

19. Thomas and Thomas, "Something Borrowed," 102–3; Nathan Hare, "The Plasma of Thinking Black," *Negro Digest* 18 (January 1969): 13, 18; Carmichael, *Stokely Speaks,* 149–52.

20. Stokely Carmichael, "Pan-Africanism—Land and Power," *Black Scholar* 1 (November 1969): 42; Ronald Walters, "The Re-Africanization of the Black American," in *Topics in Afro-American Studies,* ed. Henry J. Richards (Buffalo: Black Academy, 1971), 101; Imamu Amiri Baraka, "The Pan-African Party and the Black Nation," *Black Scholar* 2 (March 1971): 26; Robert Chrisman and Nathan Hare, eds., *Pan-Africanism* (Indianapolis: Bobbs-Merrill, 1974), 1.

21. James Turner, "Black Nationalism: The Inevitable Response," *Black World* 20 (January 1971): 12; Ernie Mkalimoto, "Revolutionary Black Culture: The Cultural Arm of Revolutionary Nationalism," *Negro Digest* 19 (December 1969): 12, 14, 17; H. Rap Brown, *Die Nigger Die!* (New York: Dial, 1969), 130; Lawrence P. Neal, "Black Power in the International Context," in Barbour, *Black Power Revolt,* 140; Julius Lester, *Revolutionary Notes* (New York: Richard W. Baron, 1969), 165, 191.

22. Larry Neal, "Black Art and Black Liberation," in *The Black Revolution: An "Ebony" Special Issue* (Chicago: Johnson, 1970), 40, 46, 49; Imamu Amiri Baraka, *Raise, Race, Rays, Raze: Essays since 1965* (New York: Vintage, 1972), 98, 126; Sherley Anne Williams, *Give Birth to Brightness: A Thematic Study in Neo-black Literature* (New York: Dial, 1972), 240; Walters, "African-American Nationalism," 27; Robert Chrisman, "The Formation of a Revolutionary Black Culture," *Black Scholar* 1 (June 1970): 6; Lester, *Revolutionary Notes,* 190.

23. Frantz Fanon, *The Wretched of the Earth* (New York: Grove, 1968), 240 (this work was originally published in France in 1961). On Fanon and his connection to black American activism of the 1960s, see Emmanuel Hansen, *Frantz Fanon: Social and Political Thought* (Columbus: Ohio State University Press, 1977); Alvin Poussaint, "An Overview of Fanon's Significance to the American Civil Rights Movement," in *International Tribute to Frantz Fanon* (New York: United Nations Centre against Apartheid, 1979), 59–66; Ted Stewart, "Fanon: New Messiah of Black Militants," *Sepia* 20 (December 1971): 30–32, 34–38; Ernest W. Ranly, "Frantz Fanon and the Radical Left," *America,* 1 November 1969, 384, 387–88; Aristide Zolberg and Vera Zolberg, "The Americanization of Frantz Fanon," *Public Interest* 9 (fall 1967): 49–63.

24. Larry Neal, "The Black Arts Movement," *Drama Review* 12 (summer 1968): 29–30.

25. Addison Gayle Jr., introduction to *The Black Aesthetic,* ed. Addison Gayle Jr. (Garden City, N.Y.: Doubleday, 1972), xxii.

26. Clyde Halisi, ed., *The Quotable Karenga* (Los Angeles: US Organization, 1967), 29; Melvin Dixon, "Black Theatre: The Aesthetics," *Negro Digest* 18 (July 1969): 43–44; Ronald Milner, "Black Theatre—Go Home!" in Gayle, *Black Aesthetic,* 293–94.

27. Carole A. Parks, "Self-Determination and the Black Aesthetic: An Interview with Max Roach," *Black World* 23 (November 1973): 69.

28. Chrisman, "Revolutionary Black Culture," 5; Neal, "Black Art and Black Liberation," 33; Halisi, *Karenga,* 30; LeRoi Jones, *Home: Social Essays* (New York: William Morrow, 1966), 173–78, 232.

29. Baraka, *Raise,* 80.

30. Neal, "Black Arts Movement," 30.

31. Larry Neal, "And Shine Swam On," in *Black Fire,* ed. LeRoi Jones and Larry Neal (New York: William Morrow, 1968), 648.

32. Milner, "Black Theatre," 293–94.

33. C. Eric Lincoln, "The Excellence of Soul," in *New Black Voices,* ed. Abraham Chapman (New York: New American Library, 1972), 585; W. A. Jeanpierre, "African Negritude—Black American Soul," *Africa Today* 14 (December 1967): 10–11; Herman S.

Hughes, "Soul," *America,* 2 August 1969, 62–63; Mercer Cook and Stephen E. Henderson, *The Militant Black Writer in Africa and the United States* (Madison: University of Wisconsin Press, 1969), 124; Al Calloway and Claude Brown, "An Introduction to Soul," *Esquire* 69 (April 1968): 79–90. For studies of *la négritude* as developed by French-speaking black intellectuals responding to the colonialism and cultural chauvinism of the 1930s and 1940s, see Lilyan Kesteloot, *Black Writers in French: A Literary History of Negritude* (Philadelphia: Temple University Press, 1974); Edward A. Jones, "Afro-French Writers of the 1930's and Creation of the *Négritude* School," *CLA Journal* 14 (September 1970): 18–34.

34. On soul "style," see Thomas Kochman, *Black and White Styles in Conflict* (Chicago: University of Chicago Press, 1981); David A. Schulz, *Coming up Black: Patterns of Ghetto Socialization* (Englewood Cliffs, N.J.: Prentice-Hall, 1969), 78–87; Kenneth R. Johnson, "Black Kinesics—Some Non-verbal Communication Patterns in the Black Culture," in *Perspectives on Black English,* ed. J. Dillard (The Hague: Mouton, 1975), 296–306; Benjamin G. Cooke, "Nonverbal Communication among Afro-Americans: An Initial Classification," in *Rappin' and Stylin' Out: Communication in Urban Black America,* ed. Thomas Kochman (Urbana: University of Illinois Press, 1972), 32–64.

35. On soul food, see Verta Mae Smart Grosvenor, "Soul Food," *McCall's* 97 (September 1970): 72–75; Verta Mae, *Vibration Cooking; or, The Travel Notes of a Geechee Girl* (New York: Doubleday, 1970); Helen Mendes, *The African Heritage Cookbook* (New York: Macmillan, 1971); Craig Claiborne, "Cooking with Soul," *New York Times Magazine,* 3 November 1968, 102, 104, 109.

36. On soul music, see Gerri Hirshey, *Nowhere to Run: The Story of Soul Music* (New York: Times, 1984); Michael Haralambos, *Right On: From Blues to Soul in Black America* (New York: Drake, 1975); Peter Guralnick, *Sweet Soul Music: Rhythm and Blues and the Southern Dream of Freedom* (New York: Harper & Row, 1986); Portia K. Maultsby, "Soul Music: Its Sociological and Political Significance in American Popular Culture," *Journal of Popular Culture* 17 (fall 1983): 51–60.

37. On these aspects of self-definition, see Geneva Smitherman, *Talkin and Testifyin: The Language of Black America* (Boston: Houghton Mifflin, 1977); J.L. Dillard, *Black English: Its History and Usage in the United States* (New York: Vintage, 1973); Alan W. Barnett, *Community Murals: The People's Art* (Philadelphia: Art Alliance, 1984); Albert B. Cleage Jr., *The Black Messiah* (New York: Sheed & Ward, 1968); James H. Cone, *Black Theology and Black Power* (New York: Seabury, 1969).

38. Barbara Ann Teer, "Needed: A New Image," in Barbour, *Black Power Revolt,* 222; John O'Neal, "Black Arts: Notebook," in Gayle, *Black Aesthetic,* 47.

39. Stokely Carmichael, "Toward Black Liberation," *Massachusetts Review* 7 (autumn 1966): 639.

40. Malcolm X, "Malcolm X at Yale," in *When the Word Is Given . . . ,* ed. Louis E. Lomax (New York: New American Library, 1964), 162–63; *Malcolm X on Afro-American History* (New York: Pathfinder, 1970), 44; *The End of White World Supremacy: Four Speeches by Malcolm X,* ed. Benjamin Karim (New York: Seaver, 1971), 133–34; *Malcolm X Speaks: Selected Speeches and Statements,* ed. George Breitman (New York: Grove, 1966), 38–40.

41. "Death of a Desperado," *Newsweek,* 8 March 1965, 24.

42. Rolland Snellings, "Malcolm X: As International Statesman," *Liberator* 6 (February 1966): 6–7; George Norman, "To Malcolm X," in *For Malcolm: Poems on the Life and the Death of Malcolm X,* ed. Dudley Randall and Margaret Burroughs (Detroit: Broadside, 1969), 23; Edward S. Spriggs, "Berkeley's Blue Black," in Randall and Burroughs, *For Malcolm,* 74.

43. James Baldwin, *No Name in the Street* (New York: Dial, 1972), 99. The screenplay was published as *One Day, When I Was Lost* (New York: Dial, 1973).

44. *The Autobiography of Malcolm X* (New York: Grove, 1966); *Two Speeches by Malcolm X* (New York: Pathfinder, 1965); *By Any Means Necessary: Speeches, Interviews, and a Letter by Malcolm X,* ed. George Breitman (New York: Pathfinder, 1970); *Message to the Grass Roots from Malcolm X,* Afro, 1264; *Ballots or Bullets,* First Amendment, 100; *Malcolm X Talks to Young People,* Douglas 795; *Malcolm X: His Wit and Wisdom,* Douglas 797.

45. John Oliver Killens, *'Sippi* (1967; reprint, New York: Thunder's Mouth, 1988), 240, 414.

46. Poems quoted here were written by Etheridge Knight, Margaret Burroughs, Christine C. Johnson, Robert Hayden, Don L. Lee, and Ted Joans and collected in Randall and Burroughs, *For Malcolm.*

47. William Wellington Mackey, *Requiem for Brother X* (1966), in *Black Drama Anthology,* ed. Woodie King and Ron Milner (New York: New American Library, 1972), 336.

48. G. Louis Heath, ed., *Off the Pigs! The History and Literature of the Black Panther Party* (Metuchen, N.J.: Scarecrow, 1976), 117.

49. Earl Anthony, *Picking up the Gun: A Report on the Black Panthers* (New York: Dial, 1970), 88.

50. Newton, *To Die,* 104, 176; Huey P. Newton, *Revolutionary Suicide* (New York: Ballantine, 1974), 127–42; Bobby Seale, *Seize the Time: The Story of the Black Panther Party and Huey P. Newton* (New York: Random House, 1970), 404–22; Reginald Major, *A Panther Is a Black Cat* (New York: William Morrow, 1971), 58; David Hilliard, "Interview with CBS News, December 28, 1969," in Foner, *Black Panthers Speak,* 133.

51. Seale, *Seize the Time,* 30–31, 368–69; "Huey Newton Talks," 60; Newton, *To Die,* 48–49; Gene Marine, *The Black Panthers* (New York: New American Library, 1969), 41; Anthony, *Gun,* 95; Heath, *Off the Pigs!* 63–64.

52. Seale, *Seize the Time,* 71; Newton, *To Die,* 175–76; Newton, *Revolutionary Suicide,* 126.

53. Marine, *Black Panthers,* 67–72; Newton, *Revolutionary Suicide,* 369; *The Harris Survey Yearbook of Public Opinion, 1970* (New York: Louis Harris & Associates, 1971), 231; *The Harris Survey Yearbook of Public Opinion, 1971* (New York: Louis Harris & Associates, 1975), 332.

54. "The Black Mood: More Militant, More Hopeful, More Determined," *Time,* 6 April 1970, 28–29; "The Tough New Breed: Ghetto Blacks under 30," *Newsweek,* 30 June 1969, 21; Daniel U. Levine, Norman S. Fiddmont, Robert S. Stephenson, and Charles Wilkinson, "Differences between Black Youth Who Support the Black Panthers and the NAACP," *Journal of Negro Education* 42 (winter 1973): 19–32; Ozzie L. Edwards, "Intergenerational Variation in Racial Attitudes," *Sociology and Social Research* 57 (October 1972): 22–31.

55. On this point, see Linda La Rue, "The Black Movement and Women's Liberation," *Black Scholar* 1 (May 1970): 36–42; Frances M. Beal, "Slave of a Slave No More: Black Women in Struggle," *Black Scholar* 6 (March 1975): 2–10; "Black Feminism: A New Mandate," *Ms.* 2 (May 1974): 97–100; "*Black Scholar* Interviews Kathleen Cleaver," *Black Scholar* 3 (December 1971): 54–59; "Panther Sisters on Women's Liberation," in Heath, *Off the Pigs!* 339–50; Louise Moore, "Black Men vs. Black Women," *Liberator* 6 (August 1966): 16–17.

56. See, e.g., "Whatever Happened to Ron Karenga?" *Ebony* 30 (September 1975): 170; Alex Poinsett, "Where Are the Revolutionaries?" *Ebony* 31 (February 1976): 84–92; Nathan Hare, "What Happened to the Black Movement," *Black World* 25 (January 1976): 20–32; Mark S. Johnson, "Open Letter to Nationalists," *Black Scholar* 6 (April 1975): 52–53.

57. Herbert H. Haines, *Black Radicals and the Civil Rights Mainstream, 1954–70* (Knoxville: University of Tennessee Press, 1988), 2–4, 184–85.

58. On the "silencing" of the black militants, see Kenneth O'Reilly, *"Racial Matters": The FBI's Secret File on Black America, 1960–1972* (New York: Free Press, 1989); Ward Churchill and Jim Vander Wall, *Agents of Repression: The FBI's Secret Wars against the Black Panther Party and the American Indian Movement* (Boston: South End, 1988); Karl Evanzz, *The Judas Factor: The Plot to Kill Malcolm X* (New York: Thunder's Mouth, 1992).

59. Public opinion polls conducted during the Black Power era revealed that the cultural thrust of the movement had broad appeal. Distinctive hairstyles, clothing, cuisine, and music won endorsement from a wide range of age groups within black America. Support for the study of African languages and culture and for the institutionalization of black studies programs also was widespread. Surveys which tested for even broader cultural concepts such as the belief that "black is beautiful" or that blacks possessed "soul" or shared a sense of collective identity reinforced these findings. See, e.g., Peter Goldman, *Report from Black America* (New York: Simon & Schuster, 1971), 156, 205, 261, 263, 264; Gary T. Marx, *Protest and Prejudice: A Study of Belief in the Black Community* (New York: Harper & Row, 1969), 228; Angus Campbell and Howard Schuman, *Racial Attitudes in Fifteen American Cities* (Ann Arbor: Survey Research Center, Institute for Social Research, University of Michigan, 1968), 19–20; *Report of the National Advisory Commission on Civil Disorders* (Washington, D.C.: U.S. Government Printing Office, 1968), 333; *Harris Survey, 1970,* 262; "Black Mood," 28; Jan E. Dizard, "Black Identity, Social Class, and Black Power," *Psychiatry* 33 (May 1970): 199–200.

Chapter Three

1. David C. Young, *The Olympic Myth of Greek Amateur Athletics* (Chicago: Ares, 1984), 111–33.

2. On ancient Greek sports and sports heroes, see H. A. Harris, *Greek Athletes and Athletics* (London: Hutchinson, 1964); Vera Olivova, *Sports and Games in the Ancient World* (London: Orbis, 1984); Michael B. Poliakoff, *Combat Sports in the Ancient World: Competition, Violence, and Culture* (New Haven: Yale University Press, 1987); E. Norman Gardiner, *Athletics of the Ancient World* (Oxford: Clarendon Press, 1930).

3. Poliakoff, *Combat Sports,* 121–22; Harris, *Greek Athletes,* 121–22; *The Iliad of Homer,* trans. Richard Lattimore (Chicago: University of Chicago Press, 1976), 468.

4. On the sociology of American sport, see Richard Lipsky, *How We Play the Game: Why Sports Dominate American Life* (Boston: Beacon, 1981); Robert Lipsyte, *SportsWorld: An American Dreamland* (New York: Quadrangle, 1975); J. Bowyer Bell, *To Play the Game: An Analysis of Sports* (New Brunswick, N.J.: Transaction, 1987); Neil D. Isaacs, *Jock Culture U.S.A.* (New York: W. W. Norton, 1978); Michael A. Messner, *Power at Play: Sports and the Problem of Masculinity* (Boston: Beacon, 1992); Allen Guttmann, *Sports Spectators* (New York: Columbia University Press, 1986).

5. "Whether You Play or Pay, Sports Are Bigger than Ever," *U.S. News and World Report,* 8 September 1975, 46–48.

6. Douglas A. Noverr and Lawrence E. Ziewacz, *The Games They Played: Sports in American History, 1865–1980* (Chicago: Nelson-Hall, 1983), 304.

7. On Nixon's relationship with athletics, see Robert M. Collins, "Richard M. Nixon: The Psychic, Political, and Moral Uses of Sport," *Journal of Sport History* 10 (summer 1983): 77–84.

8. Garry Smith, "The Sport Hero: An Endangered Species," *Quest* 19 (January 1973): 65–67.

9. Carolyn E. Thomas, *Sport in a Philosophic Context* (Philadelphia: Lea & Febiger, 1983), 111.

10. By 1980, more than 40 percent of professional football players, 45 percent of major league baseball players, and 75 percent of professional basketball players were African-Americans (Randy Roberts and James S. Olson, *Winning Is the Only Thing: Sports in America since 1945* [Baltimore: Johns Hopkins University Press, 1989], 183).

11. On these early black sports figures, see Andrew Ritchie, *Major Taylor: The Extraordinary Career of a Champion Bicycle Racer* (San Francisco: Bicycle, 1988); Arthur R. Ashe Jr., *A Hard Road to Glory: A History of the African-American Athlete, 1619–1918* (New York: Warner, 1988), 28–30; David Wiggins, "Isaac Murphy: Black Hero of Nineteenth-Century American Sport, 1861–1896," *Canadian Journal of History of Sport and Physical Education* 10 (May 1979): 15–32; John M. Carroll, *Fritz Pollard: Pioneer in Racial Advancement* (Urbana: University of Illinois Press, 1992); Harry Edwards, "Paul Robeson: His Political Legacy to the Twentieth-Century Gladiator, in *Paul Robeson: The Great Forerunner,* by the editors of *Freedomways* (New York: Dodd, Mead, 1978): 17–25.

12. Edwin B. Henderson, *The Black Athlete: Emergence and Arrival* (Washington, D.C.: Association for the Study of Negro Life and History, 1968), 56–57, 65–67; Arthur R. Ashe Jr., *A Hard Road to Glory: A History of the African-American Athlete, 1919–1945* (New York: Warner, 1988), 45, 100; Donn Rogosin, *Invisible Men: Life in Baseball's Negro Leagues* (New York: Atheneum, 1985), 25–26, 119.

13. Randy Roberts, *Papa Jack: Jack Johnson and the Era of White Hopes* (New York: Free Press, 1983), 63, 66.

14. On Johnson as badman, see William H. Wiggins Jr., "Jack Johnson as Bad Nigger: The Folklore of His Life," in *Contemporary Black Thought,* ed. Robert Chrisman and Nathan Hare (Indianapolis: Bobbs-Merrill, 1973), 53–70.

15. Finis Farr, *Black Champion: The Life and Times of Jack Johnson* (1964; reprint, Greenwich, Conn.: Fawcett, 1969), 63.

16. Al-Tony Gilmore, *Bad Nigger! The National Impact of Jack Johnson* (Port Washington, N.Y.: Kennikat, 1975), 19–20, 52.

17. Ibid., 21, 52–53, 102; Roberts, *Papa Jack,* 97–98, 146–47.

18. Frederic Cople Jaher, "White America Views Jack Johnson, Joe Louis, and Muhammad Ali," in *Sport in America: New Historical Perspectives,* ed. Donald Spivey (Westport, Conn.: Greenwood, 1985), 150; Theodore Roosevelt, "The Recent Prize Fight," *Outlook,* 16 July 1910, 550–51; Roberts, *Papa Jack,* 203.

19. Roberts, *Papa Jack,* 224, 227, 230.

20. *Joe Louis: My Life* (New York: Harcourt Brace Jovanovich, 1978), 3, 9.

21. Chris Mead, *Champion: Joe Louis, Black Hero in White America* (New York: Viking Penguin, 1986), 52–53.

22. Ibid., 133, 139; Gerald Astor, *". . . And a Credit to His Race": The Hard Life and Times of Joseph Louis Barrow, a.k.a. Joe Louis* (New York: Saturday Review/E. P. Dutton, 1974), 179.

23. Mead, *Champion,* 145.

24. E. Franklin Frazier, *Negro Youth at the Crossways: Their Personality Development in the Middle States* (1940; reprint, New York: Schocken, 1967), 178–79.

25. "Black Moses," *Time,* 29 September 1941, 60–64; *Joe Louis: My Life,* 48–49.

26. *Joe Louis: My Life,* 58. On the Ethiopian issue, see William R. Scott, *The Sons of Sheba's Race: African-Americans and the Italo-Ethiopian War, 1935–1941* (Bloomington: Indiana University Press, 1992).

27. *Joe Louis: My Life,* 63.

28. On Louis's wartime activities, see Dominic J. Capeci Jr. and Martha Wilkerson, "Multifarious Hero: Joe Louis, American Society, and Race Relations during World Crisis, 1935–1945," *Journal of Sport History* 10 (winter 1983): 15–23.

29. Anthony O. Edmonds, "The Second Louis-Schmeling Fight: Sport, Symbol, and Culture," *Journal of Popular Culture* 7 (summer 1973): 49. On the hope and frustration brought about by the war, see Pete Daniel, "Going among Strangers: Southern Reactions to World War II," *Journal of American History* 77 (December 1990): 886–911; John Modell, Marc Goulden, and Sigurdur Magnusson, "World War II in the Lives of Black Americans: Some Findings and an Interpretation," *Journal of American History* 76 (December 1989): 838–48; Richard M. Dalfiume, "The 'Forgotten Years' of the Negro Revolution," *Journal of American History* 55 (June 1968): 90–106; Harvard Sitkoff, "Racial Militancy and Interracial Violence in the Second World War," *Journal of American History* 58 (December 1971): 661–81.

30. "Joe Louis and Jesse Owens," *Crisis* 42 (August 1935): 241.

31. Astor, ". . . *And a Credit to His Race,"* 85; Joe Louis Barrow Jr. and Barbara Munder, *Joe Louis: 50 Years an American Hero* (New York: McGraw-Hill, 1988), 131, 191–93; Mead, *Champion,* 204, 231–32.

32. Barrow and Munder, *Joe Louis,* 143.

33. Joe Louis, *My Life Story* (New York: Duell, Sloan & Pearce, 1947), 187.

34. Astor, ". . . *And a Credit to His Race,"* 177–78.

35. Lena Horne and Richard Schickel, *Lena* (New York: Doubleday, 1965), 75; Maya Angelou, *I Know Why the Caged Bird Sings* (New York: Random House, 1969), 129–32; *The Autobiography of Malcolm X* (New York: Grove, 1966), 23–24; Barrow and Munder, *Joe Louis,* 239–40.

36. *Joe Louis: My Life,* 39.

37. On baseball's search for the "right type" of black athlete to successfully integrate the sport, see William Simons, "Jackie Robinson and the American Mind: Journalistic Perceptions of the Reintegration of Baseball," *Journal of Sport History* 12 (spring 1985): 39–64.

38. Jules Tygiel, "The Court-Martial of Jackie Robinson," *American Heritage* 35 (August–September 1984): 34–39.

39. Jackie Robinson and Alfred Duckett, *I Never Had It Made* (Greenwich, Conn.: Fawcett, 1974), 39–42; Branch Rickey and Robert Riger, *The American Diamond: A Documentary of the Game of Baseball* (New York: Simon & Schuster, 1965), 46.

40. Robinson and Duckett, *I Never Had It Made,* 41; Rickey and Riger, *American Diamond,* 46.

41. Harvey Frommer, *Rickey and Robinson: The Men Who Broke Baseball's Color Barrier* (New York: Macmillan, 1982), 136, 140; Robinson and Duckett, *I Never Had It Made,* 256; Jackie Robinson, "What's Wrong with Negro Baseball," *Ebony* 3 (June 1948): 18.

42. Jules Tygiel, *Baseball's Great Experiment: Jackie Robinson and His Legacy* (New York: Oxford University Press, 1983), 321–22; Carl T. Rowan and Jackie Robinson, *Wait till Next Year: The Life Story of Jackie Robinson* (New York: Random House, 1960), 199; Robinson and Duckett, *I Never Had It Made,* 80; "Chandler Requests Jackie Explain Reported Crack," *Sporting News,* 23 March 1949.

43. Robinson and Duckett, *I Never Had It Made,* 100–101; "Jackie Finds It 'Strange'–No Negroes with 3 Clubs," *Sporting News,* 13 February 1957. On Robinson's postcareer civil rights activism, see David Falkner, *Great Time Coming: The Life of Jackie Robinson, from Baseball to Birmingham* (New York: Simon & Schuster, 1995), 258–342.

44. Tygiel, *Great Experiment,* 323, 326.

45. "The Jackie Robinson Situation," *Sporting News,* 23 March 1949; Roscoe McGowen, "Robinson Steams at Boston Tea Party," *Sporting News,* 17 September 1952.

46. Tygiel, *Great Experiment,* 132, 199.

47. Public opinion polls reveal the staying power of Robinson's popularity. In a 1963 national sampling of African-American opinion on the quality of the contributions made by various individuals prominent in the struggle for black rights, he received an 80 percent approval rating. In a similar survey conducted in 1966, his rating had dropped to 66 percent but remained higher than that of all other black leaders with the exception of James Meredith (71 percent) and Martin Luther King Jr. (88 percent). See William Brink and Louis Harris, *The Negro Revolution in America* (New York: Simon & Schuster, 1964), 120–22; William Brink and Louis Harris, *Black and White: A Study of U.S. Racial Attitudes Today* (New York: Simon & Schuster, 1967), 54.

48. Tygiel, *Great Experiment,* 321; Maury Allen, *Jackie Robinson: A Life Remembered* (New York: Franklin Watts, 1987), 14.

49. Henry Aaron and Lonnie Wheeler, *I Had a Hammer: The Hank Aaron Story* (New York: HarperCollins, 1991), 14; Stan Baldwin and Jerry Jenkins, *Bad Henry* (Radnor, Pa.: Chilton, 1974), 143–44.

50. Bob Gibson and Phil Pepe, *From Ghetto to Glory: The Story of Bob Gibson* (New York: Popular Library, 1968), 35; Cleon Jones and Ed Hershey, *Cleon* (New York: Coward-McCann, 1970), 39.

51. Bill Russell and Taylor Branch, *Second Wind: The Memoirs of an Opinionated Man* (New York: Random House, 1979), 37–39; John Devaney, *Alcindor and the Big O* (New York: Lancer, 1971), 18–19, 55; Bill Libby and Vida Blue, *Vida: His Own Story* (Englewood Cliffs, N.J.: Prentice-Hall, 1972), 24, 170.

52. Russell and Branch, *Second Wind,* 15–26.

53. Devaney, *Alcindor,* 17; John Roseboro and Bill Libby, *Glory Days with the Dodgers, and Other Days with Others* (New York: Atheneum, 1978), 16.

54. Arthur R. Ashe Jr., *A Hard Road to Glory: A History of the African-American Athlete since 1946* (New York: Warner, 1988), 20; Phil Musick, *Hank Aaron: The Man Who Beat the Babe* (New York: Popular Library, 1974), 164; Joel Cohen, *Big A: The Story of Lew Alcindor* (New York: Scholastic, 1971), 6. On the historiography of blacks in American sport, see David K. Wiggins, "Clio and the Black Athlete in America: Myths, Heroes, and Realities," *Quest* 32, no. 2 (1980): 217–25.

55. Libby and Blue, *Vida,* 64; Wilma Rudolph, *Wilma* (New York: New American Library, 1977), 143; Dick Allen and Tim Whitaker, *Crash: The Life and Times of Dick Allen* (New York: Ticknor & Fields, 1989), 25.

56. Musick, *Aaron,* 142.

57. Roseboro and Libby, *Glory Days,* 180.

58. Bill Libby and Spencer Haywood, *Stand Up for Something: The Spencer Haywood Story* (New York: Grosset & Dunlap, 1972), 5.

59. Reggie Jackson and Bill Libby, *Reggie* (Chicago: Playboy, 1976), 1, 268.

60. Musick, *Aaron,* 210.

61. Libby and Blue, *Vida,* 133–34. See also Jimmy Bee, "Vida Blue," United Artists 50843, 1972.

62. Jack Tatum and Bill Kushner, *They Call Me Assassin* (New York: Avon, 1980), 7.

63. Arna Bontemps, *Famous Negro Athletes* (New York: Dodd, Mead, 1964), 15, 17, 48, 64, 81, 82, 93, 117, 118. For more general commentary on black portraiture in children's books

of the 1960s and 1970s, see Nancy Larrick, "The All-White World of Children's Books," *Saturday Review,* 11 September 1965, 63–65, 84–85; Jeanne S. Chall, Eugene Radwin, Valarie W. French, and Cynthia R. Hall, "Blacks in the World of Children's Books," *Reading Teacher* 32 (February 1979): 527–33; Dorothy M. Broderick, *Image of the Black in Children's Fiction* (New York: R. R. Bowker, 1973); Rudine Sims, *Shadow and Substance: Afro-American Experience in Contemporary Children's Fiction* (Urbana: National Council of Teachers of English, 1982).

64. Studies of this literature include Michael Oriard, *Dreaming of Heroes: American Sports Fiction, 1868–1980* (Chicago: Nelson-Hall, 1982); and Christian K. Messenger, *Sport and the Spirit of Play in Contemporary American Fiction* (New York: Columbia University Press, 1990).

65. Charles Rosen, *A Mile above the Rim* (New York: Arbor House, 1976); Jay Neugeboren, *Sam's Legacy* (New York: Holt, Rinehart & Winston, 1974), 334; Paul Hemphill, *Long Gone* (New York: Viking, 1979); Walter Kaylin, *The Power Forward* (New York: Atheneum, 1979), 47; James Whitehead, *Joiner* (New York: Alfred A. Knopf, 1971); Jay Neugeboren, *Big Man* (Boston: Houghton Mifflin, 1966).

66. Jim Bouton, *Ball Four: My Life and Hard Times Throwing the Knuckleball in the Big Leagues* (New York: World, 1970); Leonard Shecter, *The Jocks* (Indianapolis: Bobbs-Merrill, 1969).

67. Frederick Exley, *A Fan's Notes* (New York: Harper & Row, 1968), 8.

68. Aaron and Wheeler, *Hammer,* 278–79.

69. See, e.g., Willie Morris, *The Courting of Marcus Dupree* (Garden City, N.Y.: Doubleday, 1983).

70. Wilt Chamberlain and David Shaw, *Wilt: Just like Any Other 7-Foot Black Millionaire Who Lives Next Door* (New York: Warner, 1975), 239.

71. Meadowlark Lemon and Jerry B. Jenkins, *Meadowlark* (Nashville: Thomas Nelson, 1987), 158.

72. Bill Russell and William McSweeny, *Go Up for Glory* (New York: Coward-McCann, 1966), 110–11.

73. Aaron and Wheeler, *Hammer,* 278–79.

74. Jackson and Libby, *Reggie,* 88.

75. Aaron and Wheeler, *Hammer,* 40, 93; Musick, *Aaron,* 103, 125.

76. Musick, *Aaron,* 179; Aaron and Wheeler, *Hammer,* 233–34, 237; Baldwin and Jenkins, *Bad Henry,* 16.

77. Aaron and Wheeler, *Hammer,* 248.

78. On the basketball quotas, see Russell and McSweeny, *Glory,* 59, 73.

79. John W. Loy and Joseph F. McElvogue, "Racial Segregation in American Sport," *International Review of Sport Sociology* 5 (1970): 10; D. Stanley Eitzen and Norman R. Yetman, "Racial Dynamics in American Sports: Continuity and Change," in *Social Approaches to Sport,* ed. Robert M. Pankin (East Brunswick, N.J.: Associated University Presses, 1982), 159; Phillip M. Hoose, *Necessities: Racial Barriers in American Sports* (New York: Random House, 1989), 132.

80. D. Stanley Eitzen and David C. Sanford, "The Segregation of Blacks by Playing Position in Football: Accident or Design?" *Social Science Quarterly* 55 (March 1975): 948–59; Eitzen and Yetman, "Racial Dynamics," 161.

81. Roberts and Olson, *Winning,* 26–28; Martin Kane, "An Assessment of 'Black Is Best,'" *Sports Illustrated,* 18 January 1971, 75, 78–80; Hoose, *Necessities,* 72. For the effects which these views had on player salaries, product endorsement possibilities, and coaching

opportunities, see Robert G. Mogull, "Racial Discrimination in Professional Basketball," *American Economist* 18 (spring 1974): 11–15; Gerald W. Scully, "Pay and Performance in Major League Baseball," *American Economic Review* 64 (December 1974): 915–30; Kevin J. Christiano, "Salary Discrimination in Major League Baseball: The Effect of Race," *Sociology of Sport Journal* 3 (June 1986): 144–53; Anthony H. Pascal and Leonard A. Rapping, *Racial Discrimination in Organized Baseball* (Santa Monica: Rand, 1970), 40; D. Stanley Eitzen and George H. Sage, *Sociology of American Sport* (Dubuque, Iowa: William C. Brown, 1978), 251.

82. Gibson and Pepe, *Ghetto to Glory,* 103.

83. Russell and McSweeny, *Glory,* 92, 102, 163.

84. James Toback, *Jim: The Author's Self-Centered Memoir on the Great Jim Brown* (Garden City, N.Y.: Doubleday, 1971), 16.

85. Curt Flood and Richard Carter, *The Way It Is* (New York: Pocket, 1972), 25–26.

86. Chamberlain and Shaw, *Wilt,* 64; Henry Aaron and Furman Bisher, *"Aaron, r.f."* (Cleveland: World, 1968), 28, 31.

87. Arthur Ashe Jr. and Clifford George Gewecke Jr., *Advantage Ashe* (New York: Coward-McCann, 1967), 111–12; Johnny Sample, Fred J. Hamilton, and Sonny Schwartz, *Confessions of a Dirty Ballplayer* (New York: Dell, 1971), 3.

88. Willie Mays and Charles Einstein, *Willie Mays: My Life in and out of Baseball* (New York: E. P. Dutton, 1966), 26.

89. On the alleged snub, see David K. Wiggins, "The 1936 Olympic Games in Berlin: The Response of America's Black Press," *Research Quarterly for Exercise and Sport* 54 (September 1983): 285–86.

90. William J. Baker, *Jesse Owens: An American Life* (New York: Free Press, 1988), 206; William Johnson, "After the Golden Moment," *Sports Illustrated,* 17 July 1972, 41.

91. Jesse Owens and Paul Neimark, *Blackthink: My Life as Black Man and White Man* (New York: Simon & Schuster, 1971), 29, 56, 66, 69, 158, 170; "Jesse Owens' Sportstalk," *Chicago Defender,* 25 March 1961, 24.

92. Harry Edwards, *The Revolt of the Black Athlete* (New York: Free Press, 1969), 50; Johnathan Rodgers, "A Step to an Olympic Boycott," *Sports Illustrated,* 4 December 1967, 30–31; "The Black Boycott," *Time,* 23 February 1968, 61; Arnold Hano, "The Black Rebel Who 'Whitelists' the Olympics," *New York Times Magazine,* 12 May 1968, 42.

93. "Should Negroes Boycott the Olympics?" *Ebony* 23 (March 1968): 112.

94. Edwards, *Revolt,* 59; Harry Edwards, *The Struggle That Must Be: An Autobiography* (New York: Macmillan, 1980), 182; Stokely Carmichael, *Stokely Speaks: Black Power Back to Pan-Africanism* (New York: Vintage, 1971), 123.

95. Edwards, *Struggle,* 179–80; Jack Scott, "The White Olympics," *Ramparts* 6 (May 1968): 60; Jack Scott and Harry Edwards, "After the Olympics: Buying Off Protest," *Ramparts* 8 (November 1969): 16.

96. Edwards, *Revolt,* 98–99, 104; Edwards, *Struggle,* 195; "Olympic Trials: Black Athletes Prepare for Mexico City," *Ebony* 23 (October 1968): 186.

97. "'Black Power' at the Olympics," *U.S. News and World Report,* 28 October 1968, 10; Edwards, *Revolt,* 104.

98. "Black Complaint," *Time,* 25 October 1968, 62–63; Edwards, *Revolt,* 103–5; Jeremy Larner and David Wolf, "Amid Gold Medals, Raised Black Fists," *Life,* 1 November 1968, 64.

99. Harry Edwards, "Why Negroes Should Boycott Whitey's Olympics," *Saturday Evening Post,* 9 March 1968, 6; Hano, "Black Rebel," 32; Edwards, *Struggle,* 217; Harry Edwards, "The Olympic Project for Human Rights: An Assessment Ten Years Later," *Black Scholar* 10 (March–April 1979): 2.

100. Donald Spivey, "Black Consciousness and Olympic Protest Movement, 1964–80," in Spivey, *Sport in America,* 246; Jesse Owens, "The Olympics: A Preview," *TV Guide,* 12 October 1968, 10; "Jesse Owens Honored," *Chicago Defender,* 25 May 1968, 19.

101. "Owens Doubts Boycott Value," *Chicago Defender,* 10 February 1968, 15; Owens and Neimark, *Blackthink,* 61–64, 98 (the quotations I have used from *Blackthink,* published in 1971, are from 1970). A somewhat more charitable appraisal of the "black extremists" appeared a few years later in Jesse Owens and Paul Neimark, *I Have Changed* (New York: William Morrow, 1972), 92, 105.

102. Baker, *Owens,* 206; Owens and Neimark, *Blackthink,* 78, 97.

103. Scott, "White Olympics," 61.

104. Thomas Hauser, *Muhammad Ali: His Life and Times* (New York: Simon & Schuster, 1991), 269–70, 366; Budd Schulberg, *Loser and Still Champion: Muhammad Ali* (New York: Popular Library, 1972), 113; John Cottrell, *Muhammad Ali, Who Once Was Cassius Clay* (New York: Funk & Wagnalls, 1967), 96; Muhammad Ali and Richard Durham, *The Greatest: My Own Story* (New York: Random House, 1975), 19.

105. Larry Fox, *The O. J. Simpson Story: Born to Run* (New York: Dodd, Mead, 1974), 12; Rudolph, *Wilma,* 15; Libby and Haywood, *Stand Up,* 10, 15, 17, 35.

106. Ali and Durham, *The Greatest,* 38–39.

107. Ibid., 64–69, 77.

108. Ibid., 70–78.

109. Cottrell, *Muhammad Ali,* 188, 311, 322; Wilfrid Sheed, *Muhammad Ali: A Portrait in Words and Photographs* (New York: New American Library, 1976), 222–23; Hauser, *Muhammad Ali,* 189; Jack Olsen, *Black Is Best: The Riddle of Cassius Clay* (New York: G. P. Putnam's Sons, 1967), 162.

110. Hauser, *Muhammad Ali,* 135, 293.

111. Cottrell, *Muhammad Ali,* 154, 285, 336.

112. Olsen, *Black Is Best,* 183; José Torres, *Sting Like a Bee: The Muhammad Ali Story* (New York: Curtis, 1971), 152.

113. Hauser, *Muhammad Ali,* 281, 515. A 1971 Harris Poll showed Ali to be as greatly admired among blacks as Massachusetts senator Edward Brooke or Brooklyn congresswoman Shirley Chisholm. The highest-ranked sports figure in the survey, his approval rating was almost twice that of "militants" such as Stokely Carmichael and Eldridge Cleaver (*The Harris Survey Yearbook of Public Opinion, 1971* [New York: Louis Harris & Associates, 1975], 340).

114. Eldridge Cleaver, *Soul on Ice* (New York: McGraw-Hill, 1968), 91–92.

115. Ali and Durham, *The Greatest,* 64, 239, 308, 403.

116. Cottrell, *Muhammad Ali,* 39, 198; Sheed, *Muhammad Ali,* 219.

117. Schulberg, *Loser,* 41.

118. Hauser, *Muhammad Ali,* 60.

119. See, e.g., Cottrell, *Muhammad Ali,* 174; Roodevelt "Rosey" Grier and Dennis Baker, *Rosey, an Autobiography: The Gentle Giant* (Tulsa: Honor, 1986), 250–54; Archie Griffin and Dave Diles, *Archie: The Archie Griffin Story* (Garden City, N.Y.: Doubleday, 1977), 51, 75–76; Jim Brown and Steve Delsohn, *Out of Bounds* (New York: Kensington, 1989), 58; Phil Pepe, *Kareem Abdul-Jabbar* (New York: Grosset & Dunlap, 1970), 113–16; Larry Fox, *Willis Reed: Take-Charge Man of the Knicks* (New York: Grosset & Dunlap, 1970), 122; David Wolf, *Foul! The Connie Hawkins Story* (New York: Warner, 1972), 506–7.

120. Gale Sayers and Al Silverman, *I Am Third* (New York: Bantam, 1972), 132.

121. Audrey Edwards and Gary Wohl, *Muhammad Ali: The People's Champ* (Boston: Little, Brown, 1977), 4.

122. Stan Isaacs, *Jim Brown: The Golden Year, 1964* (New York: Manor, 1970), 51.

Chapter Four

1. For depictions of John Henry as a badman, see Roger D. Abrahams, *Deep Down in the Jungle . . . : Negro Narrative Folklore from the Streets of Philadelphia* (Chicago: Aldine, 1970), 75; Guy B. Johnson, *John Henry: Tracking Down a Negro Legend* (Chapel Hill: University of North Carolina Press, 1929), 11; Theodore Browne, *Natural Man,* in *Black Theater, U.S.A.: Forty-five Plays by Black Americans, 1847–1974,* ed. James V. Hatch and Ted Shine (1937; reprint, New York: Free Press, 1974), 367–78.

2. James Baldwin, *The Devil Finds Work* (New York: Dial, 1976), 100.

3. On the flaws of the early black-cast films, see Daniel J. Leab, "'All-Colored'—But Not Much Different: Films Made for Negro Ghetto Audiences, 1913–1928," *Phylon* 36 (September 1975): 321–39; Daniel J. Leab, "A Pale Black Imitation: All-Colored Films, 1930–60," *Journal of Popular Film* 4, no. 1 (1975): 57–76; Thomas Cripps, *Slow Fade to Black: The Negro in American Film, 1900–1942* (New York: Oxford University Press, 1977), 70–89, 170–202, 309–48.

4. Inventive advertising claims for the black western heroes can be sampled via promotional materials reproduced in John Kisch and Edward Mapp, *A Separate Cinema: Fifty Years of Black-Cast Posters* (New York: Noonday, 1992).

5. On NAACP lobbying efforts, see Thomas Cripps, *Making Movies Black: The Hollywood Message Movie from World War II to the Civil Rights Era* (New York: Oxford University Press, 1993), 35–63; Walter White, *A Man Called White* (New York: Viking, 1948), 198–205; Leonard C. Archer, *Black Images in the American Theatre: NAACP Protest Campaigns—Stage, Screen, Radio, and Television* (Brooklyn: Pageant-Poseidon, 1973), 183–224.

6. Joseph Morgenstern, "Spence and Supergirl," *Newsweek,* 25 December 1967, 70.

7. Maxine Hall Elliston, "Two Sidney Poitier Films," *Film Comment* 5 (winter 1969): 28.

8. Marshall Hyatt, *The Afro-American Cinematic Experience* (Wilmington, Del.: Scholarly Resources, 1983), 244–45; "U.S Black Audience–Slated Films: 25 New 1974 Titles," *Variety,* 8 January 1975, 18. Casts, credits, and plot summaries for over one hundred such films may be found in James Robert Parish and George H. Hill, *Black Action Films* (Jefferson, N.C.: McFarland, 1989). For an entertaining, somewhat more impressionistic celebration of the genre, see Darius James, *That's Blaxploitation!* (New York: St. Martin's, 1995).

9. Melvin Van Peebles quoted in James Murray, *To Find an Image: Black Films from Uncle Tom to Super Fly* (Indianapolis: Bobbs-Merrill, 1973), 165. See also "The Black Movie Boom," *Newsweek,* 6 September 1971, 66; David E. James, "Chained to Devilpictures: Cinema and Black Liberation in the Sixties," in *The Year Left 2,* ed. Mike Davis, Manning Marable, Fred Pfeil, and Michael Sprinker (London: Verso, 1987), 126–27; Jesse Algeron Rhines, *Black Film/White Money* (New Brunswick: Rutgers University Press, 1996), 42–50; Ada Gay Griffin, "Seizing the Moving Image: Reflections of a Black Independent Producer," in *Black Popular Culture,* ed. Gina Dent (Seattle: Bay, 1992), 228–33.

10. Pauline Kael, "Notes on Black Movies," *New Yorker,* 2 December 1972, 162–63.

11. Thomas Cripps, *Black Film as Genre* (Bloomington: Indiana University Press, 1978), 11–12, 128–30. See also Donald Bogle, *Toms, Coons, Mulattoes, Mammies, and Bucks: An Interpretive History of Blacks in American Films* (New York: Continuum, 1989), 241–42.

12. On Hollywood's crisis-driven recognition of black moviegoers' "consumer power," see John Izod, *Hollywood and the Box Office, 1895–1986* (New York: Columbia University Press, 1988), 171–98; Douglas Gomery, *Shared Pleasures: A History of Movie Presentation in the United States* (Madison: University of Wisconsin Press, 1992), 165–70; James P. Murray, "The Subject Is Money" (1973), in *Black Films and Film-Makers: A Comprehensive Anthology*

from Stereotype to Superhero, ed. Lindsay Patterson (New York: Dodd, Mead, 1975), 247–57; Ed Guerrero, *Framing Blackness: The African American Image in Film* (Philadelphia: Temple University Press, 1993), 82–84.

13. For a colorful survey of the various subgenres, see Richard Meyers, *For One Week Only: The World of Exploitation Films* (Piscataway, N.J.: New Century, 1983).

14. Charles Michener, "Black Movies," *Newsweek,* 23 October 1972, 77.

15. "Blacks vs. Shaft," *Newsweek,* 28 August 1972, 88.

16. Reneé Ward, "Black Films, White Profits," *Black Scholar* 7 (May 1976): 23; "How to Survive in Hollywood between Gigs," *Ebony* 33 (October 1978): 36; Bonnie Allen, "The Macho Men: What Ever Happened to Them?" *Essence* 9 (February 1979): 92; Murray, *To Find an Image,* 158.

17. Doris Black, "Hollywood's New King of Ego," *Sepia* 22 (August 1973): 42.

18. Ossie Davis, "The Power of Black Movies," *Freedomways* 14, no. 3 (1974): 230.

19. Allen, "Macho Men," 98; "Vonetta McGee's Own Story: Hollywood's Daring Mixed Romance Movie," *Sepia* 24 (March 1975): 37.

20. Black, "King of Ego," 40; "Blacks vs. Shaft," 88.

21. For additional commentary on the filmmaker-audience interface, see Thomas M. Leitch, "The Case for Studying Popular Culture," *South Atlantic Quarterly* 84 (spring 1985): 115–26; Martin Laba, "Making Sense: Expressiveness, Stylization, and the Popular Culture Process," *Journal of Popular Culture* 19 (spring 1986): 107–17; Andrea S. Walsh, *Women's Film and Female Experience, 1940–50* (New York: Praeger, 1984), 3–15.

22. For these encapsulations of the black heroic, see Robeson in *Song of Freedom* (Hammer–British Lion, 1936), Edwards in *Home of the Brave* (United Artists, 1949), Hernandez in *Intruder in the Dust* (Metro-Goldwyn-Mayer, 1949), Marshall in *Lydia Bailey* (20th Century Fox, 1952), Strode in *Sergeant Rutledge* (Warner Brothers, 1960), and Dixon in *Nothing but a Man* (Du Art, 1964).

23. For Peters's early contributions to the development of black male portraiture, see *Carmen Jones* (20th Century Fox, 1954), *Porgy and Bess* (Columbia, 1959), *To Kill a Mockingbird* (Universal-International, 1962), and *The Pawnbroker* (Landau-Unger, 1965); for Kotto's, see *Nothing but a Man* (Du Art, 1964) and *The Liberation of L. B. Jones* (Columbia, 1970); for Brown's, see *The Dirty Dozen* (Metro-Goldwyn-Mayer, 1967), *Dark of the Sun* (Metro-Goldwyn-Mayer, 1968), and *100 Rifles* (20th Century Fox, 1969).

24. On the early black film goddesses, see Horne in *Stormy Weather* (20th Century Fox, 1943), Kitt in *Anna Lucasta* (United Artists, 1958), Dandridge in *Carmen Jones* (20th Century Fox, 1954), and Bailey in *Porgy and Bess* (Columbia, 1959). On the male "gaze," see Laura Mulvey, "Visual Pleasure and Narrative Cinema," *Screen* 16 (autumn 1975): 6–18; Jackie Stacey, *Star Gazing: Hollywood Cinema and Female Spectatorship* (London: Routledge, 1994), 7–10, 20–21; E. Ann Kaplan, *Women and Film: Both Sides of the Camera* (New York: Methuen, 1983), 23–35. On the ability of female spectators to "negotiate" the reception and "read against the grain" of patriarchal texts, see Jacqueline Bobo, *Black Women as Cultural Readers* (New York: Columbia University Press, 1995), 5, 23, 89–90. For a chronology of the events, publications, and films central to the rise of feminist film studies during the 1970s, see Mary Ann Doane, Patricia Mellencamp, and Linda Williams, eds., *Re-Vision: Essays in Feminist Film Criticism* (Los Angeles: American Film Institute, 1984), 3–4; Annette Kuhn, *Women's Pictures: Feminism and Cinema* (London: Verso, 1994), 72–81. For an overview of subsequent trends and developments in feminist film scholarship, see Diane Carson, Linda Dittmar, and Janice R. Welsch, eds., *Multiple Voices in Feminist Film Criticism* (Minneapolis: University of Minnesota Press, 1994).

25. On Van Peebles's personal odyssey, see Thomas Cripps, "*Sweet Sweetback's Baadasssss Song* and the Changing Politics of Genre Film," in *Close Viewings: An Anthology of New Film Criticism,* ed. Peter Lehman (Tallahassee: Florida State University Press, 1990), 242–48; Karen Jaehne, "Melvin Van Peebles: The Baadasssss Gent," *Cineaste* 18, no. 1 (1990): 4–8.

26. "Power to the Peebles," *Time,* 16 August 1971, 47; Melvin Van Peebles, *The Making of "Sweet Sweetback's Baadasssss Song"* (New York: Lancer, 1972), 12; Horace W. Coleman, "Melvin Van Peebles," *Journal of Popular Culture* 5 (fall 1971): 369, 371, 376.

27. For a sampling of black opinion on the film, see Lerone Bennett Jr., "The Emancipation Orgasm: Sweetback in Wonderland," *Ebony* 26 (September 1971): 106–18; Huey P. Newton, "He Won't Bleed Me: A Revolutionary Analysis of *Sweet Sweetback's Baadasssss Song,*" *Black Panther,* 19 June 1971, A–L; Clayton Riley, "What Makes Sweetback Run?" *New York Times,* 9 May 1971, 11; Don L. Lee, "The Bittersweet of Sweetback; or, Shake Yo Money Maker," *Black World* 21 (November 1971): 43–48.

28. On Van Peebles's commitment to creating a politicized yet commercial film rather than a "didactic discourse," see Melvin Van Peebles, "A Black Odyssey: *Sweet Sweetback's Baadasssss Song,*" in Patterson, *Black Films,* 227.

29. Van Peebles, *Making of "Sweet Sweetback's Baadasssss Song,"* 13; "Sweet Song of Success," *Newsweek,* 21 June 1971, 89.

30. On the universality of the outlaw heroic tradition, see Eric Hobsbawm, *Bandits* (New York: Delacorte, 1969); Jack Katz, *Seductions of Crime: Moral and Sensual Attractions in Doing Evil* (New York: Basic, 1988), 227. On the outlaw-warrior connection, see Edward Tabor Linenthal, *Changing Images of the Warrior Hero in America: A History of Popular Symbolism* (New York: Edwin Mellen, 1982), xii, xvi–xvii.

31. Oscar Brown Jr., "Signifyin' Monkey," in *Talk That Talk: An Anthology of African-American Storytelling,* ed. Linda Goss and Marian E. Barnes (New York: Simon & Schuster, 1989), 456–57; Dennis Wepman, Ronald B. Newman, and Murray B. Binderman, *The Life: The Lore and Folk Poetry of the Black Hustler* (Philadelphia: University of Pennsylvania Press, 1976), 26. On the place of the Signifying Monkey in black folklore, see Henry Louis Gates Jr., *The Signifying Monkey: A Theory of African-American Literary Criticism* (New York: Oxford University Press, 1988). On Shine, see Bruce Jackson, *"Get Your Ass in the Water and Swim Like Me": Narrative Poetry from Black Oral Tradition* (Cambridge: Harvard University Press, 1974), 35–38, 191–95.

32. For exposition of the Stagolee legend, see Abrahams, *Deep Down in the Jungle,* 75–79, 129–42; Julius Lester, *Black Folklore* (New York: Richard W. Baron, 1969), 113–35. For Railroad Bill's exploits, see Paul Oliver, "Railroad Bill," *Jazz and Blues* 1 (May 1971): 12–14; Norm Cohen, *Long Steel Rail: The Railroad in American Folksong* (Urbana: University of Illinois Press, 1981), 122–28.

33. Iceberg Slim [Robert Beck], *Airtight Willie and Me* (Los Angeles: Holloway House, 1979), 94; Odie Hawkins, *Ghetto Sketches* (Los Angeles: Holloway House, 1972), 38.

34. *Super Fly* (Warner Brothers, 1972); *Willie Dynamite* (Universal, 1973).

35. Joseph Nazel, *The Iceman #2: The Golden Shaft* (Los Angeles: Holloway House, 1974), 112; Roosevelt Mallory, *Radcliff #4: New Jersey Showdown* (Los Angeles: Holloway House, 1976), 15, 20; *Riot* (Paramount, 1969); Iceberg Slim [Robert Beck], *Pimp* (Los Angeles: Holloway House, 1969), 118; Iceberg Slim, *Airtight Willie,* 200; *The Human Tornado* (Dimension, 1976).

36. Donald Goines, *Eldorado Red* (Los Angeles: Holloway House, 1974), 25–28.

37. *The Mack* (Cinerama, 1973).

38. Iceberg Slim, *Pimp,* 103, 105, 115, 164, 292; Donald Goines, *Street Players* (Los Angeles: Holloway House, 1973), 31; Donald Goines, *Whoreson: The Story of a Ghetto Pimp* (Los Angeles: Holloway House, 1972), 45, 62, 71.

39. Iceberg Slim, *Pimp,* 117–18; Donald Goines, *Inner City Hoodlum* (Los Angeles: Holloway House, 1975), 33; Donald Goines, *Black Gangster* (Los Angeles: Holloway House, 1977), 16, 69, 119; *Mister Mean* (Lone Star/Po'Boy, 1977).

40. Goines, *Black Gangster,* 119; Donald Goines, *Never Die Alone* (Los Angeles: Holloway House, 1974), 190–91.

41. Goines, *Hoodlum,* 33–37; *The Mack* (Cinerama, 1973); *Black Caesar* (American International, 1973); *Mean Johnny Barrows* (Dimension, 1975); Donald Goines, *Daddy Cool* (Los Angeles: Holloway House, 1974), 46.

42. *Thomasine and Bushrod* (Columbia, 1974); *Together Brothers* (20th Century Fox, 1974); Iceberg Slim [Robert Beck], *The Naked Soul of Iceberg Slim* (1971; reprint, Los Angeles: Holloway House, 1986), 217–18.

43. Iceberg Slim [Robert Beck], *Death Wish* (1977; reprint, Los Angeles: Holloway House, 1986), 66–67, 134, 140–41; *Cool Breeze* (Metro-Goldwyn-Mayer, 1972); *The Mack* (Cinerama, 1973); *The Black Godfather* (Cinemation, 1974).

44. Iceberg Slim, *Pimp,* 164, 194; Iceberg Slim [Robert Beck], *Trick Baby: The Biography of a Con Man* (Los Angeles: Holloway House, 1967), 166; Goines, *Street Players,* 131–33; Nathan C. Heard, *Howard Street* (1968; reprint, New York: New American Library, 1970), 184–85; Goines, *Daddy Cool,* 193.

45. Iceberg Slim, *Trick,* 126, 146, 163; *Trick Baby* (Universal, 1973).

46. Goines, *Never Die,* 73, 119, 155; *Super Fly* (Warner Brothers, 1972).

47. Roosevelt Mallory, *Radcliff #3: Double Trouble* (Los Angeles: Holloway House, 1975), 32, 170, 209–10.

48. Iceberg Slim, *Pimp,* 11–12, 120, 159; Goines, *Street Players,* 73; Iceberg Slim, *Naked Soul,* 57, 123.

49. Iceberg Slim, *Death Wish,* 117; Louise Meriwether, *Daddy Was a Number Runner* (1970; reprint, New York: Pyramid, 1971), 15, 22.

50. Nazel, *Golden Shaft,* 132; Nathan C. Heard, *To Reach a Dream* (1972; reprint, New York: New American Library, 1973), 68.

51. *Across 110th Street* (United Artists, 1972); Goines, *Black Gangster,* 256–58.

52. Goines, *Never Die,* 107; Iceberg Slim, *Death Wish,* 106.

53. Iceberg Slim, *Pimp,* 134, 176, 195; *The Human Tornado* (Dimension, 1976).

54. *The Black Godfather* (Cinemation, 1974).

55. Hawkins, *Sketches,* 18–20.

56. Iceberg Slim, *Pimp,* 152.

57. Goines, *Whoreson,* 202.

58. Iceberg Slim, *Naked Soul,* 66; Iceberg Slim [Robert Beck], *Long White Con* (1977; reprint, Los Angeles: Holloway House, 1987), 8.

59. Goines, *Street Players,* 77, 86; Iceberg Slim, *Naked Soul,* 58.

60. *The Candy Tangerine Man* (Moonstone, 1975).

61. Iceberg Slim, *Pimp,* 104, 197.

62. Ibid., 13, 62, 111, 114; Goines, *Black Gangster,* 23.

63. Iceberg Slim, *Pimp,* 109–10; Goines, *Whoreson,* 243.

64. Iceberg Slim, *Naked Soul,* 67.

65. Mallory, *Double Trouble,* 32, 36, 47.

66. *Live and Let Die* (United Artists, 1973).

67. *Hell Up in Harlem* (American International, 1973); *The Black Godfather* (Cinemation, 1974).

68. Mallory, *Double Trouble,* 117.

69. Iceberg Slim, *Airtight Willie,* 81.

70. Iceberg Slim, *Trick,* 125.

71. Mallory, *Showdown,* 77.

72. *Willie Dynamite* (Universal, 1973).

73. Goines, *Eldorado,* 211–12.

74. Goines, *Black Gangster,* 252, 255, 263; Goines, *Hoodlum,* 203.

75. Mallory, *Double Trouble,* 32; Goines, *Hoodlum,* 39.

76. Iceberg Slim, *Naked Soul,* 248.

77. Iceberg Slim, *Pimp,* 303, 305, 311.

78. *Super Fly* (Warner Brothers, 1972).

79. On these points, see Iceberg Slim, *Naked Soul,* 223–24; Bob Moore, "The Inside Story of Black Pimps," *Sepia* 21 (February 1972): 56, 58; D. B. Graham, "'Negative Glamour': The Pimp Hero in the Fiction of Iceberg Slim," *Obsidian* 1 (summer 1975): 16.

80. Sam Greenlee, *The Spook Who Sat by the Door* (1969; reprint, New York: Bantam, 1970), 88; Goines, *Black Gangster,* 27, 31–32, 90, 154–55; *The Black Godfather* (Cinemation, 1974).

81. *Uptight* (Paramount, 1968); *The Final Comedown* (New World, 1972).

82. Donald Goines, *Crime Partners* (Los Angeles: Holloway House, 1978), 49.

83. Fletcher Knebel, *Trespass* (1969; reprint, New York: Pocket, 1970), 234.

84. Barry Beckham, *Runner Mack* (1972; reprint, Washington, D.C.: Howard University Press, 1983), 140; John A. Williams, *The Man Who Cried I Am* (Boston: Little, Brown, 1967), 250.

85. Julian Moreau [J. Denis Jackson], *The Black Commandos* (Atlanta: Cultural Institute, 1967), 23–24, 40, 64.

86. *The Spook Who Sat by the Door* (United Artists, 1973); James Baldwin, *Tell Me How Long the Train's Been Gone* (New York: Dial, 1968), 73.

87. Alan Seymour, *The Coming Self-Destruction of the United States of America* (New York: Grove, 1969), 62, 235.

88. Ibid., 122–23.

89. Knebel, *Trespass,* 289; Greenlee, *Spook,* 243; Donald Goines, *Death List* (Los Angeles: Holloway House, 1974), 25.

90. Hank Lopez, *Afro-6* (New York: Dell, 1969), 112; Edwin Corley, *Siege* (New York: Stein & Day, 1969), 69.

91. Moreau, *Black Commandos,* 185; B. B. Johnson [Joe Greene], *Black Is Beautiful* (New York: Paperback Library, 1970), 12; Williams, *Man Who Cried,* 253.

92. Moreau, *Black Commandos,* 50; Dan Britain, *Civil War II: The Day It Finally Happened!* (New York: Pinnacle, 1971), 48–49.

93. Blyden Jackson, *Operation Burning Candle* (1973; reprint, New York: Pyramid, 1974), 146–50.

94. For a description of one fictional black militant who included "Third World brothers 'n sisters" and "po' ass crackers" in his revolutionary plans, see Hawkins, *Sketches,* 131.

95. D. Keith Mano, *Horn* (1969; reprint, New York: Avon, 1970), 205; *Uptight* (Paramount, 1968).

96. *The Final Comedown* (New World, 1972); Corley, *Siege,* 70.

97. Mano, *Horn,* 142, 205.

98. Beckham, *Runner Mack,* 201.

99. *Five on the Black Hand Side* (United Artists, 1973); Lopez, *Afro-6,* 36; Knebel, *Trespass,* 86; Johnson, *Beautiful,* 42–45.

100. Ann Allen Shockley, "Is She Relevant?" *Black World* 20 (January 1971): 63–64.

101. Lopez, *Afro-6,* 90–91; Henry Van Dyke, *Dead Piano* (New York: Farrar, Straus & Giroux, 1971), 35.

102. Ed Lacy, *In Black and Whitey* (New York: Lancer, 1967), 78, 80; Ed Lacy, *Harlem Underground* (New York: Pyramid, 1965), 58.

103. Goines, *Crime Partners,* 52; Lopez, *Afro-6,* 230; *Uptight* (Paramount, 1968).

104. Donald Goines, *Kenyatta's Last Hit* (Los Angeles: Holloway House, 1975), 160.

105. Goines, *Crime Partners,* 55; Lopez, *Afro-6,* 121–22.

106. Lopez, *Afro-6,* 27, 158; Goines, *Death List,* 76.

107. Greenlee, *Spook,* 107; Moreau, *Black Commandos,* 58–59.

108. Seymour, *Self-Destruction,* 152; Knebel, *Trespass,* 26; Britain, *Civil War II,* 25, 243–44.

109. Lloyd Zimpel, *Meeting the Bear: Journal of the Black Wars* (New York: Macmillan, 1971), 36; Knebel, *Trespass,* 133, 222, 234; Dan Brennan, *Insurrection!* (New York: Belmont, 1970), 183.

110. Chuck Stone, *King Strut* (Indianapolis: Bobbs-Merrill, 1970), 164; Lopez, *Afro-6,* 55; Warren Miller, *The Siege of Harlem* (1964; reprint, Greenwich, Conn.: Fawcett, 1969), 13–14.

111. Moreau, *Black Commandos,* 196–97, 209–10, 225; John A. Williams, *Sons of Darkness, Sons of Light* (1969; reprint, New York: Pocket, 1970), 140–42.

112. Corley, *Siege,* 107–9, 165, 192–94, 204.

113. Ibid., 283–88.

114. Ibid., 49, 380.

115. Miller, *Siege,* 13; Britain, *Civil War II,* 47–48, 108, 152; Moreau, *Black Commandos,* 79, 82; Stone, *King Strut,* 323–24.

116. Jackson, *Burning Candle,* 149–50, 167, 201.

117. Lopez, *Afro-6,* 74; Jackson, *Burning Candle,* 25; *Five on the Black Hand Side* (United Artists, 1973); Van Dyke, *Dead Piano,* 62.

118. Evan K. Walker, "Legacy," *Black World* 21 (December 1971): 72; Beckham, *Runner Mack,* 196.

119. Jackson, *Burning Candle,* 239; Williams, *Darkness,* 183–84.

120. Paula Hankins, "Testimonial," in *Black Short Story Anthology,* ed. Woodie King (New York: Columbia University Press, 1972), 99, 101–2; Mano, *Horn,* 72, 164–67.

121. Miller, *Siege,* 55–56, 141.

122. Zimpel, *Meeting the Bear,* 119.

123. Don Pendleton, *Revolt!* (n.p.: Bee-Line, 1968), 4–8; Seymour, *Self-Destruction,* 299; Williams, *Man Who Cried,* 367–76.

124. For additional background on the detective character in popular literature, see David Geherin, *The American Private Eye: The Image in Fiction* (New York: Frederick Ungar, 1985); Robert A. Baker and Michael T. Nietzel, *Private Eyes: One Hundred and One Knights, A Survey of American Detective Fiction, 1922–1984* (Bowling Green, Ohio: Bowling Green State University Popular Press, 1985); William Ruehlmann, *Saint with a Gun: The Unlawful American Private Eye* (New York: New York University Press, 1974); David Geherin, *Sons of Sam Spade: The Private-Eye Novel in the 70s* (New York: Frederick Ungar, 1980).

125. On the detective in popular film, see Jon Tuska, *The Detective in Hollywood* (Garden City, N.Y.: Doubleday, 1978); James Robert Parish and Michael R. Pitts, *The Great Detective Pictures* (Metuchen, N.J.: Scarecrow, 1990); Max Allan Collins and John Javna, *The Best of Crime and Detective TV* (New York: Harmony, 1988); Richard Meyers, *TV Detectives* (San Diego: A. S. Barnes, 1981).

126. On early black detective portraiture, see Frankie Y. Bailey, *Out of the Woodpile: Black Characters in Crime and Detective Fiction* (Westport, Conn.: Greenwood, 1991); Stephen F. Soitos, *The Blues Detective: A Study of African American Detective Fiction* (Amherst: University of Massachusetts Press, 1996).

127. For an introduction to these and other ethnic crime-fighters, see Bill Pronzini and Martin H. Greenberg, eds., *The Ethnic Detectives: Masterpieces of Mystery Fiction* (New York: Dodd, Mead, 1985).

128. B. B. Johnson [Joe Greene], *Death of a Blue-Eyed Soul Brother* (New York: Paperback Library, 1970), 5–6, 141; *Death Journey* (Atlas, 1976).

129. John Wyllie, *The Killer Breath* (1979; reprint, Chicago: Academy Chicago, 1986), 13, 109; J. F. Burke, *Location Shots* (New York: Harper & Row, 1974), 1–2, 46.

130. Ernest Tidyman, *Shaft* (1970; reprint, New York: Bantam, 1971), 4; Ernest Tidyman, *Shaft among the Jews* (1972; reprint, New York: Bantam, 1973), 102.

131. B. J. Mason, "The New Films: Culture or Con Game?" *Ebony* 28 (December 1972): 62.

132. Tidyman, *Jews,* 4–5.

133. Tidyman, *Shaft,* 35, 63, 158.

134. Ernest Tidyman, *Good-bye, Mr. Shaft* (New York: Dial, 1973), 24; Tidyman, *Jews,* 54, 182.

135. Ernest Tidyman, *Shaft Has a Ball* (New York: Bantam, 1973), 7; Tidyman, *Shaft,* 146; Ernest Tidyman, *Shaft's Carnival of Killers* (New York: Bantam, 1974), 20.

136. Tidyman, *Shaft,* 165.

137. Maurice Peterson, "Gordon Parks," *Essence* 3 (October 1972): 62.

138. Tidyman, *Shaft,* 26, 88, 161–62, 184; Tidyman, *Jews,* 91; Tidyman, *Ball,* 23.

139. Tidyman, *Ball,* 22, 39.

140. Ibid., 11, 31, 84–85; Tidyman, *Good-bye,* 37.

141. "'Is Shaft Really a Hero?' Co-star in the Movie Asks," *Jet,* 14 September 1972, 51; Eugenia Collier, "'TV Still Evades the Nitty-Gritty Truth!'" *TV Guide,* 12 January 1974, 7; Meyers, *TV Detectives,* 186–87.

142. Tidyman, *Shaft,* 51.

143. Ibid., 61; *Shaft's Big Score!* (Metro-Goldwyn-Mayer, 1972).

144. Bonnie Allen, "The Macho Men: What Ever Happened to Them?" *Essence* 9 (February 1979): 90; Bob Lucas, "The *Shaft* Business," *Sepia* 21 (July 1972): 37, 40.

145. On the links between Himes's early life experiences and the detective thrillers composing his Harlem Domestic Series (1957–69), see Robert E. Skinner, *Two Guns from Harlem: The Detective Fiction of Chester Himes* (Bowling Green, Ohio: Bowling Green State University Popular Press, 1989).

146. Chester Himes, *Cotton Comes to Harlem* (1965; reprint, New York: Dell, 1970), 17.

147. Chester Himes, *The Big Gold Dream* (1960; reprint, New York: New American Library, 1975), 60, 190.

148. Chester Himes, *Hot Day, Hot Night* (1969; reprint, New York: New American Library, 1975), 45.

149. Himes, *Gold,* 184.

150. Himes, *Cotton,* 162–63; Chester Himes, *The Heat's On* (1966; reprint, New York: Vintage, 1988), 14; Chester Himes, *All Shot Up* (New York: Avon, 1960), 30–31.

151. Himes, *Gold,* 47.

152. Himes, *Cotton,* 19.

153. Ibid., 116, 135–36, 163; Himes, *Heat's On,* 112.

154. *Cotton Comes to Harlem* (United Artists, 1970); Himes, *Heat's On,* 146.

155. Himes, *Gold,* 80; Himes, *Heat's On,* 55; Himes, *Hot Day,* 5, 37, 117, 149, 167–68.

156. Himes, *Hot Day,* 67; Himes, *Heat's On,* 174.

157. Himes, *Heat's On,* 174.

158. Himes, *Cotton,* 18.

159. Himes, *Gold,* 59.

160. John Ball, *The Eyes of Buddha* (Boston: Little, Brown, 1976), 27.

161. John Ball, *In The Heat of the Night* (1965; reprint, New York: Bantam, 1967), 13; John Ball, *Five Pieces of Jade* (1972; reprint, New York: Harper & Row, 1985), 124, 230; Ball, *Eyes,* 52.

162. John Ball, *Then Came Violence* (1980; reprint, New York: Harper & Row, 1988), 45; Ball, *Eyes,* 29; John Ball, *The Cool Cottontail* (Boston: Little, Brown, 1976), 19.

163. John Ball, *Johnny Get Your Gun* (Boston: Little, Brown, 1969), 135; Ball, *Heat,* 114.

164. *They Call Me Mister Tibbs!* (United Artists, 1970); Ball, *Violence,* 173.

165. *The Organization* (United Artists, 1971).

166. Ball, *Eyes,* 120.

167. Ball, *Heat,* 68.

168. Ball, *Eyes,* 57, 113, 177–78; Ball, *Cottontail,* 24.

169. Ball, *Gun,* 139, 225–26; Ball, *Cottontail,* 166.

170. Ball, *Heat,* 52; Ball, *Jade,* 104.

171. Ball, *Heat,* 121.

172. Ball, *Gun,* 111.

173. On the history of fictional female investigators, see Kathleen Gregory Klein, *The Woman Detective: Gender and Genre* (Urbana: University of Illinois Press, 1988); Maureen T. Reddy, *Sisters in Crime: Feminism and the Crime Novel* (New York: Continuum, 1988); Jane C. Pennell, "The Female Detective: Pre– and Post–Women's Lib," *Clues* 6 (fall–winter 1985): 85–98.

174. Rex Stout, "Too Many Detectives," in *Three for the Chair* (New York: Viking, 1957), 121.

175. B. B. Johnson [Joe Greene], *Bad Day for a Black Brother* (New York: Paperback Library, 1970), 22.

176. For an introduction to female sleuths Kinsey Millhone, Penny Wanawake, Sharon McCone, and V. I. Warshawski, see Sue Grafton, *"A" Is for Alibi* (New York: Holt, Rinehart, & Winston, 1982); Susan Moody, *Penny Black* (London: Macmillan, 1984); Marcia Muller, *The Cheshire Cat's Eye* (New York: St. Martin's, 1983); Sara Paretsky, *Deadlock* (New York: Dial, 1984).

177. James D. Lawrence, *The Godmother Caper* (New York: Pyramid, 1975), 6, 39, 58, 84.

178. *Sheba, Baby* (American International, 1975).

179. Sidney Frasier (Gloria Hendry) in *Black Belt Jones* (Warner Brothers, 1974).

180. Diana Jackson (Jeanne Bell) in *T.N.T. Jackson* (New World, 1975).

181. Cleopatra Jones (Tamara Dobson) in *Cleopatra Jones and the Casino of Gold* (Warner Brothers, 1975).

182. *Coffy* (American International, 1973); *Foxy Brown* (American International, 1974).

In the tradition of early female sleuths, Grier's B-movie characters tended to be detectives without portfolio but with close ties to career law enforcement professionals.

183. *Velvet Smooth* (Howard Mahler, 1976).

184. *Cleopatra Jones* (Warner Brothers, 1973).

185. *T.N.T. Jackson* (New World, 1975).

186. *Get Christie Love!* (Wolper, 1974)

187. *Sheba, Baby* (American International, 1975).

188. On these matters as they relate to film, see Molly Haskell, *From Reverence to Rape: The Treatment of Women in the Movies* (Chicago: University of Chicago Press, 1987), 40, 402; Jan Rosenberg, *Women's Reflections: The Feminist Film Movement* (Ann Arbor: UMI Research, 1983), 112.

189. *Black Samurai* (B.J.L.J. International, 1977); Marc Olden, *The Deadly Pearl* (New York: New American Library, 1974), 85; Marc Olden, *Killer Warrior* (New York: New American Library, 1974), 22.

190. Marc Olden, *The Golden Kill* (New York: New American Library, 1974), 124; Olden, *Deadly Pearl,* 9; Olden, *Killer Warrior,* 19.

191. Olden, *Golden Kill,* 92, 95; Olden, *Deadly Pearl,* 8.

192. Olden, *Golden Kill,* 19, 39; Marc Olden, *Sword of Allah* (New York: New American Library, 1975), 144.

193. Olden, *Killer Warrior,* 126.

194. Olden, *Deadly Pearl,* 153.

195. Ibid., 2, 85; Marc Olden, *The Inquisition* (New York: New American Library, 1974), 157.

196. Olden, *Deadly Pearl,* 65; Olden, *Inquisition,* 36, 91.

197. *Hit Man* (Metro-Goldwyn-Mayer, 1972); *Bucktown* (American International, 1975).

198. *Black Samson* (Warner Brothers, 1974).

199. *The Black Six* (Cinemation, 1974); *Slaughter* (American International, 1972).

200. Burke, *Location Shots,* 102.

201. Ibid., 71–72.

202. Ibid., 72; J. F. Burke, *Kelly among the Nightingales* (New York: E. P. Dutton, 1979), 170.

203. Burke, *Location Shots,* 73.

204. *No Way Back* (Atlas, 1976); Percy Spurlark Parker, *Good Girls Don't Get Murdered* (New York: Charles Scribner's Sons, 1974), 72, 94; Robert B. Parker, *Promised Land* (Boston: Houghton Mifflin, 1976), 12–14.

205. *The Take* (Columbia, 1974).

206. *Hit!* (Paramount, 1973).

207. George Baxt, *Topsy and Evil* (New York: Simon & Schuster, 1968), 61, 158; George Baxt, *A Queer Kind of Death* (1966; reprint, New York: International Polygonics, 1986), 108, 219, 246.

208. Lacy, *Harlem Underground,* 11, 22, 29; Lacy, *Black and Whitey,* 46, 95, 109.

209. Lacy, *Harlem Underground,* 143; Lacy, *Black and Whitey,* 45, 62, 81.

210. Lacy, *Harlem Underground,* 17, 146; Lacy, *Black and Whitey,* 24, 67.

Chapter Five

1. Jacques Attali, *Noise: The Political Economy of Music* (Minneapolis: University of Minnesota Press, 1985), 4–5.

2. For commentary on music as a cultural mechanism for expressing emancipatory political perspectives, see Ray Pratt, *Rhythm and Resistance: Explorations in the Political Uses of Popular Music* (New York: Praeger, 1990); Reebee Garofalo, ed., *Rockin' the Boat: Mass Music and Mass Movements* (Boston: South End, 1992).

3. Paul A. Cimbala, "Fortunate Bondsmen: Black 'Musicianers' and Their Role as an Antebellum Southern Plantation Slave Elite," *Southern Studies* 18 (fall 1979): 291–303.

4. *Twelve Years a Slave: Narrative of Solomon Northup* (1853; reprint, New York: Miller, Orton & Mulligan, 1855), 216–17.

5. Garnett Andrews, *Reminiscences of an Old Georgia Lawyer* (Atlanta: Franklin Steam Printing House, 1870), 10–11. For more on corn generals, see Roger D. Abrahams, *Singing the Master: The Emergence of African American Culture in the Plantation South* (New York: Pantheon, 1992).

6. On the black holiday celebrations, see Sterling Stuckey, *Slave Culture: Nationalist Theory and the Foundations of Black America* (New York: Oxford University Press, 1987), 74–82; Sterling Stuckey, "The Skies of Consciousness: African Dance at Pinkster in New York, 1750–1840," in *Going Through the Storm: The Influence of African American Art in History* (New York: Oxford University Press, 1994), 53–80; Joseph P. Reidy, "'Negro Election Day' and Black Community Life in New England, 1750–1860," *Marxist Perspectives* 1 (fall 1978): 102–17; Melvin Wade, "'Shining in Borrowed Plumage': Affirmation of Community in the Black Coronation Festivals of New England, ca. 1750–1850," in *Material Life in America, 1600–1860,* ed. Robert Blair St. George (Boston: Northeastern University Press, 1988), 171–82.

7. Dena J. Epstein, *Sinful Tunes and Spirituals: Black Folk Music to the Civil War* (Urbana: University of Illinois Press, 1977), 68.

8. On Greenfield, see Arthur R. LaBrew, *The Black Swan: Elizabeth T. Greenfield, Songstress* (Detroit: published by the author, 1969). On Bethune, see Geneva H. Southall, *Blind Tom: The Post–Civil War Enslavement of a Black Musical Genius* (Minneapolis: Challenge, 1979). On Aldridge, see Herbert Marshall and Mildred Stock, *Ira Aldridge: The Negro Tragedian* (London: Rockliff, 1958).

9. Surveys of African-American contributions to these popular musical forms include Eileen Southern, *The Music of Black Americans: A History* (New York: W. W. Norton, 1983); Arnold Shaw, *Black Popular Music in America* (New York: Schirmer, 1986); Samuel A. Floyd Jr., *The Power of Black Music: Interpreting Its History from Africa to the United States* (New York: Oxford University Press, 1995).

10. William Howland Kenney, *Chicago Jazz: A Cultural History, 1904–1930* (New York: Oxford University Press, 1993), 124–25.

11. J. A. Rogers, "Jazz at Home," in *The New Negro,* ed. Alain Locke (1925; reprint, New York: Atheneum, 1968), 217.

12. "Hot Society," *Time,* 17 May 1937, 50.

13. Lawrence W. Levine, "Jazz and American Culture," in *The Unpredictable Past: Explorations in American Cultural History* (1989; reprint, New York: Oxford University Press, 1993), 178–80; Neil Leonard, *Jazz and the White Americans: The Acceptance of a New Art Form* (Chicago: University of Chicago Press, 1962), 32–39.

14. On the supernatural and shamanistic aspects of jazzmen, see Neil Leonard, *Jazz: Myth and Religion* (New York: Oxford University Press, 1987).

15. On the rent party ambience, see Katrina Hazzard-Gordon, *Jookin': The Rise of Social Dance Formations in African-American Culture* (Philadelphia: Temple University Press, 1990), 94–119.

16. Robert George Reisner, ed., *Bird: The Legend of Charlie Parker* (New York: Citadel, 1962), 124.

17. On the jazzman's jargon, see Robert S. Gold, *Jazz Talk* (Indianapolis: Bobbs-Merrill, 1975); Neil Leonard, "The Jazzman's Verbal Usage," *Black American Literature Forum* 20 (spring–summer 1986): 151–60; Elliot Horne, *The Hiptionary: A Hipster's View of the World Scene* (New York: Simon & Schuster, 1963).

18. Kathy J. Ogren, *The Jazz Revolution: Twenties America and the Meaning of Jazz* (New York: Oxford University Press, 1989), 87.

19. On the limitations placed on the women of jazz, see Linda Dahl, *Stormy Weather: The Music and Lives of a Century of Jazzwomen* (New York: Pantheon, 1984), 44, 58, 80, 88, 93, 122–24.

20. Macdonald Smith Moore, *Yankee Blues: Musical Culture and American Identity* (Bloomington: Indiana University Press, 1985), 90.

21. David Levering Lewis, *When Harlem Was in Vogue* (1981; reprint, New York: Vintage, 1982), 170.

22. For a sampling of the artists' jazz-influenced work in the context of their times, see *Harlem Renaissance: Art of Black America* (New York: Studio Museum in Harlem and Harry N. Abrams, 1987). On jazzmen in film, see David Meeker, *Jazz in the Movies: A Guide to Jazz Musicians, 1917–1977* (New Rochelle, N.Y.: Arlington House, 1977); Krin Gabbard, *Jammin' at the Margins: Jazz and the American Cinema* (Chicago: University of Chicago Press, 1996).

23. James Baldwin, "Sonny's Blues" (1957), in *Going to Meet the Man* (New York: Dell, 1976), 119; John Clellon Holmes, *The Horn* (New York: Random House, 1958), 36.

24. Langston Hughes, "Trumpet Player" (1959), in *Selected Poems of Langston Hughes* (New York: Vintage, 1974), 114; Dorothy Baker, *Young Man with a Horn* (1938; reprint, New York: Readers Club, 1943), 67.

25. Jack Kerouac, "221st Chorus," in *Mexico City Blues* (New York: Grove, 1959), 223.

26. Langston Hughes, *Not without Laughter* (1930; reprint, New York: Macmillan, 1969), 297.

27. Holmes, *Horn,* 6.

28. Eudora Welty, "Powerhouse," in *A Curtain of Green* (Garden City, N.Y.: Doubleday Doran, 1943), 254.

29. Carl Van Vechten, *Nigger Heaven* (1926; reprint, New York: Harper & Row, 1971), 90, 222; Claude McKay, *Home to Harlem* (1928; reprint, New York: Pocket, 1965), 140.

30. Langston Hughes, "Jazzonia," in *The Weary Blues* (New York: Alfred A. Knopf, 1926), 25.

31. Frank Kofsky, *Black Nationalism and the Revolution in Music* (New York: Pathfinder, 1970), 144.

32. Nat Hentoff, "The New Jazz—Black, Angry, and Hard to Understand," *New York Times Magazine,* 25 December 1966, 10, 36; LeRoi Jones, "New Tenor Archie Shepp Talking," in *Black Music* (1965; reprint, New York: William Morrow, 1968), 154. As was to be expected, not all of the free jazz experimenters were perceived as avatars of societal change. Some were criticized for being "revolutionary" only in terms of their technical innovations. For a critique of the music's failure to have a "direct bearing on the political and social life of the community," see Lawrence P. Neal, "The Black Musician in White America," *Negro Digest* 16 (March 1967): 56–57.

33. Kofsky, *Black Nationalism,* 227.

34. W. C. Handy, *Father of the Blues* (New York: Macmillan, 1941), 74.

35. Houston A. Baker Jr., *Blues, Ideology, and Afro-American Literature: A Vernacular Theory* (Chicago: University of Chicago Press, 1984), 5.

36. See, e.g., *The Blues Aesthetic: Black Culture and Modernism,* ed. Richard J. Powell (Washington, D.C.: Washington Project for the Arts, 1989); Albert Murray, *The Blue Devils of Nada: A Contemporary American Approach to Aesthetic Statement* (New York: Pantheon, 1996).

37. See, e.g., "The Weary Blues" and "Blues Fantasy," in Hughes, *Weary Blues,* 23–24, 37–38; Sterling Brown, "Ma Rainey" (1932), in *The Collected Poems of Sterling A. Brown,* ed. Michael S. Harper (New York: Harper & Row, 1980), 62–63; Amina Baraka, "Birth Right" and "Blues," in *The Music: Reflections on Jazz and Blues,* by Amiri Baraka and Amina Baraka (New York: William Morrow, 1987), 28, 30.

38. See, e.g., August Wilson, *Ma Rainey's Black Bottom* (New York: New American Library, 1985); Edward Albee, *The Death of Bessie Smith* (London: S. French, 1960); Alan Greenberg, *Love in Vain* (Garden City, N.Y.: Doubleday, 1983); *Leadbelly* (Paramount, 1976); *St. Louis Blues* (RKO, 1929; Paramount, 1958).

39. See, e.g., Peter Guralnick, *Nighthawk Blues* (New York: Thunder's Mouth, 1988); Walter Mosley, *RL's Dream* (New York: W. W. Norton, 1995); Albert Murray, *Train Whistle Guitar* (New York: McGraw-Hill, 1974); Gayl Jones, *Corregidora* (New York: Random House, 1975); John Edgar Wideman, *Sent for You Yesterday* (New York: Avon, 1983); Alice Walker, *The Color Purple* (New York: Harcourt Brace Jovanovich, 1982); Clarence Major, *Dirty Bird Blues* (San Francisco: Mercury House, 1996). For a more complete exposition of blues-related themes and figures as they have appeared in various forms of popular cultural expression, see Mary Ellison, *Extensions of the Blues* (London: John Calder, 1989), 107–276.

40. Barry Lee Pearson, "'One Day You're Gonna Hear about Me': The H-Bomb Ferguson Story," *Living Blues,* no. 69 (1986): 15; Mance Lipscomb, *I Say Me for a Parable: The Oral Autobiography of Mance Lipscomb, Texas Bluesman* (New York: W. W. Norton, 1993), 51–52.

41. John Anthony Brisbin, "Big Moose Walker: Playin' All Night Long," *Living Blues* 23 (September/October 1992): 38.

42. Margaret McKee and Fred Chisenhall, *Beale Black and Blue: Life and Music on Black America's Main Street* (Baton Rouge: Louisiana State University Press, 1981), 113; Ted Olson, "'I Believe in Right at All Times': Bentonia Blues, Part One," *Living Blues* 23 (May/June 1992): 45.

43. Dorothy Schainman Siegel, *The Glory Road: The Story of Josh White* (1982; reprint, White Hall, Va.: Shoe Tree, 1991), 46–47. For a sampling of both personas, see the compilation CD *Josh White Blues Singer, 1932–1936,* Columbia/Legacy 67001.

44. Barry Lee Pearson, *Virginia Piedmont Blues: The Lives and Art of Two Virginia Bluesmen* (Philadelphia: University of Pennsylvania Press, 1990), 38–39; McKee and Chisenhall, *Beale Black and Blue,* 187–88; Michael W. Harris, *The Rise of Gospel Blues: The Music of Thomas Andrew Dorsey in the Urban Church* (New York: Oxford University Press, 1992), 96–98.

45. Barry Lee Pearson, *"Sounds So Good to Me": The Bluesman's Story* (Philadelphia: University of Pennsylvania Press, 1984), 153; McKee and Chisenhall, *Black and Blue,* 139.

46. T-Bone Walker, "Call It Stormy Monday (But Tuesday Is Just as Bad)," Black & White 122, 1948.

47. Rod Gruver, "The Blues as a Secular Religion, in *Sacred Music of the Secular City: From Blues to Rap,* ed. Jon Michael Spencer (1970; reprint, Durham: Duke University Press, 1992), 62.

48. For background on African belief systems, see John S. Mbiti, *African Religions and Philosophy* (New York: Praeger, 1969); Geoffrey Parrinder, *West African Religion* (London: Ep-

worth, 1969); Benjamin C. Ray, *African Religions: Symbol, Ritual, and Community* (Engle-wood Cliffs, N.J.: Prentice-Hall, 1976); Noel Q. King, *African Cosmos* (Belmont, Calif.: Wadsworth, 1986).

49. On this point, see Jon Michael Spencer, *Blues and Evil* (Knoxville: University of Ten-nessee Press, 1993); James H. Cone, *The Spirituals and the Blues: An Interpretation* (New York: Seabury, 1972), 108–42.

50. Robert Johnson, "Stones in My Passway," Vocalion 3723, 1937.

51. Sonny Boy Williamson, "Born Blind," Checker 883, 1957; Koko Taylor, "Wang Dang Doodle," Checker 1135, 1966.

52. John Lee Hooker, "I'm Bad like Jesse James," in *Live at Cafe Au-Go-Go*, Blues Way 6002, 1966; "Little Son" Jackson, "Evil Blues," Gold Star 663, 1949; Charley Patton, "Elder Greene Blues," Paramount 12972, 1929; Muddy Waters, "I'm Ready," Chess 1579, 1954.

53. Bessie Smith, "Nobody in Town Can Bake a Sweet Jelly Roll like Mine," Columbia 3942, 1923; Lil Johnson, "My Stove's in Good Condition," Vocalion 3251, 1936. For Carter's early-1930s material, see the compilation *Banana in Your Fruit Basket,* Yazoo 1064.

54. Michael Bane, *White Boy Singin' the Blues* (New York: Penguin, 1982), 69; John Lee Hooker, "Burnin' Hell," Sensation 21, 1949; Texas Alexander, "Justice Blues," Vocalion 2856, 1934; Kansas Joe and Memphis Minnie, "Preacher's Blues," Vocalion 1643, 1931; J. T. "Funny Paper" Smith, "Fool's Blues," Vocalion 1674, 1931.

55. Peter Guralnick, *Searching for Robert Johnson* (New York: E. P. Dutton, 1989), 17–18; David Evans, *Tommy Johnson* (London: Studio Vista, 1971), 22–23.

56. Lawrence Hoffman, "John William Hurt: 'And Daddy Would Play All Night Long,'" *Living Blues* 24 (May/June 1993): 40–41; Margey Peters, "Wild Jimmy Spruill: You Got to Move the Soul First," *Living Blues* 25 (May/June 1994): 29.

57. Tut Underwood, "Eddie Kirkland: The Energy Man," *Living Blues* 24 (September/October 1993): 15, 20–21.

58. D. Thomas Moon, "'Memphis' Charlie Musselwhite: Remembering Big Joe Williams," *Blues Review,* March/April 1995, 44–45; Lipscomb, *I Say Me for a Parable,* 230–34; McKee and Chisenhall, *Black and Blue,* 143–46.

59. Muddy Waters, "I'm Your Hoochie Coochie Man," Chess 1560, 1954.

60. John Anthony Brisbin, "Robert Plunkett: I Think I Had a Little Magic," *Living Blues* 25 (March/April 1994): 47.

61. Willie Mitchell, "Soul Serenade," Hi 2140, 1968; Booker T. & the MG's, "Soul-Limbo," Stax 0001, 1968; 5th Dimension, "Stoned Soul Picnic," Soul City 766, 1968; James Brown, "Soul Power," King 6368, 1971; Capitols, "Soul Brother, Soul Sister," Karen 1543, 1969; James Brown, "Soul Pride," King 6222, 1969; Marvin L. Sims, "Talkin' about Soul," Revue 11024, 1968.

62. R. Ernest Holmes, "Soul Music," *Liberator* 7 (December 1967): 18.

63. James Brown and Bruce Tucker, *James Brown: The Godfather of Soul* (1986; reprint, New York: Thunder's Mouth, 1990), 29.

64. Jeff Colburn, "Lost in the Shuffle: The O. V. Wright Story," *Goldmine,* 16 October 1992, 38, 42.

65. Stanley Booth, *Rythm Oil: A Journey through the Music of the American South* (New York: Pantheon, 1991), 150–51.

66. Sam & Dave, "Hold on, I'm Comin'," Stax 189, 1966.

67. Staple Singers, "Respect Yourself," Stax 104, 1971; James Carr, "Freedom Train," Goldwax 338, 1968.

68. Brown and Tucker, *James Brown,* 42–43; Cynthia Rose, *Living in America: The Soul Saga of James Brown* (London: Serpent's Tail, 1990), 126.

69. Aretha Franklin, "Spirit in the Dark," Atlantic 2731, 1970; Marvin Gaye, "Let's Get It On," Tamla 54234, 1973; Miracles, "I Gotta Dance to Keep from Crying," Tamla 54089, 1963; Impressions, "Keep on Pushing," ABC-Paramount 10554, 1964.

70. W. E. B. Du Bois, "Jefferson Davis as a Representative of Civilization" (1890), in *Writings,* ed. Nathan I. Huggins (New York: Library of America, 1986), 812; W. E. Burghardt Du Bois, *Dusk of Dawn: An Essay toward an Autobiography of a Race Concept* (1940; reprint, New York: Schocken, 1968), 153.

71. Memphis Minnie, "Man, You Won't Give Me No Money," Vocalion 3474, 1936; Smoky Babe, "Hard Times Blues," in *Country Negro Jam Sessions,* Folk Lyric 111, 1960.

72. Mary Wilson, Patricia Romanowski, and Ahrgus Juilliard, *Dreamgirl: My Life as a Supreme* (New York: St. Martin's, 1986), 26–27; Peter Benjaminson, *The Story of Motown* (New York: Grove, 1979), 141–42.

73. Juke Boy Bonner, "Life Is a Nightmare," in *Going Back to the Country,* Arhoolie 1036, 1968; B. B. King, "Chains and Things," ABC 11280, 1970; Muddy Waters, "You Can't Lose What You Ain't Never Had," Chess 1895, 1964.

74. Mance Lipscomb, *I Say Me for a Parable,* 69, 301–4, 314, 481; William Barlow, *"Looking Up at Down": The Emergence of Blues Culture* (Philadelphia: Temple University Press, 1989), 52; James Rooney, *Bossmen: Bill Monroe and Muddy Waters* (New York: Dial, 1971), 104.

75. Pleasant "Cousin Joe" Joseph and Harriet J. Ottenheimer, *Cousin Joe: Blues from New Orleans* (Chicago: University of Chicago Press, 1987), 3; Brown and Tucker, *James Brown,* 14–15; Peter Guralnick, *Sweet Soul Music: Rhythm and Blues and the Southern Dream of Freedom* (New York: Harper & Row, 1986), 133; David Ritz, *Divided Soul: The Life of Marvin Gaye* (New York: McGraw-Hill, 1985), 34.

76. On the negative experiences of the Motortown Review in the segregated South, see Otis Williams and Patricia Romanowski, *Temptations* (New York: G. P. Putnam's Sons, 1988), 78–79, 103; Wilson, Romanowski, and Juilliard, *Dreamgirl,* 120–25; Berry Gordy, *To Be Loved: The Music, The Magic, The Memories of Motown* (New York: Warner, 1994), 165–66.

77. Syl Johnson, "Concrete Reservation," Twinight 129, 1970; John Lee Hooker, "One Room Country Shack," in *Simply the Truth,* Bluesway 6023, 1968.

78. Peter Guralnick, *Feel like Going Home: Portraits in Blues and Rock 'n' Roll* (1971; reprint, New York: Harper & Row, 1989), 244.

79. Rose, *Living in America,* 18.

80. Ibid., 9.

81. Jim O'Neal, "BluEsoterica," *Living Blues* 25 (November/December 1994): 128.

82. Mothers of Invention, "Brown Shoes Don't Make It," in *Absolutely Free,* Verve 5013, 1967.

83. Brown and Tucker, *James Brown,* xv.

84. On the soulster's costumery, see Mablen Jones, *Getting It On: The Clothing of Rock 'n' Roll* (New York: Abbeville, 1987).

85. Tony Turner and Barbara Aria, *All That Glittered: My Life with the Supremes* (New York: Dutton, 1990), 4–6; Brown and Tucker, *James Brown,* 165; Guralnick, *Soul Music,* 244, 318; Mark Bego, *Aretha Franklin: Queen of Soul* (1989; reprint, London: Robert Hale, 1990), 173.

86. Phyl Garland, *The Sound of Soul* (Chicago: Henry Regnery, 1969), 159.

87. Charles Sawyer, *B. B. King: The Authorized Biography* (1980; reprint, London: Quartet, 1982), 3; Colin Escott, "The Fortunate Son: An Appreciation of B. B. King," *Goldmine,* 29 April 1994, 16.

88. Booth, *Rythm Oil,* 101.

89. Charles Keil, *Urban Blues* (Chicago: University of Chicago Press, 1966), 106.

90. Rooney, *Bossmen,* 147–49; Bob Margolin, "Blues Fans," *Blues Review,* winter 1994, 12.

91. Smokey Robinson and David Ritz, *Smokey: Inside My Life* (New York: McGraw-Hill, 1989), 115–16.

92. On Wolf's antics, see Peter Guralnick, *Lost Highway: Journeys and Arrivals of American Musicians* (1979; reprint, New York: Harper & Row, 1989), 284–87; Cub Coda, "Howlin' Wolf: The Wolf Is at the Door," *Goldmine,* 16 April 1993, 14.

93. Ritz, *Divided Soul,* 82.

94. Keil, *Urban Blues,* 108; Rooney, *Bossmen,* 107; McKee and Chisenhall, *Beale Black and Blue,* 246.

95. Turner and Aria, *All That Glittered,* 46, 82.

96. Frank C. Taylor and Gerald Cook, *Alberta Hunter: A Celebration in Blues* (New York: McGraw-Hill, 1987), 247.

97. Marvin Gaye, *Super Hits,* Tamla 300, 1970.

98. Dick Shurman, "Chicago—The Post-War Blues Scene and Patton's Heirs," in *The Voice of the Delta: Charley Patton and the Mississippi Blues Traditions,* ed. Robert Sacre (Liège, Belgium: Presses Universitaires, 1987), 277.

99. Brown and Tucker, *James Brown,* 267.

100. Helen Oakley Dance, *Stormy Monday: The T-Bone Walker Story* (Baton Rouge: Louisiana State University Press, 1987), 165–66.

101. "Junior Wells: *Living Blues* Interview," *Living Blues* 26 (January/February 1995): 16–17; Andrew M. Robble, "Rod Piazza: Flyin' High with the Master of the Chromatic," *Blues Review,* fall 1994, 40.

102. Rooney, *Bossmen,* 129.

103. B. B. King, "Worry, Worry," in *B. B. King Live at the Regal,* ABC 509, 1971; Taylor and Cook, *Alberta Hunter,* 254–55.

104. Rooney, *Bossmen,* 135.

105. Wilson, Romanowski, and Juilliard, *Dreamgirl,* 195, 203; Gerri Hirshey, *Nowhere to Run: The Story of Soul Music* (New York: Times, 1984), 277; John Swenson, *Stevie Wonder* (New York: Harper & Row, 1986), 89.

106. Rose, *Living in America,* 58.

107. Ritz, *Divided Soul,* 226–27; Sam & Dave, "I Thank You," Stax 242, 1968.

108. Carole A. Parks, "Self-Determination and the Black Aesthetic: An Interview with Max Roach," *Black World* 23 (November 1973): 69–70.

109. Michael Haralambos, *Right On: From Blues to Soul in Black America* (New York: Drake, 1975), 123–24.

110. Nina Simone, "Revolution," RCA Victor 9730, 1969.

111. Bob Dylan, "The Lonesome Death of Hattie Carroll," in *The Times They Are A-Changin',* Columbia 8905, 1964.

112. On the folk scene of the early 1960s, see Jerome L. Rodnitzky, *Minstrels of the Dawn: The Folk Protest Singer as a Cultural Hero* (Chicago: Nelson-Hall, 1976); Reebee Garofalo, "Popular Music and the Civil Rights Movement," in Garofalo, *Rockin' the Boat,* 231–40; Jeff Todd Titon, "Reconstructing the Blues: Reflections on the 1960s Blues Revival," in *Transforming Tradition: Folk Music Revivals Examined,* ed. Neil V. Rosenberg (Urbana: University of Illinois Press, 1993), 220–40; Eric von Schmidt and Jim Rooney, *Baby, Let Me Follow You Down* (Garden City, N.Y.: Anchor/Doubleday, 1979).

113. For a selection of the songs of the civil rights movement, see Pete Seeger and Bob Reiser, *Everybody Says Freedom* (New York: W. W. Norton, 1989).

114. Chi-Lites, "(For God's Sake) Give More Power to the People," Brunswick 55450, 1971; Willie Hightower, "Time Has Brought about a Change," Fame 1474, 1970; Simone, "Revolution."

115. Elvis Presley, "In the Ghetto," RCA Victor 9741, 1969; Dion, "Abraham, Martin and John," Laurie 3464, 1968; Rascals, "People Got to Be Free," Atlantic 2537, 1968.

116. James Brown, "I Don't Want Nobody to Give Me Nothing (Open Up the Door, I'll Get It Myself)," King 6224, 1969; Aretha Franklin, "Respect," Atlantic 2403, 1967; Impressions, "We're a Winner," ABC 11022, 1967; Staple Singers, "Be What You Are," Stax 164, 1973; James Brown, "Get up, Get into It, Get Involved," King 6347, 1971; Isley Brothers, "Fight the Power," T-Neck 2256, 1975; James Brown, "Say It Loud—I'm Black and I'm Proud," King 6187, 1968; Temptations, "Message from a Black Man," in *Puzzle People*, Gordy 949, 1970; Sly & the Family Stone, "Poet," in *There's a Riot Goin' On*, Epic 30986, 1971; Edwin Starr, "Stop the War Now," Gordy 7104, 1970; Freda Payne, "Bring the Boys Home," Invictus 9092, 1971; Marvin Gaye, "Inner City Blues (Make Me Wanna Holler)," Tamla 54209, 1971; Stevie Wonder, "Village Ghetto Land," in *Songs in the Key of Life*, Motown 6002, 1976; O'Jays, "Give the People What They Want," Philadelphia International 3565, 1975; Jimmy Collier, "Burn, Baby, Burn," in *Freedom Is a Constant Struggle: Songs of the Freedom Movement*, ed. Guy Carawan and Candie Carawan (1966; reprint, New York: Oak, 1968), 191.

117. Marvin Gaye, *What's Going On*, Tamla 310, 1971. A sampling of the reggae stars' work may be found in the following compilations: Bob Marley and the Wailers, *Natural Mystic (The Legend Lives On)*, Tuff Gong 41032; Peter Tosh, *The Toughest*, Capitol 90201.

118. Sherry Turner, "An Overview of the New Black Arts," *Freedomways* 9 (spring 1969): 156; Last Poets, "Run, Nigger," "Wake up, Niggers," and "Niggers Are Scared of Revolution," in *The Last Poets*, Douglas 3, 1970; Last Poets, "Opposites," in *This Is Madness*, Douglas 7, 1971; Gil Scott-Heron, *The Revolution Will Not Be Televised*, Flying Dutchman 3818, 1974; Watts Prophets, *Rappin' Black in a White World*, ALA 1971, 1971.

119. Leadbelly, "Scottsboro Boys" (1938), in *Let It Shine on Me*, Rounder 1046, 1991; Big Bill Broonzy, "When Do I Get to Be Called a Man" (1955), in *1955 London Sessions*, Collectables 5161, 1994.

120. John Lee Hooker, "Birmingham Blues," Vee Jay 538, 1963; Juke Boy Bonner, "Struggle Here in Houston," in *The Struggle*, Arhoolie 1045, 1968; liner notes to Eddy Clearwater, *The Chief*, Rooster Blues 2615, 1980.

121. Louisiana Red, "Red's Dream" (1965), in *The Best of Louisiana Red*, Evidence 26059, 1995.

122. Nina Simone and Stephen Cleary, *I Put a Spell on You: The Autobiography of Nina Simone* (New York: Pantheon, 1991), 90, 94, 100, 108–10; Ritz, *Divided Soul*, 106; Wilson, Romanowski, and Juilliard, *Dreamgirl*, 215.

123. Brown and Tucker, *James Brown*, 181; Ritz, *Divided Soul*, 132; Aretha Franklin, *Amazing Grace*, Atlantic 906, 1972; Aretha Franklin, *Young, Gifted, and Black*, Atlantic 7213, 1972; Bego, *Aretha Franklin*, 145.

124. Elaine Brown, "End of Silence," in *Seize the Time*, Vault 131, 1971.

125. Brown and Tucker, *James Brown*, 171, 183–89, 211.

126. Wilson, Romanowski, and Juilliard, *Dreamgirl*, 224.

127. Hirshey, *Nowhere to Run*, 146, 192; Ritz, *Divided Soul*, 106, 193.

128. Percy Sledge, "When a Man Loves a Woman," Atlantic 2326, 1966.

129. Donald Byrd, "The Meaning of Black Music," *Black Scholar* 3 (summer 1972): 31; Haki R. Madhubuti, *From Plan to Planet: Life Studies—The Need for Afrikan Minds and Institutions* (Chicago: Third World, 1973), 99–103; Hubert Walters, "Black Music and the Black University," *Black Scholar* 3 (summer 1972): 17–20; Garland, *Sound of Soul,* 12–13.

130. On the white minstrels' exploitation of black culture, see Robert C. Toll, *Blacking Up: The Minstrel Show in Nineteenth-Century America* (New York: Oxford University Press, 1974), 40–51; Eric Lott, *Love and Theft: Blackface Minstrelsy and the American Working Class* (New York: Oxford University Press, 1993), 38–62; Howard L. Sacks and Judith Rose Sacks, *Way up North in Dixie: A Black Family's Claim to the Confederate Anthem* (Washington, D.C.: Smithsonian Institution, 1993), 3, 169.

131. Broadway Rastus, "Whoopee Stomp," Paramount 12764, 1929. For a sampling of the early white bluesmen's work, see the compilation *White Country Blues (1926–1938): A Lighter Shade of Blue,* Columbia 47466.

132. Other black artists whose work was "covered" by the young Elvis include Kokomo Arnold, Roy Brown, Wynonie Harris, Little Richard, Arthur Gunter, and Big Mama Thornton. In the United States, blue-eyed soul acts included the Righteous Brothers, the Rascals, Hall & Oates, and the Soul Survivors.

133. Jones, *Black Music,* 205–6.

134. Bane, *White Boy,* 189–90, 192, 195; Al Kooper and Ben Edmonds, *Backstage Passes: Rock 'n' Roll Life in the Sixties* (New York: Stein & Day, 1977), 133, 149.

135. Ortiz M. Walton, *Music: Black, White, and Blue—A Sociological Survey of the Use and Misuse of Afro-American Music* (New York: William Morrow, 1972), 121, 142; Garland, *Sound of Soul,* 188; Robert Palmer, *Deep Blues* (1981; reprint, New York: Penguin, 1982), 260.

136. Robert Tyler, "The Musical Culture of Afro-America," *Black Scholar* 3 (summer 1972): 27; Olly Wilson, "The Significance of the Relationship between Afro-American Music and West African Music," *Black Perspective in Music* 2 (spring 1974): 3–22; William H. McClendon, "Black Music: Sound and Feeling for Black Liberation," *Black Scholar* 7 (January/February 1976): 24.

137. Dyke and the Blazers, "We Got More Soul," Original Sound 86, 1969; McKee and Chisenhall, *Beale Black and Blue,* 189; Bruce Cook, *Listen to the Blues* (New York: Charles Scribner's Sons, 1973), 185–86; Willie Dixon, *I Am the Blues,* Columbia 9987, 1970.

138. Bill Wyman and Ray Coleman, *Stone Alone: The Story of a Rock 'n' Roll Band* (New York: Viking Penguin, 1990), 33; David Dalton, *The Rolling Stones: The First Twenty Years* (New York: Alfred A. Knopf, 1981), 18; Ray Coleman, *Clapton!* (New York: Warner, 1986), 8, 26. For a detailed study of the British blues boom, see Bob Groom, *The Blues Revival* (London: Studio Vista, 1971).

139. The Rolling Stones and Pete Goodman, *Our Own Story* (1964; reprint, New York: Bantam, 1965), 57, 142–43.

140. On the use of black English by white bluesmen, see John M. Hellmann Jr., "'I'm a Monkey': The Influence of the Black American Blues Argot on the Rolling Stones," *Journal of American Folklore* 86 (October–December 1973): 367–73. Two of the best-known "fathers and sons" recordings are Muddy Waters, *Fathers and Sons,* Chess 127, 1969, and Howlin' Wolf, *The London Howlin' Wolf Sessions,* Chess 60008, 1971.

141. Stephen Davis, *Hammer of the Gods: The Led Zeppelin Saga* (1985; reprint, New York: Ballantine, 1986), 47–48.

142. Booth, *Rythm Oil,* 94.

143. Rooney, *Bossmen,* 145.

144. Bob Brunning, *Blues: The British Connection* (Poole, England: Blandford, 1986), 176.

145. Eric Burdon, *I Used to Be an Animal, but I'm All Right Now* (Boston: Faber & Faber, 1986), 29, 49, 142–43.

146. Stanley Booth, *Dance with the Devil: The Rolling Stones and Their Times* (New York: Random House, 1984), 131.

147. Taylor and Cook, *Alberta Hunter,* 233. On the white folklorist-fans'"rediscovery" efforts, see David Evans, "Mississippi Blues Today and Its Future," in Sacre, *Voice of the Delta,* 315–35; Samuel B. Charters, *The Country Blues* (1959; reprint, New York: Da Capo, 1975), vii–xvi; Alan Lomax, *The Land Where the Blues Began* (New York: Pantheon, 1993).

148. David Fricke, "Eric Clapton: The *Rolling Stone* Interview," *Rolling Stone,* 25 August 1988, 28. For visual documentation of the rediscovered artists' skills, see the videos *Legends of Country Blues Guitar,* vols. 1 and 2, Vestapol Productions, 13003 and 13016. For an occasionally insightful parody of the "blues revival," see Richard "Cheech" Marin and Tommy Chong's "Blind Melon Chitlin'," in *Cheech and Chong,* Warner Brothers 3250, 1971.

149. Junior Parker, *You Don't Have to Be Black to Love the Blues,* People 4, 1973.

150. Bruce Jackson, "The Folksong Revival," in Rosenberg, *Transforming Tradition,* 80; David Evans, *Big Road Blues: Tradition and Creativity in the Folk Blues* (1982; reprint, New York: Da Capo, 1987), 84.

151. Hirshey, *Nowhere to Run,* 328; *Ski Party* (American International, 1965).

152. Garland, *Sound of Soul,* 128–29.

153. On Joplin, see Myra Friedman, *Buried Alive: The Biography of Janis Joplin* (New York: William Morrow, 1973); Ellis Amburn, *Pearl: The Obsessions and Passions of Janis Joplin* (New York: Warner, 1992).

154. Tony Glover quoted in liner notes to *Jimi Hendrix: Blues,* MCA 11060, 1994. On Hendrix, see Charles Schaar Murray, *Crosstown Traffic: Jimi Hendrix and the Post-war Rock 'n' Roll Revolution* (New York: St. Martin's, 1989).

155. Gordy, *To Be Loved,* 114; Ritz, *Divided Soul,* 73.

156. Gordy, *To Be Loved,* 245.

157. Miracles, *Doin' Mickey's Monkey,* Motown 245, 1963; Isley Brothers, *This Old Heart of Mine,* Motown 269, 1966; Marvelettes, *Please Mr. Postman,* Motown 228, 1961; Mary Wells, *Bye Bye Baby,* Motown 600, 1961.

158. On the inner workings of Motown's hit-making machinery, see Nelson George, *Where Did Our Love Go? The Rise and Fall of the Motown Sound* (New York: St. Martin's, 1985).

159. Underwood, "Kirkland," 16; Pearson, *Bluesman's Story,* 46.

160. Robinson and Ritz, *Smokey,* 215–16.

161. On this point, see David Whiteis's review of *The History of the Blues* by Francis Davis, *Living Blues* 26 (May/June 1995): 111.

Conclusion

1. Screamin' Jay Hawkins, "Little Demon," Okeh 7072, 1956.

2. On these sociocultural changes, see Rowland Evans and Robert Novak, *The Reagan Revolution* (New York: E. P. Dutton, 1981); Richard Reeves, *The Reagan Detour* (New York: Simon & Schuster, 1985); Kevin P. Phillips, *The Politics of Rich and Poor: Wealth and the American Electorate in the Reagan Aftermath* (New York: Random House, 1990); Haynes Johnson, *Sleepwalking through History: America in the Reagan Years* (New York: W. W. Norton, 1991); James Combs, *The Reagan Range: The Nostalgic Myth in American Politics* (Bowling Green, Ohio: Bowling Green State University Popular Press, 1993).

3. On the disco scene, see Albert Goldman, *Disco* (New York: Hawthorn, 1978). On rap, see S. H. Fernando Jr., *The New Beats: Exploring the Music, Culture, and Attitudes of Hip-Hop* (New York: Anchor/Doubleday, 1994); Tricia Rose, *Black Noise: Rap Music and Black Culture in Contemporary America* (Hanover, N.H.: Wesleyan/University Press of New England, 1994).

4. On the "cinema of recuperation," see Ed Guerrero, *Framing Blackness: The African American Image in Film* (Philadelphia: Temple University Press, 1993), 113–55; *Star Wars, The Empire Strikes Back,* and *Return of the Jedi* (Lucasfilm/Fox, 1977, 1980, 1983); *Rocky I* to *Rocky V* (United Artists, 1976, 1979, 1982, 1985, 1990).

5. Melvin Van Peebles, *Bold Money: How to Get Rich in the Options Market* (New York: Warner, 1987).

6. See, e.g., Barbara Gibson and Ted Schwarz, *The Kennedys: The Third Generation* (New York: Thunder's Mouth, 1993); Nellie Bly, *The Kennedy Men: Three Generations of Sex, Scandal, and Secrets* (New York: Kensington, 1996).

7. "How to Survive in Hollywood between Gigs," *Ebony* 33 (October 1978): 36; *Chained Heat* (Jensen Farley, 1983).

8. James Gregory, *The Soul of the Jackson 5* (New York: Curtis, 1973), 36, 62; LaToya Jackson and Patricia Romanowski, *LaToya: Growing Up in the Jackson Family* (New York: Dutton, 1991), 1–2; J. Randy Taraborrelli, *Michael Jackson: The Magic and the Madness* (New York: Birch Lane, 1991), ix. On the Jacksons' continuing problems, see Gillian G. Gaar, "It's a Family Affair: The Triumphs and Tribulations of the Jacksons," *Goldmine,* 13 October 1995, 18–62, 194.

9. Jancee Dunn, "Liz Phair," *Rolling Stone,* 6 October 1994, 46.

10. See, e.g., James Patterson and Peter Kim, *The Day America Told the Truth: What People Really Believe about Everything That Really Matters* (New York: Prentice Hall, 1991), 207–10; Thomas Hargrove and Guido H. Stempel III, "Do We Have Heroes?" *Madison, Wisconsin, Capital Times,* 11 August 1994, A1, 14.

11. Walter Scott, "Personality Parade," *Parade,* 3 December 1995, 2.

12. Seth Shulman, "They Hunt for Heroes," *Parade,* 17 September 1995, 24.

13. *First Lady Jacqueline Kennedy Onassis, 1929–1994: Memorial Tributes* (Washington, D.C.: U.S. Government Printing Office, 1995); Wendy Leigh, *Prince Charming: The John F. Kennedy, Jr., Story* (New York: Dutton, 1993).

14. *Nixon* (Hollywood Pictures, 1995).

15. On the nationalistic politics of rap, see Joseph D. Eure and James G. Spady, eds., *Nation Conscious Rap* (New York: PC International, 1991); Clarence Lusane, "Rap, Race, and Politics," *Race and Class* 35 (July–September 1993): 41–56; Jeffrey Louis Decker, "The State of Rap: Time and Place in Hip Hop Nationalism," in *Microphone Fiends: Youth Music and Youth Culture,* ed. Andrew Ross and Tricia Rose (New York: Routledge, 1994), 99–121.

16. On black filmmakers' efforts to encapsulate history and urban reality, see Mario Van Peebles and Melvin Van Peebles, "For 'New Jack City,' It's the Same Old Story," *New York Times,* 31 March 1991, H9, 17; Karen Grigsby Bates, "'They've Gotta Have Us': Hollywood's Black Directors," *New York Times Magazine,* 14 July 1991, 15–19, 38–44; Patrick E. Cole, "Cinema Revolution," *Emerge* 3 (January 1992): 36–40; Spike Lee and Ralph Wiley, *By Any Means Necessary: The Trials and Tribulations of the Making of "Malcolm X"* (New York: Hyperion, 1992); Sheila Rule, "Young Black Film Makers Face the Aftermath of Success," *New York Times,* 11 August 1994, C13, 18; Michael Robinson, "The Van Peebleses Prowl through the Panthers' History," *American Visions* 10 (April–May 1995): 16–18.

17. "Pelé Says He Can Heal Sick Children," *Madison, Wisconsin Capital Times,* 27 August

1993, A2; Wilt Chamberlain, *A View from Above* (New York: Villard, 1991), 251–52. On the continuing role of African-American cultural productions in promoting "integrative cultural diversity," see Charles T. Banner-Haley, *The Fruits of Integration: Black Middle-Class Ideology and Culture, 1960–1990* (Jackson: University Press of Mississippi, 1994), 121–56; Richard M. Merelman, *Representing Black Culture: Racial Conflict and Cultural Politics in the United States* (New York: Routledge, 1995), 97–128. For a pictorial celebration of 1990s black culture heroes, see Paul Carter Harrison, *Black Light: The African American Hero* (New York: Thunder's Mouth, 1993).

INDEX